Dactylocnemis 	6 species. Noc taxa, restricted to the North Island and offshore islands. Moderately expanded toe pads with long distal phalanges. Rostral scale in broad contact with nostrils.	102–113
Hoplodactylus duvaucelii 	1 species. Genus contains a single species; nocturnal, large (adult size up to 165 mm SVL). Restricted to offshore islands off the north-east coast of the North Island and in Cook Strait (recently reintroduced to the mainland).	Page 114
Woodworthia 	13 species. Nocturnal (sometimes diurnal or crepuscular); terrestrial, saxicolous and semi-arboreal. Widely distributed across the North and South Islands, including many offshore islands. Broadly expanded toe pads with shorter distal phalanges than other genera; very short in some species. Rostral scale excluded from nostril in most species, or, if in contact, only just.	Pages 116–146

Skinks *Scincidae*

Oligosoma 	63 species. An extremely diverse genus, with a large variety of forms and morphological traits. Members of the genus distinguished from *L. delicata* by divided (vs. single/undivided) frontoparietal scale, and generally viviparous reproduction (with the exception of *O. suteri*).	Pages 162–293
Lampropholis delicata 	1 species. Introduced from Australia, and occurs throughout the upper North Island south to Palmerston North. Small, slender, and brown or grey-brown in colour. Frequently seen basking in the sun and very active. Distinguished from native *Oligosoma* species by single (vs. paired/divided) frontoparietal scale, and (with the exception of *O. suteri*) by oviparous reproduction.	Page 294

Dylan van Winkel, Marleen Baling and Rod Hitchmough are wildlife ecologists and herpetologists with over 60 years of combined experience researching New Zealand's reptiles and amphibians.

Dylan van Winkel is a wildlife ecologist and consultant herpetologist based in New Zealand. He has a strong interest in the natural world, specifically in reptile and amphibian conservation. Dylan has been involved in numerous research and conservation programmes, including several wildlife translocations and island restoration projects. He is also a technical advisor to the Ministry for Primary Industries, providing species identifications, biosecurity risk assessments, and eradication advice for foreign herpetofauna arriving on New Zealand's shores. Dylan currently works for Bioresearches Group Ltd.

Marleen Baling is a wildlife ecologist with a particular interest in New Zealand herpetology. She has been involved in numerous reptile research and conservation projects in the last sixteen years. She has worked with many organisations on their wildlife restoration management including reptile translocations and monitoring. She is a member of the IUCN Reintroduction Specialist Group, Oceania Section.

Rod Hitchmough is a Department of Conservation science advisor, specialising in lizard taxonomy, herpetology and conservation, and the assessment of species' conservation status. He has been involved in studies of the taxonomy of New Zealand geckos since the 1970s, and is currently preparing scientific descriptions for new species. He has also co-authored papers on skink taxonomy. Until recently he managed the process of listing species using the New Zealand Threat Classification System, running meetings of expert panels for 28 different groups of animals, plants and fungi.

Harlequin gecko, *Tukutuku rakiurae*

REPTILES AND AMPHIBIANS OF NEW ZEALAND

A FIELD GUIDE

Dylan van Winkel, Marleen Baling and Rod Hitchmough

B L O O M S B U R Y   W I L D L I F E
LONDON • OXFORD • NEW YORK • NEW DELHI • SYDNEY

Black-eyed gecko, *Mokopirirakau kahutarae*

Contents

Acknowledgements vii

Introduction 1

New Zealand herpetofauna 2

Conservation of New Zealand herpetofauna 13

Observing amphibians and reptiles 15

New Zealand's ecosystems and geographic history 18

How to use this guide 25

SPECIES ACCOUNTS

Tuatara 30

Geckos 36

Skinks 155

Frogs 303

Marine turtles 321

Marine snakes 337

Regional checklist of New Zealand herpetofauna 351

Glossary 357

Further reading 362

Index 363

Three Kings gecko, *Dactylocnemis* "Three Kings"

Whirinaki skink, *Oligosoma* "Whirinaki"

Acknowledgements

We would like to express our thanks and appreciation to all those who assisted and contributed in many different ways to the production of this guide. Foremost, we would like to acknowledge and express our gratitude to Geraldine Moore (DOC) for her tremendous efforts and time in creating the marvellous maps that enhanced the quality of this guide, and thanks to Katie Milne (also of DOC), who provided assistance.

Thank you to those who supplied images of taxa we were unable to obtain ourselves: Aaron Bauer, Trent Bell, Hal Cogger, Jamie Darbyshire, Nick Harker, Mark Jefferson, Dave Jenkins, Tony Jewell, Lisa Keene, Samantha King, Carey Knox, George Kruza, Marieke Lettink, Phil Melgren, Ken Miller, Colin Miskelly, Les Moran, Simon Pierce, Patrice Plichon, Jozef Polec, James Reardon, Ria Rebstock, Ian Southey, Jean-Claude Stahl (Te Papa), Roger Waddell (www.thegates.co.nz), Matt Walters, Chris Wedding, Sarah J. Wells and the late Tony Whitaker (via Viv Whitaker). Their specific contributions are also acknowledged beside their relevant image(s). All photographs and illustrations are by Dylan van Winkel unless otherwise stated.

We gratefully appreciate all those who provided field assistance and/or logistical support: Department of Conservation (DOC), William (Iain) Baggaley, Phil 'Brownie' Brown, Rhys Burns, Kevin Carter, Mike Chillingworth, Jessica Feickert, Neil Forrester, Richard Gibson, Pip Green, Lesley Hadley (Friends of Flora), Nick and Tim Harker, Ben Herbert, the Manawatawhi/Three Kings Islands DOC team, Chris McClure, Haley McCoskery, Don McFarlane, Lynda McGrory-Ward, Phil Melgren, Sabine Melzer, Les Moran, Irene Petrove, Miriam Ritchie, Ivan Rogers, Sara Smeaton, Ruth Smith, Laurence Sullivan, Dive Tutukaka, Graham Ussher, Megan Vercoe, Tamsin Ward-Smith and Chris Wedding; and to those who provided information relating to specific taxa: Ben Bell, Phil Bishop, Paul Doughty, Jen Germano, Brian Gill, Dan Godoy and Kate McInnes. We are also grateful to those who granted us access to private captive collections: Doug Ashby, Ivan Borich (Ti Point Reptile Park), Dave Craddock, Andrew Christie (Kelly Tarlton's Sea Life Aquarium), Richard Gibson (Auckland Zoo), Nick Harker, Dennis Keall, Joel Knight and Gary Molloy.

A special mention and thanks to Ben Barr, Marieke Lettink, and James Reardon for the company and essential assistance on excursions into the field, and for providing photographs and information on rare taxa. We also wish to thank Tony Jewell for imparting invaluable information on several lizard taxa and for his critical revision of the skink identification key.

We extend our thanks to David Chapple, Marieke Lettink, and Geoff Patterson who reviewed the entire text and provided constructive comments that greatly improved the guide. We also thank everyone at Auckland University Press, especially Sam Elworthy, Katharina Bauer, Katrina Duncan and Louisa Kasza for seeing this project through to completion. Thank you to Sue Hallas, whose copyediting skills greatly refined the guide, to Matt Turner for proofreading and Timothy Vaughan-Sanders for indexing. We also greatly appreciate the support by the Charles Fleming Publishing Award (2018) for assistance in the final stages of this guide.

Lastly, to our friends and families, your support has been overwhelming. Dylan is particularly grateful to his wife Sarah for her loving support, encouragement and assistance in the field, and to his son Zephyr for regular, but enjoyable, distractions while preparing this book. Marleen is especially grateful to Richard for his amazing patience and continual support during the many hours of her working on this guide. Rod is grateful to his DOC managers and directors for encouraging and supporting his work on this book, and to Grace, Liam, Judy and Julie for accepting his reduced availability over many weekends while this book was being prepared.

Ornate skink, *Oligosoma ornatum*, Three Kings Islands

Introduction

New Zealand is often recognised as a land of birds, particularly as a centre of diversity for seabirds, but it is New Zealand's herpetofauna – our reptiles and amphibians – that is the most diverse of all native terrestrial vertebrate groups. Moreover, for its relatively small land area, this country supports one of the most diverse lizard faunas of any temperate region in the world. The New Zealand herpetofauna is highly distinctive, and includes the sole surviving member of the ancient taxonomic order Rhynchocephalia (tuatara), a genus of archaic frogs (*Leiopelma*) and the world's largest assemblage of long-lived and live-bearing lizards (geckos and skinks).

The New Zealand herpetofauna currently comprises 123 species or taxa (here, 'taxa' is used because a large proportion of the fauna remains undescribed) from six main groups: tuatara, geckos, skinks, frogs, marine turtles and marine snakes. Most of these (89%) are endemic to New Zealand (meaning they are found only here), while others are vagrant or migrant (marine species; 8%), or are exotic (meaning they were introduced and have naturalised here; 3%). All the endemic species sit in four taxonomic families, two of which are found only in New Zealand – Sphenodontidae (tuatara) and Leiopelmatidae (frogs). All the New Zealand geckos fall within seven genera in the family Diplodactylidae (geckos), and the skinks belong to an almost-endemic genus in the family Scincidae (Eugongylinae skinks). The only species in the New Zealand skink genus *Oligosoma* that occurs outside of the country is *O. lichenigera*, on Australia's Lord Howe and Norfolk Island groups.

The herpetofauna includes some taxa that were probably present before the New Zealand landmass began drifting away from the ancient supercontinent Gondwana, about 80 million years ago (mya; tuatara and Leiopelmatid frogs). Other taxa (geckos and skinks) are probably more recent colonisers, arriving here after New Zealand's separation from all other continental landmasses, but still tens of millions of years ago. In more recent times, one exotic lizard (a skink) and three exotic frogs from Australia have successfully naturalised in New Zealand. All marine species are vagrant or migrant, and typically occur in the wider Pacific Basin.

All New Zealand's native terrestrial reptiles and amphibians produce few young per year, live relatively long, take a relatively long time to reach sexual maturity and are naïve when it comes to introduced mammalian predators (e.g. rodents, mustelids, hedgehogs, possums and cats). These unique characters, as well as the survival of ancient-lineage species, have come about because of New Zealand's complex geological history, unstable climate and the natural absence of mammalian predators for millions of years. Therefore, recent human influences – in particular, introduced mammalian predators and habitat changes (e.g. brought about by agriculture, logging and urban development) – have led to most of New Zealand's terrestrial herpetofauna suffering large-scale contractions of their ranges and localised extinctions. At present, more than 80% of our reptiles and amphibians are threatened with or at longer-term risk of extinction, and many species rely on direct conservation management to ensure their survival.

NEW ZEALAND HERPETOFAUNA

Brief historical account

Early knowledge of New Zealand's herpetofauna dates to the arrival of Polynesians in the 13th century. These first colonisers brought with them the traditional Polynesian names for reptiles and amphibians they had frequently seen during their daily activities in their Pacific homelands. Therefore, in the Māori language we find ngārara as a general term for reptiles; moko or mokomoko for lizards; and pepeke, peketua or pepeketua for frogs. Other names apply more specifically to 'types' or discrete species of reptiles, such as tuatara, niho taniwha, kumi, moko kākāriki, moko pāpā, moko pārae, moko pirirākau, moko tāpiri and kawekaweau. Reptiles, particularly tuatara and geckos, have high cultural and spiritual significance to Māori. Ngārara are cited in many of their myths and legends, with links to death, demons and the after-world. There can be great superstition and cultural fear of ngārara. For example, the presence of a moko ngārara or moko kākāriki (referring to green-coloured geckos) was seen as a bad omen, and caused tribes that were on a warpath to turn back. Some iwi (tribal groups in Māori society) also see lizards as kaitiaki (guardians) over the dead, and lizards were buried or placed near important structures such as the whare wānanga (house of learning). Reptiles are often depicted in traditional wooden carvings, petroglyphs (rock artworks), tattoos and pendants. Frogs, however, do not seem to feature in Māori myths and legends. But Māori must have been aware of the existence of native frogs, since at least six species were present in New Zealand in the early years of human colonisation.

The arrival of Europeans from the eighteenth century brought about a new interest in New Zealand's unique fauna and flora, although the herpetofauna was largely overlooked by early colonial naturalists. This oversight may have been partly due to the popularity of botany and ornithology among the naturalists, but also because the kiore (*Rattus exulans*), introduced centuries earlier by Polynesian explorers and settlers, had already decimated the mainland populations of lizards. The earliest European account of reptiles in New Zealand came from the personal journal of William Bayly in 1773, who noted 'a few small harmless lizards' in the forests around Queen Charlotte Sound. Later, in 1777, Captain James Cook noted 'two or three sorts of small harmless lizards' during his visit to New Zealand en route to the North Pacific. It was only in the early 19th century that the first lizard specimens were collected and formally described. From then on, there were several waves of interest in the taxonomy of New Zealand's herpetofauna.

The first began in the early to mid-19th century, when scientific exploration in New Zealand was rife, and many species, including tuatara (*Sphenodon punctatus*) and the first indigenous frog – Hochstetter's frog (*Leiopelma hochstetteri*) – were formally described. Duvaucel's gecko (*Hoplodactylus duvaucelii*), as well as the Pacific, forest and some 'green' (*Naultinus*) geckos, were described between 1836 and 1872. Much later, in the early 20th century, more species were added to the list, including two frogs - Hamilton's frog (*L. hamiltoni*) and Archey's frog (*L. archeyi*). It was not until half a century later that a second wave of taxonomic work began. A major revision of the New Zealand lizards in 1955 by Charles McCann more than doubled the number of described species. In the 1980s, following more extensive fieldwork and newly developed molecular genetic techniques, several cryptic species were discovered and described. The current wave of today (2000s) focuses mainly on untangling complexes of cryptic species, and has resulted in another giant increase in the number of recognised taxa, particularly of lizards. Even now, there are completely new and distinct species being discovered, and there is still a way to go to understanding the true extent of New Zealand's herpetofauna diversity.

Diversity and origins

New Zealand's 123 species/taxa of extant reptiles and amphibians fall into six groups: tuatara, geckos, skinks, frogs, marine turtles and marine snakes. Each group sits in a single taxonomic family, except for the frogs, marine turtles and snakes (Figure 1). The groups are briefly introduced here, including their origins, taxonomy, and distinguishing characteristics or behaviours.

Tuatara: Tuatara are very lizard-like in appearance, and even belong to the same major taxonomic classification that includes lizards and snakes. So, that major group - the Lepidosauria - includes the order Squamata (lizards, snakes and amphisbaenians) and the sister order

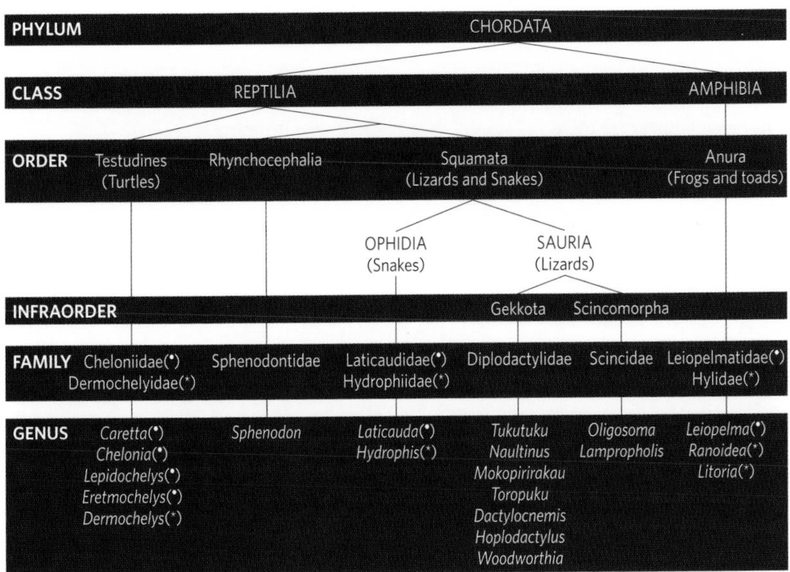

FIGURE 1 Higher taxonomic classifications for New Zealand's extant reptiles and amphibians

Tuatara, *Sphenodon punctatus*

Rhynchocephalia (tuatara). The latter is a more ancient group of reptiles, having appeared and thrived during the Mesozoic era (250–65 mya). Although Rhynchocephalians, including their more specialised forms (Sphenodontians), were once globally widespread and abundant, only one member of this diverse group, tuatara, survives today, and it is found only in New Zealand. The relatives of the tuatara are assumed to have arrived in the land that was to become New Zealand when it was part of the large supercontinent of Gondwana. However, because there are no living or recently fossilised overseas relatives, tuatara's Gondwanan origins cannot be confirmed or falsified using genetic tests of relatedness to overseas relatives, as has happened for the lizards. Evidence from subfossils (i.e. bones or remains that are not fully fossilised) indicates tuatara were once widely distributed throughout the country, but became functionally extinct on the North and South Island mainlands by c. 1840, shortly after the arrival of Europeans.

Tuatara have several anatomical features that distinguish them from other extant reptiles. These include: a distinct skull and jaw structure; the complete absence of a male intromittent organ to deliver sperm during mating; and a unique type of haemoglobin in the blood. Tuatara are one of three terrestrial reptiles in New Zealand that lay eggs (the other two are skinks).

Geckos: There are 43 extant species of New Zealand geckos (family Diplodactylidae) in seven genera (*Tukutuku, Naultinus, Mokopirirakau, Toropuku, Dactylocnemis, Hoplodactylus* and *Woodworthia*). All are endemic to New Zealand, and descended from a single common ancestor, which arrived in New Zealand some time between 53.5 and 28.9 mya. Certainly by 19–16 mya,

Northland green gecko, *Naultinus grayii*

when fossils in the Saint Bathans deposits in Otago were laid down, several species were present. Their closest relatives are in Australia. Geckos are widely distributed throughout New Zealand, occurring in all regions. In general, geckos are characterised by large eyes that are covered with transparent protective membranes rather than moveable eyelids. This means that their eyes are permanently open and geckos use a large fleshy tongue to clean the eyes and snout. Geckos are covered in small granular scales that give the skin a soft velvety appearance. Most geckos are competent and agile climbers owing to the presence of setae (microscopic hair-like structures) on the underside of their digits, and many have a prehensile tail. All New Zealand geckos are viviparous (i.e. give birth to live young).

Skinks: There are 64 extant species of New Zealand skinks, and two confirmed extinct species. All belong to the family Scincidae (subfamily Eugongylinae), and are in the single large genus *Oligosoma*. Like the geckos, all the New Zealand skinks are descended from a single colonising species. It probably arrived a little later than the ancestral gecko, but, like the geckos, the skinks were well established by the time the Saint Bathans fossil deposits were laid down. One naturalised exotic species – the plague or rainbow skink (*Lampropholis delicata*) – is part of the New Zealand skink fauna. Skinks are widely distributed throughout New Zealand, occurring in every region and almost every habitat type. Compared to geckos, skinks have moveable eyelids and narrower, pointed tongues, and their smooth overlapping scales give them a shiny or glossy appearance. Most New Zealand skinks are terrestrial (i.e. live on the ground), but many are also capable of climbing, swimming and diving below the water surface. Some skinks that climb

Copper skink, *Oligosoma aeneum*

trees (and therefore are arboreal), or rocks (and therefore are saxicolous) typically have longer toes, and some even have a prehensile tail. All but one native species, the egg-laying skink (*Oligosoma suteri*), and the exotic plague (rainbow) skink, are viviparous.

Frogs: The living New Zealand frog fauna consists of three native species (family Leiopelmatidae) and three exotic species (family Hylidae). All the native species belong to one endemic genus, *Leiopelma*, which also includes at least three extinct species (known only from subfossil bones). *Leiopelma* frogs (along with frogs of the North American genus *Ascaphus*) are the most primitive in the world, having diverged from other frog lineages more than 200 mya. Like the tuatara, they are assumed to be Gondwanan in origin and to have been present on New Zealand ever since it separated from adjacent landmasses; however, also like the tuatara, the absence of close relatives means this is difficult to confirm or falsify. Our native frog species have restricted ranges, and occur only in isolated populations across the northern North Island and on either side of the Cook Strait. These small frogs (< 52 mm snout-vent length, SVL) exhibit archaic characters that set them apart from most other frogs worldwide, such as the absence of a vocal sac (i.e. they do not call like other frogs, but may squeak or chirp), the absence of tympana (eardrums), and retention of tail-wagging muscles. The three exotic species were introduced from Australia, and are now well established in New Zealand. They differ from our native frogs by having visible tympana; being able to produce loud calls that can usually be heard over the breeding seasons; and their tadpoles are large, aquatic and free-living, and they actively feed.

Marine turtles: Marine turtles (superfamily Chelonioidea) are reptiles of the order Testudines (turtles). There are seven extant species worldwide, five of which

Hochstetter's frog, *Leiopelma hochstetteri*

PATRICE PLICHON

Green turtle, *Chelonia mydas*

have been reported in New Zealand waters. Except for the leatherback turtle (family Dermochelyidae), all marine turtles are in the family Cheloniidae. Most marine turtles seen in New Zealand waters are typically occasional visitors or stragglers. However, the leatherback is considered a regular migrant, and the green turtle has resident populations of juveniles.

The marine turtles have a protective bony shell that is hydrodynamically streamlined, and enlarged limbs or flippers that allow them to propel themselves gracefully through the water.

Marine snakes: Marine snakes are reptiles in the order Ophidia (snakes). Of the four species reported in New Zealand,

GEORGE KRUZA

Saint Giron's sea krait, *Laticauda saintgironsi*

three belong to the family Laticaudidae (sea kraits) and one to the family Hydrophiidae (true marine snakes). Sea kraits, although considered native, are not resident in New Zealand waters but instead are stragglers that have been carried by oceanic currents or storms. They are amphibious, spending much of their time in coastal waters but also coming ashore to bask and lay eggs. True marine snakes, on the other hand, live their entire lives at sea. The yellow-bellied sea snake (*Hydrophis platurus*) may be present year-round, and may even breed, in New Zealand waters to the north of the mainland. All marine snakes have a laterally flattened tail to help propel their streamlined body through the water. Most species have some ability to 'breathe' through their skin (accounting for 20–30% of their respiratory gas exchange), and all have a specialised gland, the posterior sublingual gland, that excretes excess salt. All four species from New Zealand are dangerously venomous.

Extinct fauna

The diversity of herpetofauna in New Zealand has changed markedly over geological time. In prehistoric times (before 65 mya), dinosaurs roamed through the ancient forests of New Zealand and giant plesiosaurs inhabited the surrounding oceans. However, there is an incomplete understanding of the New Zealand biota that lived during those times because of the country's poor fossil record, which in turn is probably a result of New Zealand's unstable geological history (which included violent volcanic activity and folding or uplifting of the Earth's crust, glaciations and marine submergences). These events, and subsequent erosion and deposition of tephra and gravels, would have destroyed or buried most, but not all, fossil material.

In 1981, the first New Zealand dinosaur fossil was found by Joan Wiffen (1922–2009), providing the first evidence of a pre-Pliocene land-dwelling fauna in this country. Since then, palaeontologists have revealed other fossil material, mostly originating from the Cretaceous period (c. 145–65 mya) and Early Miocene epoch (c. 23–16 mya). Fossils have been collected from sites in Hawke's Bay, Port Waikato, Kaikōura and the Chatham Islands, and include dinosaur groups such as non-maniraptoran coelurosaurs (relatively small carnivorous dinosaurs, with long tails and rudimentary feathers), titanosauriform sauropods (large herbivorous dinosaurs with small heads, and long necks and tails), ankylosaurs (armour-plated herbivorous dinosaurs, with a club-like protrusion on the end of the tail) and ornithopods (large bipedal herbivores with horny beaks). In north-west Nelson, there was even a set of dinosaur footprints left in the exposed late Cretaceous rocks. But probably the most significant dinosaur fossil site in New Zealand is the Maungataniwha Member, Tahora Formation, which is exposed at Mangahouanga Stream in Hawke's Bay. This site has yielded numerous dinosaur fossils, as well as fossil remains from pterosaurs (large flying reptiles), plesiosaurs and freshwater turtles. This was also the site where Joan Wiffen discovered the first dinosaur bone.

In central Otago at Saint Bathans, a small fragment of a crocodilian lower jaw was found in the Bannockburn Formation (Manuherikia Group) dating back to about 16 mya. The crocodilian is thought to represent a small 'blunt-snouted' crocodile (in the subfamily Mekosuchinae), similar to those that existed in Australia, Fiji, New Caledonia and Vanuatu around the same geological time period. While it is uncertain whether crocodilians lived in New Zealand permanently or were merely occasional visitors, this evidence indicates that crocodiles were present in New Zealand, at least intermittently, during the Miocene. The Saint Bathans site has also yielded fossils from other reptiles such as Rhynchocephalians (animals similar to tuatara), skinks morphologically similar to *Oligosoma* skinks, and *Hoplodactylus* (Diplodactylidae) geckos. As for 'amphibians' in New Zealand, the earliest known were the Stereospondyli. These 2-m-long amphibians had short legs, large heads with upward-facing eyes, and their large mouths were lined with needle-like teeth capable of snatching prey from the water or damp environments in which they lived. The Stereospondyli lived during the Triassic period (c. 251–199 mya), when New Zealand was probably still part of Gondwana. Other Gondwanan amphibian relicts include two Leiopelmatids and a neobatrachian frog (an 'advanced' frog, similar in morphology to typical frogs living today) that survived during the Early Miocene.

Since the beginning of the Quaternary period (< 2.6 mya), New Zealand's geology has remained relatively stable, which has led to a rich accumulation of subfossils. Reptile and amphibian subfossil bones from the late Pleistocene–Holocene epochs (< 100,000 years ago) have been found in dunes, caves and tomos across the country. Two large (140–170 mm SVL) extinct skinks (*Oligosoma northlandi* and *O.* indet.) are known only from subfossil remains. The subfossil amphibian fauna consists of three species of frogs of the genus *Leiopelma*, including *L. auroraensis, L. markhami* and *L. waitomoensis.* All were larger and more robust than today's Leiopelmatid frogs,

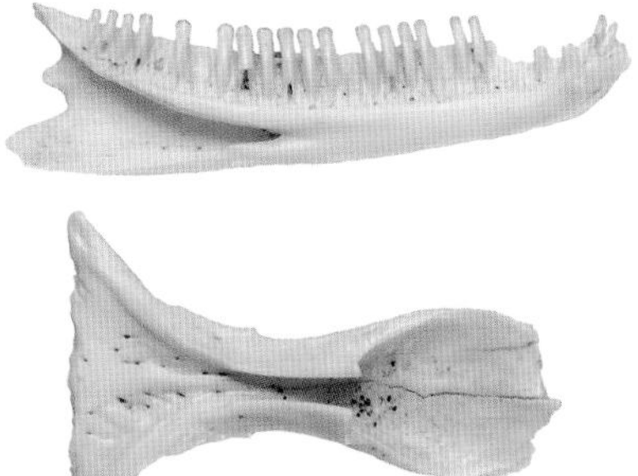

Oligosoma northlandi, subfossil bones

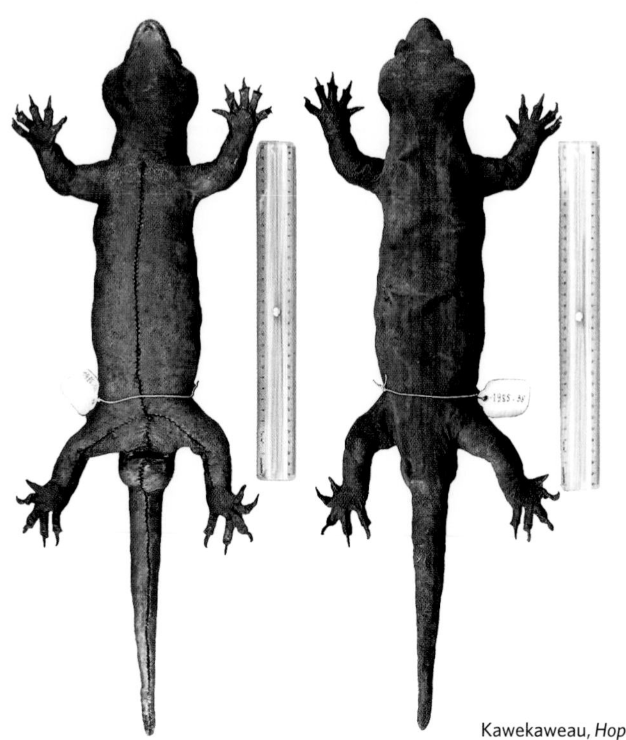

AARON BAUER

Kawekaweau, *Hoplodactylus delcourti*

and lived up to 1000–2000 years ago. *Leiopelma waitomoensis*, the largest of the three (at c. 100 mm SVL), was found in the North Island, while *L. auroraensis* occurred only in the South Island. *Leiopelma markhami* lived in both the North and South Islands. Unfortunately, many other bone fragments collected from these dune and cave sites remain unidentified and it is likely that New Zealand was home to further, undiscovered extinct reptile and amphibian species.

One further lizard, a giant gecko referred to as kawekaweau or Delcourt's gecko (*Hoplodactylus delcourti*), is known only from a 62-cm-long, poorly preserved specimen currently held in the Musée d'Histoire Naturelle de Marseille (Natural History Museum of Marseille) in France. The genus *Hoplodactylus* is endemic to New Zealand, and it has long been suggested that this gecko came from New Zealand. Māori folklore provides some support for such claims, referring to large arboreal lizards with dull red longitudinal stripes – a description which appears to closely match that of the preserved kawekaweau specimen. However, the specimen's lack of collection information, and the absence of New Zealand fossil remains of geckos of that size, mean that its origin remains a mystery. Additionally, recent molecular research has suggested that *H. delcourti* aligns more closely with the New Caledonian gecko fauna.

Exotic species

Exotic (alien or non-native) species are those living outside their native geographic range, having arrived at a new location via human activities. The list of exotic herpetofauna reported in New Zealand is assorted and extensive, comprising c. 200 species. These species arrived in New Zealand through generally one of three pathways: i) legal importation, either for aesthetic purposes (e.g. by acclimatisation societies, to stock zoological parks or by captive-animal enthusiasts) or research purposes; ii) accidental introduction, such as when species arrive as stowaways with imported cargo or people; or iii) intentional and illegal smuggling.

Over 50 species of exotic reptiles and amphibians are currently present in captivity in New Zealand. Fortunately, for many, the risk of invasion to and establishment in New Zealand is low given their subtropical or tropical origins and New Zealand's temperate climate. Some species, however, can tolerate cooler temperatures and there have been occasional reports of exotic reptiles and amphibians seen in the wild, such as the red-eared slider (*Trachemys scripta elegans*), eastern water dragon (*Intellagama lesueurii lesueurii*), Australian blue tongue skink (*Tiliqua scincoides*), eastern bearded dragon (*Pogona barbata*), and eastern snake-necked turtle (*Chelodina longicollis*). Prompt intervention by regional and national authorities has usually resulted in the rapid removal of individuals from the wild. However, sometimes more

Alpine newt, *Ichthyosaura alpestris apuanus*

Blue tongue skink, *Tiliqua scincoides*

Plague (rainbow) skink, *Lampropholis delicata*

intensive management has been required to extirpate small populations, for example, of White's tree frog (*Litoria caerulea*), eastern banjo frog (*Limnodynastes dumerilii*) and red-eared slider.

Only five exotic species have managed to naturalise in New Zealand, including the plague (rainbow) skink, the green and golden bell frog (*Ranoidea aurea*), the southern bell frog (*R. raniformis*), the brown (whistling) tree frog (*Litoria ewingii*) and the alpine newt (*Ichthyosaura alpestris apuanus*). The first four species are native to Australia, have had a relatively long presence in New Zealand and are well established. Establishment of the alpine newt is more recent, occurring probably around the turn of the century. An intensive eradication programme is underway to remove the single known population from New Zealand.

Exotic species can threaten our native species in many ways, such as: through the introduction or spread of novel diseases, pathogens or parasites (external or internal); directly through predation; or as competitors for important resources. Chytridiomycosis is an infectious disease of amphibians caused by the chytrid fungus *Batrachochytrium dendrobatidis* (*Bd*). It is responsible for many declines in amphibian populations worldwide, and has been implicated in the decline of one of New Zealand's native frogs, Archey's frog. However, the relationship between the presence of chytrid and the decline in Archey's frog remains unclear. Fortunately, *Bd* has not yet been detected in New Zealand's other two endemic frog species. It is possible that *Bd* was introduced to New Zealand via African clawed frogs (*Xenopus*) that were once imported in large numbers for human pregnancy testing. *Bd* could then have escaped to the wild via infected exotic *Ranoidea* frogs that were released by captive-animal keepers. *Ranoidea* frogs are also known to prey on native lizards, and since these frogs coexist with many of our native taxa, including some that are highly endangered, these frogs could negatively affect New Zealand's lizard populations. In terms of exotic reptiles

Red-eared slider, *Trachemys scripta elegans*

and amphibians competing with indigenous species for important resources such as food and shelter sites, the plague (rainbow) skink is capable of reaching extremely high population densities, saturating available resources, and it could out-compete or drive out our native species.

New Zealand faces ongoing challenges from exotic species, and more research is required to investigate the effects of exotic reptiles and amphibians on our endemic herpetofauna. Some of the key challenges include:

- preventing the spread of current naturalised exotic species to other more sensitive areas of New Zealand (e.g. protected offshore islands)
- finding ways to control or eradicate naturalised exotic species
- preventing further exotic species from naturalising (e.g. red-eared slider)
- preventing the arrival and establishment of new exotic species from overseas.

National authorities such as the Department of Conservation, regional councils and the Ministry for Primary Industries are instrumental in tackling such challenges, but public reporting of exotic reptiles and amphibians in the wild remains essential for rapid response and attempts at control.

CONSERVATION OF NEW ZEALAND HERPETOFAUNA

New Zealand's terrestrial herpetofauna has suffered major declines since the arrival of humans, so now over 80% of our taxa are threatened with, or are at longer-term risk of, extinction. When humans arrived here, they introduced mammalian predators (e.g. cats, hedgehog, pigs, mustelids, possums, rodents) and other exotic species that harboured diseases and pathogens (e.g. *Ranoidea* frogs). In addition, humans are responsible for land-use changes (e.g. deforestation, forestry, agriculture, urban development, mining) that have caused significant loss and fragmentation of habitats. These anthropogenic effects have resulted in severe range contractions, population fragmentation, and both localised and national extinctions of native species. Many taxa have managed to persist only where these influences are lessened or absent, such as on offshore islands and at high altitudes. Other taxa survive only through active management to conserve them.

Current management strategies have primarily been aimed at removing the pressures exerted by mammalian predators on New Zealand's native reptiles and amphibians. Two techniques have been relatively successful – intensive and sustained control of the mammalian predators, and translocation of native species to protected, mammal-free sites (i.e. mainland sanctuaries or offshore islands). Specifically, controlling mammalian predators has entailed excluding predators from sites (e.g. by erecting mammal-proof fences) or severely suppressing predator numbers. These techniques are the first steps towards restoring sites for herpetofauna conservation. Large-scale, intensive predator control programmes, to trap and poison predators, have been successful in some places, but disappointing in others. To benefit lizards, the programmes need to effectively target not just purely carnivorous predators but also rodents. In some habitats, mice can have severe impacts on lizard populations, and these rodents are extremely difficult to control consistently over large areas, particularly when their own predators are removed.

For native species that have undergone local extinction, conservation translocation is an increasingly common solution. Individuals are either collected from another wild sub-population, or raised in captivity to sufficient numbers, and then released at the new site. Most translocations of reptiles and amphibians in New Zealand have been wild-to-wild

Predator-free sanctuary, Auckland

translocations; however, more recently, captive breeding has also contributed to successful conservation programmes, including for tuatara, geckos (e.g. barking (*Naultinus punctatus*), elegant (*N. elegans*) and Duvaucel's geckos), skinks (e.g. shore (*Oligosoma smithi*), grand (*O. grande*) and Otago (*O. otagense*) skinks) and frogs (e.g. Archey's and Hamilton's frogs).

Habitat loss is a serious threat to New Zealand's herpetofauna. New Zealand's native forest cover has been reduced from 80% (before human occupation) to just 24%. Large areas of land continue to be cleared and developed for agriculture, urban use and other human-associated activities. All native herpetofauna and their habitats are protected under the Wildlife Act 1953 and Resource Management Act 1991 respectively, which means it is illegal to deliberately disturb them without specific authorisation. In practice, any land development, especially of sites supporting threatened native species or habitat that is significant for native species, is legally required to avoid, reduce or mitigate negative environmental impacts. While some regional authorities are diligently attempting to ensure compliance with these laws, monitoring across many regions of New Zealand is not consistent, and the result is a net loss of biodiversity, often including the loss of indigenous herpetofauna.

Two of the novel diseases, pathogens and parasites threatening the reptiles and amphibians of New Zealand are chytridiomycosis in frogs (mentioned above) and dermatomycosis, caused by *Paranannizziopsis australasiensis*, in tuatara. Research on chytrid fungi, both in New Zealand and overseas, has been extensive owing to their devastating effects on amphibians worldwide. Recent experimental work in New Zealand suggests that under laboratory conditions, all three *Leiopelma* frogs can carry chytrids but survive infection, and the full effects of chytrids on wild frog populations are yet to be determined. Recently, *P. australasiensis* – a member of the fungal group *Chrysosporium* anamorph of *Nannizziopsis vriesii* (CANV) complex – has been detected in both captive and wild tuatara. It causes dermatitis and skin lesions which can threaten the welfare and conservation of tuatara. However, at this stage it is unknown whether *P. australasiensis* is endemic in New Zealand, or is an imported exotic pathogen.

OBSERVING AMPHIBIANS AND REPTILES

In New Zealand, all native reptiles and amphibians are protected by law, under the Wildlife Act 1953. This protection status means that it is illegal to capture, collect, hold in possession or deliberately disturb them without a wildlife permit (technically, a Wildlife Act Authorisation) issued by the Department of Conservation. Before venturing into the field to search for reptiles or amphibians, ensure that you have the necessary permissions (e.g. permission from landowners and iwi, a wildlife permit).

Locating and observing wild herpetofauna can be extremely difficult, relatively easy and anything in between, depending on where you are in the country, the taxa found there and the environmental conditions. Many taxa are highly cryptic, and some have very restricted distributions or are present in low numbers, and thus can be hard to find. Others are relatively common and are frequently observed at

Tuatara faeces (top), gecko faeces (middle) and skink faeces (bottom)

easily accessible sites, such as in urban or suburban areas, regional parks, reserves or publicly accessible pest-free islands. When searching, it is also worth looking for the signs left by lizards, such as sloughed skin or faeces.

Marine reptiles are more difficult to observe, but can occasionally be seen while you are diving or snorkelling, or can be found (less frequently) stranded on beaches. For marine reptiles, whether you are in a boat or in the water, you must adhere to the Wildlife Act and remain at least 5 m away from the subject. Never attempt to touch the animal, especially marine snakes, since there is both a risk of you causing them distress or them causing you harm (all marine snakes are dangerously venomous).

What to do if you encounter a native reptile or amphibian

If you encounter a native reptile or amphibian, note down the observation and submit the record to the Department of Conservation's Amphibian and Reptile Distribution Scheme (ARDS). Visit the DOC website (www.doc.govt.nz) for more information on the Scheme and to download an 'ARDS card' (a submission form).

Keeping reptiles and amphibians in captivity in New Zealand

As indicated already in this chapter, it is illegal to catch and hold wild native reptiles and amphibians in New Zealand without authorisation (i.e. a permit), under the Wildlife Act 1953. However, it is possible to keep some species/taxa of captive-bred native lizards under a 'General Authorisation to hold common species'. You simply apply for the General

Gecko slough

Authorisation through the Department of Conservation website (www.doc.govt.nz), where you will also find information on the application process and other useful guidelines. Captive native reptiles cannot be sold, but can be rehomed to other authorised holders or passed to the Department of Conservation.

Permits are generally not required to hold non-native reptiles and amphibians that are currently available, in captivity, in New Zealand. The exceptions are: those listed as 'unwanted organisms' under the New Zealand Biosecurity Act 1993; those considered a 'containment animal' (e.g. certain species held by zoos); and species listed in regional pest management plans. At the time of printing, two species are listed as 'unwanted organisms': the plague (rainbow) skink and the alpine newt. For these species, it is illegal to knowingly move, spread, release, breed, display or sell them without permission from the Ministry for Primary Industries.

Regional pest management plans/strategies aim to prevent the establishment or spread of other high-risk reptiles by prohibiting their sale, breeding, distribution, release or exhibition. Some regions, such as Auckland, have lists of 'surveillance pest' species, for which trade is regulated. There, for example, bearded dragons, red-eared sliders, shingleback lizards (*Tiliqua rugosa*) and eastern water dragons are declared pests when outside of secure confinement, and regional authorities respond to remove these animals from the wild when they are reported. The Ministry for Primary Industries is developing a National Pest Pet Biosecurity Accord to regulate the domestic trade of high-risk pets and encourage responsible pet ownership. No species are currently regulated under the accord, but it is likely that several commonly kept reptile and amphibian species will be affected by it in future.

Illegal collection from the wild

As highlighted above, New Zealand native reptiles are unique by world standards, and green geckos (*Naultinus*) in particular differ markedly from other geckos as they are brightly coloured, diurnal and exhibit unusual life history traits (they are live-bearing and long-lived). Further, many of our taxa are rare, and all these factors make New Zealand's reptiles particularly interesting and desirable to private collectors overseas.

Small numbers of native reptiles, including tuatara and probably four species of geckos, were previously exported legally. Their limited availability in the international pet trade has meant that private international keepers receive high prices for these taxa. But the low numbers overseas and the animals' slow reproductive rates mean that traders are unable to satisfy the huge demand. This has resulted in the illegal collection of New Zealand's wild reptiles for smuggling. Illegal collection from the wild is a serious problem for many of New Zealand's native lizard taxa because it can compromise the long-term viability of populations, particularly of those taxa that occur in small accessible populations or are naturally in decline. Illegal collection may even lead to the extinction of sub-populations.

Many of New Zealand's lizards are targeted, but those taxa with attractive markings – such as the jewelled gecko (*N. gemmeus*) – are prioritised for collection. High pressure from smugglers has resulted in all *Naultinus* taxa being listed under Appendix 2 of the Convention on International Trade in Endangered Species (CITES), which aims to manage trade by making it illegal to trade these reptiles without official CITES documents. All other New Zealand geckos are listed under Appendix 3. But even this level of protection does not deter poachers, and animals continue to leave the country each year. New Zealand wildlife investigators monitor international trade and investigate and intercept poaching whenever possible, and smugglers who are caught are prosecuted. Public reporting of any suspicious activity to the Department of Conservation is important.

NEW ZEALAND'S ECOSYSTEMS AND GEOGRAPHIC HISTORY

New Zealand is a small archipelago, comprising two main islands (North and South Islands) and over 650 smaller islands and islets around them. It is long and narrow, extending from 37°S to 47°S latitude, and is over 1600 km long along its north–south axis and c. 400 km across at its widest point. New Zealand is part of the submerged subcontinent of Zealandia, which broke away from Gondwana approximately 80 mya. During the Pliocene epoch, the southern North Island was submerged under the Manawatu Strait. The coastline of the southern North Island ran across the Central Plateau region, from present-day Taranaki to Hawke's Bay, and the strait created a significant barrier between the then North and South islands. During the late Pliocene and early Pleistocene epochs, tectonic activity uplifted the southern North Island, resulting in the draining of Manawatu Strait. Vast expanses of lowland forest gradually covered the area, and subsequent sea level fluctuations allowed intermittent land bridges to form between the two islands, across the Cook Strait. The uplift of the South Island's iconic longitudinal backbone mountains, the Southern Alps, also occurred during the Pliocene and early Pleistocene epochs, with movement along the Alpine Fault thrusting mountains up from previously low-lying land. These mountainous regions offered new habitats, such as montane tussock grassland and true alpine zones, for local species to exploit. Throughout the mid- and late Pleistocene, a series of climatic fluctuations – long cold glacial periods interrupted by warmer interglacials – strongly shaped the structure and diversity of New Zealand's vegetation and habitats. The development of new habitat, and fragmentation or isolation of other habitats, due to these cyclic patterns in turn affected animal movement (i.e. gene flow) between these land areas. High faunal diversity and high species endemism within the regions were a consequence (Figure 2). In some cases, human impacts causing local extinctions and contractions of species' ranges may have exaggerated these regional effects, but there's good evidence that most of the local endemism is natural.

New Zealand, in its current state, has several ecosystem types, each with a distinct assemblage of species. For the purposes of this field guide, ecosystem types have been broadly categorised into altitudinal zones.

Marine and coastal (sea level–c. 200 m ASL)

New Zealand's marine environment is exposed to three major water fronts: the Tasman, the Subtropical and the Subantarctic. The first two bring warm surface currents from the west, which bathe

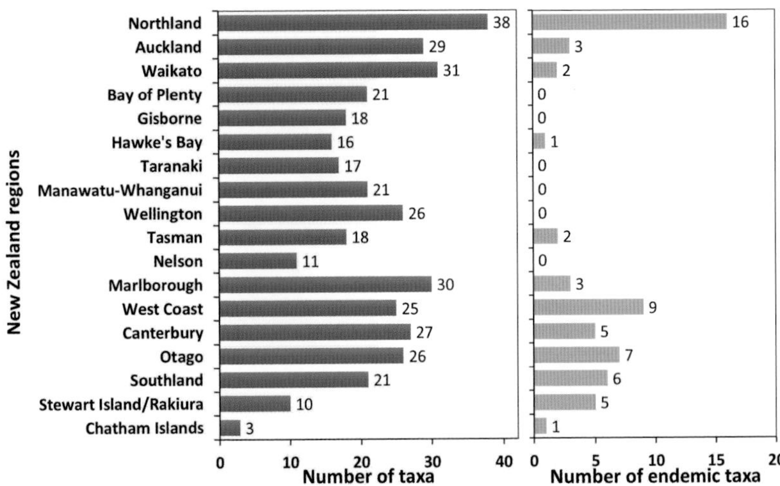

FIGURE 2 Numbers of reptile and amphibian taxa per region, showing (left) all taxa and (right) taxa endemic to the region.

the North Island's coasts and travel down the west coast and around the bottom of the South Island. The cooler Subantarctic Front and associated Antarctic Circumpolar Current flow north-eastwards along the deep ocean floor east of the Campbell Plateau and Chatham Rise, bringing cold water to the seas off the southern and south-eastern coast of the South Island.

The 30° latitudinal spread of New Zealand's seascapes encompasses subtropical to subantarctic waters. Coupled with New Zealand's isolation from large landmasses, this creates a particularly rich and complex marine environment that supports a diversity of habitats and species assemblages. It is mostly because of these fronts and currents that marine turtles and snakes are found in New Zealand's waters. Some individuals are passively carried (drifting) with the currents, while others rely on oceanic currents to assist in their movement towards important feeding or nursery areas.

The coastline of New Zealand extends for 15,000 km, and includes many habitat types such as estuarine mudflats; sandy, gravel or boulder beaches; dunelands; and rocky shores and platforms. The littoral or intertidal zone is heavily influenced by tidal activity, and is continually being inundated and then exposed during the daily tidal cycles. The few reptiles that live in this demanding and hostile environment have adapted to the challenges of exposure to breaking waves and the desiccating effects of wind, sunlight, and high salinity. Of the terrestrial reptiles, only three species of skinks are strictly confined to these harsh habitats (shore skink, egg-laying skink and Fiordland skink (*O. acrinasum*)), although several others frequently inhabit the shoreline and the adjacent coastal scrub or forest.

The habitat structure changes markedly as you move from the littoral zone inland, and you may encounter areas of coastal duneland or suddenly come upon scrubland

Base map: Geographx

or coastal forest. The vegetation here is dominated by plants that can tolerate wind and salt spray, such as spinifex (*Spinifex sericeus*), wire vine (*Muehlenbeckia complexa*), flax (*Phormium tenax*), and trees and shrubs like ngaio (*Myoporum laetum*), taupata (*Coprosma repens*), pōhutukawa (*Metrosideros excelsa*) and patē (*Schefflera digitata*). Further inland, more sheltered sites are dominated by species like pūriri (*Vitex lucens*), karaka (*Corynocarpus laevigatus*) and kawakawa (*Macropiper excelsum*). This coastal zone supports a diversity of herpetofauna including tuatara and many species of lizard.

Offshore islands and smaller islets are also included in the coastal zone. Islands that have never had exotic mammals support a rich biodiversity of reptiles and amphibians. These pest-free islands represent examples of relatively unmodified ecosystems in New Zealand, and act as refugia for rare species that have been extirpated on the mainland (e.g. robust skink (*O. alani*), and New Zealand's rarest frog, Hamilton's frog). The abundance of

Coastal habitat, Auckland

Rocky shore on an offshore island, Northland

the herpetofauna on these mammal-free islands can be extraordinary, and so these islands do provide good examples of what the New Zealand mainland might have looked like in pre-human history (although predatory native birds such as wēkā (*Gallirallus australis*), and other now extinct species, may have reduced mainland densities somewhat).

Lowland (< 500 m ASL)

New Zealand's lowland environments make up approximately half of the total land area, and their habitat types and species assemblages can vary greatly depending on their location. Generally, these areas receive relatively high rainfall (less on the east than the west coast) and experience warm temperatures that encourage the growth of forests and the formation of wetlands, swamps, marshes, pakihi and bogs. Wetlands generally support sedges, rushes and reeds, and are surrounded by scrubland, including mānuka (*Leptospermum scoparium*), kānuka (*Kunzea* species), mingimingi (*Leucopogon fasciculatus*), pōhuehue (*Muehlenbeckia australis*), and māpou (*Myrsine australis*), and forests containing kahikatea (*Dacrycarpus dacrydioides*), pukatea (*Laurelia novae-zelandiae*), cabbage tree (*Cordyline australis*), and silver pine (*Manoao colensoi*). Numerous lizard species are associated with these habitats, including green and cryptic skinks (*O. chloronoton* and *O. inconspicuum*, respectively), which prefer damp environments, and forest (*Mokopirirakau* species) and green (*Naultinus* species) geckos found in the surrounding scrubland and forests.

The warmer climate in the northern part of New Zealand produces mixed podocarp-broadleaf forests. Here there is a rich diversity of trees, and they are dominated by emergent podocarps, such as rimu (*Dacrydium cupressinum*), mātai

Lowland forest, Westland

(*Prumnopitys taxifolia*), tōtara (*Podocarpus totara*), kauri (*Agathis australis*) and miro (*Prumnopitys ferruginea*), and broadleaved species like taraire (*Beilschmiedia taraire*), tawa (*B. tawa*) and maire (*Nestegis cunninghamii*). Typically, the sub-canopy supports kohekohe (*Dysoxylum spectabile*), māhoe (*Melicytus ramiflorus*), kāmahi (*Weinmannia racemosa*), nīkau (*Rhopalostylis sapida*) and various vines, such as kiekie (*Freycinetia banksii*), with ferns and herbaceous species cloaking the ground. In the cooler parts of New Zealand, these forests are replaced by other combinations such as tawa, rimu, mataī, tōtara and northern rātā (*Metrosideros robusta*). In the South Island, beech (*Fuscospora and Lophozonia* species), broadleaved and podocarp forests dominate, and coastal forests support a ferny, moss-covered understory with a dense leaf-litter layer. Lowland environments support a rich diversity of herpetofauna, including Hochstetter's and Archey's frogs, several species of green geckos, *Woodworthia* or *Dactylocnemis* geckos, members of the forest gecko group, and leaf-litter dwelling skinks. However, the coverage of lowland native forests across New Zealand has been drastically reduced to make way for human-associated land use, and as a result, the number of lowland herpetofauna taxa is much reduced today.

Montane/subalpine (500–1000 m ASL)

Nestled between the lowland forest and harsh alpine areas, the subalpine zone is generally drier than less elevated land and exposed to a wider range of temperatures, from below freezing to over 30 °C. The subalpine zone covers c. 19% of New Zealand's land area, and is an iconic landscape of the South Island, and to a lesser degree, areas of the North Island's Central Plateau. This zone generally

Subalpine pākihi swamp, Westland

Subalpine shrubland, Canterbury

supports tussock grassland, e.g. snow and red tussock (*Chionochloa* species); native herbs; dense shrubland, e.g. tūpare/leatherwood (*Olearia colensoi*), snow tōtara (*Podocarpus nivalis*), mountain toatoa (*Phyllocladus alpinus*), porcupine shrub (*Melicytus alpinus*), matagouri (*Discaria toumatou*), and the little mountain heath (*Pentachondra pumila*); and subalpine scrubland, e.g. *Dracophyllum menziesii* and mountain beech (*Fuscospora cliffortioides*). The montane/subalpine zone supports a very high diversity of lizards, particularly *Oligosoma* skinks, but *Woodworthia* geckos are also common in this zone. Rocky outcrops, tors and screes scattered throughout the montane/subalpine zone provide suitable crevices and rocky basking sites for lizards, and the dense shrublands are preferred habits of the arboreal green geckos. During the harsh winters, lizards take refuge in rocky crevices and screes, or in dense vegetation thickets, to escape heavy frosts and snow.

Alpine (> 1000 m ASL)

The alpine zone typically includes areas that occur above the regional treeline, and below the subnival zone, which is permanently covered in snow. The altitudinal range of the alpine zone varies with latitude, being lower in the more southerly parts of New Zealand and higher in the warmer northern regions. That said, the alpine zone can be considered to be above 1000 m ASL. Approximately 11% of New Zealand's land area falls in the alpine zone, which is primarily in the North Island's Central Plateau and the South Island's Southern Alps and axial ranges. Some plant species (e.g. low-growing herbs, mosses and liverworts) survive the cold temperatures by being small and compact. Rock outcrops, boulder fields and screes are common in this zone, and avalanches heavily affect this environment. Separated by lowlands, the alpine zone preserves pockets of biodiversity, but New Zealand's alpine herpetofauna is poorly known, and currently limited to a handful of gecko

Alpine zone, Kahurangi National Park

SARAH J. WELLS

Alpine zone, Canterbury

and skink taxa. Some – like the black-eyed gecko (*Mokopirirakau kahutarae*) and Sinbad skink (*Oligosoma pikitanga*) – appear to be exclusive alpine specialists, while others also occur at lower altitudes, in the montane/subalpine zone (e.g. the Southern Alps gecko (*Woodworthia* "Southern Alps") and scree skink (*Oligosoma waimatense*)). These alpine lizards survive in the harsh conditions, where avalanches, rock falls and snow cover are features of their habitat for six or more months of the year, by taking refuge in deep rock crevices and having an ability to be active at very low temperatures.

HOW TO USE THIS GUIDE

Several guides exist on New Zealand's reptiles and amphibians, and this book builds upon the works of previous authors, presenting the most up-to-date view of the ever-increasing information on New Zealand's herpetofauna. The aim of this book is to help you, the reader, identify reptiles and amphibians encountered in New Zealand, particularly in the field, where species identification can be challenging. Although some species are iconic and easily identified (e.g. tuatara and Hochstetter's frog), for others, identification may require closer attention to body shape, colour and patterning, and scale features, and to the animal's behaviour or habitat because many taxa appear very similar to each other. Also, knowledge of where the animal was found can be vital for distinguishing between closely related or similar-looking species. This field guide differs from other guides by presenting each species or taxon on a uniform white background, highlighting its morphological characters, to allow rapid and clear comparisons between different species or taxa. While it is generally possible to determine the identity of a specimen in hand, it is often helpful to take high-quality photographs that can be referred to later.

This book covers six major groups: tuatara, geckos, skinks, frogs, marine turtles and marine snakes, each of which is in a separate 'species account' section. Each section begins with a general introduction to the biology and behaviour of taxa in that group, followed by a series of illustrations that highlight important morphological features and then detailed accounts of each of the taxa. An identification key is provided at the end of each section.

Photographing Lizards for Identification Purposes

As mentioned above, several subtle features are important for identification, and this is especially true of lizards, including colour pattern, scale numbers and scale arrangements. Therefore, taking a series of high-quality close-up photographs that are in focus will help you and experts to accurately identify the species or taxon encountered.

Important features for lizards include:

- dorsal, lateral and ventral colour patterning
- arrangement of scales on the head and tip of the snout, including the rostral scale that lies between the nostrils
- colouration of the inside of the mouth and tongue
- underside of the hind foot showing the lamellae (broad transverse scales)
- vent region, on the underside between the hind legs.

Photographs of the following will allow these important features to be clearly visible:

- close-up of the side and top of the head
- the entire lizard showing the dorsolateral aspect
- of the ventral (underside) surface
- close-up of the underside of the hind foot.

Species name

The taxon's common and scientific or 'tag name' lead the account. The common names follow the standardised names as listed by Bell (2014). A tag name is a temporary name used where a scientific name for a taxon has not been formally assigned. Tag names generally begin with the genus followed by the specimen's general locality, e.g. *Mokopirirakau* "southern forest", *Woodworthia* aff. *maculata* "Muriwai", or reference to a specific characteristic in double quote marks, e.g. *Oligosoma* "cobble", *Mokopirirakau* "pygmy". As high as 45% of the known 'species' in New Zealand have not been formally described, thus tag names are in frequent use. The specific name is followed by the name of author(s) and year in which the species description was published, e.g. *Naultinus elegans* Gray, 1842. Where a species name has been re-classified to a different genus from which it was originally described, the original author name and date are in parentheses, e.g. *Oligosoma moco* (Duméril & Bibron, 1839). The origin and meaning (i.e. etymology) of the common and specific or tag names, and where relevant, the Māori names, are provided.

Some species of lizard have been found (usually using genetic research) to include several different taxa of similar appearance. Until the genetic relationships between the taxa and their diagnostic morphological features are determined, these groups are referred to as **species complexes**. For example, the green skink is in the process of being formally split into four or five taxa, so is currently referred to as the '*Oligosoma chloronoton* species complex'. In this book, these taxa are treated separately and are given tag names, even though they have not been formally described. The abbreviation "aff." (meaning 'affinis' or 'has an affinity to') is used to denote members of a species complex (*Oligosoma* aff. *chloronoton* "West Otago"). For groups of very closely related species that have been formally described (e.g. *O. lineoocellatum, O. elium, O. prasinum* and *O. kokowai*), these are referred to as **species groups** (e.g. *O. lineoocellatum* species group).

Description

The taxon description begins with a measurement of the body length, generally measured on the ventral surface of the animal, from the tip of the snout to the vent (cloacal opening). This measurement is commonly referred to as the 'snout-vent length' (SVL), and values provided in this book are generally the upper limit for sexually mature individuals. Individuals seen in the field will usually be smaller than the sizes stated here, although occasional individuals may be slightly larger. Where available, weights of mature, non-gravid (i.e. not containing eggs or young) adults are provided. There are general descriptions of body colouration and pattern, including pertinent features that distinguish the species/taxon from similar ones. This includes the arrangement of colour markings on the dorsal, lateral and ventral surfaces, and specific scale characters such as the arrangement of scales on the head. In skinks and snakes, the number of mid-body scale rows (MSRs) - the scales encircling the middle of the body - are often helpful for distinguishing between closely related taxa, and where appropriate the number of MSRs is provided. For lizards, the number and shape of lamellae on the underside of the fourth toe of the hind foot vary between taxa, and often are a diagnostic feature.

Distribution

Text explains where the species/taxon can be found in New Zealand and a map of New Zealand depicts the known (and for some taxa, the predicted) ranges. For exotic species, descriptions of their distributional ranges in their native countries are also provided.

Maps

A distribution map is provided for each species/taxon. The predicted, and in many cases potential range is shown in green for terrestrial species and blue for marine ones (see key below, which applies to all distribution maps). A darker shade indicates predicted range - based on database records surrounded by a 40 km buffer, except where this would include areas where the species/taxon is absent. A lighter shade is used for areas adjacent to the predicted range where the species/taxon is likely to be present - these are crude estimates and should be regarded as general hypotheses only. Arrows highlight species presence in small areas not clearly visible at the map scale, such as islands, island groups, some mainland sites such as sanctuaries where species/taxa have been reintroduced, or where species/taxa are limited to a narrow coastal margin. Where a species/taxon occupies many sites in a small area, arrows are indicative only.

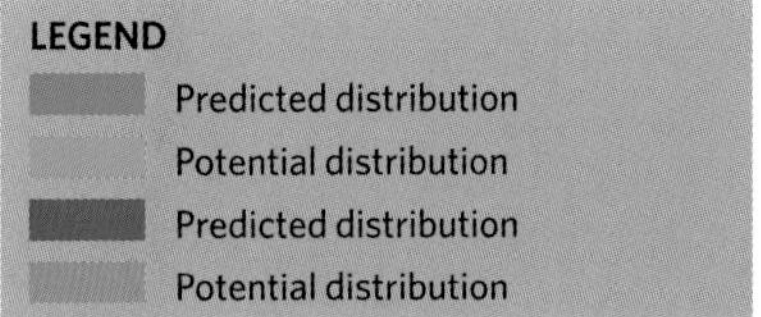

Variation and similar species

Since many taxa vary considerably in body colour patterning, both within and between populations, a description of this intraspecific variation is provided. Similar-looking or confusing taxa found in the same area are also described here, to enable quick comparisons and accurate identification.

Habitat

The taxon's habitat type, based on altitude, is stated using these categories: coastal (0–200 m ASL), lowland (200–500 m ASL), montane/subalpine (500–1000 m ASL) and alpine (> 1000 m ASL) as described above. This is followed by descriptions of the areas and microhabitat in which the species/taxon can be found.

Natural history

Text highlights some typical aspects of the natural history of the taxon such as its activity period, behaviour, reproductive biology, diet and other interesting information.

Photograph

Photographs present the typical morphology of the species/taxon. A series of photographs is provided where considerable morphological variation is known, and captions are provided to indicate locations or variant names.

Identification key

An identification key is provided at the end of each major group. Each key provides a stepwise method to accurately identify each species or taxon. You are presented with two contrasting characters, only one of which should apply to the specimen being identified, and you are to choose one. Each choice determines the next step and the next couplet of characters to consider, until a species/taxon is identified. Once a specimen has been successfully keyed out, the specific name is listed at the end of the key, and you can refer to the respective species account in the guide. For some taxa, the identification key ends at the genus or species group level (e.g. *Oligosoma infrapunctatum* group). Here, you will need to refer to the species accounts for all members of the specific genera or species group where descriptions of each taxon will help you identify the specimen.

If neither of the characters in a couplet fits, there are a few possibilities:

- you have made an incorrect decision in an earlier couplet, so start again and see if you end up at the same place
- the specimen has characters that fall outside the general description of the taxon (for some taxa, considerable morphological variation exists between individuals and identification keys may not accurately describe all variations)
- there may be an error in the key
- the specimen may represent a species new to science.

In these last two cases, consider contacting a professional herpetologist for advice.

Elegant gecko, *Naultinus elegans*

Tuatara, *Sphenodon punctatus*, Hauraki Gulf

TUATARA

TUATARA

Tuatara belong to the large taxonomic superorder Lepidosauria, a group that also includes lizards and snakes. Although it is very lizard-like in its appearance, the tuatara is rather the sole surviving member of an ancient lineage of Sphenodontid reptiles. It is classified within its own order, Rhynchocephalia, and its closest relatives are the extinct Rhyncocephalians represented only by fossil bones from the Mesozoic era (250–65 mya).

Tuatara have Gondwanan origins, and have retained a number of ancestral features, including:

- a pronounced parietal eye ('third eye') on the top of the head, which functions as a light-sensing organ
- no ear opening or eardrum
- amphicoelous vertebrae (shaped more like those of fish)
- uncinate processes – small hook-like structures that attach muscles to the ribs
- gastralia or 'abdominal ribs' – bones in the skin layer of the ventral surface
- two rows of teeth on the upper jaw, and one row of teeth on the lower jaw. The resulting specialised jaw movement allows the teeth to exert a shearing effect
- no intromittent organ in males (i.e. males lack the paired hemipenes found in lizards).

Tuatara are long-lived reptiles, and have very low reproductive rates. Generation time (the average interval between the birth of an individual and the birth of its offspring) is usually regarded as 30 years, one of the longest of any known terrestrial reptile. In the wild, sexual maturity is reached at 10–15 years of age, and females are capable of breeding only every 2–5 years owing to the long time it takes to produce eggs. Eggs can take 10–16 months to hatch. The sex of hatchlings is temperature dependent, with warmer incubation temperatures ($\geq$ 22.2 °C) tending to produce males, and cooler temperatures ($\leq$ 21.2 °C) females. At 22 °C, there is an equal probability of an egg developing into a male or a female.

Sphenodon punctatus, juvenile

Tuatara were once widely distributed throughout New Zealand. However, numbers have declined significantly, and mainland and many island populations disappeared following the arrival of Pacific rats/kiore (*Rattus exulans*) with early Polynesian settlers, and since then, with the arrival of further predatory mammals (including other rat species) with Europeans. Rats probably had a dual effect on tuatara numbers via direct predation (by kiore preying on small-sized tuatara and tuatara eggs) and competition (between tuatara and rats for food resources). The very rapid extinction of tuatara in the 1970s from Whenuakura Island (near Whangamata) when Norway rats (*Rattus norvegicus*) reached the island indicates that this species preys on adult tuatara as well.

The tuatara is currently restricted to a total of 32 isolated offshore islands, off the east of the North Island (Bay of Plenty to Northland) and in the Cook Strait. And those island populations are thriving, with an estimated 100,000 wild tuatara in total. Some offshore islands have population densities reaching 2732 tuatara per hectare (e.g. Stephens Island/ Takapourewa). These encouraging numbers are partly a result of conservation efforts over the last two decades to remove the threats of predation and competition by rats from several islands. Tuatara were then introduced to some protected islands, and to a small handful of pest-free mainland sanctuaries.

The tuatara is an iconic species for New Zealand, and is of great significance to Māori culture. They feature in some Māori legends, traditional paintings and sculptures, and, for some iwi, tuatara represent the guardians of knowledge.

DAVE JENKINS

Sphenodon punctatus, hatching

Tuatara

Sphenodon punctatus (Gray, 1842) **Endemic**

Cook Strait

DESCRIPTION

200–280 mm SVL; females up to 0.5 kg, males up to 1 kg weight

New Zealand's largest reptile; closely resembles a lizard. **Dorsal surface** typically slate-grey, olive-green, yellowish or brick-red. Body often finely speckled (more prominent in juveniles), with crest of soft spines (usually white) along mid-line of neck, body and tail. Crest more strongly developed in males. **Ventral surface** uniform (occasionally lightly speckled) pale grey. No ear opening. Top of head with parietal eye ('third eye'), having photoreceptive abilities (more pronounced in juveniles). Males generally larger, and with broader and more triangular heads, than females. Hatchlings have blunt snouts and white denticulate markings along lower jawline. **Feet** with narrow digits; each toe with a large claw on the end.

DISTRIBUTION

North and South Islands. Occurs on several offshore islands off the east coast of the North Island and in Cook Strait. Translocated populations also established at several mainland localities, in fenced mammal-free sanctuaries.

VARIATION AND SIMILAR SPECIES

For some years considered two separate species (tuatara, *S. punctatus*; and Brother's Island or Gunther's tuatara, *S. guntheri*) based on morphology and genetics, but in 2009 *S. guntheri* was synonymised with *S. punctatus*. Now treated as a single species, informally split into northern and Cook Strait groups. The Cook Strait animals frequently with bolder and more contrasting colour markings. Unlike any other New Zealand reptile, so unlikely to be confused with other reptile species.

HABITAT

Coastal, Lowland

Inhabits shoreline, beaches, open grassland, shrubland, herbfields and coastal forest. Frequently found living among seabird colonies on offshore islands.

NATURAL HISTORY

Nocturnal, but readily sun-basks (in burrow entrances or out in the open) during the day. Active at temperatures lower than those normally tolerated by many other reptiles, down to 5 °C (with optimal body temperature 16–21 °C). Terrestrial, but also climbs into lower branches of trees. Typically, a sedentary predator feeding on ground-dwelling invertebrates including beetles, spiders, wētā, snails, millipedes and centipedes, and earthworms. Also known to prey on native skinks, geckos, frogs, passerines, seabird chicks and eggs, and to scavenge on carrion. Male tuatara can mate every year; females reproduce only every 2–7 years depending on food resources. In summer, males defend home ranges and fight off rival males. Male initiates courtship behaviours when female arrives, erecting a crest and inflating body and gular region, and circling towards female with the *stolzer Gang* ('proud walk'). Male then mounts female, and contact between cloacal regions transfers sperm to female. Copulation may last up to 90 minutes. Females remain gravid over winter; clutch of 1–18 (usually 4–13) eggs laid in spring in a burrow dug in friable soil. Eggs are covered over, and remain buried for up to 16 months. Young hatch and dig their way out of burrows. Sexual maturity reached at 170 mm (female) or 180 mm (male) SVL (13–17 years). Longevity largely unknown but thought to be at least 60 years, and potentially over 100 years in the wild.

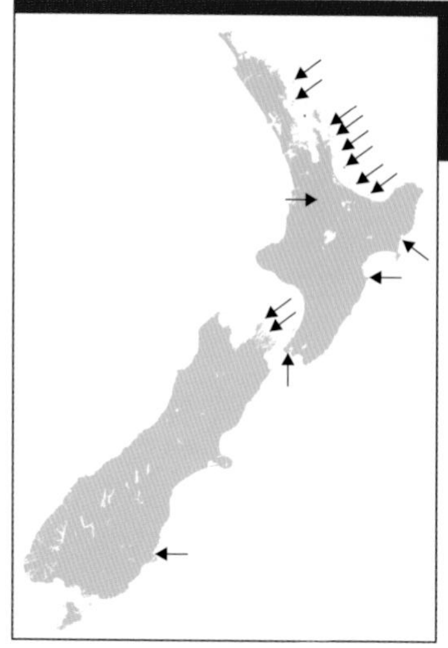

ETYMOLOGY

Specific name (Latin) meaning 'speckled' or 'spotted'. **Common name** (Māori) means 'peaks on the back' (tua = 'back', tara = 'spiny'), referring to the triangular folds of skin that form a crest along the dorsal midline.

Poor Knights Islands, Northland

GECKOS

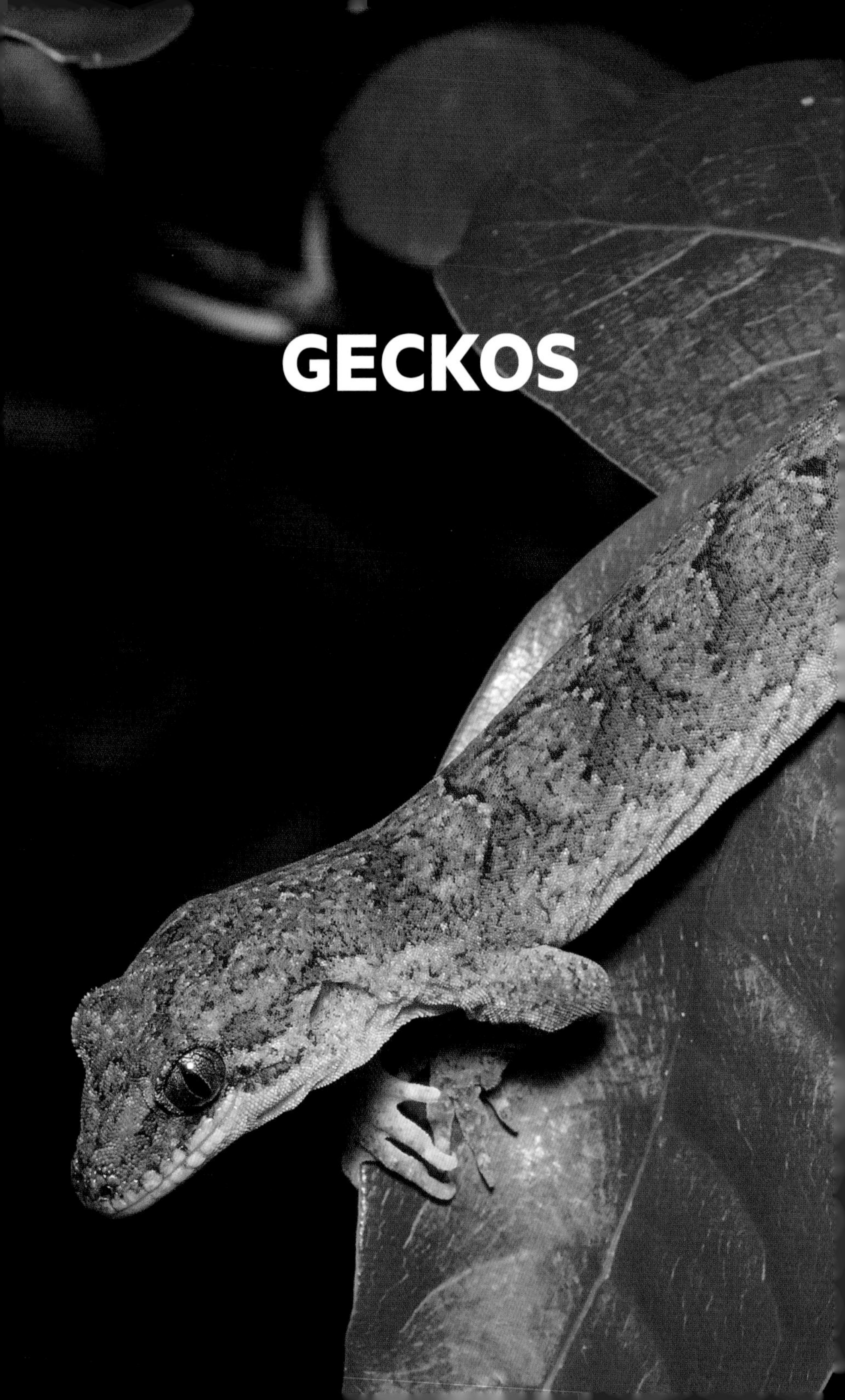

Mokohinau gecko, *Dactylocnemis* "Mokohinau". SARAH J. WELLS

Contents

Harlequin gecko *Tukutuku rakiurae* 48
Aupouri gecko *Naultinus* "North Cape" 50
Northland green gecko *Naultinus grayii* 52
Elegant gecko *Naultinus elegans* 54
Barking gecko *Naultinus punctatus* 56
Marlborough green gecko *Naultinus manukanus* 58
Rough gecko *Naultinus rudis* 60
Starred gecko *Naultinus stellatus* 62
West Coast green gecko *Naultinus tuberculatus* 66
Jewelled gecko *Naultinus gemmeus* 68
Forest gecko *Mokopirirakau granulatus* 72
Ngahere gecko *Mokopirirakau* "southern North Island" 76
Cupola gecko *Mokopirirakau* "Cupola" 78
Broad-cheeked gecko *Mokopirirakau* "Okarito" 80
Open Bay Islands gecko *Mokopirirakau* "Open Bay Islands" 82
Cascade gecko *Mokopirirakau* "Cascades" 84
Tautuku gecko *Mokopirirakau* "southern forest" 86
Orange-spotted gecko *Mokopirirakau* "Roys Peak" 88
Takitimu gecko *Mokopirirakau cryptozoicus* 92
Cloudy gecko *Mokopirirakau nebulosus* 94
Black-eyed gecko *Mokopirirakau kahutarae* 96
Northern striped gecko *Toropuku* "Coromandel" 98
Southern striped gecko *Toropuku stephensi* 100
Matapia gecko *Dactylocnemis* "Matapia" 102
Te Paki gecko *Dactylocnemis* "North Cape" 104
Pacific gecko *Dactylocnemis pacificus* 106
Three Kings gecko *Dactylocnemis* "Three Kings" 108
Mokohinau gecko *Dactylocnemis* "Mokohinau" 110
Poor Knights gecko *Dactylocnemis* "Poor Knights" 112
Duvaucel's gecko *Hoplodactylus duvaucelii* 114
Raukawa gecko *Woodworthia maculata* 116
Muriwai gecko *Woodworthia* aff. *maculata* "Muriwai" 120
Waitaha gecko *Woodworthia* cf. *brunnea* 122
Pygmy gecko *Woodworthia* "pygmy" 124
Minimac gecko *Woodworthia* "Marlborough mini" 126
Kaikouras gecko *Woodworthia* "Kaikouras" 128
Kahurangi gecko *Woodworthia* "Mount Arthur" 130
Southern Alps gecko *Woodworthia* "Southern Alps" 132
Schist gecko *Woodworthia* "Central Otago" 134
Kawarau gecko *Woodworthia* "Cromwell" 136
Korero gecko *Woodworthia* "Otago/Southland large" 138
Short-toed gecko *Woodworthia* "southern mini" 142
Goldstripe gecko *Woodworthia chrysosiretica* 144
Key to New Zealand geckos 147

Duvaucel's gecko, *Hoplodactylus duvaucelii*, Cook Strait

Rough gecko, *Naultinus rudis*

NEW ZEALAND GECKOS

New Zealand geckos have some unique and remarkable characters compared to other members of the large and diverse infraorder Gekkota (geckos), most of which have evolved in response to living in a cool, temperate climate, and in varied and diverse landscapes. Some taxa such as the harlequin gecko (*Tukutuku rakiurae*) of Stewart Island/Rakiura can be active in temperatures not much above freezing, at c. 4 °C. This gecko is found at latitudes as far south as 47°S, making it the second-most southerly occurring species in the world after Darwin's marked gecko (*Homonata darwini*, which has been recorded at 52°S in Patagonia).

Most New Zealand geckos are nocturnal, although the vast majority (probably all) will sun-bask, exposing all or only part of their bodies, for at least part of the day to warm up. Interestingly, all taxa in the genus *Naultinus* are strictly diurnal, and most are brightly coloured - traits that are uncommon among other geckos worldwide. Globally, only about 25% of all geckos are diurnally active, and only one other genus, *Phelsuma*, has bright green species.

Another feature of all New Zealand geckos is that they are viviparous, a characteristic found in only two other geckos in the world (the tough-snouted giant gecko (*Rhacodactylus trachycephalus*) and the rough-snouted giant gecko (*R. trachyrhynchus*) of New Caledonia). So, instead of laying eggs, female New Zealand geckos retain the embryos inside their bodies and give birth to live young. Along with all but one of the native skinks, New Zealand lizards represent the largest assemblage of live-bearing lizards worldwide. During the long gestation phase

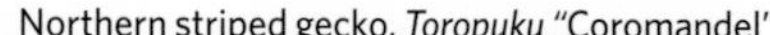

Northern striped gecko, *Toropuku* "Coromandel"

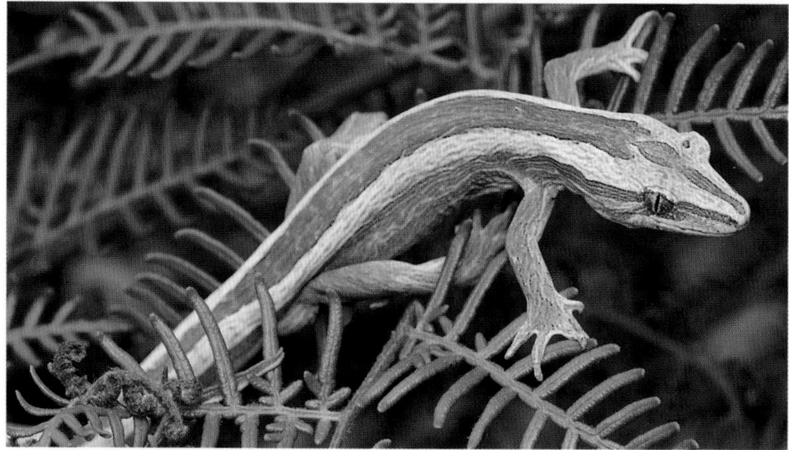

(3 to at least 14 months), females can actively regulate their body temperature (e.g. by sun-basking or moving into shade), and so provide a more stable environment for the embryos developing in the oviduct. They can also move the embryos from risk of predators.

Other distinctive characteristics of our geckos include: being the only geckos worldwide born without specialised egg teeth; having very low rates of annual reproduction (i.e. two young – in extreme exceptions, three – are born per year, and in some large or southerly species, young are born only every 2 or 3 years); and having unusually long lifespans (up to at least 53 years in the wild).

Most New Zealand geckos are omnivorous, and feed primarily on insects and other small invertebrates. Soft fruits, berries, honeydew and nectar from flowers are eaten seasonally. This frequent consumption of fruit and nectar means that geckos are important seed dispersers and pollinators (ecological roles that are more commonly associated with birds). Geckos

TOP LEFT **Raukawa gecko eating cicada.** TOP RIGHT **Duvaucel's gecko licking honey dew.** BOTTOM **Forest gecko licking nectar.**

SVL AND PORE LOCATION

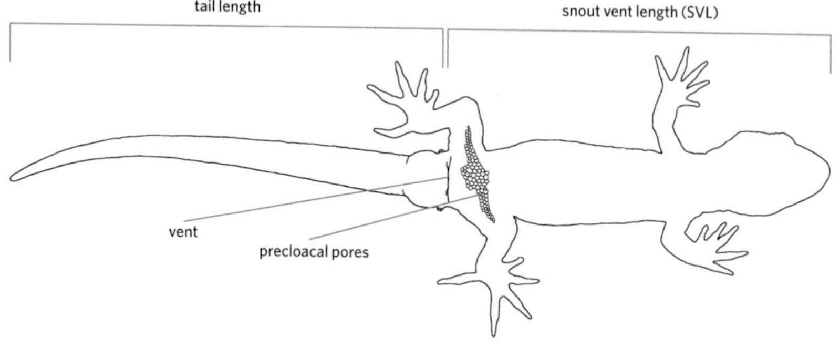

GECKO HEAD SCALES

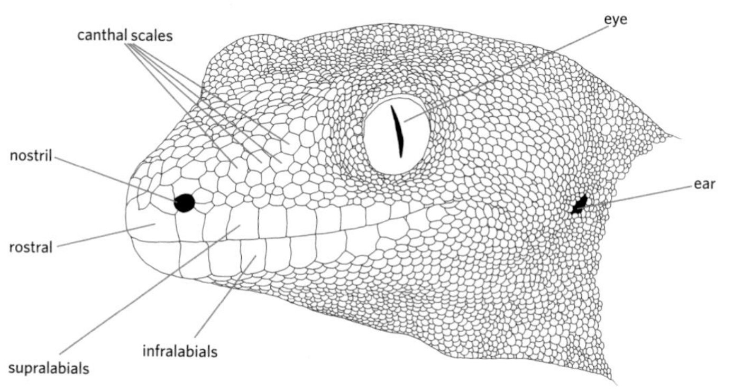

ROSTRAL SCALE OF GECKOS

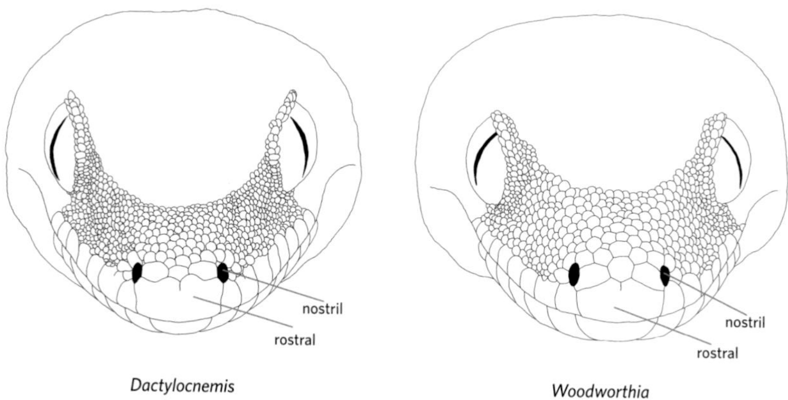

Dactylocnemis *Woodworthia*

GECKO FEET BY GENERA

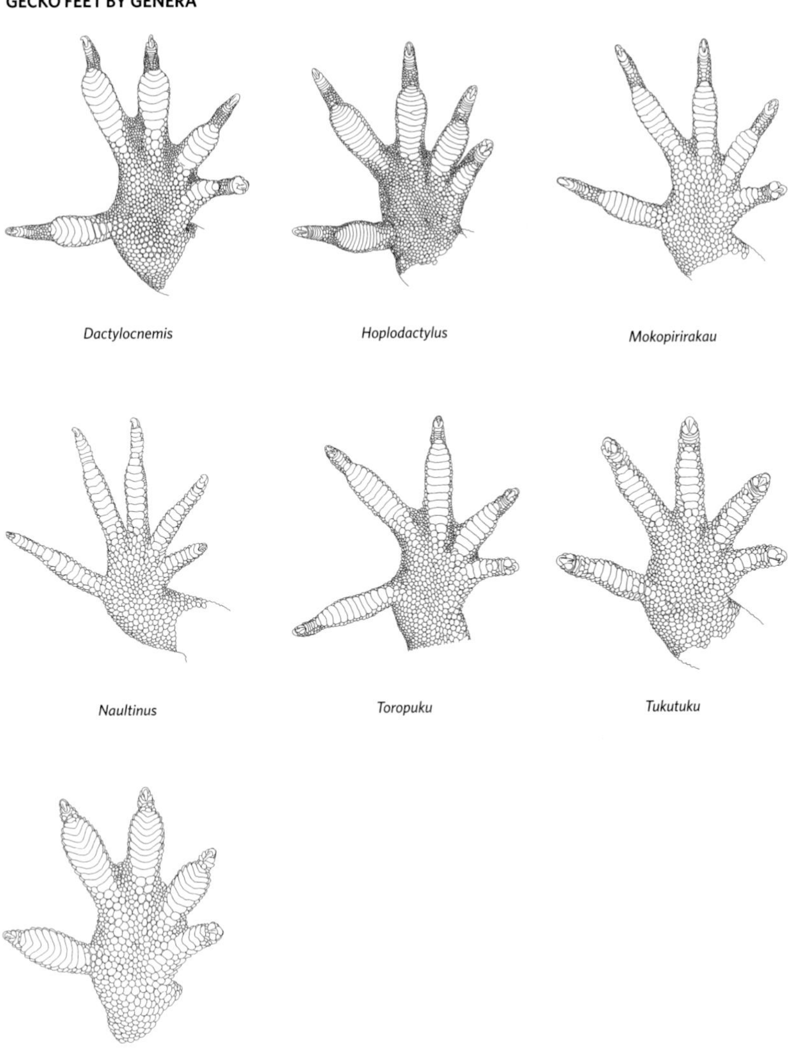

Dactylocnemis

Hoplodactylus

Mokopirirakau

Naultinus

Toropuku

Tukutuku

Woodworthia

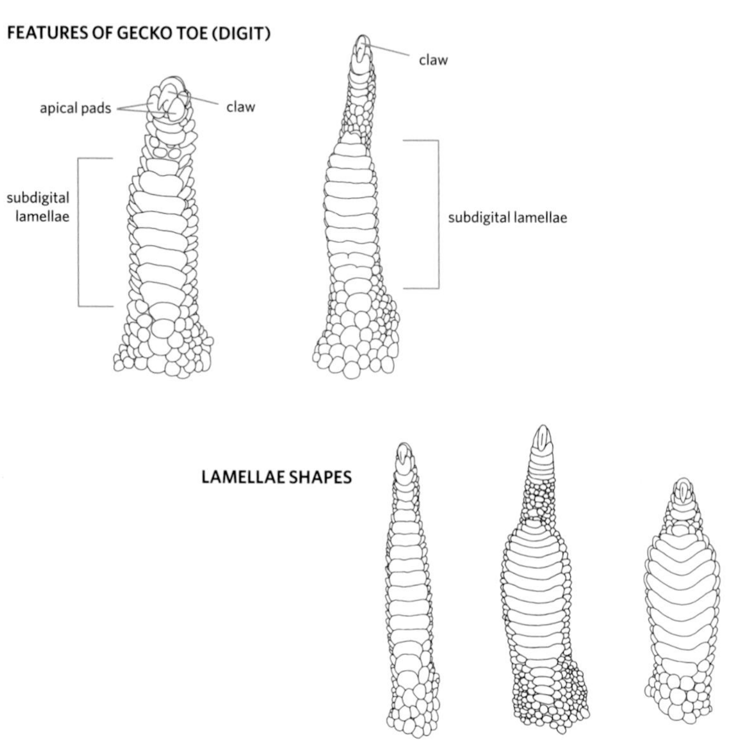
FEATURES OF GECKO TOE (DIGIT)
apical pads
claw
subdigital lamellae
claw
subdigital lamellae
LAMELLAE SHAPES
straight
curved
strongly curved

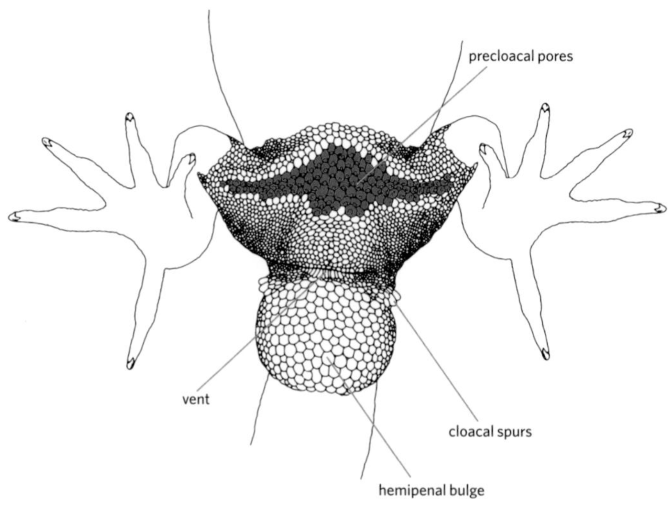
GECKO SEXUAL FEATURES
precloacal pores
vent
cloacal spurs
hemipenal bulge

CLOACAL SPURS

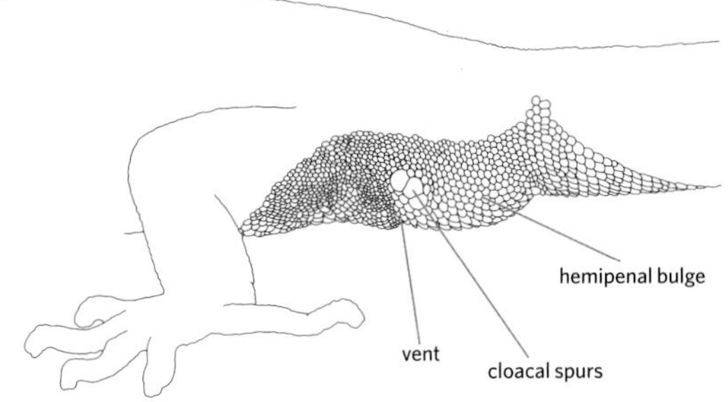

TAIL ANNULI

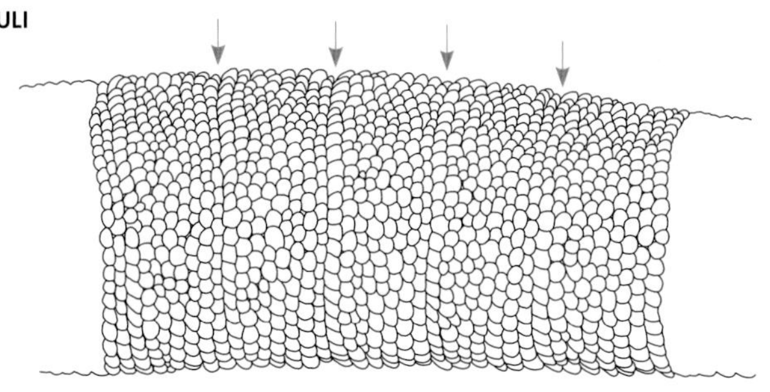

can inadvertently transfer pollen between flowers because it readily sticks to the scales on their head and throat when the reptiles feed on the flowers' nectar.

Male and female geckos generally look very much alike, although in some *Naultinus* species, body colouration may differ between the sexes (e.g. starred gecko (*N. stellatus*)). In some species, males may be larger than females, or vice versa. In all taxa, males have bulges behind the vent in which are tucked the hemipenes (sexual organs). Males also have a series of pores between the hind limbs close to the cloaca (precloacal pores) and extending onto the underside of the hind limbs (femoral pores). These pores exude a waxy substance during the breeding season. Although the role of this exudate is poorly known, it is probably related to pheromone delivery (e.g. for attracting mates or marking territories). Females lack these bulges and pores, but instead often have pits in the scales in the same position. During late spring and summer, gravid females (those carrying embryos) can usually be readily distinguished by their greatly distended abdomen. As all geckos grow, their skin is shed or sloughed, usually coming off in one complete inside-out piece. This happens several times per year in fast-growing juveniles and subadults, and still happens at least once a year in adults.

In common with most geckos, New Zealand geckos are competent and agile climbers, owing to the presence of setae (hair-like structures) on the underside of their digits. These setae branch further

Scanning electron microscope images of gecko lamellae.

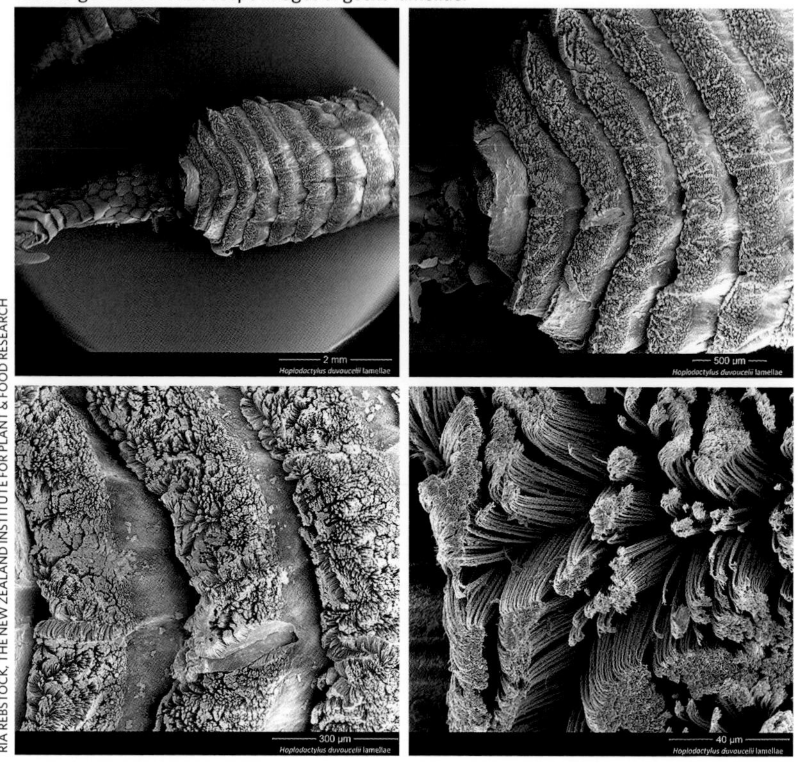

RIA REBSTOCK, THE NEW ZEALAND INSTITUTE FOR PLANT & FOOD RESEARCH

into hundreds of nano-sized tips called septulae, each of which generates molecular interactions (van der Waals forces) that create a strong adhesive force with the substrate, allowing geckos to walk up smooth surfaces. *Woodworthia* species and Duvaucel's gecko (*Hoplodactylus duvaucelii*) have broadly expanded toe pads compared to other strongly arboreal genera (e.g. *Naultinus, Mokopirirakau*). The variation in toe pad shape is likely influenced by the different requirements of climbing over rocks and in trees and shrubs. Many taxa also have a prehensile tail that can grasp branches and foliage.

Geckos are generally known for their ability to vocalise, and New Zealand geckos are no different. The sounds produced by different native taxa range from chirps and squeaks to loud croaks or barks. These sounds are often produced in series of short, harsh loud notes, usually in response to threats such as predators. Some geckos accompany these calls with a raised and inflated body posture, vigorous tail wagging, mouth gaping to reveal the contrastingly coloured interior, and rapid lunges in the direction of the threat.

Forest gecko, *Mokopirirakau granulatus*, Westland

Mokohinau gecko, *Dactylocnemis* "Mokohinau" SARAH J. WELLS

Harlequin gecko

Tukutuku rakiurae (Thomas, 1981) **Endemic**

DESCRIPTION

Up to 71 mm SVL; up to 13 g weight

A beautiful and distinctive little gecko from Stewart Island/Rakiura. **Dorsal surface** basal colour brown, green, olive, white, yellow, orange or red; complex and distinctive herringbone markings, bounded by dorsolateral stripes, embellish dorsal surface. Markings usually outlined by a network of fine white, pale green or grey lines. A broad V-shaped marking on top of head between eyes; snout with a longitudinal or oblong-shaped marking medially. **Lateral surfaces** either with an extension of dorsum's herringbone pattern, or mottled with blotches of colour outlined in white or grey. **Ventral surface** grey or pale brown, either uniform or with green or brown speckling. **Eye** colour mustard- to bright yellow. **Mouth lining** pink (but roof of mouth dark grey or blue); **tongue** indigo or dark purple-blue. **Intact tail** equal to or shorter than body length (SVL). Tail annuli distinct on intact tail. **Toes** narrow, without greatly expanded pads. Paired enlarged apical plates at distal end of all digits. **Subdigital lamellae** 10–12. **Soles of feet** cream or orange-brown.

DISTRIBUTION

Stewart Island/Rakiura only. Occurs in the southern half of Stewart Island from the Tin Range southwards, and west to Doughboy Bay.

VARIATION AND SIMILAR SPECIES

Highly variable in basal and pattern colours, but herringbone pattern almost invariable. Colour varies from red, orange and yellow to green; some individuals more grey-white with dark (black) outlines. Some evidence that lowland populations are smaller (67–68 mm) and more brown than individuals from higher altitudes, which are larger (> 70 mm) and more green in colour; alternatively, differences may be due to different ages of animals. Unlikely to be confused with any other species.

HABITAT

Lowland, Montane/subalpine

Inhabits lowland and alpine herbfields,

heathland, wetlands and open hill-top fellfield habitats where sphagnum moss, cushion plants, mānuka, little mountain heath, *Olearia* species, tangle fern (*Gleichenia dicarpa*) and sedges grow. Occasionally occurs under slabs of granite on bare rock outcrops.

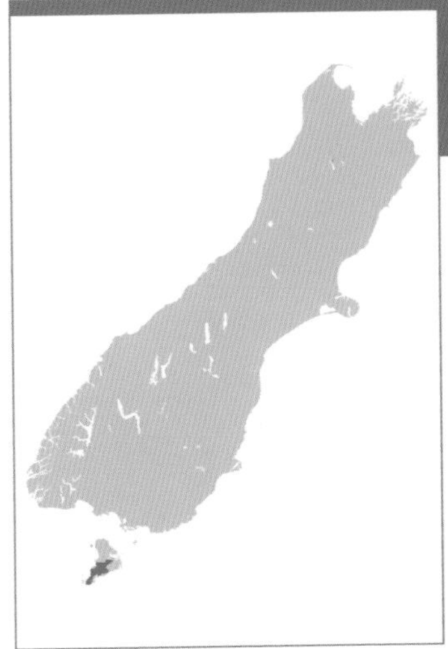

NATURAL HISTORY

Cathemeral (diurnal and nocturnal; active in the early hours after dark but only on warm nights). Terrestrial, and partially arboreal. Readily sun-basks in the open on vegetation or on branches just above ground. Will also thermoregulate beneath warm objects such as rock slabs (thigmothermic behaviour). Generally active at temperatures above 12 °C, but can be active in temperatures as low as 4 °C. Does not reproduce every year. Gravid females reported year-round, and 1 or 2 young born probably late summer–early autumn. Vocalises with a harsh 'chittering' sound during the day, from dense vegetation (perhaps advertising territory); makes soft chirps and squeals when distressed. One of the most southerly-distributed geckos in the world. Feeds on small invertebrates (*Hemiandrus* ground wētā, spiders, cockroaches, amphipods) and known to eat the bright red berries of little mountain heath. Also eats nectar from flowers.

ETYMOLOGY

Generic name (Māori) meaning 'intricate' and 'beautiful ornamental latticework', referring to the unique dorsal markings of this species. **Specific name** is a Latinisation of the Māori word Rakiura for Stewart Island, where this species is endemic. **Common name** refers to the complex and brightly coloured dorsal patterns.

Aupouri gecko

Naultinus "North Cape"

Endemic

DESCRIPTION

Up to 70 mm SVL

A small slender green gecko from the far north of Northland. **Dorsal surface** bright lime green, either uniform or patterned with rows of white spots or stripes finely edged in black. **Lateral surfaces** more yellow-green that fades to pale green, blue-green or white ventrally. Typically has longitudinal white stripes between sides and belly, between fore- and hind limbs. **Ventral surface** pale green in females, flushed with blue in males. Chin, throat and belly may be uniform or marked with large blotches of white. **Eye** colour olive, orange- or murky-brown. **Rostral and canthal scales** enlarged and domed. **Mouth lining** orange and pale lavender; **tongue** bright orange or red. Inside lining of lips and nostrils orange, extending to external corners of the mouth. **Cloacal spurs** green. **Intact tail** slender, prehensile; longer than body length (SVL). **Subdigital lamellae** 16–17. **Soles of feet** pale green with a yellow tinge.

DISTRIBUTION

North Island only. Restricted to the northern areas of the Aupouri Peninsula in Northland. Not known to occur on offshore islands.

VARIATION AND SIMILAR SPECIES

Markings on dorsal surface variable; uniform yellow (xanthic) variants are known. Superficially similar to **elegant gecko** (*N. elegans*) and **Northland green gecko** (*N. grayii*), but geographically isolated from these species, and can be distinguished by presence of orange colour lining the lips (visible at corner of the mouth even when mouth is closed) and nostrils (absent in the other two species). Similar in body size to elegant gecko but considerably smaller than Northland green gecko.

HABITAT

Costal, Lowland

Occurs in scrubland, and coastal forest. Frequently found in foliage of kānuka, mānuka and māpou, particularly along shrubland edges with easy access to sun-basking sites.

NATURAL HISTORY

Diurnal; arboreal. Strongly heliothermic (avid sun-basker). Remains inactive in vegetation overnight, but may retreat to the ground, sheltering beneath objects and dense vegetation, in inclement weather and during winter. Little known about reproductive biology, but 2 young born mid-summer (1–2 months earlier than in Northland green gecko). Occasionally vocalises when threatened or distressed.

ETYMOLOGY

Common and **tag names** both references to the geographic range of this species: North Cape and northern areas of Aupouri Peninsula.

Northland green gecko

Naultinus grayii Bell, 1843 **Endemic**

DESCRIPTION

Up to 95 mm SVL; up to 23 g weight

A large but slender green gecko found from the Bay of Islands to the southern part of Aupouri Peninsula. **Dorsal surface** vivid lime green, either uniform or marked with paired rows of white, green or pale yellow spots or blotches, or with continuous or broken stripes. Most individuals with a pair of elongate white, green or yellow markings on head, extending from behind eyes to usually over shoulders and forelimbs. Dorsal and head markings outlined in golden yellow or black. Rarely, individuals are entirely bright yellow with white markings edged in black. **Lateral surfaces** bright vivid green with large white, green or pale yellow spots edged with golden yellow or black. A white stripe may be present along interface of lateral and ventral surfaces. Males may have pale blue flanks, especially around axillae. **Ventral surface** pale green or yellow-green, and either uniform or with large pale blotches or longitudinal stripes. Ventral markings may be particularly bold in juveniles. **Eye** colour orange or orange-brown, without filigree pattern. **Canthal scales** enlarged, pentagonal and flat. **Mouth lining** blue; **tongue** vivid orange or red. Infralabial scales on lower lip usually white. **Intact tail** slender, prehensile; longer than body length (SVL). **Toes** slender and tapering, without greatly expanded pads. **Subdigital lamellae** 11–17. **Soles of feet** grey-green, and toes outlined in yellow.

DISTRIBUTION

North Island only. Restricted to Northland, from the Bay of Islands northwards to just south of Houhora Harbour. Not known to occur on offshore islands.

VARIATION AND SIMILAR SPECIES

Some naturally occurring variation in colour (e.g. lime green, and rare yellow (xanthic) individuals) and colour of markings, and very variable in the degree and extent of markings (uniform, blotches, stripes). Not known to occur with other members of the *Naultinus* genus. Similar in appearance to **Aupouri gecko** (*N.* "North Cape") but distinguished by its much larger adult size; flatter, more triangular head; bluish colour on lateral surfaces in males; and absence of orange colouration at corners of mouth and around nostrils. Also, similar to **elegant gecko** (*N. elegans*) and **barking gecko** (*N. punctatus*), but easily distinguished by combination of blue mouth lining and orange-red tongue (vs. dark blue mouth and dark blue or purple-black tongue in the other two species); flatter, more wedge-shaped head; and large flattened scales on snout (vs. domed).

HABITAT

Coastal, Lowland

Inhabits scrubland (including mānuka and kānuka), and lowland forest. Spends most of its time among the foliage but will bask on branches, and occasionally disperse across the open ground to reach neighbouring vegetation.

NATURAL HISTORY

Diurnal; arboreal. Strongly heliothermic (avid sun-basker). Females establish small home ranges, but may move in response to weather conditions; whereas males are more free-ranging. Reproduces annually, mating late July–September. Gestation (may include a period of sperm storage before fertilisation) c. 7.5 months; 1 or 2 young born in March, c. 35 mm SVL (1 g) when born. Sexually mature at c. 1.5–2 years. Defensive posturing (raised and inflated body, mouth gaping, aggressive lunges and tail waving), and vocalisation common when threatened. Feeds primarily on invertebrates but will eat fruits (berries) and consume nectar from flowers (e.g. mānuka).

ETYMOLOGY

Specific name (Latinisation) after John Edward Gray (1800–1875), a zoologist at the British Museum in London, who scientifically described several New Zealand lizards. **Common name** refers to the Northland Region, where this species occurs.

Elegant gecko

Naultinus elegans Gray, 1842

Endemic

Auckland

DESCRIPTION

Up to 75 mm SVL; up to 15 g weight

A species from the upper North Island, easily recognisable by its brilliant green colouration, relatively small size and slender build. **Dorsal surface** either uniform green (less commonly bright yellow), or marked with rows of paired white, pale green, dull yellow or pale pink blotches or stripes (continuous or broken). Blotches or stripes sometimes outlined in black. A white lower lip common, but may be uniform green. **Lateral surfaces** vivid green with or without large white, pale green spots sometimes edged with black. A white stripe may be present along interface of lateral and ventral surfaces. **Ventral surface** generally pale green in females; white or pale blue in males. Belly may have green and white longitudinal stripes or swirls (particularly in juveniles). **Eye** colour light orange-brown. **Rostral scale** 2.5x as wide as high at centre. **Canthal scales** on snout dome shaped, with posterior head scales becoming smaller and more granular. **Mental scale** usually square or oblong, bordered posteriorly by 3 or more postmentals. **Mouth lining** and **tongue** blue-black (rarely with tongue tip orange or yellowish in northernmost part of range). **Intact tail** slender, prehensile; longer than body length (SVL). **Subdigital lamellae** 10–16. **Soles of feet** pale green or grey-white.

DISTRIBUTION

North Island only. Widely distributed throughout upper half of the North Island, from Whanganui across to East Cape, northwards to south of Bay of Islands. Currently known to occur naturally on four large offshore islands within the Hauraki Gulf and off Northland.

VARIATION AND SIMILAR SPECIES

Extent of dorsal and lateral markings variable (e.g. uniform, blotched or striped). Rare yellow (xanthic) and off-white (amelanotic) variants occur naturally, resulting from natural genetic mutations inhibiting pigment expression. Previously considered a subspecies (i.e. *N. elegans*

elegans) but has been raised to species status. Distinguished from other North Island *Naultinus* by a combination of: the blue-black mouth lining and tongue; its smaller size (compared to **barking gecko** (*N. punctatus*), and **Northland green gecko** (*N. grayii*)); and pale green or grey-white soles of feet. Refer to key to distinguish this species from geographically separated *Naultinus* taxa.

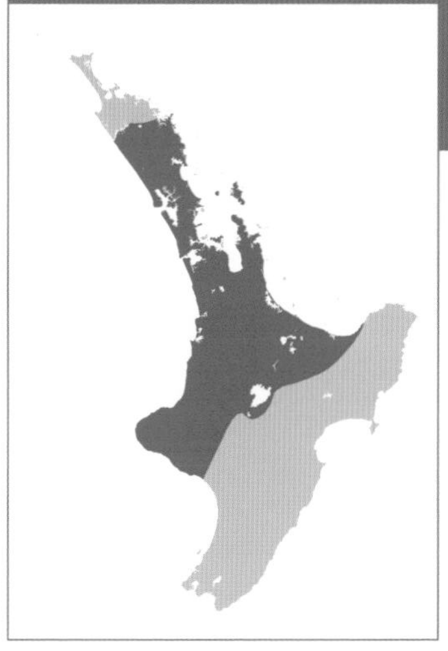

HABITAT

Coastal, Lowland

Occurs in gumland, scrubland and forested habitats. Can still be found in relatively high densities, and co-inhabits many sites with forest gecko (*M. granulatus*). Prefers to remain in dense foliage but will use tree trunks and branches, and may disperse across open ground. During inclement weather or over winter, may retreat beneath objects (e.g. logs) or dense vegetation on the ground.

NATURAL HISTORY

Diurnal; arboreal. Heliothermic (avid sun-basker). Mating occurs August–September. Females give birth to 2 young in early spring (August–October) the following year. Males remain close to females and mate with them soon after the birth. Sexually mature at 3 years and females can breed annually. Lifespan more than 20 years. When threatened, may mouth gape, vocalise (bark or chirp), and leap or drop from branches to escape. Primarily insectivorous but will lick nectar from flowers and honeydew.

ETYMOLOGY

Specific name (Latin) meaning 'elegant'. **Common name** also refers to the slender, elegant body form and colour. **Māori name** is moko kākāriki; translates to 'green-coloured lizard'.

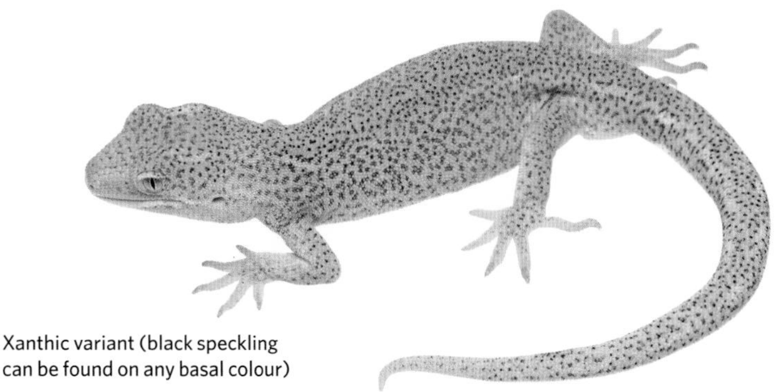

Xanthic variant (black speckling can be found on any basal colour)

Barking gecko

Naultinus punctatus Gray, 1843

Endemic

DESCRIPTION

Up to 95 mm SVL

A large 'stocky' pugnacious species from the lower North Island. **Dorsal surface** light to mid-bluish-toned green, either uniform or with two rows of light blue-green (in adults), white or pale yellow (in juveniles and subadults) patches or stripes either side of midline. Patches or stripes may continue down intact tail. **Lateral surfaces** generally green, but in males lower lateral surfaces (flanks), especially around axillae, pale blue. **Ventral surface** uniform pale green including chin and throat. **Eye** colour light orange-brown, without filigree pattern. **Canthal scales** on snout enlarged and domed. **Mouth lining** vibrant blue; **tongue** dark blue-black. **Intact tail** prehensile; longer than body length (SVL). **Toes** narrow and tapering, without expanded pads. **Subdigital lamellae** 11–18. **Soles of feet** yellow, and toes with yellow margins.

DISTRIBUTION

North Island only. Occurs widely throughout the south-eastern areas of the North Island, from East Cape to Whanganui, southwards to Wellington. Occurs naturally on Kapiti Island, and populations have been translocated to Mana and Matiu/Somes Islands.

VARIATION AND SIMILAR SPECIES

Basal colour variable (green to yellow) as is extent of dorsal markings (e.g. uniform green, sparse pale spots or patches, or distinct pale stripes that can be broken or continuous). Some individuals entirely yellow (xanthic). Very similar in appearance to **elegant gecko** (*N. elegans*), which occurs further north, but distinguished by much larger adult size; more robust build; distinctive bluish shade of green in most adults; pale blue flanks and axillae in males; and yellow soles of feet and toes. Adults larger, more robust in build, lacking enlarged conical scales, and with blue mouth lining and bluish-black tongue compared to **Marlborough green gecko** (*N. manukanus*). Refer to key to distinguish this species from geographically separated *Naultinus* taxa.

HABITAT

Coastal, Lowland

Occupies scrubland, including mānuka and kānuka shrubland, and lowland forest where it lives among the foliage, where it remains stationary at night. May retreat to the ground during inclement weather and in winter.

NATURAL HISTORY

Diurnal; arboreal but may shelter or disperse between trees on the ground. Strongly heliothermic (avid sun-basker). Mating occurs July–August, and females give birth to 1 or 2 young the following April–May. Renowned for its defensive threat displays that include a raised and inflated body, wide mouth gaping to reveal blue interior, aggressive lunges and loud vocalisations (chirps or barks). Feeds primarily on insects (e.g. beetles, flies and moths) and spiders but will eat fruits and consume nectar from flowers.

ETYMOLOGY

Specific name (Latin) meaning 'spotted', referring to the scattered blackish scales sometimes present on the dorsal surface. **Common name** refers to the species' loud defensive vocalisations.

NICK HARKER

Marlborough green gecko

Naultinus manukanus (McCann, 1955) **Endemic**

DESCRIPTION

Up to 81 mm SVL; up to 12.5 g weight

A relatively plain green gecko, usually with enlarged and raised conical or domed scales, particularly on snout, head and base of tail (pelvic area), but also in dorsolateral rows in some populations. **Dorsal surface** typically uniform green, or with paired rows of pale green, white or yellow spots or thin irregular-shaped markings either side of midline. Some individuals with similar markings on head. **Lateral surfaces** generally green, sometimes with irregular-shaped white blotches. **Ventral surface** of adults pale yellow-green in females; pale blue-green or blue-white in males. Juveniles have uniform green ventral surface, changing colour with maturation. **Eye** colour light brown or olive-brown, without filigree pattern. **Enlarged scales** typically present on snout, head, nape and along dorsolateral surfaces. Snout deep and blunt; white or yellow stripe may be present along lower lip (i.e. white or yellow infralabial scales). **Mouth lining** pale lavender, pink or orange; **tongue** pink or yellow. **Intact tail** narrowly tapering, prehensile; longer than body length (SVL). **Toes** narrow, without expanded pads. **Subdigital lamellae** c. 16. **Soles of feet** yellow.

DISTRIBUTION

South Island only. Occurs in Marlborough, as far south as the Wairau River, and as far west as the Bryant and Richmond Ranges. Also present on islands in the Marlborough Sounds, including Stephens Island/Takapourewa, Arapawa Island and Rangitoto ki te Tonga (d'Urville Island). Translocated populations established on Motuara Island and Wakaterepapanui Island.

VARIATION AND SIMILAR SPECIES

Geographically variable in pattern and extent of enlarged, raised conical scales. Some individuals may be green-yellow or entirely yellow (xanthic). Populations from outer Marlborough Sounds uniform green, and have few enlarged scales, whereas populations further south with bold and variable colour patterns, and distinctive enlarged conical or domed scales over body. Sexually dimorphic in size: males (64–68 mm SVL) smaller than females (69–79 mm SVL). Marlborough green gecko typically more uniformly coloured, and less patterned than most other South Island *Naultinus*, except for **jewelled gecko** (*N. gemmeus*) from the far south and **starred gecko** (*N. stellatus*) from the far north-west. Can be distinguished from all other *Naultinus* species (except the **rough gecko**, *N. rudis*) by enlarged conical scales on head, nape and dorsolateral regions of body. Most similar to rough gecko, especially where the species' distributions abut, but distinguished by the raised, conical scales being restricted to head, nape and dorsolateral regions (vs. over entire body); by mouth and tongue colour; by the absence of a grey or brown morph; and by Marlborough green gecko males having blue-white bellies.

HABITAT

Coastal, Lowland

Inhabits shrubland and coastal and/or lowland forest, as well as vineland (*Muehlenbeckia* thickets).

NATURAL HISTORY

Diurnal; arboreal. Strongly heliothermic (avid sun-basker). Visually and behaviourally cryptic, due to its colouration matching foliage, and generally static behaviour and slow movements (i.e. does not move large distances, usually 1–3 m per day). Movement usually associated with positioning itself in a sunny spot and retreating into denser vegetation during inclement weather. Mating occurs June–October (in captivity), and females give birth in February–April to 2 young, 26–35 mm SVL. Maturity at 3 and 4 years in males and females, respectively. Long lived, in excess of 30 years (captive record). Employs a sit-and-wait foraging strategy, eating primarily small invertebrates.

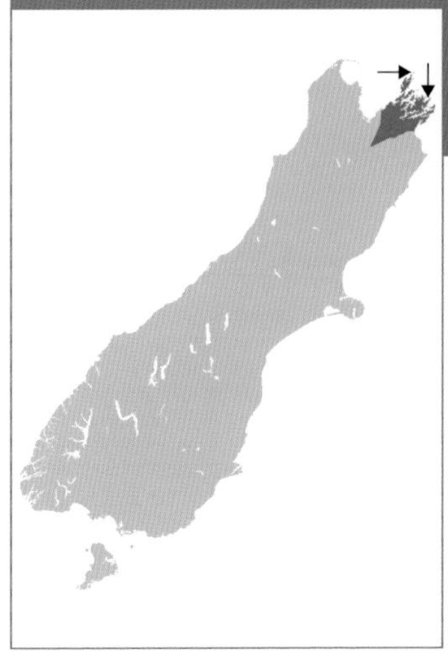

ETYMOLOGY

Specific name a reference to mānuka (*Leptospermum scoparium*), a shrub frequently used by this species. **Common name** refers to the Marlborough Region where this species occurs.

Rough gecko

Naultinus rudis (Fischer, 1882) **Endemic**

DESCRIPTION

Up to 77 mm SVL; c. 12 g weight (gravid female up to 15.5 g)

A striking gecko characterised by greatly enlarged conical scales, giving a rough spiny appearance. **Dorsal surface** variable from light to dark green, to grey-brown, with series of paired irregular pale blotches, white diamonds, transverse bands or broken dorsolateral stripes often edged in black. Markings begin on head and continue down intact tail. **Lateral surfaces** green or grey with black-edged white blotches. **Ventral surface** brown or light grey, often with white blotches, speckles or longitudinal streaks. **Eye** colour light brown or olive-green. **Canthal scales**, neck and body, covered in raised conical or domed scales that often continue down intact tail. **Mouth lining** and **tongue** dark blue, mauve or purple; tongue tip may be pinkish red, green-yellow or orange. **Intact tail** slender and prehensile; longer than body length (SVL). **Toes** narrow, without expanded pads. **Subdigital lamellae** 12–19. **Soles of feet** white or pale grey.

DISTRIBUTION

South Island only. Occurs from southern Marlborough (south of the Wairau Valley) to northern Canterbury, east of the Main Divide.

VARIATION AND SIMILAR SPECIES

Colour variable within and between populations, from grey to bright green. Possible sexual dichromatism, with males displaying more browns and greys, and females more greens, but all colour combinations can occur in both males and females. Similar to **Marlborough green gecko** (*N. manukanus*) but more robust in build, with bolder colour patterns; a greater abundance of raised scales over entire body; darker mouth and tongue colour; and males lack bluish colour on belly. Distinguished from **starred gecko** (*N. stellatus*) by presence of raised tubercles on nape and body. Refer to key to distinguish this species from geographically separated *Naultinus* taxa.

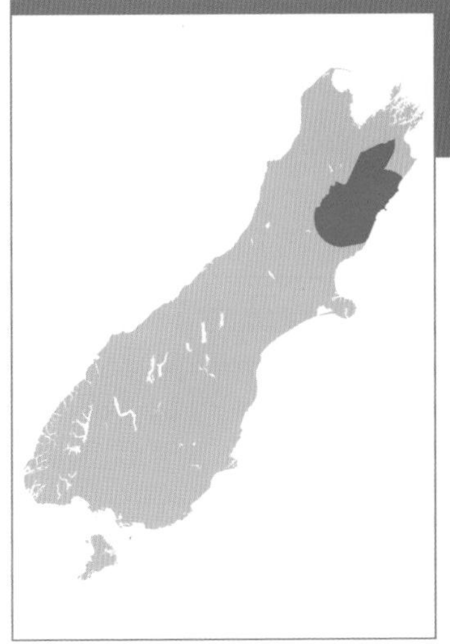

HABITAT

Coastal, Lowland, Montane/subalpine, Alpine
Inhabits shrubland, lowland and montane forest, shrublands in old riverbeds and subalpine shrubland. Found among dense foliage above ground.

NATURAL HISTORY

Diurnal; arboreal. Strongly heliothermic (avid sun-basker). Mating occurs early spring (August–October); gestation over summer; in March–May, females give birth to 1 or 2 young. Vocalises loudly with squeaks, chirps or barks when disturbed or threatened. Vocalisations often coupled with a threat display that involves a raised posture, inflated body, mouth gaping and aggressive lunges. Feeds on small invertebrates (e.g. spiders, moths, flies, beetles) and may eat nectar from flowers (e.g. mānuka).

ETYMOLOGY

Specific name (Latin) meaning 'rough'. **Common name** also refers to the enlarged scales covering the body and giving a rough texture to the skin.

Starred gecko

Naultinus stellatus Hutton, 1872

Endemic

Female, Nelson Lakes

Male, Nelson Lakes

DESCRIPTION

Up to 80 mm SVL

A small to moderate-sized gecko with highly variable colours and patterning, often very contrasting and striking, but can be uniform green. **Dorsal surface** green, brown, white or grey, and usually marked with paired large white, green or yellow blotches or star-shaped patches either side of midline that continue down intact tail; blotches often with a darker broad outline, or a dark green, brown or black outline. Individuals with almost uniform colouration either lack prominent dorsal markings or with joined blotches that form paired stripes either side of midline. **Lateral surfaces** with large circular or irregular blotches of colour, similar to those on dorsum. Usually a green or white stripe extending from eye to ear opening. Young born dark green with bold white markings, developing complex colouration and patterning as they mature. **Ventral surface** white, grey, pale green or blue-green, either uniform or mottled with white. Limbs blotched with white, green or white. **Eye** colour olive, olive-green, orange-brown or murky yellow. **Mouth lining** pale lavender, pink or orange; **tongue** yellow or red-orange. **Intact tail** slender and tapering; highly prehensile, and often held coiled when animal is sheltering or threatened. Intact tail equal to or slightly longer than body length (SVL). **Subdigital lamellae** 9–15. **Soles of feet** yellow or grey.

DISTRIBUTION

South Island only. Occurs throughout the Nelson and Tasman regions, from the Maitai Valley east of Nelson to the northern West Coast, and southwards to Nelson Lakes.

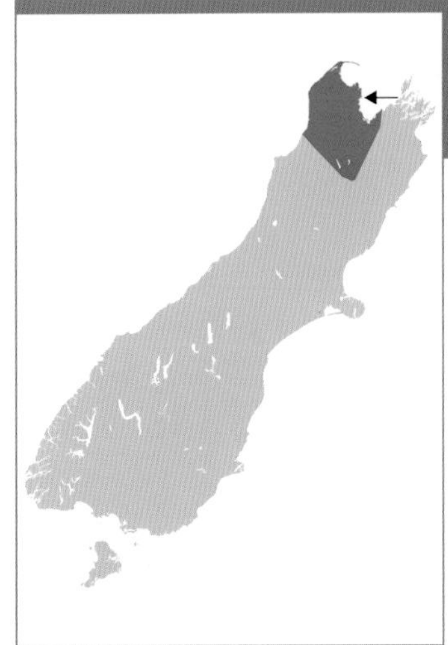

VARIATION AND SIMILAR SPECIES

Extraordinarily variable in morphology, colouration and reproductive cycle. Much variation is geographic, with smaller, more weakly marked individuals from north-west Nelson (this population was commonly misidentified in the 1960s to 1980s as *N. tuberculatus*), and larger, more grey or brownish specimens in the Nelson Lakes area. A blue-coloured individual was reported near Golden Bay, and xanthic (yellow) individuals occur in the wild. Three distinct local forms are unofficially recognised by captive holders but probably represent points along a more or less continuous cline, which occurs from north to south across the whole width of the species' range, rather than isolated populations:

1. ***Sandy Bay***: Individuals smaller (50–60 mm SVL), with relatively long thin tails. **Dorsal surface** green or blue-green, either uniform or with light green or green-yellow rows of blotches. **Mouth lining** orange-pink with some pale blue; **tongue** orange-pink. **Soles of feet** grey or pale-yellow.
2. ***Nelson Lakes***: Individuals larger (70–80 mm SVL), with shorter tails, and have complex colour patterns. Nelson Lakes population somewhat sexually dichromatic. **Dorsal surface** of females with more green or olive-green basal colour (sometime light grey), overlaid with green markings; males with a

Sandy Bay

Matai Valley

darker sepia-brown or silver-grey basal colour, overlaid with green blotches. **Mouth lining** pale lavender, with orange on inside of lips; **tongue** red-orange. **Soles of feet** yellow. Similar animals were photographed on the Stockton Plateau, West Coast.

3. ***Maitai Valley***: Individuals show DNA evidence of past hybridisation with Marlborough green gecko (*N. manukanus*). Medium-sized (65–70 mm SVL). **Dorsal and lateral surfaces** green or brown-green and weakly marked with paired lighter green or yellow-green spots or blotches. **Ventral surface** may be pale blue-green or whitish. **Mouth lining** pink-orange; **tongue** orange-red. **Soles of feet** off-white or brownish. Similar animals found near Upper Takaka, and in the Mokihinui catchment on the northern West Coast.

Starred geckos were in the past confused with **West Coast green geckos** (*N. tuberculatus*), but can be readily differentiated by orange or lavender mouth lining (vs.dark blue or black), smaller size, and plain or almost plain bright green colouration. Populations from the northern West Coast somewhat similar-looking to **Marlborough green gecko** from outer Marlborough Sounds but are distinguished from that species and **rough gecko** (*N. rudis*) by the absence of enlarged tubercles on dorsal and lateral surfaces.

HABITAT

Coastal, Lowland, Montane/subalpine
Occupies scrub, kānuka and mānuka shrubland, beech forest, subalpine shrubland and herbfields. Usually found among foliage but will shelter on the ground beneath rocks and logs, or in dense

low-growing vegetation during inclement weather and in winter, especially when snow covers large areas of their habitat.

NATURAL HISTORY

Diurnal. Arboreal, but may spend time on the ground, especially during inactive winter phase. Strongly heliothermic (avid sun-basker). Annual reproductive cycle, mating in late winter and spring (late August–November). Females give birth to 1 or 2 young the following year (March–May). Some variation in birthing season between populations (Sandy Bay populations have been recorded giving birth in March–April; Maitai Valley and Nelson Lakes populations in April–May). Lifespan up to 47 years (in captivity). Feeds primarily on invertebrates, and known to lick honeydew. May also eat fruit (berries) and consume nectar from flowers.

ETYMOLOGY

Specific name (Latin) meaning 'set like stars'. **Common name** also refers to the star-like patterns on the dorsal surface.

Juvenile, Nelson Lakes

SAMANTHA KING

Farewell Spit

West Coast green gecko

Naultinus tuberculatus (McCann, 1955)

Endemic

DESCRIPTION

Up to 85 mm SVL; up to 14.5 g weight

A relatively large and intricately marked gecko, with patterns and colours that resemble moss. Snout relatively long and shallow. **Dorsal surface** green, dark green to brown-green, usually with green-yellow dorsolateral rows of diamond- or irregular-shaped spots, streaks or even longitudinal stripes. Markings may be outlined in darker green, olive or black. Top of head with a pair of pale semi-circular markings. Thin pale green mid-dorsal stripe may be present. Some individuals overlaid with fine black speckles. A white or pale green canthal stripe and usually a white or pale yellow-green stripe from eye to ear opening. **Lateral surfaces** with circular or irregular spots or blotches, similar to those on dorsal surface but smaller. Occasionally, lateral markings joined, forming a broad mid-lateral longitudinal stripe. **Ventral surface** pale green or green-white, either uniform or mottled with dull green irregular-shaped blotches. **Eye** colour olive or orangey-brown; relatively small. **Rostral and canthal scales** enlarged domed (conical) or tuberculate scales. **Mouth lining** dark blue; **tongue** black or dark blue. **Intact tail** slender, prehensile and frequently held in tight coil when sheltering or threatened; longer than body length (SVL). **Toes** narrow, without enlarged pads. **Subdigital lamellae** 14–18. **Soles of feet** white, off-white or pale green to yellow-green.

DISTRIBUTION

South Island only. Occurs in Westland, from Stockton southwards to at least the Hokitika district, and probably to Haast, and eastwards to the Lewis Pass area.

VARIATION AND SIMILAR SPECIES

No sexual dichromatism, except for subtly darker males in the Denniston population. Xanthic (yellow) individuals known to occur in the wild. Two distinct geographic forms:

1. ***Lewis Pass***: (previously considered a separate species, *N. poecilochlorus*) from eastern Lewis Pass to Reefton. Population shows genetic evidence of past hybridisation with rough gecko (*N. rudis*). Large (up to 85 mm SVL)

and robust, and with a bolder and more intricate pattern of white or pale green blotches or longitudinal patches outlined in darker green or olive, or rarely black. Fine black speckling on dorsal and lateral surfaces common. Overall pattern may be reminiscent of moss.

2. ***West Coast***: Smaller (up to 78 mm SVL) and generally more green or yellow-green overall, with less bold markings on dorsal and lateral surfaces. Dorsal markings can be large pale green or yellow-green diamond- and cross-shaped blotches.

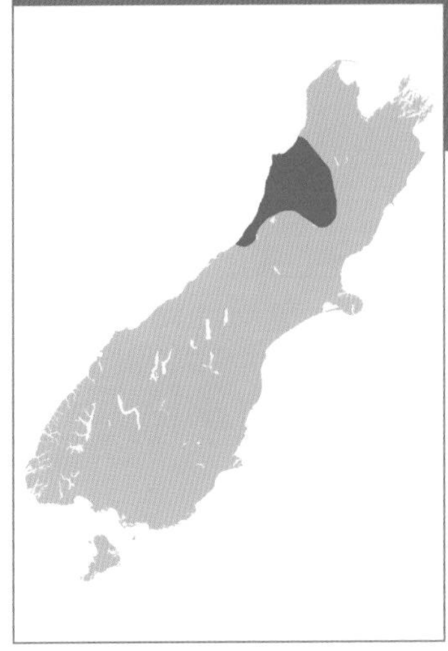

Readily distinguished from **starred gecko** (*N. stellatus*) by its black or blue tongue (vs. yellow or red-orange in starred gecko) and longer, shallower snout. Distinguished from **rough gecko** (these species abut each other east of Lewis Pass) by the absence of enlarged scales.

HABITAT

Lowland, Montane/subalpine

Occupies canopy of kānuka and mānuka scrub, complex divaricating bushes and shrubs (e.g. matagouri), fernland, clearings or edges of beech forest, and prostrate vegetation in subalpine zone, including 'coal measures' vegetation.

NATURAL HISTORY

Diurnal. Arboreal, but will take refuge on the ground beneath prostrate vegetation, or beneath rock slabs during inclement weather (snowfall) and winter. Strongly heliothermic (avid sun-basker). Frequency of reproduction unknown. In captivity, mating occurs September–October, and 1 or 2 young born in autumn (March–May). When threatened, may inflate its body, raise and arch its back, perform mouth gaping, vocalise loudly (barks) and lunge aggressively. Feeds on small invertebrates and may eat berries or nectar.

ETYMOLOGY

Specific name (Latin) meaning 'warty or tuberculate', referring to the enlarged domed scales on the snout and head, and very strongly pointed body scales. **Common name** refers to the West Coast area where this species occurs.

Lewis Pass

Jewelled gecko

Naultinus gemmeus (McCann, 1955) **Endemic**

Otago Peninsula

DESCRIPTION

Up to 80 mm SVL

The southernmost green gecko species. **Dorsal surface** variable, usually green, but grey to brown in many adult males in Canterbury, with a series of pale diamond- or cross-shaped markings or continuous stripes. Paired white or yellow crescent-shaped markings on top of head, which may be edged in black or yellow. Pale canthal stripe usually present. **Lateral surfaces** uniform green or frequently with circular or irregular-shaped white or light green spots or blotches. Occasionally, lower lateral markings joined, forming a broad pale longitudinal stripe. **Ventral surface** grey, pale brown, green or yellow-green. **Eye** colour olive-green to brown, sometimes outlined in white. **Mouth lining** pink, mauve, deep blue or purple-blue; **tongue** pink, orange, deep blue or black. **Intact tail** slender, tapering and prehensile; usually longer than body length (SVL). **Subdigital lamellae** c. 19. **Soles of feet** brown, yellow or pale grey.

DISTRIBUTION

South Island only. Occurs widely from northern Canterbury southwards through Banks Peninsula, and Otago. Historic sightings from Southland, and it could occur in Fiordland. Also found on islands in Foveaux Strait and on Codfish Island/ Whenuahou, and may occur on mainland Stewart Island/Rakiura.

VARIATION AND SIMILAR SPECIES

Geographically isolated from all other *Naultinus* species, thus misidentification is unlikely. Large variation in colour and pattern both amongst and between populations. Several geographic colour variants recognised, including populations from:

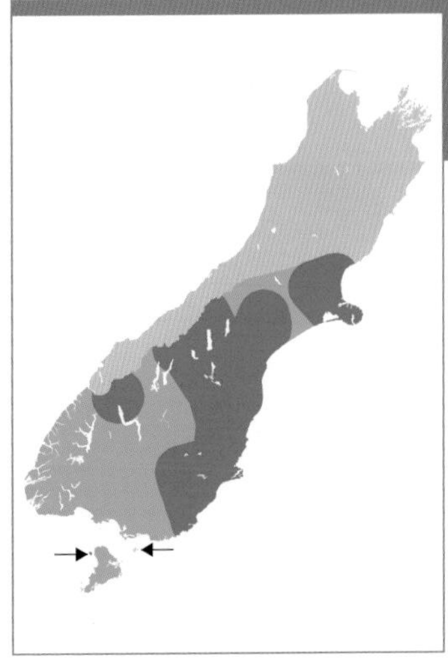

1. ***Canterbury***: **Dorsal surface** green or olive (most males turn grey or brown over first year of life) with a series of white, yellow, grey or pink diamond-shaped markings or stripes, edged in black, yellow or lime green. Strong sexual dichromatism at Banks Peninsula: males nearly always brown or grey; females nearly always green or olive. Dichromatism more variable further south. **Lateral surfaces** usually with a series of large pale blotches between fore- and hind limbs. Dorsal and lateral surfaces often flecked with green, yellow or grey. **Ventral surface** grey, green, pale yellow, brown, or bluish with pale longitudinal streaks. Lower jaw edged with white. **Mouth lining** pink or mauve; **tongue** pink or orange. **Soles of feet** brown, yellow or pale grey.
2. ***Otago***: **Dorsal surface** deep emerald green, either with paired longitudinal yellow or white stripes, finely edged with black or paired series of white or yellow diamond-shaped markings, edged in yellow or black. Inland Otago individuals generally more green overall

Codfish Island

JAMES REARDON

Female, Banks Peninsula

Female, Banks Peninsula

Male, Banks Peninsula

(i.e. base colour of emerald green with lime green diamond- or cross-shaped markings, edged in black and often connected together, along dorsal surface. Head markings, including on lower jaw, and lateral blotches lime green). No sexual dichromatism. **Lateral surfaces** usually with a series of large pale blotches between fore- and hind limbs. Lower jaw white. **Ventral surface** grey or yellow-green, often with white blotches or longitudinal streaks. **Mouth lining** and **tongue** deep blue. Inland Otago individuals have light pink or mauve-coloured mouth linings. **Soles of feet** yellow.

3. ***Codfish Island/Fouveaux Strait***: Large and sturdily built. **Dorsal surface**

uniform green with a faint pale canthal stripe and paired crescent-shaped markings on head, and white lower lip band; usually no other dorsal markings. Limbs and tail more brownish. No sexual dichromatism. **Ventral surface** uniform yellow-green. **Mouth lining** deep blue; **tongue** black. **Intact tail** shorter than SVL.

HABITAT

Costal, Lowland, Montane/subalpine, Alpine
Inhabits dense shrubland, and beech and podocarp (e.g. tōtara/mataī) forests. Most often seen in foliage of kānuka and mānuka, and of dense, divaricating matagouri and *Coprosma* shrubs. Also occurs in alpine tussock, but this may represent a surrogate habitat in a landscape once dominated by shrubland.

NATURAL HISTORY

Diurnal. Arboreal, but will retreat into denser foliage or take refuge on the ground beneath rocks or logs, and will disperse over open ground between patches of vegetation. Strongly heliothermic (avid sun-basker), and very cryptic due to highly effective camouflage. Mating occurs July-September; typically, 2 young, 30-32 mm SVL, born in late summer or autumn (March-May) or in spring (September-November) in montane/subalpine populations. Sexually mature at 3-4 years. Adults tolerant of juveniles, and individuals may be seen basking together on top of one another. Primarily insectivorous but will consume fruits (berries) and possibly nectar from flowers.

ETYMOLOGY

Specific name (Latin) meaning 'set with gems' or 'resembling gems'. **Common name** also refers to the diamond- or jewel-shaped markings on the dorsum. **Māori name** is moko kākāriki; translates to 'green-coloured lizard'.

West Otago

CAREY KNOX

Forest gecko

Mokopirirakau granulatus (Gray, 1845)

Endemic

Auckland

DESCRIPTION

Up to 98 mm SVL; up to c. 16 g weight

A large, intricately marked inhabitant of forest and shrubland, from the northern half of the North Island and the north and west of the South Island. **Dorsal surface** large granular scales, especially on the rostrum. Grey, brown, olive or greenish, occasionally with bright yellow, orange or pink patches. Specimens from Westland highly variable in colour and patterning, often striking. Dorsum usually with transverse W-shaped markings continuing down intact tail, patterning often resembling lichen or tree bark. Capable of dramatic changes in colour tone. V-shaped marking on top of head; white stripe on either side of head, from eye to ear opening. **Lateral surfaces** with blotches and lichen-like markings, similar to those on dorsal surface. **Ventral surface** cream with dark speckles or blotches. **Eye** colour grey, olive or brown, overlaid with black filigree pattern. **Mouth lining** bright orange or orange-yellow, turning black towards throat; **tongue** orange or pale red. **Intact tail** often longer than body length (SVL). **Subdigital lamellae** 11–14. **Soles of feet** pale yellow or cream.

DISTRIBUTION

North and South Islands. Widespread throughout the upper North Island from South Taranaki to southern part of Bay of Islands, including some offshore islands; absent from northern Northland and Aupouri Peninsula. In the South Island, occurs from Marlborough to Nelson, Tasman and Westland.

VARIATION AND SIMILAR SPECIES

Highly variable in colour and patterning. North Island animals usually predominantly grey, although central North Island specimens can have distinctive white and pink markings. South Island animals can be strikingly colourful, particularly Westland populations. Some specimens from the Denniston Plateau (West Coast) have unique pale longitudinal stripes. Outwardly similar to **ngahere gecko** (*M.* "southern North Island") but distinguished by its longer snout; bolder markings that are continuous across dorsal midline; and more precloacal pores. Easily distinguished from ***Dactylocnemis* species** by its speckled ventral surface; often distinctive W-shaped markings on dorsum; and orange mouth lining and tongue. Refer to key to distinguish this species from geographically separated *Mokopirirakau* taxa.

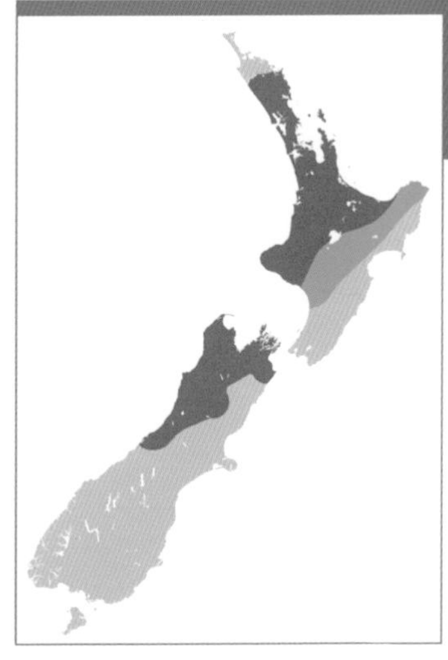

HABITAT

Coastal, Lowland, Montane/subalpine, Alpine

Inhabits forest, scrublands, herbfields, and rocky bluffs and sandstone pavements. Commonly found in mānuka or kānuka

West Coast

West Coast
West Coast

scrub and on trunks, branches or foliage of trees. Takes refuge beneath bark, in dense foliage, in hollow tree trunks, in the crowns of ferns and beneath rock slabs or in crevices during the day. Also known to inhabit peri-urban areas, where it lives in gardens and takes refuge beneath outdoor furniture, woodpiles or timber decking. May disperse across open ground, even rural roads, to reach new habitat.

NATURAL HISTORY

Cathemeral. Mainly arboreal but will also move on ground. Mating occurs in autumn (April–May), and 1 or 2 young born in late summer (January–April), occasionally outside this period. Neonates c. 35 mm SVL. Will mouth gape, displaying bright orange interior, when distressed. Eats primarily invertebrates but also consumes nectar, fruit and honeydew.

ETYMOLOGY

Specific name (Latin) referring to the granular scales on the body. **Common name** is a reference to its habitat. **Māori name** pirirākau translates to 'lizard that clings to trees'.

Auckland

Ngahere gecko

Mokopirirakau "southern North Island"

Endemic

DESCRIPTION

Up to 85 mm SVL

Extremely similar in appearance to the forest gecko, despite the two not being particularly close relatives. **Dorsal surface** grey, brown or olive, with two rows of pale cream-yellow or orange-brown blotches, or smudges either side of midline that sometimes meet on spine, creating a series of chevron or W- or H-shapes, which may be edged in black anteriorly. Markings often overlaid with smaller irregular mustard-yellow, dull red or brown patches. Prominent V-shaped marking on head behind eyes; white stripe extending from behind eye to ear opening. **Lateral surfaces** with blotches and coloured patches, similar to the dorsal surface. **Ventral surface** pale cream or white, marked with grey speckles. **Eye** colour grey, brown or olive, overlaid with dark filigree pattern. **Mouth lining** and **tongue** bright orange or yellow, turning black towards throat. **Intact tail** longer than body length (SVL). **Tail annuli** obvious on intact tail. **Subdigital lamellae** 8–10. **Soles of feet** grey or yellow-grey.

DISTRIBUTION

North Island only. Distributional limits poorly understood, but occurs from Gisborne area and Hawke's Bay southwards to the Tararua Ranges, Kapiti Island and Wellington. Introduced to Matiu/Somes and Mana Islands.

VARIATION AND SIMILAR SPECIES

Highly variable in colour and patterning. Extremely similar to (but genetically very distinct from) the **forest gecko** (*M. granulatus*), which occurs north and south of ngahere gecko. Distinguished by its shorter snout; lower numbers of precloacal and femoral pores; and a strong tendency for dorsal markings to not meet at the midline (vs. markings nearly always continuous across the midline in forest gecko). Refer to key to distinguish this taxon from geographically separated *Mokopirirakau* taxa.

HABITAT

Coastal, Lowland

Inhabits forests, scrub and shrublands, including understorey ferns or flax. Occurs on trees (trunks and branches), high in forest canopies, but can be found closer to ground at forest edges or shrubs. Also uses stone piles, woodpiles, rock crevices, bases of plants, crevices in clay banks, and artificial rock walls in suburban landscapes.

NATURAL HISTORY

Cathemeral, and sun-basks close to retreat entrances; arboreal, terrestrial. Some individuals seldom stray far from particular large trees or structures (e.g. rock walls). Feeds mainly on insects, but will eat soft fruits (including berries) and likely nectar. Gravid females reported in January.

ETYMOLOGY

Tag name referring to the southern North Island area, where the species is known to occur. **Common name** (Māori) meaning 'forest'.

TRENT BELL

Cupola gecko

Mokopirirakau "Cupola"

Endemic

ROGER WADDELL

Nelson Lakes National Park

DESCRIPTION

Body length unknown (potentially up to 85 mm SVL)

A poorly known gecko, from the mountainous regions of far south-western Nelson; only two individuals recorded. **Dorsal surface** mid- to dark grey, with two bold rows of light grey triangular or W-shaped markings either side of midline, edged in black, and continuing down intact tail. Light grey patches on fore- and hind limbs, and on toes. Bold, well-defined markings on head, including a prominent dark V-marking on top of head behind eyes and T-shaped marking on rostrum (i.e. dark grey transverse band joining eyes, and thin longitudinal line towards tip of snout). **Lateral surfaces** mid- to dark grey with a series of pale grey patches or vertical bands between fore- and hind limbs. **Ventral surface** grey, and lightly speckled with black. **Eye** colour olive-grey, overlaid with fine black filigree pattern. **Mouth lining** and **tongue** colour unknown. **Intact tail** equal to or longer than body length (SVL). **Subdigital lamellae** unknown. **Soles of feet** cream or pale yellow.

DISTRIBUTION

South Island only. Range poorly known. Mountainous areas of Nelson Lakes National Park, including the Travers and Sabine Ranges.

VARIATION AND SIMILAR SPECIES

Variation in colour and pattern unknown. Most similar to the **Cascade**

gecko (*M.* "Cascades") but taxa are geographically isolated from each other. Similar to **forest gecko** (*M. granulatus*) but distinguished by its bold markings on snout, shorter snout, more triangular head and more uniform ventral surface.

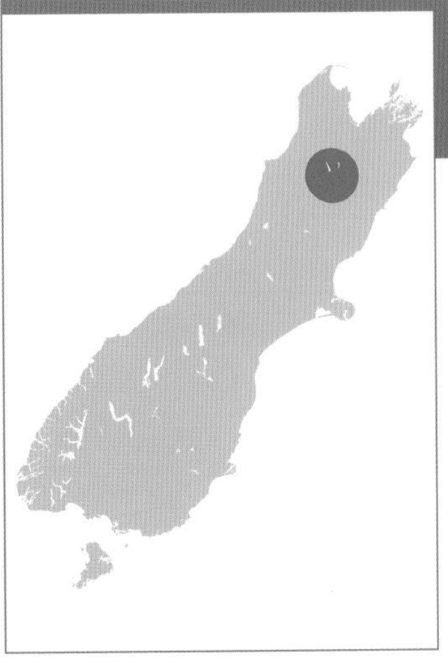

HABITAT

Montane/subalpine, Alpine

Occurs in screes, and boulder fields surrounded by alpine shrubland (snow tōtara, celery pine, *Coprosma* species, mountain flax and snowberry) and *Chionochloa* tussock grassland. Also may occur at lower altitudes, in beech forest or river flat grasses and shrubs.

NATURAL HISTORY

Cathemeral; terrestrial, and saxicolous. Natural history, including reproductive biology, unknown. Several dedicated searches have failed to detect further animals.

ETYMOLOGY

Common and **tag names** referring to Cupola Basin, one of the locations where the species was found.

Nelson Lakes National Park

ROGER WADDELL

Broad-cheeked gecko

Mokopirirakau "Okarito"

Endemic

MATTHEW WALTERS

Paringa

DESCRIPTION

Up to 79 mm SVL

A poorly known taxon from the dense forests and shrublands of the West Coast near Ōkārito, south to near Haast Pass. **Dorsal surface** shades of brown, pink-brown or grey, with lighter W- or H-shaped markings, often edged in black posteriorly, from neck to end of intact tail. Occasionally with orange-brown (brick red) smudges, and small black spots along dorsal surface. Broad cheeks when viewed from above, and short snout. **Lateral surfaces** similar colour to dorsal surface, with or without a series of paler patches, vertical bands or darker speckling between fore- and hind limbs. **Ventral surface** shades of grey with dark speckling, and occasionally small cream or pale yellow blotches. Chin, neck and base of tail may be lighter cream or pale yellow, with dark speckling. Some labial scales may be uniform cream or pale yellow forming a crude denticulate pattern. **Eye** colour brown, overlaid with fine black filigree pattern. **Rostral scale** broadly in contact with nostrils. **Mouth lining** and **tongue** bright orange. **Intact tail** equal to body length (SVL). **Feet** large. **Subdigital lamellae** unknown. **Soles of feet** pale yellow.

DISTRIBUTION

South Island only. Restricted to the West Coast. Distribution limits poorly known, but currently reported from Westland Tai Poutini National Park south of Ōkārito Lagoon to the Paringa River (Douglas Range), north of Haast. Replaced by forest gecko (*M. granulatus*) to the north and

Cascade gecko (*M.* "Cascades") to the south; Open Bay Islands gecko (*M.* "Open Bay Islands") also occurs near the southern limit of range.

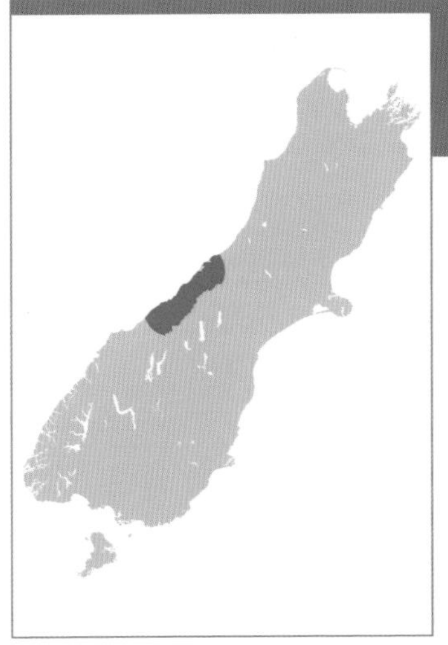

VARIATION AND SIMILAR SPECIES

Highly variable in colour and patterning, but all specimens with a short snout, broad head behind eyes (i.e. expanded cheeks), robust build and relatively short wide toes. Similar to **forest gecko** and **Cascade gecko**, but distinguished by its more robust body, shorter snout, broad head and cheeks, shorter and wider toes, and more heavily speckled ventral surface. Distinguished from the **Open Bay Islands gecko** by its larger size, darker colour and larger granular scales on body (vs. much finer scales). Refer to key to distinguish this taxon from geographically separated *Mokopirirakau* taxa.

HABITAT

Coastal, Lowland, Montane/subalpine

Inhabits dense wet forest, on trunks and branches of large trees beneath the canopy. May also occur in subalpine scrubland and on prostrate vegetation.

NATURAL HISTORY

Nocturnal, but may sun-bask cryptically. Arboreal. Reproductive biology unknown, but likely to be similar to that of other South Island *Mokopirirakau* species.

ETYMOLOGY

Common name referring to the 'broad cheeks' when viewed from above, a characteristic feature of this taxon. **Tag name** is after the Ōkārito area, one of the locations where this taxon occurs.

Ōkārito

IAN SOUTHEY

Ōkārito

GLENN LILLEY

Open Bay Islands gecko

Mokopirirakau "Open Bay Islands"

Endemic

TONY WHITAKER

DESCRIPTION

Up to 77 mm SVL; up to 10.7 g weight

A slender gecko, the smallest *Mokopirirakau* taxon. Known from a single, small, isolated island off the coast of the southern West Coast, west of Haast. **Dorsal surface** light brown or olive, with beige dorsolateral stripes and indistinct transverse bands between them. Stripes continue down intact tail. Distinctive brown V-shaped marking on top of head between and behind eyes. Broad pale stripe extending from behind eye to ear opening. Dorsal scales granular but noticeably smaller than in other *Mokopirirakau* species. **Lateral surfaces** typically uniform light brown or olive, or with series of vertical beige bands between fore- and hind limbs. **Ventral surface** uniform cream. **Eye** colour brown or olive-grey, overlaid with dark filigree pattern. **Rostral scale** in narrow contact with nostrils. **Mouth lining** and **tongue** bright orange. **Intact tail** shorter than or equal to body length (SVL). **Subdigital lamellae** c. 11. **Soles of feet** pale orange-yellow.

DISTRIBUTION

South Island only. Known only from Taumaka Island in the Open Bay Islands group. Because Taumaka is in shallow water, and would have been connected to the mainland until the last few thousand years, this species probably formerly lived on the adjacent mainland, and could possibly still occur there.

VARIATION AND SIMILAR SPECIES

Unlikely to be confused with other species owing to distinctive colour pattern. A close relative of **Cascade gecko** (*M.* "Cascades") but their geographic ranges do not overlap. Smaller, colour much paler and warmer, and patterning less intricate (lacking speckling and red or mustard-yellow on dorsum) compared to Cascade gecko.

Scales on dorsal surface small and fine compared to the larger granular scales of Cascade gecko and **forest gecko** (*M. granulatus*). Refer to key to distinguish this taxon from geographically separated *Mokopirirakau* taxa.

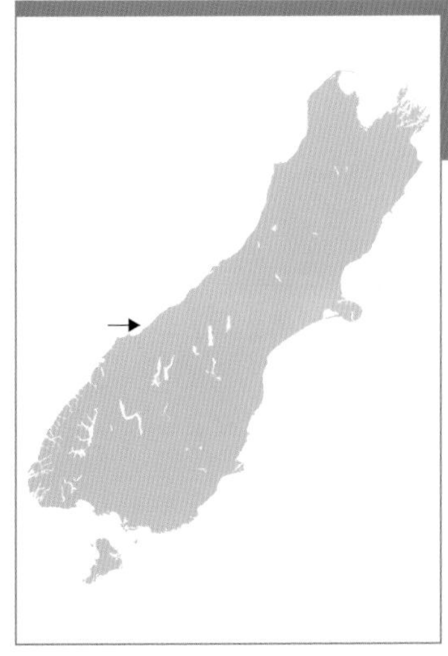

HABITAT

Coastal, Lowland

Inhabits coastal forest and shrubland, including kiekie, māhoe, patē and pōhuehue vines. May take refuge in crevices, hollows of branches and trunks, and beneath bark during the day.

NATURAL HISTORY

Nocturnal; arboreal. Females gravid in March, and give birth to 1 or 2 young (annually or biennially). Potentially threatened by wēkā (*Gallirallus australis*) but taxon's nocturnal habits may reduce risk of predation. Nothing else known of its reproductive biology or behaviour.

ETYMOLOGY

Common and **tag names** referring to the taxon's only known locality, the Open Bay Islands off the West Coast. **Māori name** is moko taumaka, translating to 'lizard of Taumaka Island'.

COLIN MISKELLY

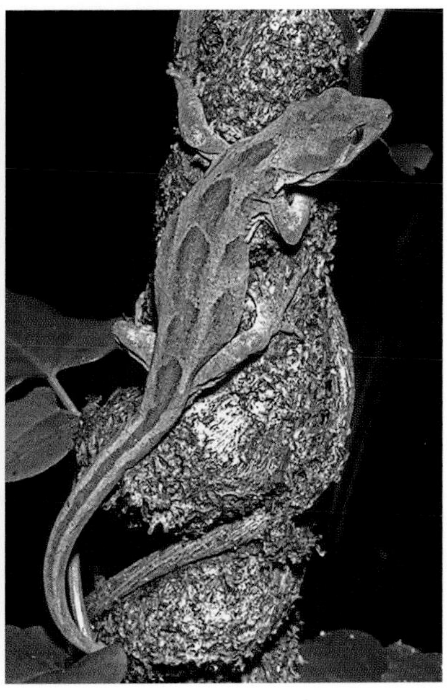

TONY WHITAKER

Cascade gecko

Mokopirirakau "Cascades"

Endemic

MARIEKE LETTINK

DESCRIPTION

Up to 88 mm SVL; up to 19 g (gravid female) weight

A slender, usually boldly marked gecko often found on alpine rock walls in north-eastern Fiordland. **Dorsal surface** brown or grey, or mixture of both, with paired paler blotches either side of midline that join medially to form a series of W or H shapes, or occasionally with pale transverse bands usually finely edged in black on anterior margins. Dorsal markings continuous from behind head to tip of intact tail. Occasionally, rusty red, orange or mustard-yellow smudges are present on nape, and interspersed between the pale dorsal markings. **Lateral surfaces** may be uniform brown or grey, or have pale spots and blotches. Distinctive dark V-shaped marking on top of head, behind eyes; a white stripe from eye to ear opening. Bold markings on snout, usually with short pale stripes from nostril to eye. **Ventral surface** grey or pale brown, either uniform or boldly marked with dark speckles, streaks or sometimes bold longitudinal stripes. **Eye** colour brown or olive, overlaid with fine black filigree pattern. **Mouth lining** and **tongue** bright orange. **Intact tail** longer than body length (SVL). **Subdigital lamellae** c. 9. **Soles of feet** grey or orange-grey.

DISTRIBUTION

South Island only. Occurs in south Westland (Cascade Plateau and Haast Range), and Fiordland (Darran Mountains, Llawrenny Peaks, and surrounding areas).

VARIATION AND SIMILAR SPECIES

Morphology varies geographically, with lowland Westland individuals smaller (< 75 mm SVL), slenderer in build, and with strong markings on ventral surface; members of alpine populations larger (≤ 85 mm SVL), more robustly built and with weaker ventral markings or entirely uniform colouration. Range abuts those of the broad-cheeked gecko (*M.* "Okarito") to the north and Takitimu gecko (*M. cryptozoicus*) near the Rees Valley and in eastern Fiordland. Distinguished from **broad-cheeked gecko** by its more slender build, longer snout, lack of broadly inflated cheeks, smoother scales, and more slender toes with longer distal phalanges. Distinguished from **Open Bay Islands gecko** (*M.* "Open Bay Islands") by its darker colour, and more contrasting markings, larger scales and larger body size. Distinguished from **Takitimu gecko** by more prominent eye, distinctive markings on snout and head, more slender toes with longer distal phalanges, longer tail, and usually also by lack of dark grey tongue tip. Refer to key to distinguish this taxon from geographically separated *Mokopirirakau* taxa.

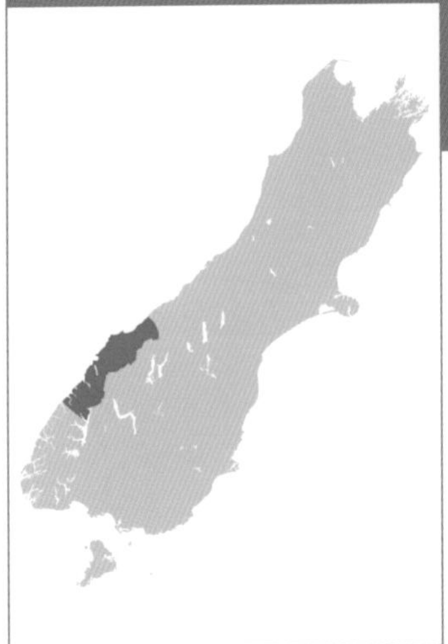

HABITAT

Lowland, Montane/subalpine, Alpine

Occupies subalpine shrubland and herbfields, alpine snow tussock grassland, boulder fields, creviced granite rock bluffs and outcrops, and ultramafic rock areas and forest (although now very uncommon in forest). Can live with 5–6 °C average annual temperatures, with frequent ground frosts, snowfall, landslides and avalanches.

TONY JEWELL

TONY JEWELL

NATURAL HISTORY

Cathemeral; partially nocturnal but will sun-bask at retreat entrances. Terrestrial, and at least partially arboreal, and saxicolous. Reproduction likely to be biennial since females of same populations have been reported in various states of pregnancy (i.e. not gravid, early to mid-term and late term) in mid-March. Diet probably consists of invertebrates (insects, spiders, molluscs) and soft fruits (berries) of alpine shrubs.

ETYMOLOGY

Common and **tag names** referring to both the high rainfall and waterfall landscapes in which the gecko lives, and the Cascade Plateau – one of the locations where it occurs.

Tautuku gecko

Mokopirirakau "southern forest"

Endemic

DESCRIPTION

Up to 88 mm SVL; up to c. 14 g weight

A cryptic species from the Catlins, resembling the forest gecko (*M. granulatus*) but more closely related (genetically similar) to the orange-spotted gecko (*M.* "Roys Peak"). **Dorsal surface** shades of grey, brown, olive or brick red, with distinctive transverse W- or H-shaped blotches that are pale or bright yellow. Frequently with irregular orange or red blotches on dorsum. Colour and patterning very reminiscent of lichen. Markings may be outlined in black. Distinctive V-shaped marking on top of head between eyes. **Lateral surfaces** with irregular-shaped pale yellow, cream or brick red blotches overlaying basal colour. **Ventral surface** light grey to yellow with dark speckles or mottling. **Eye** colour brown or brown-grey, but temporarily a distinctive blue in some individuals. **Mouth lining** and **tongue** bright orange (tongue sometimes pinkish). **Intact tail** equal to or slightly longer than body length (SVL). **Subdigital lamellae** 11–14. **Soles of feet** yellow or pale orange.

DISTRIBUTION

South Island only. Currently known from Southland (the Catlins) to south-east Otago, but likely to exist elsewhere. Museum specimens from Riverton have also been identified as this species.

VARIATION AND SIMILAR SPECIES

Body colour patterning variable. Geographically isolated from all other *Mokopirirakau* taxa but may be confused with the **Takitimu gecko** (*M. cryptozoicus*) and **cloudy gecko** (*M. nebulosus*). Distinguished from both these taxa by its uniform orange tongue, a tail length longer than SVL, and complex colour patterns. Refer to key to distinguish this taxon from geographically separated *Mokopirirakau* taxa.

HABITAT

Lowland

Inhabits dense podocarp-hardwood rainforest (rimu and kāmahi), shrubland (mānuka, kānuka, *Coprosma* species), and crown ferns. Most often seen at forest edges (but this may reflect visibility rather than abundance). Seeks refuge in crevices, trees, or beneath rock slabs on large boulders, where available, at night and during the day.

NATURAL HISTORY

Cathemeral; arboreal, semi-terrestrial. Forages at night among shrubs and rocks and on branches of trees, for small invertebrates. Sun-basks at retreat entrances during day. Females gravid in March–April, and produce 1 or 2 young. Given the cool climate, may reproduce biennially.

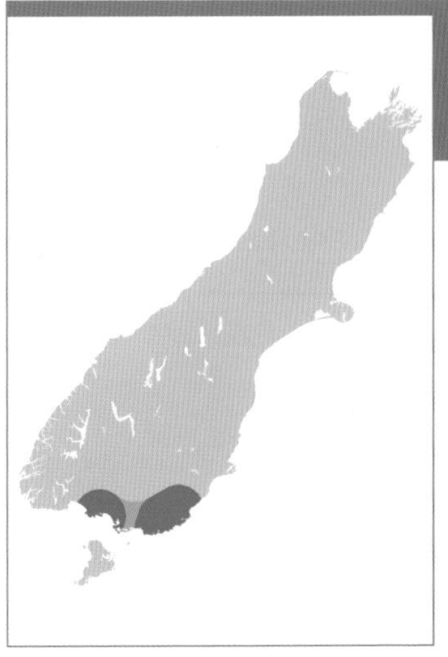

ETYMOLOGY

Common name (Māori) meaning 'low hill', referring to the hilly Tautuku Forest area, where this species occurs. **Tag name** is a reference to the extreme southern distribution.

TRENT BELL

Orange-spotted gecko

Mokopirirakau "Roys Peak"

Endemic

TRENT BELL

Crown Range

DESCRIPTION

Up to 95 mm SVL

A high-altitude species, discovered only in 1997. **Dorsal surface** grey, grey-brown, olive-brown or rusty orange, with broad pale dorsolateral stripes, or bands, or alternating blotches or smudges. Some individuals with transverse butterfly-shaped bands (i.e. enlarged paired blotches that narrow and meet over midline). Often with irregular blotches or spots of orange, black, brown or white; can be predominantly orange. Distinctive V-shaped marking on top of head behind eyes. White stripe extending from eye to ear opening. **Lateral surfaces** with a broad brown or orange lateral band, changing abruptly to grey or olive-brown ventrally. **Ventral surface** grey to pale orange, with faint or bold blotches, spots or longitudinal streaks. **Eye** colour from brown to pinkish, overlaid with fine black filigree pattern. **Mouth lining** and **tongue** bright orange. **Intact tail** usually shorter than or equal to body length (SVL), occasionally slightly longer. **Subdigital lamellae** 9–14. **Soles of feet** pale orange-yellow.

DISTRIBUTION

South Island only. Confined to mountainous areas of western Otago, including Richardson Mountains, Crown Range, Hector Mountains and Dunstan Mountains.

VARIATION AND SIMILAR SPECIES

Individuals can drastically change their colour tone. Three geographic variants recognised:

1. ***Crown Range***: Small (70–80 mm SVL), with slender build and broad shallow head. Markings usually drab and

streaked, although some individuals boldly marked. Two cloacal spurs on either side, and precloacal pores c. 28 pores wide. Subdigital lamellae 13–14. Found among large rocks and boulders.

2. ***Richardson Mountains***: Large (up to 92 mm SVL), and robust in build. Only one specimen known, with striking butterfly-shaped grey and olive markings, without orange spots. Subdigital lamellae 9–11. Individual was found beneath rocks among tussock grassland.
3. ***Dunstan Mountains***: Large (85–95 mm SVL), and moderately robust in build. Markings variable,

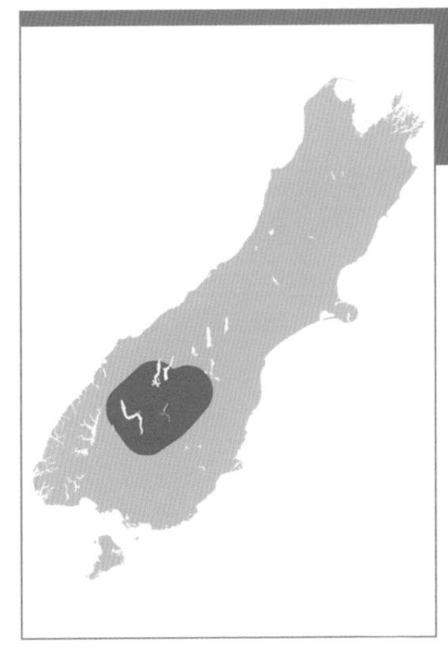

Crown Range

TRENT BELL

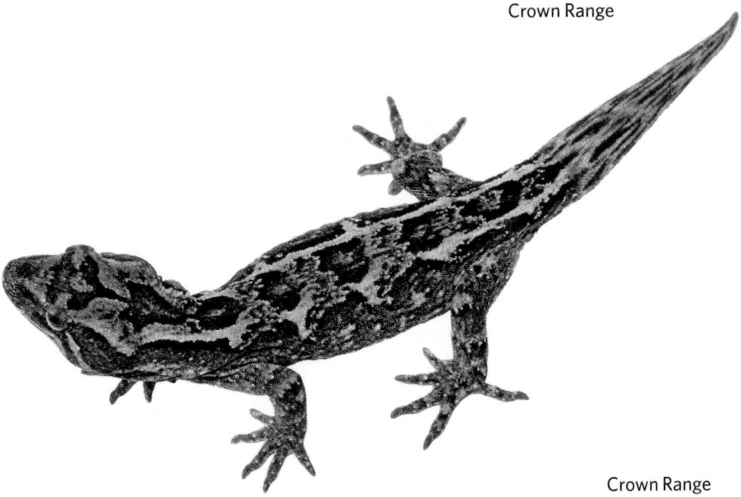

Crown Range

TONY JEWELL

Richardson Mountains

and usually prominent with some orange spots on dorsal surface. Three or four cloacal spurs on either side, and precloacal pores c. 28–37 pores wide. Lives among rock piles.

Geographically isolated from all other *Mokopirirakau* taxa. Distinguished from **Takitimu gecko** (*M. cryptozoicus*) by its uniform orange tongue (vs. pink or grey), and from **Cascade gecko** (*M.* "Cascades") by its broader toes with shorter distal phalanges, and absence of very prominent contrasting markings on snout. Most closely related to **Tautuku gecko** (*M.* "southern forest"), but with very different habitat (alpine vs. lowland forest) and ecology, and distinguished by its orange (vs. yellow) markings, more uniformly mid-grey (vs. highly mottled) background colour and shorter tail. Refer to key to distinguish this taxon from geographically separated *Mokopirirakau* taxa.

HABITAT

Alpine

Occupies boulder fields, rock falls, scree slopes and schist rock outcrops, surrounded by tussock grassland and alpine herbs and shrubs. Also found beneath rock slabs. Deep screes probably offer refuge from low temperatures and snowfall in winter.

NATURAL HISTORY

Nocturnal, but may sun-bask cryptically (although individuals have been observed basking in the open, this is considered rare); terrestrial, saxicolous. Reproduction biennial, probably an adaptation to cold, harsh environments; 1 or 2 young born October–November. Age at sexual maturity not known, but probably at least a decade.

ETYMOLOGY

Common name referring to the orange spots or smudges of colour present on many specimens. **Tag name** refers to Roys Peak, at the northern end of the Crown Range, where this species was first discovered.

CAREY KNOX

Crown Range

TONY JEWELL

Dunstan Mountains

Takitimu gecko

Mokopirirakau cryptozoicus (Jewell & Leschen, 2004) **Endemic**

TONY JEWELL

South Fiordland

DESCRIPTION

Up to 87 mm SVL; up to 18 g weight

A robust and poorly known gecko from Otago and Southland. **Dorsal surface** slate grey, with paler herringbone markings, frequently joined by longitudinal stripes. Two-toned orange blotches and spots on some specimens, others with purple-grey markings outlined in black. Patterns extend down length of intact tail. Dark V-shaped marking on top of head between eyes; indistinct pale canthal stripes and pale stripe from eye to ear opening. Series of pale lateroventral spots usually present. **Lateral surfaces** slate grey with irregular-shaped grey, purple-grey or orange blotches. **Ventral surface** pale grey or pale yellow-pink, with mottling and flecks. **Eye** colour brown or pinkish, overlaid with fine black filigree pattern. **Mouth lining** bright orange; **tongue** pink with greyish tip. **Intact tail** noticeably shorter than body length (SVL). Tail annuli clearly visible on intact tail. **Subdigital lamellae** 7–12 (usually 9–11). **Soles of feet** brown-orange.

DISTRIBUTION

South Island only. Occurs from western Otago to Southland, including the Takitimu Mountains, Rees Valley, northern Richardson Mountains and Waitutu Forest (South Fiordland).

VARIATION AND SIMILAR SPECIES

Variable in colour and patterning. Orange colouration (dorsal surface) currently known only from males. Most similar to **cloudy gecko** (*M. nebulosus*, closest relative) from Stewart Island/Rakiura, but distinguished by its smaller size (SVL), shorter tail, the colour and patterning, and habitat preferences. Refer to key to distinguish this taxon from geographically separated *Mokopirirakau* taxa.

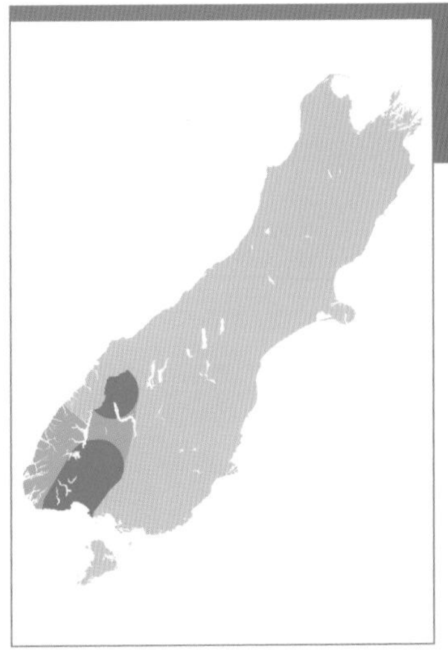

HABITAT

Lowland, Montane/subalpine, Alpine

Inhabits bluffs, rock outcrops and screes surrounded by alpine herbfields and tussock grassland. Also known from forest. Takes refuge in rock crevices, and in deep screes from which it seldom emerges.

NATURAL HISTORY

Nocturnal, and partially diurnal; terrestrial and saxicolous. Little known about reproductive biology but probably a biennial breeder. A gravid female with two embryos has been recorded in January. Nothing else known of life history or behaviour.

ETYMOLOGY

Specific name (Greek) meaning 'hidden' and 'living', referring to the cryptic lifestyle of the gecko. **Common name** refers to the Takitimu Mountains, the type locality of this species.

Rees Valley

TONY JEWELL

Takitimu Mountains

TONY JEWELL

Cloudy gecko

Mokopirirakau nebulosus (McCann, 1955) **Endemic**

JAMES REARDON

Codfish Island

DESCRIPTION

Up to 90 mm (usually smaller) SVL; up to 26 g weight

A cryptic and poorly known species from the southern islands of New Zealand. Body moderately robust, and head with short blunt snout. **Dorsal surface** dark brown, olive-grey, grey, dark green or pink-brown, with broad irregular-shaped pale patches either side of midline, forming W-shaped, herringbone or transverse chevron markings, often running together to form indistinct longitudinal stripes. Light dorsal markings often embellished with black speckles, and black posterior edges. Distinctive dark V-shaped marking on top of head behind eyes. Pale stripe extending from behind eye to ear opening. **Lateral surfaces** same colour as dorsal surface, either uniform or with irregular-shaped pale blotches sometimes partially edged in black. **Ventral surface** uniform cream or grey, speckled with brown or black, or with longitudinal stripes; chin and throat mottled. **Eye** colour olive-grey. **Rostral scale** in contact with nostrils. **Mouth lining** and **tongue** yellow to bright orange; tongue may be pinkish below and with grey tip. **Intact tail** equal to, shorter or slightly longer than body length (SVL). **Subdigital lamellae** 11–14. **Soles of feet** grey or cream.

DISTRIBUTION

Restricted to Stewart Island/Rakiura, and its outlying islands and islets, including Codfish Island/Whenuahou, and the Tītī/Muttonbird Islands. Not reported from the Hazelburgh island group in central Foveaux Strait.

VARIATION AND SIMILAR SPECIES

Colour and patterning vary between individuals and among populations. Individuals larger on some islands;

individuals from Codfish Island have more yellow colour in the irregular-shaped pale markings either side of dorsum midline, and these markings often outlined in black. Unlikely to be confused with other species owing to geographic isolation from all other members of the genus *Mokopirirakau*. Narrow lamellae pads differentiate it from ***Woodworthia* species** (which are also absent from its range). Refer to key to distinguish this species from geographically separated *Mokopirirakau* taxa.

HABITAT

Coastal, Lowland

Occupies scrub, shrubland and lowland forest, where it actively forages on the ground and in vegetation above ground. Takes shelter beneath bark of trees, in hollows and in epiphytes.

NATURAL HISTORY

Nocturnal. Arboreal, terrestrial. May sun-bask in late afternoon, and forages in trees and shrubs and on ground at night. Little known of reproductive biology. Known to vocalise with soft squeaks. Primarily insectivorous, but may consume nectar.

ETYMOLOGY

Specific name (Latin) meaning 'cloudy'. **Common name** also refers to the greyish dorsal colour and patterning.

Kundy Island

PHIL MELGREN

Black-eyed gecko

Mokopirirakau kahutarae (Whitaker, 1984) **Endemic**

Kahurangi National Park

DESCRIPTION

Up to 91 SVL; up to 15 g weight

A very distinctive gecko from the alpine zone, characterised by its large black eyes, and absence of enlarged apical plates on the toes. **Dorsal surface** olive-grey fading to lighter grey along the flanks, with white speckles. Six or seven lighter grey transverse bands across dorsal surface of body, and bands continue down intact tail (recently discovered Otago animals have more, narrower bands). Scales on body small and granular. Labial scales pale yellow or orange. **Lateral surfaces** light grey with white speckles. **Ventral surface** uniform white. **Eye** colour black. Prominent 'eyebrows'. **Mouth lining** and **tongue** pink or pale red, with orange at corners of mouth. **Intact tail** about equal to body length (SVL). **Precloacal pores** 6 rows, and **femoral pores** 2 rows. **Toes** slender, on large feet. **Subdigital lamellae** 8–14. **Soles of feet** white or cream; toe tips pale yellow.

DISTRIBUTION

South Island only. Known from the Seaward and Inland Kaikōura Ranges (Marlborough), Nelson Lakes National Park, Mt Arthur (north-west Nelson) and Matiri Range (Tasman). A population has recently been discovered in north Otago, significantly extending the species' range. May occur more widely in the South Island.

VARIATION AND SIMILAR SPECIES

Minor variation and unlikely to be confused with any other species owing to combination of large black eyes, dorsal colouration and long slender toes.

Individuals from north Otago differ, with fewer subdigital lamellae, shorter tail, rounder eyes and less distinct dorsal markings.

HABITAT

Alpine

Occurs only in alpine and subalpine bluffs, and rock outcrops, particularly greywacke and marble rock formations where deep crevices provide refuge from harsh alpine environment. Low-growing alpine shrubs, tussocks and spaniards grow sparsely on the bluffs and screes. Occasionally found beneath rock slabs during the day and on 'warm' alpine nights (i.e. > 7 °C). Forages openly on rock faces.

NATURAL HISTORY

Nocturnal, but frequently emerges during day to sun-bask on rock faces either fully or partially exposed to the sunlight. Saxicolous. Reproductive biology unknown. Feeds on invertebrates, including spiders, beetles, wētā and micro-molluscs.

ETYMOLOGY

Specific name from the type locality, the Kahutara Saddle in the Seaward Kaikōura Ranges. **Common name** refers to this species' large jet-black eyes.

North Otago

CAREY KNOX

Northern striped gecko

Toropuku "Coromandel"

Endemic

DESCRIPTION

Up to 88 mm SVL

A medium-sized and distinctive gecko from the Coromandel Region, with a slender build, long snout and webbed feet. **Dorsal surface** golden brown or tan, with broad sand-coloured dorsolateral stripes, with fine striations, from nostrils over eyes and shoulders to tip of intact tail. Dorsolateral stripes edged above and below with narrow red-brown, yellow or fine black stripes. Red-brown medial stripe extending from tip of snout to top of head between eyes, leading into paired dark crescent markings on top of head just behind eyes. Red-brown upper lateral stripe running from nostril, through eye and ear opening to tip of tail. Lower **lateral surfaces** with a series of longitudinal striations. Limbs brown with pale mottling and short dark striations and flecks. **Ventral surface** opaque light sand colour, with many fine black striations or flecks. **Eye** colour golden brown, overlaid with dark filigree pattern. **Rostral scale** in contact with nostrils. **Frontal scales** conical. **Mouth lining** and **tongue** pink; tongue tip sometimes ruby red or grey. Lips yellow-orange; corners of mouth pink. **Intact tail** prehensile; longer than body length (SVL). Tail annuli distinct on intact tail. **Cloacal spurs** 3 on either side; enlarged, pointed. **Precloacal pores** 5 rows, and **femoral pores** 2 or 3 rows, and extending along thighs. **Toes** of hind foot with prominent webbing. **Subdigital lamellae** 12–16. **Soles of feet** light brown or cream.

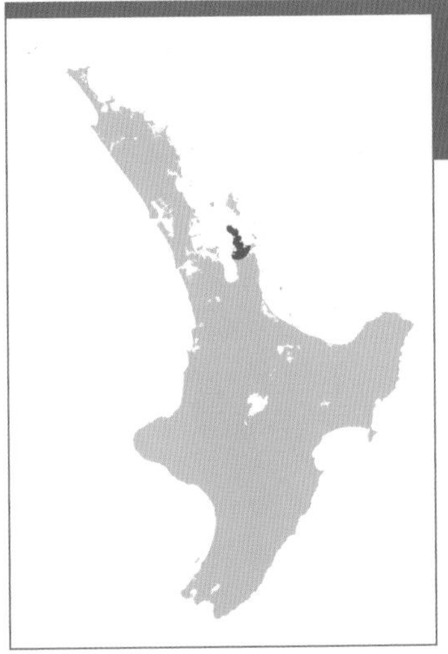

DISTRIBUTION

North Island only. Confined to the Coromandel Peninsula, from Manaia to Mt Moehau. Distribution poorly understood; species probably formerly more widespread in lowland forest habitats in the North Island; discoveries of additional populations quite likely.

VARIATION AND SIMILAR SPECIES

Similar to **southern striped gecko** (*T. stephensi*), but taxa distributions do not overlap. Distinguished from southern striped gecko by its distinctly conical (vs. domed) frontal scales, a longer snout, fewer precloacal and femoral pore rows, and paired crescent-shaped markings on top of head joined posteriorly at midline (vs. usually straighter and narrowly separated). Unlikely to be confused with other gecko species, e.g. goldstripe (*W. chrysosiretica*); Raukawa (*W. maculata*); Pacific (*D. pacificus*); and forest (*M. granulatus*), owing to distinctive markings, extent of toe webbing and presence of orange on inside of lips. Refer to key to distinguish this taxon from other geckos.

HABITAT

Lowland

Occurs in dense forest, where it appears to be strongly associated with kiekie. May also use lower-growing vineland, bracken and shrubland. Several individuals have been found crossing roads at night, and on residential buildings in remote locations.

NATURAL HISTORY

Nocturnal, but will sun-bask cryptically (gravid females sun-bask more as they near parturition). Arboreal, and very competent moving through vegetation and vineland, readily leaping between branches and foliage. May seek refuge beneath bark, in tree hollows or beneath objects on the ground during winter. Reproduction probably biennial. Mating period not known but 2 young born in May. Feeds on invertebrates and actively but stealthily pursues prey.

ETYMOLOGY

Generic name from the Māori word meaning 'secret and stealthy', referring to the gecko's cryptic habits and elusive behaviour. **Common** and **tag names** refer to the geographic range in the Coromandel Region of the North Island.

Southern striped gecko

Toropuku stephensi (Robb, 1980)

Endemic

JAMIE DARBYSHIRE

Maud Island

DESCRIPTION

Up to 81 mm SVL; up to 13.5 g weight

A medium-sized gecko with distinctive stripes on dorsal surface. **Dorsal surface** fawn, tan or golden brown with a broad red-brown stripe down midline that continues down intact tail. Broad sand-coloured dorsolateral stripes, with fine striations, from nostrils over eyes and shoulders to tip of intact tail. Dorsolateral stripes edged above and below with narrow red-brown, yellow or fine black stripes; marked with brown flecks and striations, giving a textured bark-like appearance. Red-brown medial stripe or oblong-shaped marking on snout; a brown V-shaped marking on head behind eyes. Red-brown upper lateral stripe running from nostril, through eye and ear opening to tip of tail. Lower **lateral surfaces** with a series of longitudinal striations. Limbs brown with pale mottling and short dark striations and flecks. **Ventral surface** opaque; light sand colour, with numerous fine black striations or flecks. **Eye** colour golden brown or grey-brown, overlaid with dark filigree pattern. **Rostral scales** in contact with nostrils. **Frontal scales** domed. **Mouth lining** pink with orange inside lips; **tongue** pink with ruby red or grey tip. Lips and corners of mouth yellow-orange. **Intact tail** prehensile; equal to or longer than body length (SVL). **Precloacal pore** length 6–9 rows, and **femoral pore** length 4–5 rows, extending to hind limbs. **Toes** long, with moderately expanded pads and basal webbing; feet large. **Subdigital lamellae** 11–15. **Soles of feet** cream or pale brown.

DISTRIBUTION

South Island only. Occurs on Stephens Island/Takapourewa in Cook Strait and Maud Island in the Marlborough Sounds.

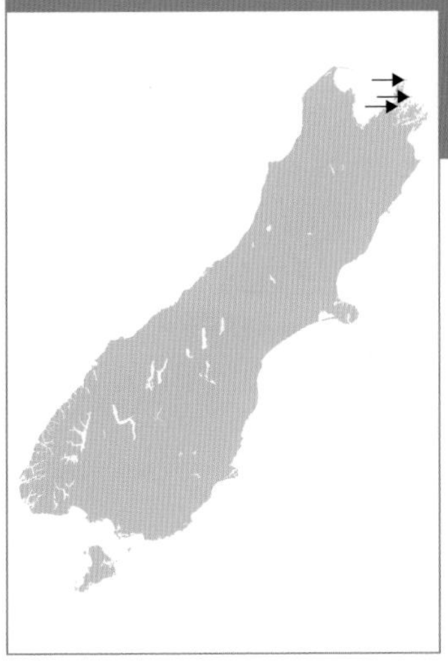

VARIATION AND SIMILAR SPECIES

Sexually dimorphic in body shape, with males being bulkier (mass relative to SVL) than females. Minor morphological differences between this species and **northern striped gecko** (*T.* "Coromandel"), including domed (vs. conical) scales on frontal region, shorter snout, more precloacal and femoral pore rows, and with the paired straight markings on top of head narrowly separated posteriorly at midline (vs. joined and usually crescent-shaped). These taxa do not overlap in distribution (i.e. they are allopatric) and, therefore, confusion unlikely. Unlikely to be confused with other gecko species because of its distinctive markings, extent of toe webbing, and presence of orange on lips inside mouth. Refer to the key to distinguish this taxon from other geckos.

HABITAT

Coastal, Lowland

Inhabits shrubland, coastal and lowland forests dominated by broadleaved tree species, and pōhuehue vineland. Usually occurs in lower-growing vegetation or on mature trees, up to about 3.5 m above the ground, but has been found on the ground.

NATURAL HISTORY

Nocturnal; arboreal, but will move down to ground. Able to change colour tone relatively rapidly (e.g. from light tan to darker brown in a matter of minutes). Very active and agile, climbing quickly through vegetation, and readily leaping between branches. Reproduction may be biennial, and females reportedly gravid in March, with 1 or 2 young born late summer. Sexual maturity reached at around 60 mm SVL. Longevity at least 10–16 years. Diet includes invertebrates (beetles, moths, spiders); may also consume nectar from flowers, and fruit.

ETYMOLOGY

Specific name (Latinisation) and **common name** referring to Stephens Island (Takapourewa) in the Cook Strait, the first reported locality of this species.

Matapia gecko

Dactylocnemis "Matapia"

Endemic

DESCRIPTION

Up to 60 mm SVL

A small, slender and quite distinctive gecko from far northern New Zealand. **Dorsal surface** golden brown to dark olive in Aupouri Peninsula populations, usually with two pronounced pale stripes extending from nostrils, over eyes and continuing down tail; stripes often bordered by thinner dark brown lines. Colour darker and patterning more variable in Karikari Peninsula populations. Prominent pale markings on top of head. Long, pointed snout. **Lateral surfaces** with a broad brown lateral band changing abrupty to cream below. **Ventral surface** uniform cream; occasionally with faint dark speckling. Chin, throat and tail uniform cream. **Eye** colour walnut brown with olive or yellow flecking. **Rostral scale** in broad contact with nostrils. **Mouth lining** light pink; **tongue** with dark grey tip (the only mainland *Dactylocnemis* to have this). **Intact tail** prehensile; longer or equal to body length (SVL). **Cloacal spurs** pointed, 3–4 on each side. **Femoral pores** absent. **Toes** more broadly expanded than in other *Dactylocnemis* species, more like many *Woodworthia*, being broadest near tip of expansion; distal phalange shorter than in other *Dactylocnemis* species. **Subdigital lamellae** 8–15. **Soles of feet** whitish.

DISTRIBUTION

North Island only. Confined to the Aupouri and Karikari Peninsulas in Northland, and present on some islands off the Te Paki area and western Northland.

VARIATION AND SIMILAR SPECIES

Populations in Karikari Peninsula dark grey, and often have transverse markings, compared to warm golden tone and longitudinally striped patterning commonly seen in Te Paki area. Smaller body size on offshore islands. May be confused with **Te Paki gecko** (*D.* "North Cape"), with overlapping distribution, but noticeably smaller, with broader toes and fewer subdigital lamellae, and lighter and warmer colour. Much smaller than all other *Dactylocnemis* species. Dark tongue tip diagnostic within *Dactylocnemis,* and this species never has mustard-yellow nape marking common in all its congeners. Superficially resembles some *Woodworthia*, but distribution ranges do not overlap and generic diagnostic features allow ready separation (e.g. rostral scale in contact with nostrils and reduction of precloacal pores to a small central patch).

HABITAT

Coastal, Lowland

A habitat generalist; found in scrub, shrubland, sedgeland, and rocky cliffs, and in crevices within clay banks.

NATURAL HISTORY

Nocturnal; terrestrial and arboreal. Known to sun-bask at retreat entrances. Very agile and acrobatic; frequently leaps between branches, and moves rapidly through foliage when disturbed. Reproductive biology unknown, but probably similar to that of Te Paki gecko and Pacific gecko (*D. pacificus*).

ETYMOLOGY

Common and **tag names** referring to Matapia Island where it was first found in sympatry with *D.* "North Cape", leading to the recognition that it is a distinct species.

Te Paki gecko

Dactylocnemis "North Cape"

Endemic

DESCRIPTION

Up to 80 (rarely up to 84) mm SVL

A cryptic species superficially very similar to Pacific gecko (*D. pacificus*); consequently, distributions of the two in northern Northland are poorly understood. **Dorsal surface** brown, olive or grey, with pale irregular-shaped blotches, transverse bands, or pale longitudinal dorsolateral stripes. Dorsal markings continue down intact tail, usually outlined in dark brown or black. Brown upper lateral band extending from nostrils through eye and over shoulder, with wavy or straight edges, and with or without white spots. Short white or pale stripe connecting eye and ear opening. Often has a bright mustard-yellow crescent on nape of neck, with similarly coloured blotches along rest of body and tail. Lower **lateral surfaces** pale whitish or grey, and may be uniform or flecked with black. **Ventral surface** pale white or grey, either uniform or occasionally flecked with black (especially under-surface of tail). Throat may be flushed with orange. **Eye** colour brown or orange-brown. **Rostral scale** in broad contact with nostrils. **Mouth lining** and **tongue** pink. **Intact tail** equal to body length (SVL). **Cloacal spurs** pointed, 3–4 on each side. **Femoral pores** absent. **Subdigital lamellae** 10–12. **Soles of feet** brownish white.

DISTRIBUTION

North Island only. Confirmed only from northern Aupouri Peninsula, Northland (north of Houhora). However, there is a large area between northern Aupouri Peninsula and Bay of Islands where *Dactylocnemis* geckos are present but their specific identity requires confirmation.

VARIATION AND SIMILAR SPECIES

Highly variable in body colour patterning. Distinguished from **Raukawa gecko** (*W. maculata*) by its rostral scale in broad contact with nostril (vs. excluded). Easily confused with sympatric **Matapia gecko** (*D.* "Matapia") but usually much larger; more grey or darker brown on dorsum; more commonly with blotches rather than stripes; smaller, more asymmetrical distal pad on first digit; longer distal phalange; and absence of dark pigment on tongue tip. Refer to key to distinguish this taxon from geographically separated *Dactylocnemis* taxa.

HABITAT

Coastal, Lowland

Inhabits scrub and forest, including mānuka and kānuka shrubland, clay banks and lowland kauri forest. Also found in mangroves – the only New Zealand gecko so far known from that habitat. Forages among foliage and on the ground at night, and takes refuge in crevices and hollows in trees, beneath bark, or under rocks and logs during day.

NATURAL HISTORY

Nocturnal, but will sun-bask cryptically. Terrestrial and arboreal. Reproductive biology like that of its close relative the Pacific gecko (*D. pacificus*), with 2 young born late January–early February.

ETYMOLOGY

Common and **tag names** referring to the Te Paki area of North Cape, where it is found.

Pacific gecko

Dactylocnemis pacificus (Gray, 1842)

Endemic

Auckland

DESCRIPTION

Up to 80 mm SVL; up to c. 13 g weight

A secretive species from the North Island. **Dorsal surface** variable in body colour and patterning; but generally brown, grey-brown or olive with pale grey or brown longitudinal dorsolateral stripes, transverse bands or blotches, or chevron-shaped markings. Large irregular-shaped blotches continue down intact tail. For striped individuals, dorsolateral stripes merge at tail base, and blotches continue to tail tip. Some specimens have a mustard-yellow crescent or lunar-shaped marking on nape. Dark V-shaped marking on top of head behind eyes. Pale stripe extending from eye to ear opening. Open with dark denticulate markings on lips. **Lateral surfaces** with light and dark brown blotches and, frequently, black speckles or small spots. Pale lower lateral stripe may be present. **Ventral surface** pale grey, cream or yellowish; either uniform or lightly speckled with black. Chin and vent may be flushed with yellow. Shallow (dorso-ventrally flattened) snout and head, and snout relatively long. **Eye** colour brown, overlaid with fine black filigree pattern. **Rostral scale** in contact with nostrils. **Mouth lining** and **tongue** pink. **Intact tail** usually longer than body length (SVL). **Cloacal spurs** pointed, 3–4 on either side. **Femoral pores** absent. **Toes** slender, with expanded toe pads and narrow distal phalange. **Subdigital lamellae** 10–16. **Soles of feet** buff, pinkish or whitish.

DISTRIBUTION

North Island only. Widely distributed throughout the North Island from Bay of Islands to Whanganui, and on many offshore islands. Records from Palmerston North and Upper Hutt may represent accidental human-assisted movements. Populations scattered, and often sparse throughout range. The specific identity of *Dactylocnemis* geckos occurring between southern Aupouri Peninsula and Bay of Islands requires confirmation.

VARIATION AND SIMILAR SPECIES

Highly variable in both colour and patterning, from uniform to blotched or striped. Distinguished from sympatric **Raukawa gecko** (*W. maculata*) by rostral scale in broad contact with nostrils (vs. excluded); narrower expanded toe pads; longer distal phalanges; and more enlarged, pointed and numerous cloacal spurs (3–4 vs. 1–2). Differs from sympatric **goldstripe gecko** (*W. chrysosiretica*) by having narrower toes and rostral scale in contact with nostrils. Not known to co-exist with other *Dactylocnemis* species. Refer to key to distinguish this species from geographically separated *Dactylocnemis* taxa.

HABITAT

Coastal, Lowland

Occupies a broad range of habitats from the coast, where occurs on boulder beaches, beneath driftwood and beached seaweed, to scrubland, flaxland and lowland forest. Also frequently seen on clay banks, creviced rock bluffs and rocky outcrops. By day, takes refuge beneath loose bark, and in tree hollows, flax bases, rock crevices or accumulations of debris in crooks of branches in forest. Forages on tree branches and among foliage by night.

NATURAL HISTORY

Nocturnal; terrestrial and arboreal. May sun-bask cryptically. Can occur at very high densities, particularly on mammal-free offshore islands. Annual reproductive cycle, with mating in autumn (March–May), and females giving birth to 1 or 2 young in summer and early autumn (February–March). Neonates 26–30 mm SVL. Sexually mature at 3–4 years. Nervous and flighty in nature, and readily dashes away, jumps or drops from vegetation when disturbed. Vocalisations limited to soft squeaks; usually when distressed. Omnivorous, feeding on invertebrates, soft fruits (berries), nectar (flax, hebe) and honeydew.

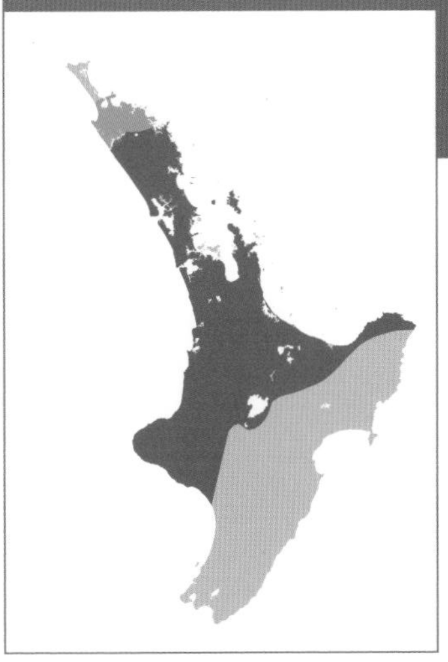

ETYMOLOGY

Specific name (Latinisation) and **common name** most likely referring to the Pacific Ocean, and the species' occurrence in the 'South Seas Islands' (i.e. New Zealand).

Auckland

Three Kings gecko

Dactylocnemis "Three Kings"

Endemic

DESCRIPTION

Up to 100 mm SVL

A large, robust gecko endemic to Manawatāwhi/Three Kings Islands. Highly variable in colour and patterning. **Dorsal surface** dull brown with longitudinal stripes, transverse bands or chevron-shaped markings. Often has a bright mustard-yellow crescent on nape of neck, with same-colour blotches along rest of body and tail. **Lateral surfaces** shades of brown or grey-brown with fine pale flecks. **Ventral surface** uniform cream or pale brown. **Eye** colour gold or brown, overlaid with black filigree pattern. **Rostral scale** in broad contact with nostrils. **Mouth lining** and **tongue** pink, tongue often with grey tip. **Intact tail** length equal to, shorter than or longer than body length (SVL). **Cloacal spurs** pointed, 3 on either side. **Femoral**

pores absent (i.e. precloacal pores do not extend onto hind limbs). **Subdigital lamellae** 15–16. **Soles of feet** pale brown or white.

DISTRIBUTION

North Island only; island endemic. Restricted to Manawatāwhi/Three Kings Islands. Occurs on all vegetated islands in the group.

VARIATION AND SIMILAR SPECIES

Highly variable in colour patterning (stripes, blotches or fairly uniform). Only gecko on Manawatāwhi/Three Kings Islands. Geographically isolated from other members of *Dactylocnemis*. Refer to key to distinguish this taxon from geographically separated *Dactylocnemis* taxa.

HABITAT

Coastal, Lowland

Occupies a range of habitats from the shoreline to flaxland, scrub and coastal forest. Takes refuge under logs and debris and in rocky crevices.

NATURAL HISTORY

Nocturnal; terrestrial and arboreal. Tolerant of conspecifics, and large aggregations of individuals (juveniles, males and females) found together in refuges. Little known about reproductive biology, but suspected to be biennial, and embryonic development in museum specimens suggests birth period likely to be in autumn. Insectivorous but also feeds on nectar and fruits (berries).

ETYMOLOGY

Common and **tag names** referring to Manawatāwhi/Three Kings Islands, where species is endemic.

Mokohinau gecko

Dactylocnemis "Mokohinau"

Endemic

DESCRIPTION

Up to 90 mm SVL

A large and stout gecko with variable body colours and patterning. **Dorsal surface** various shades of brown or grey; some individuals beige or olive, with blotches or bands black-edged anteriorly, or with prominent pale stripes. Markings extending down intact tail. Often has a bright mustard-yellow crescent on nape of neck, with same-colour blotches along rest of body and tail. White stripe from behind eye to ear opening. White flecks along dorsal and **lateral surfaces**. Labial scales often lighter (cream or white) than surrounding scales. **Ventral surface** (including chin, neck and tail) uniform cream, or with dark speckling. **Eye** colour brown or olive. **Rostral scale** in broad contact with nostrils. **Mouth lining** and **tongue** pink. **Intact tail** equal to or shorter than body length (SVL). **Cloacal spurs** large and pointed, 3–4 on each side. **Femoral pores** absent. **Toes** relatively long and slender; small distal pad present on both sides of claw of first toe. **Subdigital lamellae** 10–14. **Soles of feet** cream or grey.

DISTRIBUTION

North Island only; island endemic. Occurs only on the Mokohinau Islands off eastern Auckland.

VARIATION AND SIMILAR SPECIES

Body colour patterning extremely variable. Distinguished from sympatric **Duvaucel's gecko** (*H. duvaucelii*) by its smaller adult size, and significantly fewer subdigital lamellae (10–14 vs. 15–25). Distributions do not overlap with those of other *Dactylocnemis* species. Refer to key to distinguish this taxon from geographically separated *Dactylocnemis* taxa.

HABITAT

Coastal, Lowland

Nocturnal, but may sun-bask close to retreat entrances. Both arboreal and terrestrial. Shelters beneath rocks, in rock crevices, or below dense vegetation or debris during the day; active on shrubs, trees, flaxland, *Muehlenbeckia* vineland and rocky cliffs at night.

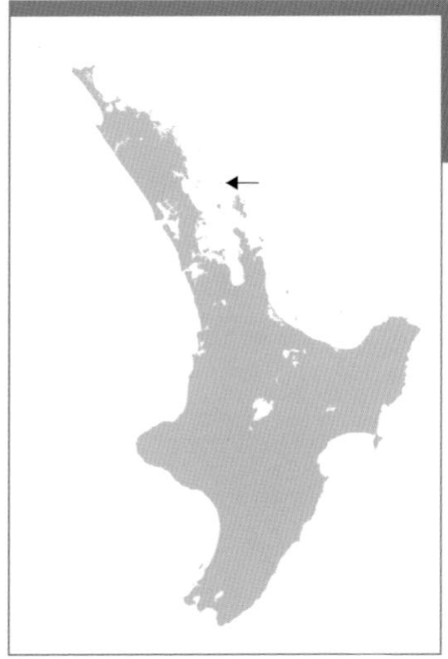

NATURAL HISTORY

Occurs at high densities (c. 1 per square metre), and appears particularly tolerant of conspecifics. Average of 2 young born once a year, in late summer to possibly mid-autumn (February–April).

ETYMOLOGY

Common and **tag names** based on Mokohinau (Pokohīnau) Islands, to which the taxon is endemic.

SARAH J. WELLS

Poor Knights gecko

Dactylocnemis "Poor Knights"

Endemic

DESCRIPTION

Up to 90 (rarely up to 95) mm SVL

A large, robust gecko endemic to the Poor Knights Islands Nature Reserve. Highly variable in colour and patterning. **Dorsal surface** dull brown with longitudinal stripes, transverse bands or chevron-shaped markings. Often has a bright mustard-yellow crescent on nape of neck, with same-colour blotches along rest of body and tail. **Lateral surfaces** shades of brown or grey-brown, often with fine pale flecking. **Ventral surface** uniform cream or pale brown. **Eye** colour brown with extensive gold flecking, overlaid with black filigree pattern. **Rostral scale** in broad contact with nostrils. **Mouth lining** and **tongue** pink. **Intact tail** length equal to or longer than body length (SVL). **Cloacal spurs** small and pointed, 2–3 on either side. **Femoral pores** absent (i.e. pores do not extend to hind limbs). **Subdigital lamellae** 11–16. **Soles of feet** white or off-white.

DISTRIBUTION

North Island only. Restricted to the islands of the Poor Knights Islands (Aorangi Island, Tawhiti Rahi Island, and associated islets, Sugarloaf Rock, and High Peak Rocks).

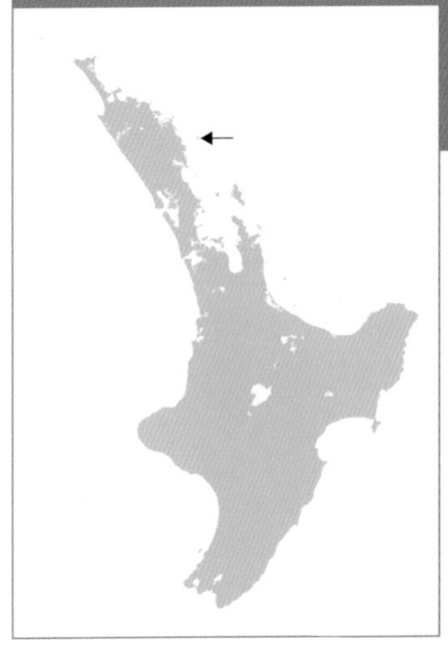

VARIATION AND SIMILAR SPECIES

Highly variable in colour patterning (stripes, blotches or fairly uniform). Population on Sugarloaf Rock has some unique scale features around jaws, and a unique behaviour of diurnal scavenging on seabird regurgitations, but genetic separation only minor between populations. Geographically isolated from other members of *Dactylocnemis*. Refer to key to distinguish this taxon from geographically separated *Dactylocnemis* taxa.

HABITAT

Coastal, Lowland

Occupies a range of habitats from the shoreline to flaxland, scrub and coastal forest.

NATURAL HISTORY

Nocturnal, although will sun-bask cryptically close to retreat entrances. Populations on small rock stacks cathemeral. Terrestrial, arboreal. Reproduction unknown. Insectivorous, but also feeds on nectar, and fruits (berries). On small island rock stacks, feeds on regurgitated fish from seabirds.

ETYMOLOGY

Common and **tag names** referring to the Poor Knights Islands, where the species is endemic.

Duvaucel's gecko

Hoplodactylus duvaucelii (Duméril & Bibron, 1836) **Endemic**

Coromandel

DESCRIPTION

Up to 165 mm SVL; up to 118 g weight

New Zealand's largest gecko, and a species particularly susceptible to mammalian predators. Robust stout build. Head large and robust. **Dorsal surface** mostly grey, olive or dull grey-brown with lighter grey smudges, or transverse bands (never striped). Often with pale spots on dorsolateral surfaces, and on tail base. Tail less marked, but occasionally with darker brown blotches. **Lateral surfaces** grey or olive-brown with fine pale and dark flecking or small blotches. **Ventral surface** uniform pale cream, occasionally lightly speckled. **Eye** colour olive, green or brownish; prominent 'eyebrows'. **Mouth lining** and **tongue** pink. **Intact tail** stout, shorter than or equal to body length (SVL). **Cloacal spurs** 3–4 on each side. **Femoral pores** extend in a narrow series along the hind limbs. **Toes** with greatly expanded pads; feet relatively large. **Subdigital lamellae** 15–20. **Soles of feet** white or cream.

DISTRIBUTION

Subfossil evidence indicates a wide historic distribution from Northland to North Otago. However, now predominantly restricted to offshore islands. Northern populations: off east coast of the North Island (islands off northern Northland, Poor Knights Islands, Hens and Chicken Islands, Mokohinau Islands, Hauturu/Little Barrier Island, Great Barrier Island (Aotea Island), Mercury Islands, islands off Bay of Plenty). Introduced to several islands in the Hauraki Gulf, and a mainland sanctuary north of Auckland. Reintroduced to Mana Island off Wellington. A single specimen reported from the Waikato in 2010, suggesting relict individuals might still occur on the mainland. Southern (Cook Strait) populations: The Brothers, Chetwode Islands, Trio Islands (Kuru Pongi) and Sentinel Rock.

VARIATION AND SIMILAR SPECIES

Northern specimens larger, more robust and generally less prominently marked or patterned. Cook Strait animals smaller

(95–120 mm SVL; c. 41 g weight) and often more boldly marked, with distinct light grey transverse markings from nape to tail base, and more distinct white dorsolateral spots. Adult unlikely to be confused with other species owing to large size. Juveniles may be confused with sympatric **Pacific gecko** (*D. pacificus*) and **Raukawa gecko** (*W. maculata*), but distinguished by their proportionately larger head, and by foot features (e.g. more subdigital lamellae and longer distal phalanges).

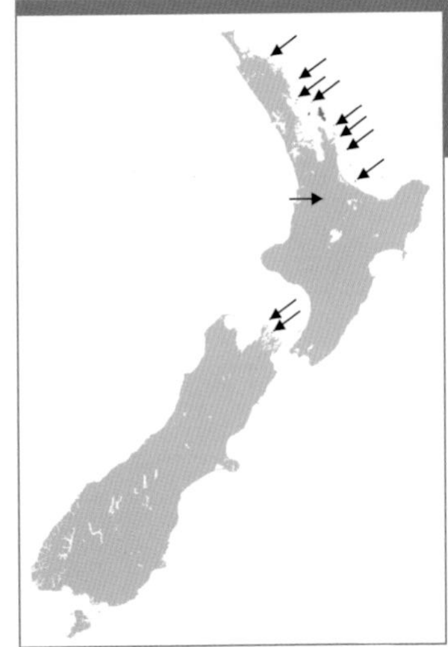

HABITAT

Coastal, Lowland

Primarily lowland forest dwelling but will inhabit scrubland, flaxland and rocky cliffs, taking refuge in deep crevices. On offshore islands may forage close to the shoreline on rocky platforms, and boulder beaches in littoral zone. Takes refuge in hollows in trunks and branches, seabird burrows, flax bases and beneath rocks.

NATURAL HISTORY

Nocturnal; terrestrial, saxicolous or arboreal. Cryptic sun-basker. Low reproductive rate; sexual maturity at 4–7 years. Mating occurs September–October, and females generally give birth biennially, February–May. Females produce 1 or 2 young (c. 50 mm SVL at birth); adults known to cannibalise young, although in the wild often social, forming aggregations of up to eight individuals (e.g. a single male, several females, and juveniles of all ages, but never more than one male in a single aggregation). Lifespan may be more than 50 years. Forages on large invertebrates, fruits (kawakawa) and berries (*Coprosma* species), nectar (pōhutukawa, flax) and honeydew, and known to prey on other lizards, including members of its own species.

Cook Strait

ETYMOLOGY

Specific name in recognition of Alfred Duvaucel (1793–1825), a French naturalist and collector who explored India.

Raukawa gecko

Woodworthia maculata (Gray, 1845)

Endemic

Nelson

DESCRIPTION

Up to 82 mm SVL; up to 14 g weight

A very common gecko in some parts of its range, reaching exceptionally high abundances on mammal-free offshore islands, but now rare over large areas of the mainland. Variable in colour and patterning. **Dorsal surface** usually dull brown or grey, with longitudinal or transverse stripes, blotches or chevron markings. If striped, stripes usually variable in width down body. Head short with blunt snout. **Lateral surfaces** shades of brown or grey with lighter coloured blotches, spots or flecks. **Ventral surface** brown to grey, uniform or lightly speckled. **Eye** colour green, green-brown or yellow-brown. Most with very spiny 'eyebrows'. **Rostral scale** separated from nostrils, very rarely barely in contact. **Mouth lining** pink; **tongue** pink with grey tip. **Intact tail** longer than or equal to body length (SVL). **Toes** straight distally, longer than in most other *Woodworthia*, with greatly expanded toe pads with curved lamellae. **Subdigital lamellae** 11–15. **Soles of feet** light grey.

DISTRIBUTION

North and South Islands. Widely distributed from Northland to northern South Island (Marlborough and Nelson, just at the northern margins of Westland and Canterbury), including many offshore islands.

VARIATION AND SIMILAR SPECIES

Highly variable in colour and patterning. Individuals from coastal environments typically much smaller (e.g. 55–60 mm SVL). Leucistic (all white) individuals known in the wild. Can be difficult to distinguish from congeners. Sympatric species distinguished as follows. **Goldstripe gecko** (*W. chrysosiretica*) overall lighter, more greenish or golden in colour, with dorsolateral stripes of uniform width on body (may be very distinct or very faint) continuing down tail (vs. breaking up at tail base); rostral scale broader, shallower. **Minimac gecko** (*W.* "Marlborough mini") smaller, and distinguished by warmer, lighter background colour, distinctive head markings (narrow stripe from nostril through eye continuing straight back to back of head), 11 or fewer subdigital lamellae and less spiny 'eyebrows'. **Pygmy gecko** (*W.* "pygmy") much smaller, with narrow toes and far fewer lamellae (7–9). **Kahurangi gecko** (*W.* "Mount Arthur") most similar in scalation, but is grey or grey-green, with subtle darker and lighter markings yet without strong contrast or black markings (whereas South Island Raukawa geckos in particular usually have highly contrasting black and brown markings), with shorter distal phalanges, and less spiny 'eyebrows'. Found at

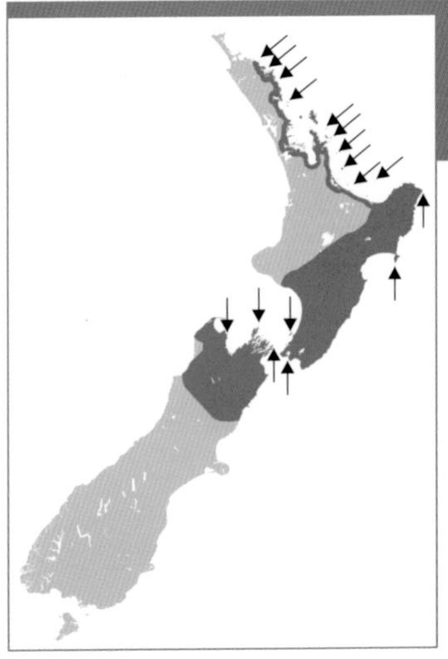

higher altitudes than the Raukawa gecko. **Waitaha gecko** (*W.* cf. *brunnea*) overlaps only very marginally with Raukawa gecko, but they occupy similar habitats and have been found together at one site. Similar in size and colour but Waitaha gecko has

Leucistic variant

Nelson

a shorter snout, slightly stockier build, fewer subdigital lamellae (10–12), shorter distal phalanges, less spiny 'eyebrows', and rostral scale narrowly contacts nostrils. **Southern Alps gecko** (*W.* "Southern Alps") overlaps only very marginally; is found at higher altitudes, is grey or grey-green, with subtle darker and lighter markings but usually without strong contrast (whereas South Island Raukawa gecko in particular usually has highly contrasting black and brown markings); has fewer subdigital lamellae (10–12), much shorter distal phalanges, less spiny 'eyebrows'; and rostral scale narrowly contacts nostrils.

HABITAT

Coastal, Lowland

Littoral zone to forest. Occurs on coastal sand dunes, coastal cliffs and rock outcrops, boulder beaches; in flaxland, kānuka and regenerating shrubland, and in old-growth forest.

NATURAL HISTORY

Nocturnal; terrestrial, arboreal, saxicolous. Thigmothermic or may occasionally sun-bask, usually just with head protruding from crevice. Annual reproduction; mating occurs February-May, with 2 young born in following summer (February). Lifespan up to 27 years documented in wild populations (likely to be longer) and 37 years in captivity. Large social aggregations (e.g. > 50 animals) commonly formed wherever this species is sufficiently abundant. Insectivorous but frequently seeks out fruits, nectar, sap and honeydew.

ETYMOLOGY

Specific name (Latin) meaning 'spotted', in reference to the rather unusual markings of the type specimen, which is patterned with small black spots. **Common name** refers to Māori name for Cook Strait (Raukawa, or Te-Moana-o-Raukawa), where the surrounding land area is the stronghold for this species.

Hauraki Gulf

Hauraki Gulf

Muriwai gecko

Woodworthia aff. *maculata* "Muriwai" **Endemic**

Muriwai

DESCRIPTION

Up to 69 mm SVL

A range-restricted and poorly known gecko from Auckland's west coast. **Dorsal surface** light to mid-sandy brown to grey, usually with a broken or indistinct thin pale mid-dorsal stripe running from neck to hind limbs. Broad and distinctive brown or grey dorsolateral stripes extending from nostrils through eye to tail base; stripes may be relatively smooth-edged, broken or notched, and are bordered above and below by thinner pale stripes. Upper stripes merging together at tail base; a series of pale medial smudges continuing length of intact tail. Usually with prominent darker brown or grey markings on head, including a line down centre of snout, and an inverted V-shape between eyes. Lower **lateral surfaces** pale brown or grey with blotches and spots. **Ventral surface** uniform pale brown, pink-brown or pale grey. **Eye** colour brown, green or yellow, overlaid with black filigree pattern. **Rostral scale** excluded from nostrils. **Mouth lining** pink; **tongue** pink with grey tip. **Intact tail** prehensile; longer than body length (SVL). **Cloacal spurs** conical and paired. **Precloacal pore**s 4 rows, and **femoral pores** extend to about a third of length of humerus. **Toes** with extremely short distal phalanges (the shortest of all *Woodworthia* species). **Subdigital lamellae** 12–15. **Soles of feet** light brown.

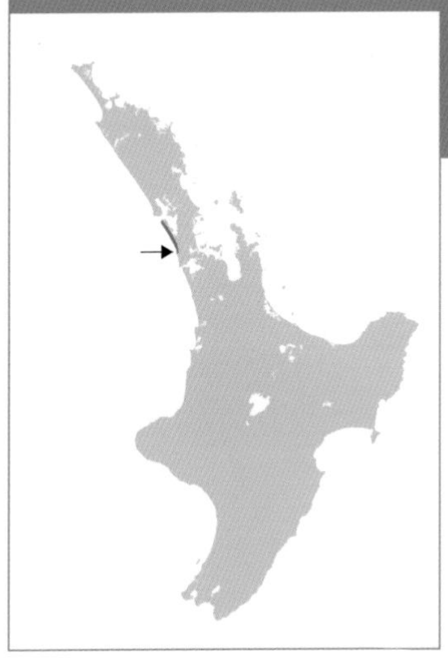

DISTRIBUTION

North Island only. Restricted to the western coastline of the Auckland Region, from Muriwai Beach northwards to South Kaipara Head, and on Oaia Island.

VARIATION AND SIMILAR SPECIES

Basal colouration appears to vary with substrate (i.e. populations from the mainland living in sand dune habitats are tan in colour, whereas those from offshore rock stacks are more grey). Outwardly similar to **Raukawa gecko** (*W. maculata*) but geographically isolated and distal phalanges very distinctly shorter.

HABITAT

Coastal, Lowland

Occupies coastal duneland, and open areas or edges of exotic (pine) forest, where it takes refuge beneath dense foliage or debris or in clumps of exotic pampas. Also occurs under loose rocks and prostrate vegetation and in rock crevices, predominantly on eastern (inland sheltered) side on Oaia Island.

NATURAL HISTORY

Nocturnal; terrestrial. Cryptic sun-basker always remaining close to dense vegetative cover. Females in late-stage pregnancy in March. Nothing else known of its life history or reproductive biology.

ETYMOLOGY

Common and **tag names** referring to the Muriwai area of Auckland's western coastline, where this species occurs.

Oaia Island

CHRIS WEDDING

Waitaha gecko

Woodworthia cf. *brunnea*

Endemic

TRENT BELL

DESCRIPTION

Up to 80 mm SVL

The commonest gecko on Banks Peninsula, around Christchurch and on the central Canterbury Plains. **Dorsal surface** brown, or olive with paler blotches, chevrons, or longitudinal or transverse stripes, and large black patches especially on intact tail. Dark spots may also be present on dorsum. A paler canthal stripe running from nostril to eye usually present. **Lateral surfaces** shades of brown or olive with darker blotches or spots. **Ventral surface** pale, uniform or occasionally spotted. **Eye** colour brown or yellow. **Rostral scale** in contact or virtually in contact with nostrils. **Mouth lining** pink; **tongue** pink with grey tip. **Toes** with straight distal phalanges. **Intact tail** equal to body length (SVL). **Subdigital lamellae** 9–12. **Soles of feet** light grey.

DISTRIBUTION

South Island only. Occurs from southern Marlborough to mid-Canterbury and Banks Peninsula, as well as inland on Canterbury Plains and coastal hills south to at least Rakaia River. Locally abundant, particularly around Banks Peninsula and the Port Hills of Christchurch, but has probably disappeared from large areas of the Canterbury Plains because of loss of habitat.

VARIATION AND SIMILAR SPECIES

Highly variable in colour and patterning. Individuals from coastal environments generally smaller (53–68 mm SVL) than those from inland forest or hill country environments (65–80 mm SVL). Over most of its range, the only *Woodworthia* species present, but overlaps with minimac gecko (*W*. "Marlborough mini") and possibly pygmy gecko (*W*. "pygmy") in north

Canterbury and south Marlborough. Overlaps very narrowly with the Raukawa gecko (*W. maculata*) in south Marlborough and abuts the Southern Alps gecko (*W.* "Southern Alps") in the foothills of the Southern Alps and Kaikōuras. **Minimac gecko** smaller, distinguished by warmer, lighter background colour, distinctive head markings (narrow stripe through eye continuing to back of head), ≤ 11 subdigital lamellae, rostral scale well separated from nostrils. **Pygmy gecko** much smaller, with narrow toes and far fewer lamellae (7–9); rostral scale well separated from nostrils. Occupies similar habitats to Raukawa gecko and they have been found together at one site. Similar in size and colour but **Raukawa gecko** with longer snout, a slightly less stocky build, rostral scale usually well excluded from nostrils, longer distal phalanges, and more spiny 'eyebrows'. **Southern Alps gecko** found at higher altitudes and is grey or grey-green, with subtle darker and lighter markings but usually without strong contrast (vs. highly contrasting black and brown markings), and with shorter distal phalanges.

HABITAT

Coastal, Lowland, Montane/subalpine

Inhabits a wide variety of habitats from boulder beaches to shattered rock outcrops, screes, boulder fields, talus slopes and lowland forest. Also inhabits seabird burrows on predator-free islands. Frequently found in modified environments (e.g. under inorganic debris, buildings) close to human habitation.

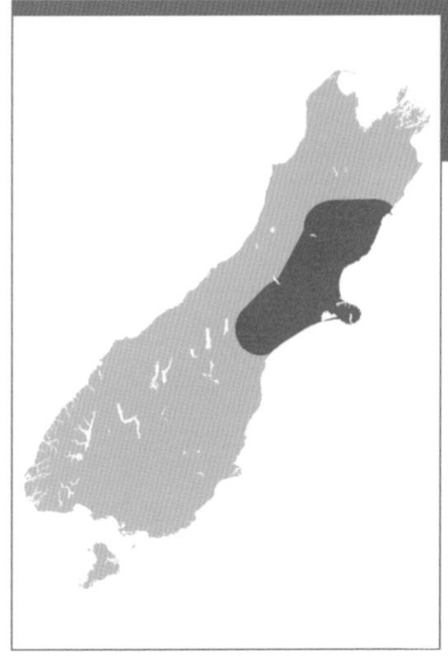

NATURAL HISTORY

Nocturnal; terrestrial, saxicolous or arboreal. Can be abundant in areas without predators and will form large social aggregations. Highest recorded longevity of any New Zealand gecko: 53 years in the wild. Females give birth to 2 young late February–March. Primarily insectivorous but also feeds on fruit (berries).

ETYMOLOGY

Specific name (Latin) meaning 'brown', referring to the brown basal colour. The name *brunnea* has yet to be confirmed for this taxon, but there is strong evidence that it is applicable. **Common name** is the Māori name for the Canterbury Region, where it is found. Also known as the 'Canterbury gecko'.

Pygmy gecko

Woodworthia "pygmy"

Endemic

DESCRIPTION

Up to 50 mm SVL

An extremely small species of *Woodworthia*, the smallest of all New Zealand's geckos. **Dorsal surface** drab grey-buff colour, with indistinct markings, usually in slightly lighter and darker shades rather than dramatic contrast, sometimes almost uniform in colour. Occasionally with boldly contrasting pale longitudinal stripes. Distinct narrow dark stripe down side of head from nostril through eye to nape. Top of head unmarked. **Lateral surfaces** drab grey-buff with small pale speckles. **Ventral surface** uniform buff or grey-buff. **Eye** colour brown. **Rostral scale** well excluded from nostrils. **Mouth lining** and **tongue** pink. **Intact tail** longer than body length (SVL). **Subdigital lamellae** 7–9. **Toes** narrow and tapering rather than expanding towards tip of digital pad. **Soles of feet** buff coloured.

DISTRIBUTION

South Island only. Found in inland areas of Marlborough south of the Wairau Valley, and of north Canterbury, with an outlying population of distinctive, even smaller-bodied (c. 38–42 mm SVL) individuals in the Rangitata Valley–Ashburton Lakes area.

VARIATION AND SIMILAR SPECIES

Individuals in Rangitata area populations extremely small in size, and usually with a series of paired, slightly lighter blotches either side of dorsal surface. Quite similar-looking to **minimac gecko** (*W.* "Marlborough mini") but is smaller, has fewer subdigital lamellae (7–9 vs. 9–11), and most importantly has less broadly expanded digital pads that taper to the tip (vs. widest near the tip). Pygmy gecko also less boldly marked on average, although there is considerable overlap. Easily distinguished from all other *Woodworthia* with overlapping distributions by the combination of very small size, indistinct markings, narrow tapering toes with very few lamellae (7–9), and having rostral scale well excluded from nostrils.

HABITAT

Lowland to (mainly) Montane/subalpine, Alpine

Low-rainfall, rain-shadow habitats; occupies open rocky areas such as river terraces and rock tumbles below fractured bluffs, from valley floors to above the treeline. Occasionally found in crevices in trees in dry, open, sunny forest.

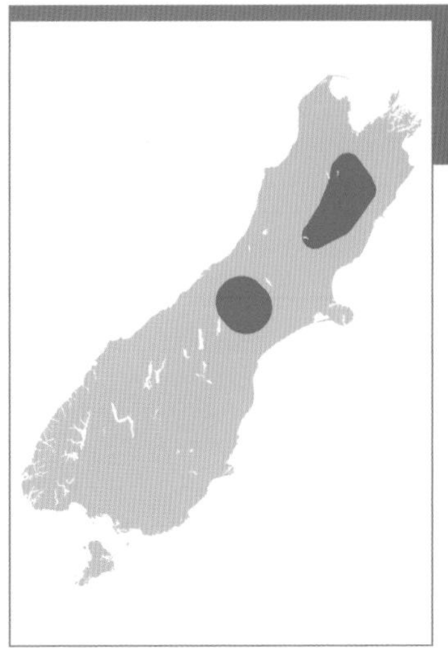

NATURAL HISTORY

Nocturnal; may bask in partial concealment at retreat entrances. Terrestrial, saxicolous. Can be abundant, but seldom forms the large aggregations seen in some other *Woodworthia*. Females observed to be heavily gravid in January.

ETYMOLOGY

Common and **tag names** referring to its tiny size.

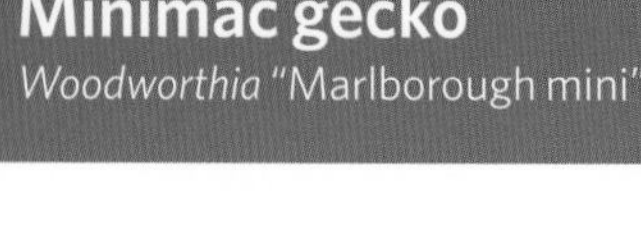

Minimac gecko

Woodworthia "Marlborough mini"

Endemic

NICK HARKER

Wellington

DESCRIPTION

Up to 65 mm SVL

A small and delicate gecko. **Dorsal surface** buff coloured, with markings in lighter and darker shades rather than dramatic contrast, occasionally almost uniform in colour. Distinct narrow dark stripe down side of head from nostril through eye to nape. Top of head usually unmarked. **Lateral surfaces** buff coloured with pale speckles or indistinct darker brown blotches. **Ventral surface** shades of light brown to grey, either uniform or lightly speckled with brown. **Eye** colour brown. **Rostral scale** well separated from nostrils. **Mouth lining** and **tongue** pink, tongue with grey tip. **Intact tail** equal to body length (SVL). **Toes** with tapering distal phalanges (occasionally straight); pads distinctly dilated, broadest near tip. **Subdigital lamellae** 9–11. **Soles of feet** grey-brown.

DISTRIBUTION

North and South Islands. Found in coastal and less arid but non-forested areas of Marlborough, north-eastern Nelson and north Canterbury, east of the distribution of pygmy gecko (*W.* "pygmy"), and has an outpost on the coast west of Wellington in the North Island.

VARIATION AND SIMILAR SPECIES

Some variation in size and boldness of patterning between populations. Individuals from Nelson Boulder Bank population stand out as particularly large and dark in colour. Quite similar to **pygmy gecko** (*W.* "pygmy"), but that species even smaller; with fewer subdigital lamellae (7–8 vs. 9–11); and, most importantly, with narrow tapering toes. More boldly marked than pygmy gecko on average, although there is considerable overlap. Distributions abut in the Kaikōura Ranges and in north

Canterbury, with pygmy gecko replacing minimac gecko further inland; probably a narrow zone of hybridisation where distributions meet. Range also abuts that of **Southern Alps gecko** (*W.* "Southern Alps") in the southern Seaward Kaikōuras, with latter found at higher altitudes; larger; grey or grey-green (vs. buff); has different head markings, with a dark V behind eyes on top of head; has a pale canthal stripe (vs. a dark stripe through eye); and rostral scale narrowly contacts nostrils (vs. excluded). Also overlaps with Raukawa gecko (*W. maculata*) and Waitaha gecko (*W.* cf. *brunnea*) in lowlands, but these larger species tend to occupy more forested (or formerly forested) habitats. **Raukawa gecko** much larger; darker in colour with more contrasting markings; has a longer snout and longer distal phalanges; more lamellae (12–14 vs. 9–11); and more spiny 'eyebrows'. **Waitaha gecko** much larger; with bolder, more contrasting markings; and rostral scale narrowly contacts nostrils (vs. excluded). Range of the minimac gecko also completely overlaps and surrounds that of **Kaikouras gecko** (*W.* "Kaikouras"), known from only a handful of localities in the Kaikōura Ranges and Haldon Hills. Kaikouras gecko similar-looking to minimac gecko, but a little larger and has bolder more contrasting markings (transverse stripes); most importantly, with much narrower toes which do not expand towards tip of dilated portion, and more lamellae (10–12, usually 11–12 vs. 9–11, usually 9–10).

HABITAT

Coastal, Lowland, Montane/subalpine
Inhabits boulder beaches, screes, river terraces, talus slopes, creviced rock outcrops in open habitat, from tideline to above treeline.

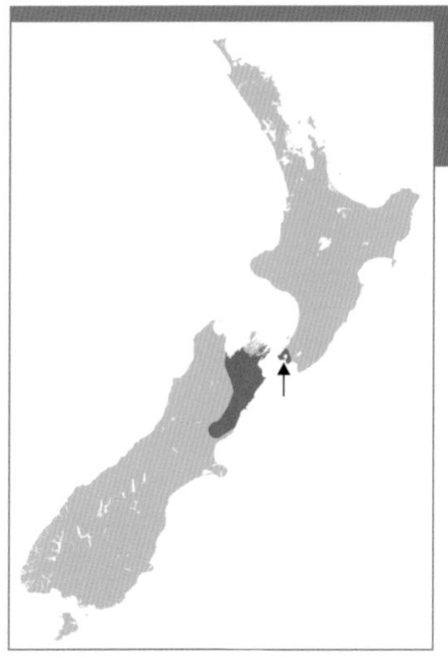

NATURAL HISTORY

Nocturnal; terrestrial, saxicolous. May bask in partial concealment at retreat entrances. Can be abundant, but seldom forms the large aggregations seen in some other *Woodworthia*. Two young born February–March.

ETYMOLOGY

Common name referring to its small 'mini' body size and relationship to the *W. maculata* ('mac') species-complex. **Tag name** refers to its core area of distribution.

NICK HARKER

Kaikouras gecko

Woodworthia "Kaikouras"

Endemic

JOZEF POLEC

DESCRIPTION

Up to 65 mm SVL

A small to medium-sized gecko, with bold markings, from eastern Marlborough. **Dorsal surface** with alternating pale and dark transverse markings with an overall warm brown tone, and a dark stripe from nostril through eye to back of head, combined with a dark V-shaped marking on top of head behind eyes. Some individuals may be more grey than brown. **Lateral surfaces** with irregular-shaped pale blotches; uniform cream on lower lateral surfaces. **Ventral surface** uniform cream. **Eye** colour brown or olive-green. **Rostral scale** well separated from nostrils. **Mouth lining** and **tongue** pink, tongue sometimes with grey tip. **Intact tail** length shorter than body length (SVL). **Toes** with tapering distal phalanges (occasionally straight); pads narrow but moderately expanded, and do not broaden towards tip. **Subdigital lamellae** 10–12. **Soles of feet** white, cream or grey.

DISTRIBUTION

South Island only. Eastern Marlborough; known from only a handful of localities in the Kaikōura Ranges and Haldon Hills.

VARIATION AND SIMILAR SPECIES

Too poorly sampled to understand full extent of variation. Most likely to be confused with much more common **minimac gecko** (*W.* "Marlborough mini"), with which it is sometimes sympatric, but distinguished by its larger size; darker, more contrasting colouration; higher lamellae count (vs. 10–11 in minimac gecko); and narrower toes not expanding towards tip of dilated portion. Mental scale at tip of chin narrow and triangular (vs. usually broader and quadrangular in minimac gecko) (occasional exceptions, so this should not be relied on alone). Range abuts that of **Southern Alps gecko** (*W.* "Southern Alps") to the south; that species larger; grey or grey-green (vs. buff); has a pale canthal stripe (vs. a dark stripe through eye); and rostral scale narrowly contacts nostrils (vs. excluded). **Raukawa gecko** (*W. maculata*) present (though uncommon) in same general area but: occurs at lower altitude, in more forested habitats; is larger and darker in colour; has more contrasting and blotchy markings; has a longer snout and longer distal phalanges; and has more spiny 'eyebrows'.

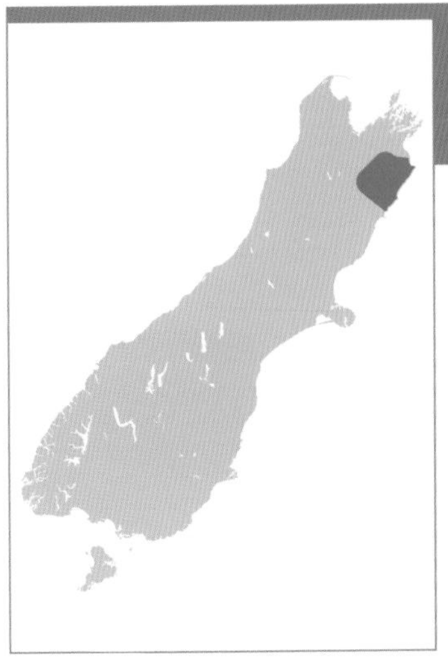

HABITAT

Lowland, Montane/subalpine

Inhabits screes, talus slopes, rock outcrops and boulder fields in montane tussock grassland and herbfields.

NATURAL HISTORY

Nocturnal; terrestrial, saxicolous. Very little known about life history and reproductive biology.

ETYMOLOGY

Common and **tag names** refer to the Kaikōura Ranges in Marlborough, where this taxon occurs.

JOZEF POLEC

Kahurangi gecko

Woodworthia "Mount Arthur"

Endemic

DESCRIPTION

Up to 68 mm SVL

Small dull-coloured gecko from the Tasman Region alpine zone. **Dorsal surface** green-grey or olive-brown with paler chevron-shaped transverse markings, overlaid with fine black speckles. Dark stripe going straight through eyes to back of head. Fairly long snout. **Lateral surfaces** drab grey or olive-brown with fine black speckles or irregular-shaped grey blotches. **Ventral surface** grey. **Eye** colour brown or olive-green. **Rostral scale** only occasionally in contact with nostrils; in western populations, scale divided down middle. **Mouth lining** and **tongue** pink, tongue usually with grey tip. **Intact tail** equal to or longer than body length (SVL). **Toes** with tapering distal phalanges. **Subdigital lamellae** 11–14. **Soles of feet** grey.

DISTRIBUTION

South Island only. Occurs from Mt Owen and Mt Arthur and surrounding ranges westward in Kahurangi National Park to the Anatoki, Douglas and Snowdon Ranges (Tasman).

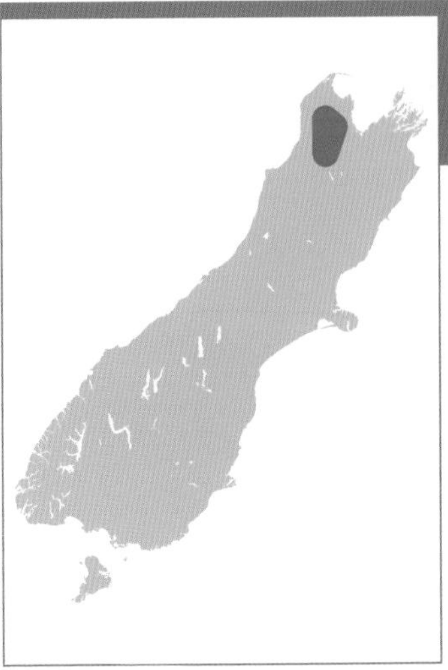

VARIATION AND SIMILAR SPECIES

Western populations have a split rostral scale; those from Mt Arthur, Mt Owen and surrounding ranges do not. **Raukawa gecko** (*W. maculata*) replaces this species in surrounding lowlands; usually with more contrasting black and brown markings, distinctly longer distal phalanges, longer intact tail, spiny 'eyebrows' and brown (vs. green) eyes. **Southern Alps gecko** (*W.* "Southern Alps") occupies similar habitat further south; is similar in size and colour, but with shorter snout, usually fewer lamellae, rostral scale not usually excluded from nostrils; substantial gap between the two species' known ranges.

HABITAT

Montane/subalpine, Alpine

Occurs in subalpine karst habitat, living beneath exfoliating marble slabs and in argillite screes.

NATURAL HISTORY

Nocturnal: terrestrial, saxicolous. Occurs in abundance (and aggregates) in argillite screes, and in crevices and below rock slabs on marble rock faces and outcrops. Little known of reproductive biology but probably reproduces biennially, similar to other high-altitude *Woodworthia* populations.

ETYMOLOGY

Common and **tag names** referring to the Kahurangi National Park area, including Mt Arthur, where this taxon occurs.

Southern Alps gecko

Woodworthia "Southern Alps"

Endemic

Canterbury

DESCRIPTION

Up to 72 mm SVL (usually < 65 mm)

A relatively abundant and variably marked gecko occurring widely in the South Island, on the eastern side of the Main Divide. **Dorsal surface** greyish (sometimes suffused with green or pink) with cross-banding or alternating dorsal blotches (longitudinal striping rare); markings often finely divided, and usually darker and lighter shades of background colour rather than contrasting. Often with a pale narrow mid-dorsal stripe, particularly in southern populations. **Lateral surfaces** greyish with pale or darker coloured blotches, flecks or streaks. **Ventral surface** light brown, grey or sometimes with greenish hue. **Mouth lining** pink. **Eye** colour grey to (commonly) distinctly green. **Rostral scale** in contact or virtually in contact with nostrils. **Intact tail** equal to or usually slightly longer than body length (SVL). **Toes** with tapering distal phalanges. **Subdigital lamellae** 9–12. **Soles of feet** light brown to grey.

DISTRIBUTION

South Island only. Eastern side of Southern Alps from southern Marlborough (Nelson Lakes) to Waitaki Valley.

VARIATION AND SIMILAR SPECIES

Two major sub-clades, found north and south of the Rakaia River:

1. ***Northern group:*** Often a little larger, darker grey in colour, and less stocky, with noticeably longer neck, less finely divided markings and usually lacking the mid-dorsal stripe.
2. ***Southern group:*** Individual populations vary in body size over quite short distances (e.g. between areas around Lakes Tekapo and Pukaki).

Over much of its range, the only *Woodworthia* species present, but overlaps widely with **pygmy gecko** (*W.* "pygmy") in the Rangitata Valley, in north Canterbury and in south Marlborough – the two are frequently found together under same rock. **Pygmy gecko** much smaller, with narrower toes and fewer lamellae (7–9), and rostral scale well separated from nostrils. Also narrowly overlaps with **Waitaha gecko** (*W.* cf. *brunnea*) at edges of the Canterbury Plains, but usually separated by altitude, and that species brown (vs. grey), and with more contrasting markings, slightly longer narrower distal phalanges and brown to yellow (vs. green to grey) eye. Range abuts that of **korero gecko** (*W.* "Otago/ Southland large") in the Waitaki Valley and at northern end of the Dunstan Mountains, but korero gecko bigger, usually very substantially so. Also abuts range of **Kawarau gecko** (*W.* "Cromwell") around Wanaka and at northern end of the Dunstan Mountains, but that species more slender, with longer narrower toes and distinctly longer distal phalanges. Where it overlaps with **Southern Alps gecko**, it is also larger (although can be smaller away from contact zone). Overlaps marginally with **minimac gecko** (*W.* "Marlborough mini") and **Raukawa gecko** (*W. maculata*) in the Kaikōuras, but minimac gecko smaller, distinguished by warmer lighter background colour, and with distinctive head markings (narrow stripe through eye continuing to back of head) and rostral scale well separated from nostrils. Raukawa gecko found at lower altitudes, and usually with more contrasting black and brown markings, distinctly longer distal phalanges, a longer snout, longer intact tail, spiny 'eyebrows' and brown (vs. green) eyes.

TRENT BELL

Otago

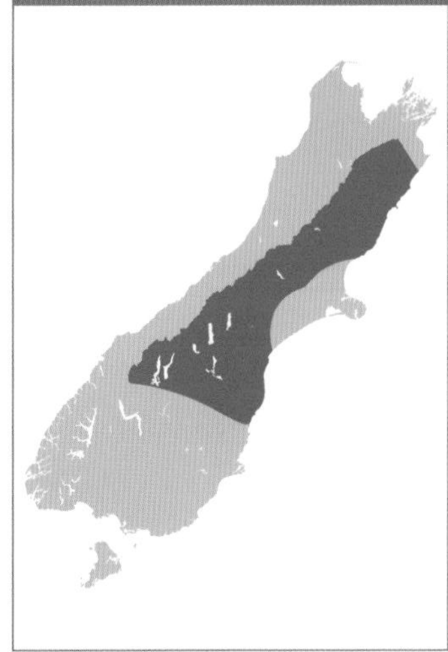

HABITAT

Lowland, Montane/subalpine, Alpine

Inhabits talus slopes, screes and shattered outcrops in open lowland (but absent from the Canterbury Plains). Northern outlier population in Wairau Valley.

NATURAL HISTORY

Nocturnal; saxicolous, terrestrial. May sun-bask in partial concealment at retreat entrances. Occasionally in shrublands where may be partially arboreal. Reproduction unknown, but likely to be biennial, at least in high-altitude populations. Can be abundant, but seldom forms the large aggregations seen in some other *Woodworthia*.

ETYMOLOGY

Common and **tag names** referring to the species' core distribution, although it extends north beyond the Southern Alps into Marlborough.

Schist gecko

Woodworthia "Central Otago"

Endemic

TRENT BELL

DESCRIPTION

Up to 71 mm SVL

Small to medium-sized, relatively slender and somewhat dorso-ventrally flattened gecko, confined to a small part of the driest area of Central Otago. **Dorsal surface** brown, or olive-brown, with irregular pale brown blotches or series of transverse bands, and with random small pale or black blotches, flecks, spots or speckles. Markings continue down intact tail. Some individuals with bold markings on head, including a brown V-shaped marking behind eyes and a pale stripe from eye to ear opening. **Lateral surfaces** with pale blotches, spots or flecks. **Ventral surface** speckled, sometimes uniform. **Mouth lining** and **tongue** pink, tongue with grey tip. **Eye** colour brown, green-grey to yellow. **Rostral scale** in contact or virtually in contact with nostrils. **Intact tail** length about equal to body length (SVL). **Toes** relatively slender for a *Woodworthia*; long straight distal phalanges; a well-developed **distal pad** on first toe, about equal in width to widest part of toe. **Subdigital lamellae** 9–11. **Soles of feet** pale greyish buff.

DISTRIBUTION

South Island only. Confined to an area including the Clutha Valley between Clive and Beaumont (including the northern slopes of the Old Man and adjacent ranges), the Raggedy Range south of where it is crossed by the Ida Burn, and Rough Ridge, and including the low dry hill country between these ranges.

VARIATION AND SIMILAR SPECIES

Variable in colouration and patterning, especially boldness of dorsal markings. Range not shared with any other *Woodworthia*; at most, just very narrow overlap where range abuts those of others. Geographically close to **Southern Alps gecko** (*W.* "Southern Alps") at northern end of North Rough Ridge, but alluvial valley separates them. Southern Alps gecko distinguished by stockier build, shorter broader toes and distinctly shorter distal phalanges. To the west, replaced by very similar-looking **Kawarau gecko** (*W.* "Cromwell"). Their ranges abut west of Clive, at south-eastern end of the Cromwell Gorge; typical examples of the two species have been collected only about 1 km apart with no obvious barrier between them; where the species meet south of the gorge not yet known. Kawarau gecko usually darker, and with denser black speckling on ventral surface; pad around claw on first digit noticeably less well-developed. Range is surrounded by that of **korero gecko** (*W.* "Otago/Southland large"), which is generally noticeably bigger, usually very substantially so, and with broader toe pads. However, korero gecko in northern section of the Raggedy Range has similar body size to schist gecko, but distinguished by broader toe pads and shorter distal phalanges. A population of geckos occurs at Glenavon, south of Middlemarch, perhaps derived from an ancient hybridisation between schist and korero geckos (based on morphology and genetics).

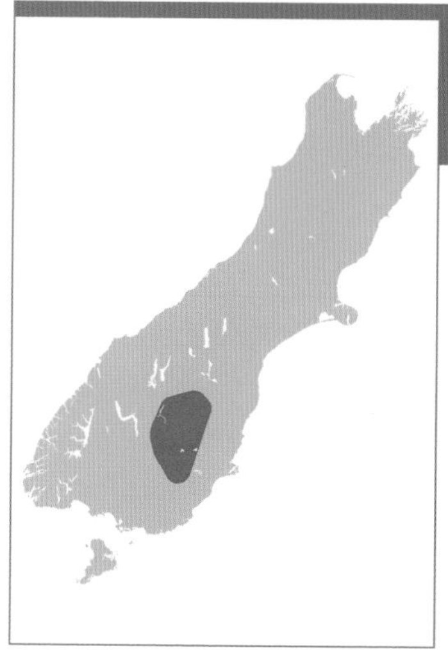

HABITAT

Lowland, Montane/subalpine

Strongly associated with schist rock outcrops in dry open country, where it occupies deep crevices and hides under loose slabs.

NATURAL HISTORY

Nocturnal forager; saxicolous, terrestrial. May sun-bask in partial concealment at retreat entrances. Can form large aggregations when abundant. Sexually mature at c. 4 years. Annual reproduction, mating immediately after the birth season; 2 young born in February the following year. Insectivorous, but may also feed on fruits.

ETYMOLOGY

Common name referring to the schist rock outcrops with which this taxon is strongly associated. **Tag name** refers to its distribution in Central Otago.

Kawarau gecko

Woodworthia "Cromwell"

Endemic

DESCRIPTION

Up to 78 mm SVL

A species with a restricted range in western Otago; average body size increases dramatically with altitude. **Dorsal surface** grey, brown, with blotches or occasionally longitudinal stripes. A broad or triangular pale canthal stripe running from nostril to eye. **Lateral surfaces** with irregular-shaped pale blotches, overlaid with black speckles, or in striped individuals, a broad brown lateral band that changes abruptly to light brown or grey ventrally. **Ventral surface** light brown to grey, may be lightly speckled. **Eye** colour shades of brown, olive or green-brown, occasionally yellow. **Rostral scale** contacting or excluded from nostrils. **Mouth lining** pink; **tongue** pink with diffuse grey tip. **Intact tail** equal to body length (SVL). **Toes** with weakly developed distal pads on first digits; distal phalanges straight. **Subdigital lamellae** 9–11. **Soles of feet** light brown.

DISTRIBUTION

South Island only. Occurs from the Dunstan Mountains, Cairnmuir Range, Old Woman Range, across to Queenstown and Wanaka (including Ruby Island in Lake Wanaka).

VARIATION AND SIMILAR SPECIES

Colour and size vary between populations, and across their ranges. Similar looking to **schist gecko** (*W.* "Central Otago") but with a pale canthal stripe running from nostril to eye. Also, schist gecko usually slightly lighter in colour, with less black speckling on belly, and pad around first digit's claw noticeably more well developed. Distribution overlaps with that of much larger **korero gecko** (*W.* "Otago/Southland large") on southern and western slopes of the Dunstan Mountains, and probably at northern end of The Remarkables. Korero gecko also with broader toe pads compared to Kawarau gecko. Range also abuts or narrowly overlaps that of **short-toed gecko** (*W.* "southern mini") at northern end of Remarkables; overlaps narrowly with **Southern Alps gecko** (*W.* "Southern Alps") near Wanaka; and abuts that of the very similar schist gecko near Clive. Southern Alps gecko has stockier build, shorter broader toes and distinctly shorter distal phalanges. But in area of overlap, Southern Alps gecko generally smaller, although smaller Kawarau geckos can be found in other areas.

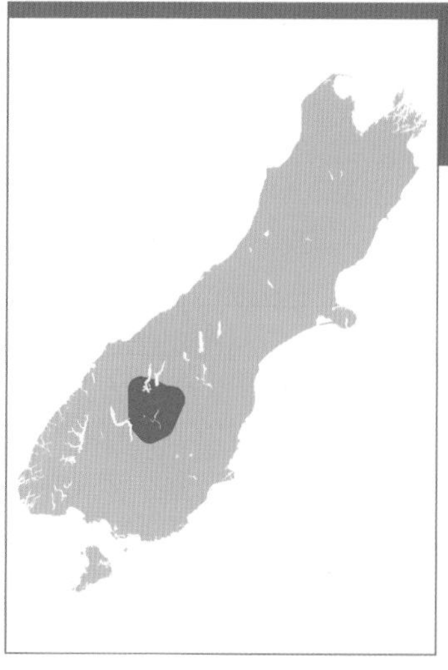

HABITAT

Lowland, Montane/subalpine, Alpine

Occupies crevices in schist rock, or below rock slabs covered in vegetation or on dry, dusty slopes. On Ruby Island occupies low vegetation (e.g. flax and cabbage trees).

NATURAL HISTORY

Nocturnal; saxicolous, terrestrial. May sun-bask in partial concealment at retreat entrances. Can form large aggregations when abundant, including males, females and juveniles. Sexual maturity reached in c. 4 years in lower-altitude populations; c. 5 years at higher altitudes. Annual reproduction, yielding 2 young usually in late January–early February. Feeds on invertebrates, and potentially berries.

ETYMOLOGY

Common and **tag names** both referring to geographic locations where this taxon occurs.

Korero gecko

Woodworthia "Otago/Southland large"

Endemic

Rock and Pillar Range

DESCRIPTION

Up to 90 mm SVL

A large, robust *Woodworthia* found over much of Otago and Southland. Highly variable in appearance and comprising three distinct geographic groups (see 'Variation and similar species' below for descriptions).

DISTRIBUTION

South Island only. Found throughout much of Otago and Southland, from the ranges immediately south of the Waitaki Valley to islands in Foveaux Strait but absent from Stewart Island/Rakiura and its offshore islands. A record from Port Pegasus has been discredited. Reaches the eastern edge of Fiordland, but thought to be absent from Fiordland proper.

VARIATION AND SIMILAR SPECIES

A very variable taxon, which may require further taxonomic splitting. Two morphologically distinguishable, distinct geographic groups of populations that are also readily distinguishable using genetics; third group has considerable geographic variation in size and appearance.

1. ***Northern Raggedy Range group*:** (≤ 68 mm SVL) Genetically most distinctive group. Confined to northern Raggedy Range, north of the Ida Burn. Populations are smaller-bodied than others of the species, closer in size to schist gecko (*W.* "Central Otago"), which abuts them to the south. Dark grey in colour, and superficially somewhat reminiscent of forest gecko (*M. granulatus*) in build, colour and markings. Eye colour brown, with pale yellow mottling, and black filigree pattern. Digits on feet moderately expanded and pads broadest near tip; distal phalanges relatively short.
2. ***Western group*:** (to 90 mm SVL) Includes populations from higher altitude areas of the block of country bounded by Clutha Valley, Kawarau Valley and areas surrounding Lake

Wakatipu in the north, the Waimea Plains in the south, and the high mountains of Fiordland in the west. Stout bodied when mature, and very large for *Woodworthia*, with large feet, broadly expanded digital pads, high subdigital lamellae counts (usually 12–13), 3 rows of precloacal pores extending well onto thighs, and very short distal phalanges. Grey in colour, with green eyes; overall, they look like a very large Southern Alps gecko (*W.* "Southern Alps").

3. ***Eastern and southern group:*** (to 80 mm SVL). Most widespread group. Highly variable in appearance. Includes Jewell's Dansey's Pass gecko and his eastern and southern forms of the korero gecko. Distribution completely surrounds that of group (1): animals found in the Dunstan Mountains, around Dansey's Pass, the Kakanui Mountains and the Horse Range, and on tops of the Rock and Pillar Range. Individuals of northern- and western-most populations large, robust and grey, superficially similar to the western group (2), but with fewer subdigital lamellae (8–13, usually 10–11), precloacal pores 2 rows (occasionally 3, extending only slightly onto thighs), and longer distal phalanges. Eye colour distinctly brown to gold. A little to the south-east, where they live in narrow crevices in highly foliated schist rock, animals much more flattened in build. Farther to the south and east, rather nondescript; like a larger version of Northern Raggedy population.

JEREMY ROLFE

North Raggedy Range

TONY JEWELL

Danseys Pass

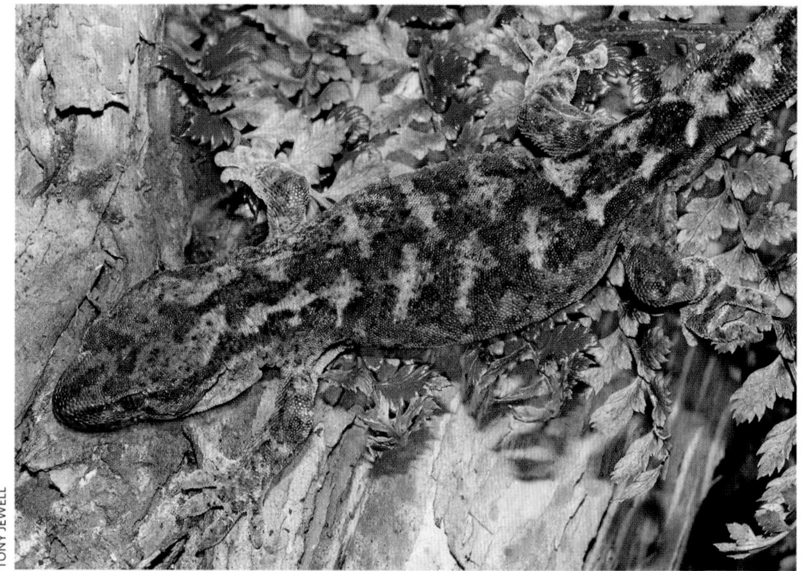
TONY JEWELL

Catlins

In the north, range abuts that of **Southern Alps gecko** (*W.* "Southern Alps") along boundary between exposures of schist and greywacke rocks; this species occupies schist, and the Southern Alps gecko greywacke, with occasional very narrow overlap. Bigger than Southern Alps gecko, usually very substantially so, and populations near area of overlap with somewhat longer distal phalanges. In driest parts of Central and western Otago, replaced by the smaller **schist gecko** and **Kawarau gecko** (*W.* "Cromwell"); often narrow zones of overlap where species' distributions meet. Both schist and Kawarau geckos smaller and more slender, with narrower toes and distinctly longer distal phalanges. There is a population of geckos at Glenavon, south of Middlemarch, with morphology and genetics suggesting it derived from an ancient hybridisation between schist gecko and korero gecko. Large western form overlaps extensively with **short-toed gecko** (*W.* "southern mini"), and they are often found together. Short-toed gecko the only species with extensive overlap - extremely distinct in appearance: dull light olive-green to fawn in colour, uniform or with indistinct longitudinal stripes, and small (< 65 mm SVL) rather than large (> 73 mm SVL), whereas western korero gecko in area of sympatry is dark grey with distinct transverse markings.

HABITAT

Lowland, Montane/subalpine

Usually under loose rocks or in crevices in rock bluffs and tors, but also occupies holes and crevices in tree trunks and branches in forest.

NATURAL HISTORY

Nocturnal, but may sun-bask in partial concealment at retreat entrances. Terrestrial. Can form large aggregations when abundant, including mix of males, females and juveniles. Mating generally occurs February. Annual reproduction in lowland populations, with 2 young born in early February; reproduction biennial in higher-altitude populations, with 2 young born about November.

ETYMOLOGY

Common name (Māori) meaning 'to talk or speak', referring to the frequent vocalisations of this taxon. **Tag name** refers to Otago-Southland distribution and that most populations are larger-bodied than the sympatric or adjacent *Woodworthia* taxa.

Short-toed gecko

Woodworthia "southern mini"

Endemic

JAMES REARDON

DESCRIPTION

Up to 65 mm SVL (usually smaller, 48–58 mm SVL)

A small poorly marked but distinctive gecko. Its closest relative is goldstripe gecko (*W. chrysosiretica*) of the North Island. Very short and stocky in all dimensions. **Dorsal surface** pale or dull olive to olive-grey, or sometimes deep olive-brown; usually uniform or almost so; occasionally with dull or indistinct dorsolateral stripes. Pale stripes may become more bold and distinct over hips and continue down intact tail. Occasionally with broad dark triangular stripes on either side of head from nostril to eye. Also occasionally with small bright orange spots on dorsum or on upper sides of limbs and feet. **Lateral surfaces** uniform olive-grey or olive-brown, sometimes overlaid with indistinct pale flecks. **Ventral surface** pale olive with scattered individual black scales. **Eye** colour dark brown. **Rostral scale** particularly wide and shallow (similar to *W. chrysosiretica*), excluded from nostrils. **Mouth lining** and **tongue** pink, but tongue may have greyish tip. **Intact tail** shorter than body length (SVL). **Toes** with very short distal phalanges, making them appear stumpy. **Subdigital lamellae** 10–13. **Soles of feet** cream with yellow or pink hue.

DISTRIBUTION

South Island only. Mountainous areas in western Southland and Otago. Westwards from the Garvie Mountains and Mt Rosa to the Livingstone Mountains, including areas to the south-west and south-east of Lake Wakatipu (Humboldt Mountains, Mt Mavora, Thompson Mountains and Eyre Mountains, Hector Mountains, The Remarkables, Mt Rosa, Slate Range and Mataura Range).

VARIATION AND SIMILAR SPECIES

Minor variation in extent of stripes on dorsal surface, and spots on ventral surface. Some individuals may lack colour, some appearing almost translucent. Unlikely to be confused with sympatric **korero gecko** (*W.* "Otago/Southland large") or **Kawarau gecko** (*W.* "Cromwell") because of its small size, dull colouration and very stocky build.

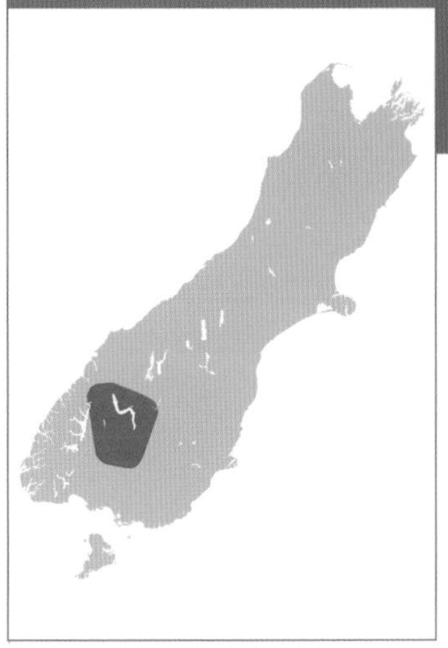

HABITAT

Montane/subalpine, Alpine

Occurs among scree, rock piles and talus slopes, beneath loose rocks and in creviced rock bluffs; usually surrounded by subalpine and alpine tussock grassland.

NATURAL HISTORY

Nocturnal; terrestrial, saxicolous. Shy and cryptic, remaining hidden beneath rocks or in crevices by day. May climb low-growing shrubs at night while foraging. Birth may occur late summer (February-March), or occasionally October; 1 or 2 young produced annually. Does not aggregate in large groups but rather lives singly or in pairs. Frequently shares retreat sites with other *Woodworthia* species.

ETYMOLOGY

Common name referring to the short stumpy appearance of the toes. **Tag name** referring to the species' southern distribution and small size.

MARIEKE LETTINK

Goldstripe gecko

Woodworthia chrysosiretica (Robb, 1980)

Endemic

DESCRIPTION

Up to 80 mm SVL; up to 13.5 g weight

One of the few native geckos quite commonly found in ornamental gardens, where it occupies tuft-forming plants such as flax (*Phormium tenax*), agapanthus (*Agapanthus praecox*) and red-hot pokers (*Kniphofia* species). **Dorsal surface** light golden brown, or olive- or green-brown to dark brown, with broad pale dorsolateral stripes from nostrils, forming the canthal stripes, passing over eye and continuing to tail base where stripes come together; canthal stripe bordered below by dark olive or brown stripe. Longitudinal pale stripes may be dull or contrasting white, and usually edged in dark brown; occasionally flecked with short darker streaks, and generally continuing down intact tail. **Lateral surfaces** uniform light golden brown or with a broad green- or olive-brown lateral band and indistinct thin longitudinal stripes below. **Ventral surface** pale cream, either uniform or flecked/speckled with dark markings on belly and tail; chin and throat uniform pale cream, and never flecked or speckled. **Eye** colour light brown or hazel. **Rostral scale** large, and widely excluded from nostrils. **Mouth lining** and **tongue** pink, but tip of tongue can be darker red. **Intact tail** length about equal to body length (SVL). **Toes** with broadly expanded pad and straight distal phalanges. **Subdigital lamellae** 12–18. **Soles of feet** cream.

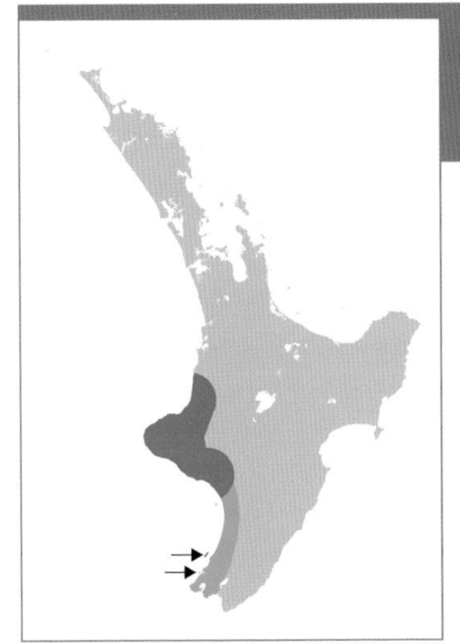

DISTRIBUTION

North Island only. Widespread from north Taranaki to Kapiti, including Kapiti and Mana Islands. An isolated record from near Te Kuiti indicates further

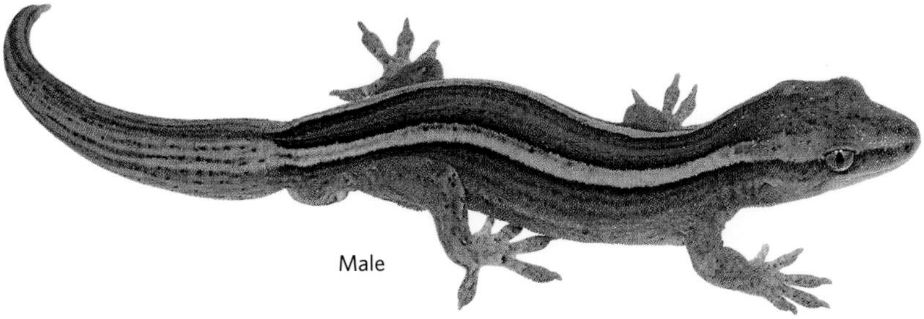

Male

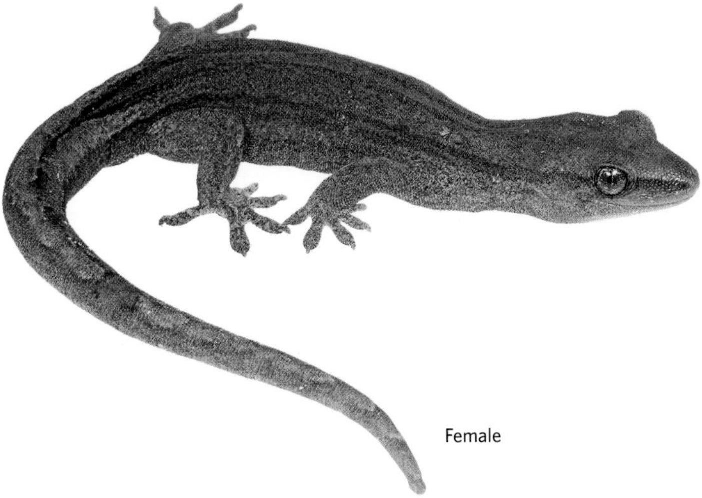

Female

survey needed - species could be more widespread, or might have been accidentally translocated.

VARIATION AND SIMILAR SPECIES

Variation between individuals generally limited to the degree of dorsal shading from golden brown to dark brown, and drabness of dorsolateral stripes. Melanotic (dark) individuals rarely reported. Similar in appearance to striped sympatric **Raukawa gecko** (*W. maculata*) and **Pacific gecko** (*D. pacificus*), but distinguished from former by continuous pale dorsolateral stripes extending down tail, and dark speckling on belly and/or tail; and from latter by rostral scale not in contact with nostrils (vs. rostral contacting nostrils).

HABITAT

Coastal, Lowland

A generalist, inhabiting flaxland, vineland, coastal forest and scrubland. Often found in farmland, and close to habitation, where it takes refuge in vegetation and beneath debris and in woodpiles.

NATURAL HISTORY

Cathemeral; arboreal and terrestrial. May live alone but generally tolerates conspecifics, and several individuals may share same flax bush or communal refuge sites. Populations can exist at high density. Sexual maturity reached at 4–5 years; mating occurs in April. Females gravid until late summer (February–March), when 2 young are born, c. 30 mm SVL. Particularly active and agile; usually climbing and jumping between branches and foliage while foraging. Partially prehensile tail and expanded toe pads allow it to climb very smooth surfaces (e.g. waxy flax leaves). May vocalise with short squeals when disturbed. Primarily insectivorous, but in summer, when flax is flowering, many individuals forage on nectar high above the ground among inflorescences.

ETYMOLOGY

Specific name (Greek) from the words *chrysos* meaning 'gold' and *seiretion* meaning 'stripe'. **Common name** also relating to appearance.

Goldstripe gecko on flax flower

Key to New Zealand geckos

GENERA

1	**Lamellae** straight across toes to slightly curved nearest tip; **mouth lining** with at least some yellow, orange, lavender or dark blue pigmentation	2
	Lamellae nearest the toe tip distinctly curved or V-shaped; **mouth lining** pink, with or without diffuse dark pigmentation on the tongue tip	5
2	**Lamellae** extend uninterrupted to base of claws	**7 (*Naultinus*)**
	Lamellae form a pad which stops before end of toe	3
3	**Apical plate** present on undersides of toes around base of claws of all digits; **dorsal body patterning** complex, including both herringbone markings and dorsolateral stripes of equal prominence, and including elements of bright green, yellow or reddish colour; southern Stewart Island/Rakiura only	***Tukutuku rakiurae***
	Apical plate present on undersides of toes around the base of claw of first digit only, or entirely absent; **dorsal body pattern** with either chevrons or transverse or longitudinal stripes predominating, without bright green components, and with any yellow or orange pigment as superimposed blotches, not part of underlying pattern	4
4	**Dorsal pattern** of very uniform-width longitudinal stripes; **mouth pigmentation** weak; **ventral scales** of tail about twice as large as dorsal tail scales	**15 (*Toropuku*)**
	Dorsal pattern usually with transverse bands or chevrons predominant, very rarely uniformly longitudinally striped; **mouth pigmentation** strong yellow to orange and dark blue-black; **ventral and dorsal scales** of tail similar in size	**16 (*Mokopirirakau*)**
5	**Ventral skin** opaque; **body size** large to very large (adults > 100 mm SVL); islands off north-eastern North Island and in Cook Strait, and in a few fenced mainland sanctuaries	***Hoplodactylus duvaucelii***
	Ventral skin translucent, particularly at night when active; **body size** small to medium (SVL ≤ 100 mm)	6
6	**Rostral scale** broadly contacting nostrils; **precloacal pores** confined to small central patch, not extending onto thighs	**25 (*Dactylocnemis*)**
	Rostral scale excluded from or very narrowly contacting nostrils; **precloacal pores** extending onto at least base of thighs	**30 (*Woodworthia*)**

Naultinus

7	**Dorsal body scales** strongly heterogeneous, some greatly enlarged	8
	Dorsal body scales more or less homogeneous	9

8	**Enlarged scales** distributed over entire dorsal area (although may be more prominent in dorsolateral rows); **mouth lining** and **tongue** dark blue, mauve or purple, tongue tip may be pinkish red, green-yellow or orange; **soles of feet** grey; **adults** sometimes brown or grey; south Marlborough (south of Wairau Valley) to north Canterbury	***N. rudis***
	Enlarged scales confined to dorsolateral rows or to back of head and pelvic area; **mouth lining** pale lavender, pink and/or orange, **tongue** pink or yellow; **soles of feet** yellow; **adult males** green with pale bluish belly (rarely yellow with white belly); Marlborough north of Wairau Valley	***N. manukanus***
9	**Canthal scales** > 4x diameter of scales on head behind eye; **dorsal scales** pointed	**10 (remaining South Island species)**
	Canthal scales ≤ 3x diameter of scales on head behind eye; **dorsal scales** fine, granular	**12 (North Island species)**
10	**Eye** small and **snout** relatively long and shallow (length about 3x eye diameter); **dorsal body** has intricate pale markings, including at least fragments of a longitudinal mid-dorsal stripe, on dull dark green or brown-green background; **scales** sharply conical; West Coast south of Stockton, including Lewis Pass area	***N. tuberculatus***
	Eye larger and **snout** shorter and deeper (length about 2.5x eye diameter); **dorsal body** markings, if any, large and bold; **scales** conical but with rounded tips	**11**
11	**Dorsal markings** stripes or rows of more or less irregular spots, bold and single-coloured apart from scattered dark scales, separated from uniformly bright green **background colour** by a narrow outline of dark scales (background colour turns brown or grey in most Canterbury males as they approach maturity); if plain green then large and sturdily built; mid-Canterbury southwards to Southland east of Main Divide, including islands around Stewart Island/Rakiura	***N. gemmeus***
	Dorsal markings large and circular, often with complex concentric rings of colour, with dark outline broader than in other species; **background colour** usually mottled and seldom bright green except in north-westernmost populations. Clinal variation with little resemblance in colour between extremes of cline - see species text. If plain green then small and slender with a very long original tail; Nelson, Tasman, West Coast north of Stockton, narrowly into Marlborough near Nelson Lakes	***N. stellatus***
12	**Body size** large (up to c. 95 mm SVL, and 23 g); **adult males** with light green belly and bluish lateral band	**13**
	Body size medium (up to c. 75 mm SVL, and 15 g); **adult males** with bluish belly	**14**

13	Scales on dorsal surface of **snout** large and flat, snout shallow and wedge-shaped; colour typically bright green; **markings** usually strongly contrasting cream or yellow and with blackish or deeper yellow margin; Northland from latitude of Bay of Islands to Kaimaumau Swamp	***N. grayii***
	Scales on dorsal surface of **snout** rounded, snout deeper and rounded; colour typically dark bluish green; adult **markings** if present usually a paler tone of background colour rather than strongly contrasting, and without contrasting margin (juveniles have bolder marking which fade during growth); southern and eastern North Island east and south of a line running from around Whanganui to National Park, then south of Lake Taupō to near East Cape	***N. punctatus***
14	**Mouth lining** and **tongue** very dark blue (tip of tongue occasionally yellowish to orange); no suggestion of orange colouration at corners of mouth or around nostrils; from southern Bay of Islands and area around Dargaville to west and north of a line running from around Whanganui to National Park, then south of Lake Taupō to near East Cape	***N. elegans***
	Mouth lining orange and pale lavender; **tongue** orange or red; orange colouration visible at corners of mouth and around nostrils; from about Houhora north	***N.* "North Cape"**

Toropuku

15	**Scales on frontal region** distinctly conical; Coromandel Peninsula	***T.* "Coromandel"**
	Scales on frontal region domed; islands in Marlborough Sounds	***T. stephensi***

Mokopirirakau

16	**Body colour** olive-grey with 6–7 lighter transverse bands (more, narrower bands in recently discovered Otago population); **eye colour** black; no **apical plate** on any digits; alpine areas of South Island ranges	***M. kahutarae***
	Body colour not as above, usually with complex mottled pattern overlain by blotches or chevrons, occasionally longitudinal stripes; **eye colour** not black, **apical plate** usually present on digit 1 (but see couplet 19)	**17**
17	**Small scales on top of thigh** near knee transitioning abruptly into much larger (3x as large) scales on front of thigh	**18**
	Small scales on top of thigh near knee transitioning gradually into larger (2x as large) scales on front of thigh	**19**
18	**Dorsal tail scales** large, hexagonal to rectangular, wider than long; **dorsal body scales** smooth, granular, beadlike; alpine areas of western Otago and north-western Southland	***M.* "Roys Peak"**
	Dorsal tail scales small, rectangular, with rounded rear margins, longer than wide; **dorsal body scales** distinctly conical; Catlins and lowland Southland east of about Waiau River	***M.* "southern forest"**

19	**Apical plate on digit 1** much reduced, and not sheathing claw base; Stewart Island and surrounding islands	***M. nebulosus***
	Apical plate on digit 1 swollen, at least partly sheathing claw base	**20**
20	**Scales between eye and nostril** uniform, granular, ≥ 15 in series; western Southland, and eastern and southern Fiordland	***M. cryptozoicus***
	Scales between eye and nostril heterogeneous in size and/or shape, usually ≤ 14 in series	**21**
21	**Dorsal body scales**, particularly those towards hind legs, dimpled to compressed (front to rear), sometimes sharply conical; **cheeks** extremely inflated; West Coast from Ōkārito south to at least Paringa	***M.* "Okarito"**
	Dorsal body scales granular or slightly conical, but not dimpled, compressed or sharply conical; **cheeks** not unusually inflated	**22**
22	**Scale rows marking** borders of break points in tail squarish to rectangular, differentiated from more rounded to oval or granular intervening scale rows, **scales on snout** conical; Haast Range and Cascade Plateau south to western and central Fiordland	***M.* "Cascades"**
	Nelson Lakes National Park	***M.* "Cupola"**
	Scale rows marking borders of break points in tail squarish to broadly rectangular, similar in size and shape to intervening scale rows, or caudal segments not clearly discernible; **scales on snout** domed	**23**
23	**Ventral surface** usually unmarked; **apical plate of digit 1** of front foot highly asymmetrical, absent on outer surface of digit; up to about 77 mm **SVL**; **dorsal body scales** small and fine; Open Bay Islands	***M.* "Open Bay Islands"**
	Ventral surface mottled or streaked; **apical plate of digit 1** of front foot slightly asymmetrical, but present on outer surface of digit; up to c. 98 mm **SVL**; **dorsal body scales** large and granular	**24**
24	**Precloacal-femoral pore patch** extends broadly onto thigh, usually with 3 rows of pores throughout most of its length; **ventral surface** usually boldly mottled and streaked with black; scales behind femoral pore series on hind limb much smaller than those in front of femoral pore series; **dorsal patterning** usually continuous across mid-dorsal line; **snout** long, shallow, slightly concave, squared across when viewed from above; North Island from southern Bay of Islands and area around Dargaville to west and north of a line running (roughly) from around Whanganui to National Park, then south of Lake Taupō to near East Cape; South Island: Marlborough, Nelson, Tasman and West Coast south to about Lake Ianthe	***M. granulatus***

	Precloacal-femoral pore patch extends only onto base of thigh, usually with 2 rows of pores throughout most of its length; **ventral surface** with subdued grey mottling; scales behind femoral pore series on hind limb only slightly smaller than those in front of femoral pore series; **dorsal patterning** usually broken across mid-dorsal line; **snout** moderate length and depth, not concave, rounded at end when viewed from above; southern and eastern North Island; exact boundary of distribution poorly understood, but roughly east and south of a line running from around Whanganui to National Park, then south of Lake Taupō to near East Cape	***M.* "southern North Island"**

Dactylocnemis

25	**Claw of first digit of hind foot** almost completely sheathed within large, symmetrical or near-symmetrical **apical plate**; dark pigmented **tongue** tip; **adult** < 60 mm SVL; **digits** relatively short and broad with pad broadest near the tip, similar to those of some *Woodworthia*; **colour patterning** uniformly longitudinally striped or usually at least with stripes predominating over background blotches; Aupouri and Karikari Peninsulas and nearby islands only	***D.* "Matapia"**
	Claw of first digit of hind foot exposed, **apical plate** reduced or very asymmetrical; **tongue** pink (except in some *D.* "Three Kings"); **adult** > 60 mm SVL; **digits** longer and narrower; **colour patterning** including darker chocolate-brown or grey-brown components; blotches or transverse stripes usually predominating in pattern, although rarely longitudinally striped	**26**
26	**Adult** usually ≤ 80 mm SVL; **mainland and inshore islands** only	**27**
	Adult ≥ 80 mm SVL; Three Kings, Poor Knights and Mokohinau/Pokohīnau island groups only	**28**
27	**Snout** shallow (below level of centre of eye) from immediately in front of eye and distinctly longer than distance from eye to ear, with 19–21 **scales between nostril and eye**; **chin shields** reduced in area, merging into small throat granules by end of second labial scale; narrow **distal phalange** ≥ 1/3 length of toe; Taranaki, Waikato and Bay of Plenty to central Northland	***D. pacificus***
	Snout deep (level with centre of eye or higher) immediately in front of eye and more or less same length as distance from eye to ear, with 15–16 **scales between nostril and eye**; **chin shields** large and flattened back to level of third or fourth infralabial scale, then changing abruptly to small throat granules; narrow **distal phalange** < 1/3 length of toe; Aupouri Peninsula and nearby islands only	***D.* "North Cape"**
28	15–16 **subdigital lamellae** on fourth digit of hind foot; adults usually > 90 mm and up to 100 mm **SVL**; **distal phalange** c. 1/4 length of toe; long **snout** with 22–24 scales between nostril and eye; Manawatāwhi/Three Kings Island group only	***D.* "Three Kings"**

	10–14 (rarely to 16) **subdigital lamellae** on fourth digit of hind foot; adults ≤ 90 mm **SVL**; **distal phalange** c. 1/3 length of toe; shorter snout with < 22 loreal granules in series between postnasal scale and edge of orbit	29
29	**Digit** moderately narrowing beyond toe pad (at base more than half maximum diameter of pad); males with 2 (rarely 3) moderate-sized **cloacal spurs**; moderately long **snout** with c. 20 scales between nostril and eye; **distal toe pad** completely absent from claw 1 of hind foot or reduced to very small remnant on outer side only; Poor Knights Islands only	***D.* "Poor Knights"**
	Digit strongly narrowing beyond toe pad (at base less than half maximum diameter of pad); males with 3–4 large **cloacal spurs**; short **snout** with c. 15 scales between nostril and eye; **distal toe pad** present on both sides of claw on first digit of hind foot; Mokohinau Island group only	***D.* "Mokohinau"**

Woodworthia

30	**Rostral scale** > 2.5x as wide as deep; **colour** mainly light drab olive green or buff; **markings,** if any, are lighter uniform longitudinal stripes; **toe** pads always broad	31
	Rostral scale < 2.5x as wide as deep; **colour** usually includes significant grey, dark brown or blackish components; **markings** usually include at least a component of blotches, chevrons or transverse stripes; longitudinal stripes, if present, usually with wavy margins or overlie transverse patterning (or in the very rare exceptions to these colour rules, **toes** are narrow and tapering)	32
31	Stocky build; **adult** < 65 (usually < 60) mm SVL; **distal phalanges** < 1/5 length of digit; western Otago and north-western Southland	***W.* "southern mini"**
	Moderately slender build; **adult** > 60 mm SVL; **distal phalanges** c. 1/4 length of digit; western North Island to Kapiti and Mana Islands	***W. chrysosiretica***
32	Distinct narrow dark **stripe** from nostril to eye, continuing straight back behind eye	33
	Broad dark **stripe** from nostril to eye diffuse to absent, if present sloping downward and/or broadening behind eye	36
33	**Toes** narrow, tapering or only slightly dilated, with pads more or less uniform in width throughout length	34
	Toe pads in adults broadly dilated, broadest near tip	35
34	**Adult** ≤ 50 mm SVL, (usually < 45 mm); 7–9 **subdigital lamellae** on digit 4 of hind foot; pads narrow and tapering, **distal lamellae** only slightly curved; **body patterning** usually very diffuse; inland basins and ranges of South Marlborough to central Canterbury	***W.* "pygmy"**

	Adults > 50 mm SVL; 10–12 **subdigital lamellae of** digit 4 of hind foot; pads narrow but not tapering, **distal lamellae** strongly curved to V-shaped; **body patterning** of boldly contrasting transverse bands; Kaikōura Ranges and other coastal ranges south of the Wairau Valley	***W.* "Kaikouras"**
35	9–11 **subdigital lamellae** on digit 4 of hind foot); **body colour** warm buff/brown; coastal ranges and coastlines of north Canterbury, eastern Marlborough, Nelson and Wellington	***W.* "Marlborough mini"**
	11–14 **subdigital lamellae** on digit 4 of hind foot ; **body colour** greyish or greenish; Mts Owen and Arthur and associated ranges, and ranges of inland Kahurangi National Park	***W.* "Mount Arthur"**
36	**Rostral scale** usually obviously excluded from nostril; obvious suture between first nasal and first **infralabial scales**; several to many small spines at posterior end of **'eyebrow'**; east coast of North Island from central Northland south; inland areas south of East Cape, the central North Island high country and Taranaki; coasts and coastal ranges of Nelson, Tasman and Marlborough	***W. maculata***
	Rostral scale contact variable, but usually either just contacting the nostril at its corner or just excluded by narrow contact between first nasal and first **infralabial scales**; few or no spines at posterior end of **'eyebrow'**	**37**
37	**Infralabial scales** in continuous series, gradually decreasing in size from mental to below eye, and much larger than adjacent throat granules	**38**
	Infralabial scales rapidly decreasing in size and ceasing to be larger than adjacent scales in front of the level of eye; adjacent chin shields enlarged	**39**
38	**Distal phalanges** > 1/5 length of digit; ≥ 5 scale rows between claw and end of pad; **apical plate on digit 1** of hind foot very asymmetrical; **colour** predominantly brown with prominent black spots and blotches, especially on original tail; pale canthal stripe less prominent to absent; Canterbury lowlands and coastal ranges, including Banks Peninsula	***W.* cf. *brunnea***
	Distal phalanges < 1/5 length of digit; c. 3 scale rows between claw and end of pad; **apical plate on digit 1** of hind foot symmetrical; **colour** predominantly grey without prominent black spots and blotches on original tail; pale canthal stripe prominent; inland ranges and basins from Marlborough south of the Wairau valley to the Waitaki Valley and Wanaka area	***W.* "Southern Alps"**
39	**Adults** usually < 65 mm SVL	**40**
	Adults > 65 (usually > 70) mm SVL	**42**
40	**Toe pads** strongly dilated, dilation widest near tip; pad > 75% length of toe; confined to Northern Raggedy Range, north of the Ida Burn	***W.* "Otago/Southland large" Northern Raggedys population**
	Toe pad only moderately dilated, dilation widest about halfway down toe	**41**

41	**Apical plate on digit 1** of hind foot small (narrower than widest part of toe); west Otago west of the Dunstan Mountains and Clyde to Wanaka and northern end of The Remarkables Range	***W.* "Cromwell"**
	Apical plate on digit 1 of hind foot well developed (as wide as widest part of toe); Central Otago north of the Old Man and Umbrella Ranges from Beaumont to Clyde and northwards to the Ida Burn in the Raggedy Range and Rough Ridge	***W.* "Central Otago"**
42	3 rows of **precloacal pores**, extending well onto thighs; up to 90 mm **SVL**; **subdigital lamellae** 12–13; length of **distal phalange** < width of pad; from west Otago (Old Man Range to around Lake Wakatipu), and northern Southland north of the Waimea Plains	***W.* "Otago/Southland large" western populations**
	2 (occasionally 3) rows of **precloacal pores**, extending only to base of thighs; up to 80 mm **SVL**; **subdigital lamellae** 8–13 (usually 10–11); length of **distal phalange** ≥ width of pad; from eastern Otago, Southland and islands in Foveaux Strait	***W.* "Otago/Southland large" eastern and southern populations**

SKINKS

Striped skink, *Oligosoma striatum*

Contents

Chevron skink *Oligosoma homalonotum* 162
Egg-laying skink *Oligosoma suteri* 164
Fiordland skink *Oligosoma acrinasum* 166
Sinbad skink *Oligosoma pikitanga* 168
Barrier skink *Oligosoma judgei* 170
Awakopaka skink *Oligosoma awakopaka* 172
Otago skink *Oligosoma otagense* 174
Taumaka skink *Oligosoma taumakae* 176
Scree skink *Oligosoma waimatense* 178
Grand skink *Oligosoma grande* 180
Burgan skink *Oligosoma burganae* 182
Eyres skink *Oligosoma repens* 184
Nevis skink *Oligosoma toka* 186
Okuru skink *Oligosoma* "Okuru" 188
Te Kakahu skink *Oligosoma tekakahu* 190
Cryptic skink *Oligosoma inconspicuum* 192
Southern skink *Oligosoma notosaurus* 196
McCann's skink *Oligosoma maccanni* 198
Small-eared skink *Oligosoma stenotis* 200
Green skink (Southland green skink) *Oligosoma chloronoton* 202
Lakes skink *Oligosoma* aff. *chloronoton* "West Otago" 204
Otago green skink *Oligosoma* aff. *chloronoton* "Eastern Otago" 206
Stewart Island green skink *Oligosoma* aff. *chloronoton* "Stewart Island" 208
Canterbury spotted skink *Oligosoma lineoocellatum* 210
Northern spotted skink *Oligosoma kokowai* 212
Mackenzie skink *Oligosoma prasinum* 214
Marlborough spotted skink *Oligosoma elium* 216
Northern long-toed skink *Oligosoma longipes* 218
Roamatimati skink *Oligosoma* aff. *longipes* "southern" 220
White-bellied skink *Oligosoma hoparatea* 222
Northern grass skink *Oligosoma polychroma* 224
Waiharakeke grass skink *Oligosoma* aff. *polychroma* Clade 2 226
South Marlborough grass skink *Oligosoma* aff. *polychroma* Clade 3 228

Copper skink, *Oligosoma aeneum*, Waikato

Canterbury grass skink *Oligosoma* aff. *polychroma* Clade 4 230
Southern grass skink *Oligosoma* aff. *polychroma* Clade 5 232
Speckled skink *Oligosoma infrapunctatum* 236
Alborn skink *Oligosoma* aff. *infrapunctatum* "Alborn" 240
Chesterfield skink *Oligosoma* aff. *infrapunctatum* "Chesterfield" 242
Cobble skink *Oligosoma* aff. *infrapunctatum* "cobble" 244
Crenulate skink *Oligosoma* aff. *infrapunctatum* "crenulate" 246
Hokitika skink *Oligosoma* aff. *infrapunctatum* "Hokitika" 248
Westport skink *Oligosoma* aff. *infrapunctatum* "Westport" 250
Hawke's Bay skink *Oligosoma* aff. *infrapunctatum* "Hawke's Bay" 252
Kupe skink *Oligosoma* aff. *infrapunctatum* "southern North Island" 254
Falla's skink *Oligosoma fallai* 256
Chathams skink *Oligosoma nigriplantare* 258
Shore skink *Oligosoma smithi* 260
Tātahi skink *Oligosoma* "Three Kings, Te Paki, Western Northland" 262
Small-scaled skink *Oligosoma microlepis* 264
Striped skink *Oligosoma striatum* 266
Moko skink *Oligosoma moco* 268
Whirinaki skink *Oligosoma* "Whirinaki" 270
Glossy brown skink *Oligosoma zelandicum* 272
Copper skink *Oligosoma aeneum* 274
Slight skink *Oligosoma levidensum* 276
Hardy's skink *Oligosoma hardyi* 278
Aorangi skink *Oligosoma roimata* 280
Ornate skink *Oligosoma ornatum* 282
Whitaker's skink *Oligosoma whitakeri* 284
Marbled skink *Oligosoma oliveri* 286
Hauraki skink *Oligosoma townsi* 288
Robust skink *Oligosoma alani* 290
McGregor's skink *Oligosoma macgregori* 292
Plague (rainbow) skink *Lampropholis delicata* 294
Key to New Zealand skinks 297

Marbled skink, *Oligosoma oliveri*, Poor Knights Islands

NEW ZEALAND SKINKS

New Zealand skinks are the largest taxonomic group of New Zealand reptiles and amphibians. All the skinks fit within a large, almost endemic genus - *Oligosoma*, which encompasses more than 60 taxa. The single non-New Zealand member of the genus (*O. lichenigera*) is found on the Lord Howe and Norfolk Island groups, and is the sister species to the New Zealand radiation. Skinks occupy almost every part of New Zealand and are present on both the mainland and most offshore islands, with the exception of the Kermadec and Subantarctic Islands. They also occupy a wide range of habitats, from the littoral zone and lowland forests to subalpine shrubland and alpine rocky habitats. Some taxa even occur in highly modified agricultural or urban landscapes.

Although a small proportion (fewer than 10%) of taxa are considered generalist in their habitat distribution (e.g. the Canterbury spotted skink (*O. lineoocellatum*) occurs from coastal boulder banks all the way up into alpine shrublands and screes), most have a more defined habitat range. The egg-laying (*O. suteri*) and Fiordland (*O. acrinasum*) skinks, for example, are found only in the coastal zone, whereas the Barrier (*O. judgei*) and Sinbad (*O. pikitanga*) skinks are confined to the high alpine zone. However, there is a high degree of species overlap (sympatric diversity) within each of New Zealand's habitat zones, which is unusual for a temperate region. So, tussock grassland habitats in the South Island may support up to six species of skink and some small northern offshore islands are known to support seven species. This is possible only because of the high ecological diversity within the New Zealand skink fauna, which exhibits a wide range of body sizes and forms (50–150 mm SVL, and 2–c.130 g weight), a range of activity patterns (e.g. diurnal, nocturnal, crepuscular), differing microhabitat preferences (e.g. saxicolous - inhabiting rocks, arboreal, fossorial - using burrows) and minor differences in diet (insectivorous, omnivorous).

SVL AND PORE LOCATION

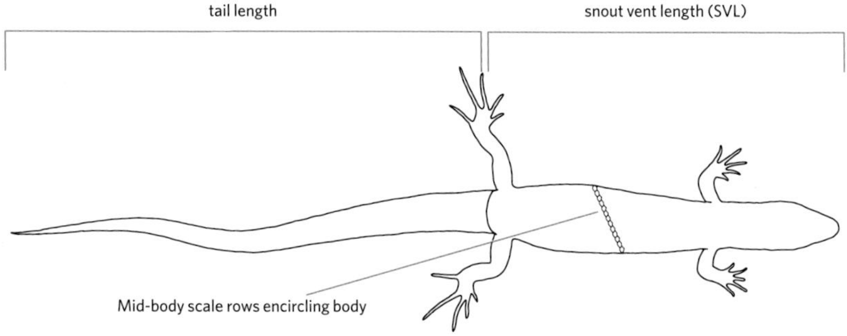

tail length

snout vent length (SVL)

Mid-body scale rows encircling body

SKINK HEAD SCALES

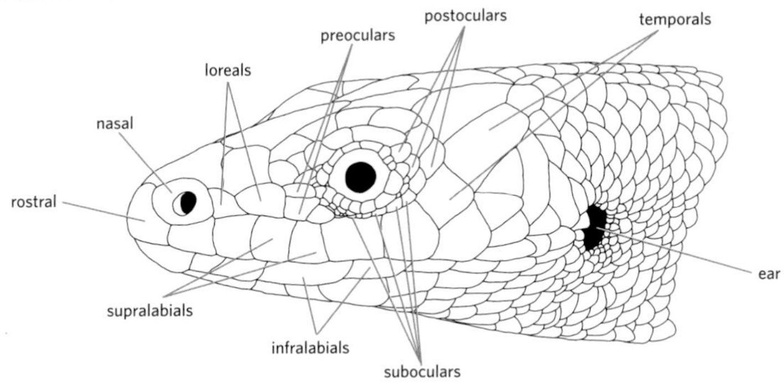

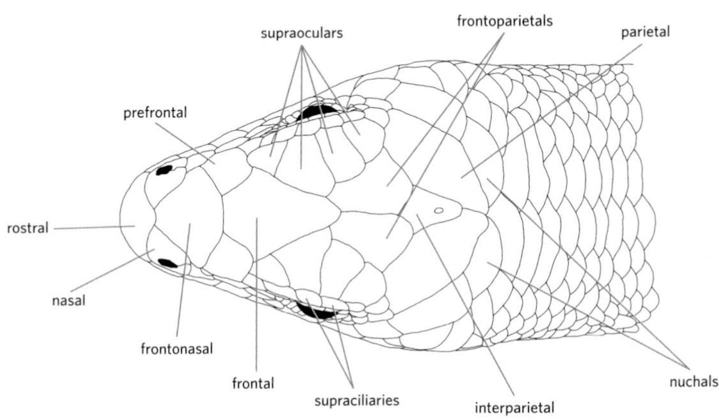

SKINK COLOUR STRIPES

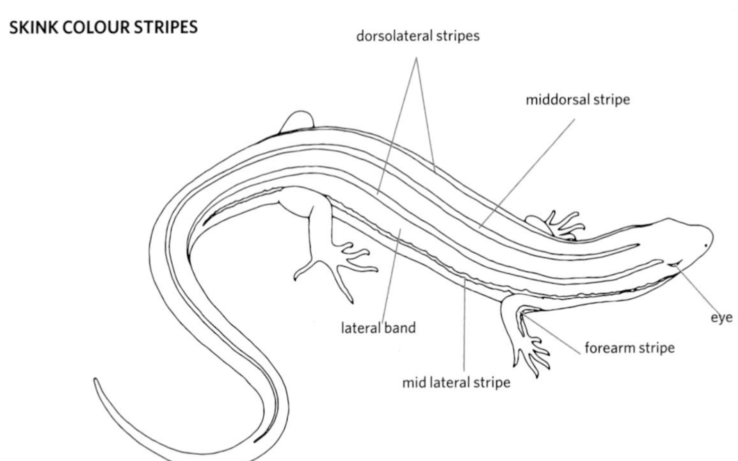

SKINK FOOT

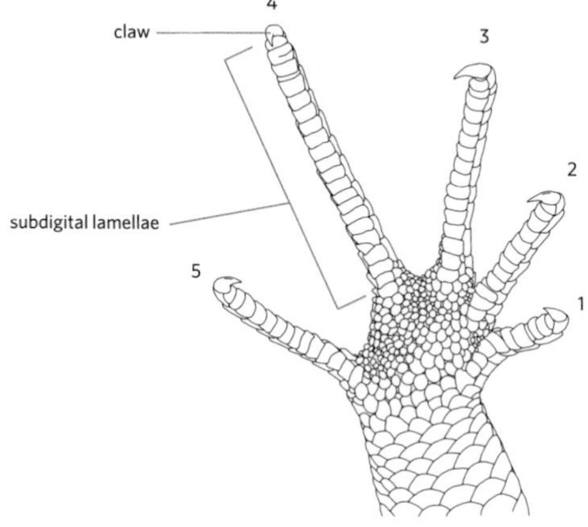

New Zealand skinks are primarily insectivorous, but can feed on other invertebrates, smaller reptiles and even flowers. Many New Zealand skinks also consume berries and nectar. One species, the moko skink (*O. moco*), is known to feed on fruits of pōhuehue (*Muehlenbeckia complexa*) and grand skinks (*O. grande*) eat the berries of porcupine shrub (*Melicytus alpinus*). In feeding on fruits, New Zealand skinks act in a similar way to birds, inadvertently dispersing seeds away from the parent plants, allowing them to germinate elsewhere. Compared to New Zealand geckos, few species of skink are known to take nectar from flowers, and their role, if any, as pollinators is largely unknown.

All but one species (the egg-laying skink) are viviparous, giving birth to small litters of live young, no more than once per year. Viviparity in cold or temperate climates can increase the chances of young surviving because, by retaining embryos in the oviduct and actively regulating their body temperature (e.g. sun-basking or moving into shade), females are able to provide a more stable environment for embryo development. The oviparous egg-laying skink is restricted to coastal boulder shorelines in the upper North Island that receive high sunshine hours, and the warmer annual temperatures are important for successful incubation of the eggs. The only other oviparous species is the plague (rainbow) skink (*Lampropholis delicata*), which has been introduced from Australia and is now naturalised in New Zealand.

Shore skink, *Oligosoma smithi*, Little Barrier Island

Scree skink, *Oligosoma waimatense*

Chevron skink

Oligosoma homalonotum (Boulenger, 1906) **Endemic**

DESCRIPTION

Up to 146 mm SVL; up to 40 g weight

A large distinctive species, and New Zealand's longest skink (total length > 340 mm). A broad, bold vertical white or yellowish teardrop marking, bordered either side with black, below eye, and spanning upper and lower jaws. **Dorsal surface** red-brown, copper or grey-brown, with distinctive repeated pale cream or golden chevron markings, often edged with black, continuing down intact tail. **Lateral surfaces** golden or grey-brown with pale blotches, and often fine black flecking. Side of head and neck may be more grey. Anterior regions of upper and lower jaws with black and white denticulate markings. **Ventral surface** pale with scattered dark spots especially on the chin and throat. **Eye** colour orange. **Intact tail** slender and long (about 1.5x longer than body). **Subdigital lamellae** 18–23. **Soles of feet** red- or pink-brown.

DISTRIBUTION

Offshore islands – only Great Barrier Island (Aotea Island) and Hauturu/Little Barrier Island. Subfossil evidence indicates a wide historical distribution throughout Northland. A single museum specimen (previously referred to as *O. gracilocorpus*), collected from Hokianga in Northland, now considered to be a mainland *O. homalonotum*.

VARIATION AND SIMILAR SPECIES

Little variation, although chevron patterning may fade to a more uniform pale brown or grey in older adults. Adults unlikely to be confused with other species. Juveniles may be confused with **ornate skink** (*O. ornatum*), but can be distinguished by their much wider and bolder teardrop marking (spans upper and lower jaws), much longer snout, very long tapering tail and more elongate torso.

HABITAT

Coastal, Lowland

Inhabits native forest and dense undergrowth; frequently found in association with stream margins, debris dams and boulders. Also uses clay banks, where it takes refuge in unoccupied kingfisher and spider holes. Susceptible to cutaneous water loss, therefore requires humid and/or moist environments. May venture onto ridges during rainfall events.

NATURAL HISTORY

Diurnal. Terrestrial, with arboreal tendencies: will climb tree ferns and trees, especially during heavy rainfall to escape flooding. Heliothermic, though may be cryptic when sun-basking. Sexual maturity at 3–5 years, and up to 8 young born in mid- to late summer (late February–March). Life expectancy can exceed 20 years. Tail prehensile and may assist in climbing. When disturbed, will flee by diving into streams, and can remain beneath the water surface for several minutes. Frequently vocalises with squeaks and chirps when distressed. Feeds on invertebrates, with spiders forming large part of diet.

ETYMOLOGY

Specific name (Greek) meaning 'smooth back'. **Common name** refers to the distinctive chevron markings on the dorsal surface of the species. **Māori name** is niho taniwha; meaning 'dragon's teeth' or 'teeth of the taniwha'.

Juvenile

Egg-laying skink

Oligosoma suteri (Boulenger, 1906)

Endemic

DESCRIPTION

Up to 126 mm SVL; c. 15.8 g weight (but can be much heavier)

A shoreline species frequently inhabiting the splash zone, and may even dive below the water surface in rock pools to escape danger or to forage. Body dorso-ventrally flattened, and scales typically very glossy. Snout long. Prominent brow above eye, and cheek region may appear swollen when viewed from above. **Dorsal surface** typically brown or grey but sometimes uniformly light cream; some individuals almost entirely black. Dorsal and **lateral surfaces** heavily marked with large irregular-shaped brown, golden or black blotches; never striped. **Ventral surface** grey, pink or orange; occasionally lightly speckled with black. **Eye** colour dark brown or black. **Intact tail** equal to or longer than body length (SVL). **Subdigital lamellae** 17–22. **Soles of feet** pale brown.

DISTRIBUTION

North Island only. Widespread but very fragmented remnant distribution on the mainland from North Cape to Coromandel Peninsula. Also occurs on the Manawatāwhi/Three Kings Islands, and numerous offshore islands off the North Island's east coast.

VARIATION AND SIMILAR SPECIES

Highly variable in colour pattern, from uniform cream to almost uniform black. Juveniles may be mistaken for **shore skink** (*O. smithi*), but distinguished by their more robust body form, glossier scales, and larger eyes with more prominent brows.

HABITAT

Coastal

Occupies splash zone at boulder and shingle beaches, rock talus and rocky platforms. Takes refuge in spaces between boulders, beneath rocks, in crevices and beneath low-growing vegetation and coastal vines. Will enter rock pools, either moving over top of aquatic vegetation or diving below the surface, holding its breath for up to 20 minutes while clutching onto substrate.

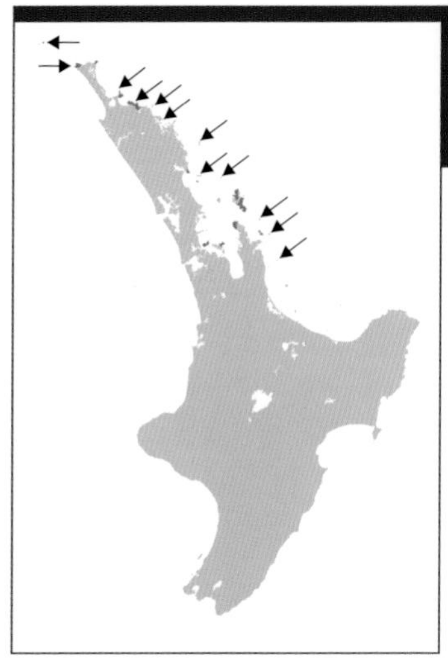

NATURAL HISTORY

Nocturnal; terrestrial. Heliothermic; may sun-bask cryptically from beneath cover or indirectly under warm boulders. Takes cover under rocks and seaweed during the day. Oviparous; the only endemic lizard to lay eggs. Annual reproduction. Mating occurs October–November; gestation period about 2 months within females, and eggs develop over 3 months in nest. Females lay 3–6 small (c. 18.5 x 13.5 mm) white leathery eggs in fine talus or sand beneath boulders or rocks, late January–February; hatching March–April. Sexual maturity at 3 years. Longevity recorded at 12 years. Occurs in high abundance in boulder beach habitats, particularly on offshore islands. Primarily insectivorous but also known to feed on amphipods (small crustaceans), and to scavenge on carrion washed ashore (e.g. fish, seabird or dolphin carcases). Can excrete excess salt from their food via nasal salt glands.

ETYMOLOGY

Specific name (Latinisation) acknowledging Henry Suter (1841–1918), a Swiss-born naturalist and conchologist, renowned for work on New Zealand molluscs. **Common name** recognises the significance of this species as the only endemic New Zealand lizard to lay eggs.

Fiordland skink

Oligosoma acrinasum (Hardy, 1977)

Endemic

JAMES REARDON

DESCRIPTION

Up to 88 mm SVL; 8.5 g weight

A sleek, dark coloured skink from the extremely harsh environment of southern Fiordland. **Dorsal and lateral surfaces** uniform dark glossy brown, frequently with yellow-green or green iridescent flecks (sometimes giving a greenish appearance to body). Green flecks occasionally more sparse along lateral edge, appearing like a broad brown dorsolateral line from ear to hind limb, and sometimes continuing down tail. **Ventral surface** mottled with green-grey, and with or without black speckling. **Eye** colour black. **Intact tail** longer than body length (SVL). **Subdigital lamellae** 16–19. **Soles of feet** black.

DISTRIBUTION

South Island only. Occurs only in southern Fiordland, on several exposed islands between Nancy and Dusky Sounds.

VARIATION AND SIMILAR SPECIES

Little variation. Similar to **Barrier skink** (*O. judgei*), but geographic distributions are not known to overlap. In addition, adult Fiordland skinks are smaller, with a more slender snout, a grey (vs. whitish) ventral surface and finer flecking on body compared to Barrier skink.

HABITAT

Coastal, Lowland

Littoral zone only, living on exposed rocky foreshores, boulder beaches, low-growing littoral vegetation, and where coastal scrub meets shoreline. Shelters in deep horizontal crevices in rocks and deep below boulders.

NATURAL HISTORY

Diurnal; terrestrial, saxicolous. Strongly heliothermic (avid sun-basker). Reproductive biology poorly known, but 2–6 young born in January–March. Occurs at high densities and sun-basks communally, with dozens sharing the most suitable basking sites. May dive into rock pools when disturbed; a strong swimmer and can remain submerged for up to 5 minutes. Known to produce high-pitched squeaks from within crevices or when disturbed. Preys on invertebrates in littoral zone, including small snails.

ETYMOLOGY

Specific name (Latin) meaning 'sharp nose', in reference to the pointed snout. **Common name** refers to the Fiordland region, where this species occurs.

JAMES REARDON

Sinbad skink

Oligosoma pikitanga Bell & Patterson, 2008

Endemic

TRENT BELL

DESCRIPTION

Up to 91 mm SVL; up to 15 g weight

A rare and beautiful green and black glossy skink from the alpine zone in Fiordland. Closest relative is the Barrier skink (*O. judgei*). Slenderly built. **Dorsal surface** glossy black with bright green irregular dorsal blotches extending from head to hind limbs. Black mid-dorsal stripe may be present. Olive-green dorsolateral stripes from behind eye and progressively breaking up around mid-body, then reforming to continue in olive- or golden brown down intact tail. **Lateral surfaces** with a black lateral band from nostril to hind limb, with bold salmon-pink spots, graduating into a pinkish lower lateral surface, heavily blotched with black. **Ventral surface** vivid orange-red, and chin and throat pale grey. **Eye** colour black. **Nasal scales** narrowly separated. **Intact tail** noticeably longer than body length (SVL). **Toes** proportionately long. **Subdigital lamellae** 20–23. **Soles of feet** black.

DISTRIBUTION

South Island only. Known only from the Sinbad Gully (Llawrenny Peaks) in Fiordland – an extremely steep glacially carved valley characterised by near-vertical granite cliffs. May occur elsewhere in Fiordland.

VARIATION AND SIMILAR SPECIES

Unlikely to be confused with any other lizard. Occurs with the **"mahogany skink"** (variant of **cryptic skink** *O. inconspicuum*) and **Cascade gecko** (*Mokopirirakau* "Cascade").

HABITAT

Alpine

Lives in damp alpine cliffs and vertical rock bluffs, in crevices or among clumps of alpine herbs, ferns and tussock grasses. Uses rock crevices as refuges. Climate harsh, with high rainfall, low temperatures, low number of sunshine hours and heavy snowfall; landscape avalanche-prone.

NATURAL HISTORY

Diurnal; terrestrial, saxicolous. Heliothermic, sun-basking close to shelter. Very agile and fast moving, especially after basking. Nothing known of its reproductive biology. Almost certainly viviparous. Feeds on invertebrates.

ETYMOLOGY

Specific name (Māori), meaning 'mountain climber', referring to the saxicolous nature of this species, and its occurrence in the alpine zone. **Common name** refers to the Sinbad Valley in Fiordland, the only known location for this species.

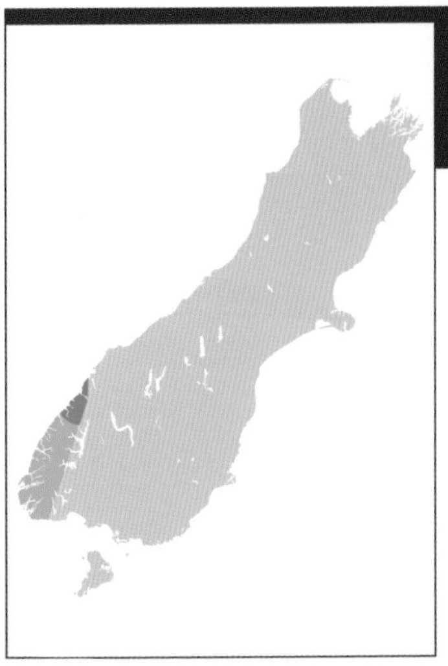

TONY JEWELL

Barrier skink

Oligosoma judgei Patterson & Bell, 2009 **Endemic**

TRENT BELL

DESCRIPTION

Up to 91 mm SVL; up to 15.4 g weight

A truly alpine skink, with stout body proportions, surviving in remarkably harsh conditions. **Dorsal surface** black with bright green, yellow or cream dorsal speckling, and thin golden yellow dorsolateral stripes from nostril over eye, progressively breaking up along body, then reforming and continuing down intact tail. Mid-dorsal stripe absent. Scales on top of head outlined or blotched with yellow or green. **Lateral surfaces** with a broad black lateral band flecked with yellow or green; flecks may join to form short longitudinal striations. Lower lateral surface heavily flecked or blotched with yellow or green. **Ventral surface** (including chin and throat) white or cream and finely flecked with black. **Eye** colour black. **Nasal scales** widely, or moderately widely, separated. **Intact tail** slightly longer than body (SVL). **Subdigital lamellae** 24–25. **Soles of feet** black.

DISTRIBUTION

South Island only. Very limited distribution; known from Barrier Knob and Students Peak in Fiordland, and the Cheviot Faces in the Takitimu Mountains. Currently known distribution may be an artefact of poor survey effort in a largely inaccessible landscape.

VARIATION AND SIMILAR SPECIES

Little variation in colour and pattern observed between populations. Most similar to **grand skink** (*O. grande*), but is smaller, with a relatively smaller ear opening separated from the primary temporal scale by 6 scale rows (vs. 4 scale rows in the grand skink). Also similar to **Sinbad skink** (*O. pikitanga*) but distinguished by its stouter body, finer flecking, more dull (vs. glossy) appearance of scales, lack of orange blotches on flanks, and a white or cream ventral surface with flecking (vs. uniform and flushed with orange). Also, similar to **scree skink** (*O. waimatense*) but distinguished by an absence of transverse bands on dorsal surface.

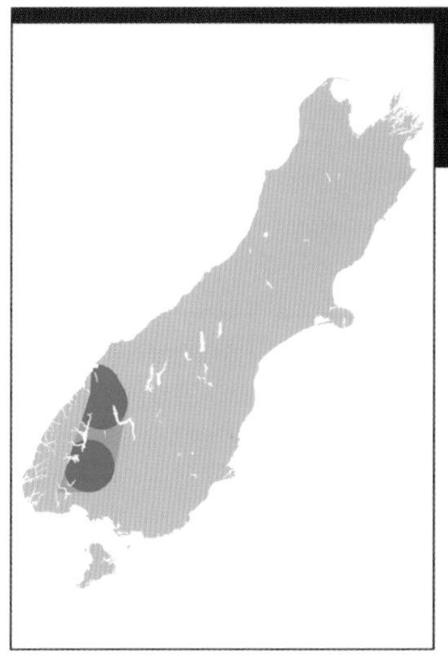

HABITAT

Alpine

Occurs on rocky cliffs (in the Darran Mountains) or scree slopes (in the Takitimu Mountains), and does not appear to be strongly associated with vegetation, although will retreat into snow tussock. Climate is extreme, with very high rainfall, much snowfall in winter, low number of sunshine hours, very low temperatures and strong winds. Rock crevices provide important thermal refuges from the elements.

NATURAL HISTORY

Diurnal; terrestrial, saxicolous. Strongly heliothermic, conspicuous sun-basker. Little known of its reproductive biology although almost certainly viviparous. Females observed to be gravid in February–March, and neonates have been observed in March.

ETYMOLOGY

Specific name (Latinisation) in recognition of Murray and Bronwyn Judge, rock climbers who rediscovered this species after 39 years of obscurity. **Common name** refers to the type locality.

TONY JEWELL

Awakopaka skink

Oligosoma awakopaka Jewell 2017 **Endemic**

TONY JEWELL

DESCRIPTION

60 mm SVL (may grow to 75–95 mm)

A rare alpine species, known only from a single individual. Elongate limbs and digits. **Dorsal surface** chestnut brown and heavily flecked with black or with ocelli (yellow-brown scales with central black spot). Indistinct pale dorsolateral stripe, edged below with black, at least anteriorly over shoulder. **Lateral surfaces** darker brown with complex arrangement of black, brown and pale flecks and spots. **Ventral surface** bright yellow and finely flecked with black. Chin and throat light grey. Underside of tail yellow-brown with heavy black flecking. **Eye** colour black. **Intact tail** slightly longer than body length. **Subdigital lamellae** 18–19. **Soles of feet** black.

DISTRIBUTION

South Island only. Known only from Homer Saddle in Fiordland's Darren Mountains; full extent of range unknown.

VARIATION AND SIMILAR SPECIES

Variation not known. Differentiated from congeners by a combination of scale counts and morphological characters, and genetically very distinct. Similar-looking to **Taumaka skink** (*O. taumakae*) but geographically isolated from it, occupies very different habitat, and distinguished by its more ovoid eye shape and 2 anterior subocular scales (vs. 3).

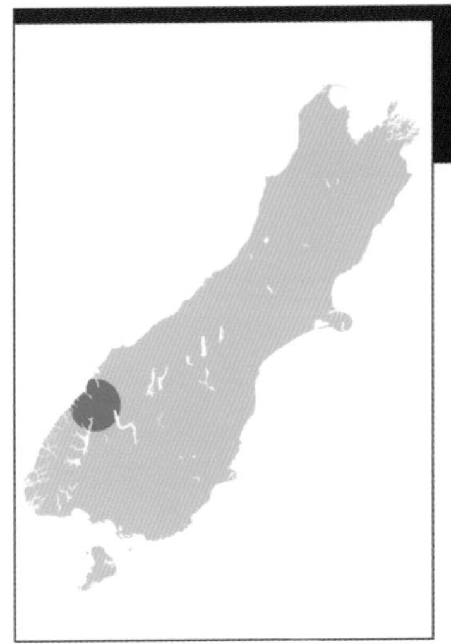

HABITAT

Alpine

Inhabits alpine zone where vegetation comprises grasses, herbs and small shrubs. Takes refuge under rocks and boulders in areas with regular avalanche and rock-fall activity.

NATURAL HISTORY

Presumably diurnal. Terrestrial and potentially saxicolous. Nothing known of its natural history or reproductive biology.

ETYMOLOGY

Specific name and **common name** (Māori) meaning 'glacier'; intended meaning is the 'skink that lives in the footprints of mighty glaciers'.

TONY JEWELL

Otago skink

Oligosoma otagense (McCann, 1955)

Endemic

Western

DESCRIPTION

Up to 130 mm SVL; up to 43.5 g weight

Large, robust and beautifully marked skink from the central Otago Region. One of New Zealand's longest skinks, reaching more than 300 mm in total length. Body and head dorso-ventrally flattened; snout long, pointed and shallow. **Dorsal and lateral surfaces** very dark brown or black with large distinctive pale yellow, grey, gold or greenish blotches that continue down intact tail. Pale blotches may join together on intact tail, making tail almost uniformly pale. Irregular-shaped pale blotches on limbs. A large pale longitudinal blotch on snout, from nostril and over eye. Upper and lower jawlines pale. **Ventral surface** off-white or pale cream, with black flecking or mottling, or large irregular black blotches. **Eye** colour black. **Intact tail** noticeably longer than body length (SVL). **Toes** very long. **Subdigital lamellae** 23–31. **Soles of feet** grey to black.

DISTRIBUTION

South Island only. Occurs in Central Otago, in the Lindis Pass–Lake Hawea (western) and Macraes Flat–Middlemarch (eastern) areas. Previously more widespread throughout Central Otago.

VARIATION AND SIMILAR SPECIES

Genetic variation occurs between the western and eastern populations. Western population with generally smaller pale blotches. Black background colouration of eastern population tends to fade with age, becoming more flecked with yellow or brown; western populations seem to retain black background colour. However, some larger western individuals may look similar to those of eastern populations. Similar in body form to the closely related **scree skink** (*O. waimatense*) but colour patterns differ markedly. Hybrid *O. otagense*–*O. waimatense* individuals occur in north Otago, appearing intermediate in morphology. Unlikely to be confused with other species as colour patterning is unique. Distinguished from **grand skink** (*O. grande*) by the presence of large pale blotches of colour on body (vs. short longitudinal striations).

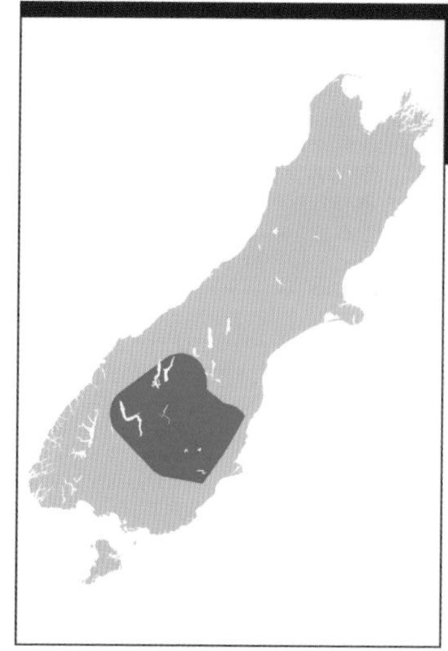

HABITAT

Lowland, Montane/subalpine

Exclusively associated with schist rock outcrops; inhabits rock crevices and fissures, and sun-basks either at crevice entrances or out in the open on rock faces.

NATURAL HISTORY

Diurnal; terrestrial and saxicolous. Strongly heliothermic (avid sun-basker). Annual or biennial reproduction. Reaches sexual maturity at 4–6 years. Mating occurs in about March, followed by sperm storage by the female; gestation period 4–5 months, 1–4 young born in late summer (February–March). Longevity in the wild reported up to 21 years (44 years in captivity). Omnivorous; both a sit-and-wait predator and will actively forage for invertebrates, fleshy fruits (i.e. berries; e.g. *Leucopogon fraseri* and *Coprosma taylorae*), and other lizards. An important seed disperser of divaricating shrubs (e.g. porcupine shrub). Occurs in social groups (2–5 individuals), often seen in male-female pairs, and family groups (including juveniles). Territorial towards other species (e.g. grand skink) inhabiting same rock tors.

ETYMOLOGY

Specific name (Latinisation) and **common name** referring to the Otago Region, where this species occurs.

Western

Taumaka skink

Oligosoma taumakae Chapple & Patterson, 2007 **Endemic**

MARIEKE LETTINK

DESCRIPTION

Up to 96 mm SVL; up to 20 g weight (but usually much less, c. 15 g)

This rare skink is confined to islands off southern Westland, and wēkā (*Gallirallus australis*) introduced to these islands threaten the taxon's survival on the two northernmost islands. **Dorsal surface** brown, grey-brown, or olive-brown with darker brown and black flecking. Narrow pale dorsolateral stripes with notched margins. **Lateral surfaces** with a broad darker brown lateral band with black and white flecks and bordered below by narrow lighter grey stripe with toothed margins. **Ventral surface** pale yellow with dark speckling. **Intact tail** longer than body length (SVL). **Eye** colour dark brown. **Subocular scales (anterior)** 3; **supraciliary scales** 5, forming an 'eyebrow'. **Subdigital lamellae** 21. **Soles of feet** dark brown.

DISTRIBUTION

South Island only. Restricted to Taumaka and Popotai Islands in the Open Bay Islands, as well as the Barn Islands off southern Westland. Full extent of possible geographic range unknown.

VARIATION AND SIMILAR SPECIES

Variation poorly known. Geographically isolated from similar species but morphologically similar to **speckled skink** (*O. infrapuncatum*) complex, from which it can be distinguished by its larger front feet (c. 25% larger) and lower supraciliary count (5 vs. 6–9). Similar to **Awakopaka skink** (*O. awakopaka*) but with 3 subocular scales (vs. 2) and round (vs. ovoid) eye.

HABITAT

Coastal

Inhabits coastal forest, shrubland and

littoral vegetation, including ferns, sedges and tussocks. Also found among creeping vines growing over limestone rock slabs.

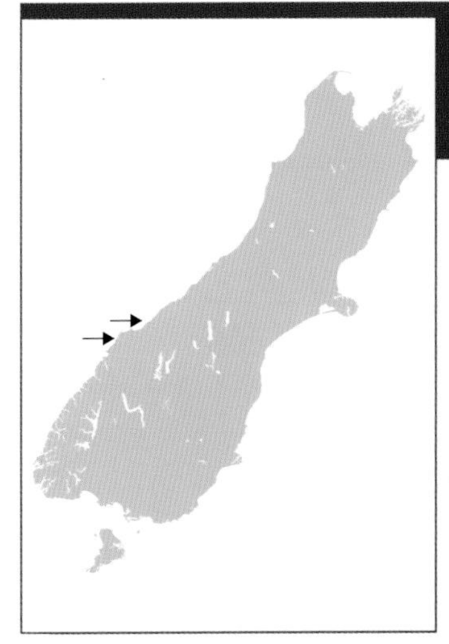

NATURAL HISTORY

Diurnal; terrestrial. Heliothermic, often sun-basking in high densities. Little known about reproductive biology; viviparous, sexual maturity estimated to be c. 4 years. Takes cover quickly when disturbed (e.g. to escape depredation by wēkā). Likely to be primarily insectivorous.

ETYMOLOGY

Specific name (Māori) and **common name** referring to Taumaka Island in the Open Bay Islands, off the South Island's West Coast (the type locality).

MARIEKE LETTINK

Scree skink

Oligosoma waimatense (McCann, 1955)

Endemic

TRENT BELL

DESCRIPTION

Up to 110 mm SVL

Large conspicuous species, related to Otago skink. **Dorsal surface** light or darker grey, brown or creamy yellow, with black transverse markings, streaks or bands that may continue onto lateral surfaces or heavily blotched with irregular-shaped banding. Some individuals with black transverse bands interrupted along dorsolateral margins by indistinct pale dorsolateral stripes. **Lateral surfaces** grey, with upper lateral surfaces blotched, banded or speckled with black, but gradually fading to more uniform grey or lightly flecked lower lateral surfaces. **Ventral surface** uniform grey, or sometimes flushed with pink or orange. Chin and throat grey and may be lightly flecked with black. **Eye** colour black. **Body scales** small (i.e. high number of mid-body scale rows; 50–68 rows) giving a smooth, glossy appearance. **Intact tail** noticeably longer than body length (SVL). **Toes** proportionately long. **Subdigital lamellae** 30–34. **Soles of feet** brown, grey or black.

DISTRIBUTION

South Island only. Inland areas east of the Main Divide, from north Marlborough through Canterbury to northern Otago.

VARIATION

Variable in colour patterning within and between populations across range. Easily distinguished from all other species by a combination of large size, colour patterning and high mid-body scale count (50–68 rows). Distinguished from closely related **Otago skink** (*O. otagense*) by the less heavily built body and markedly different colour pattern (i.e. in *O. waimatense* the paler colour patches on dorsal and lateral surfaces are broken into smaller clusters, and ventral surface uniform (vs. blotched or mottled) and often flushed with pink or orange (vs. never flushed with pink or orange)). Hybrid *O. waimatense–O. otagense* individuals occur in north Otago, appearing intermediate in morphology.

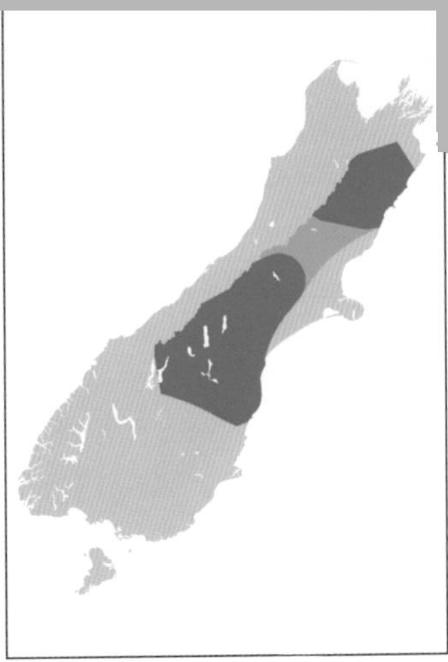

HABITAT

Lowland, Montane/subalpine, Alpine

Generally inhabits dry rocky areas, including greywacke and limestone screes, talus slopes, rock outcrops and bluffs, boulder river terraces and banks, montane tussock grassland and shrubland.

NATURAL HISTORY

Diurnal; terrestrial and saxicolous. Strongly heliothermic, readily sun-basking in the open. Little known about reproductive biology but may breed annually or biennially. Diet includes invertebrates (e.g. spiders, centipedes, millipedes, insects, crustaceans), fruits of low-growing shrubs (e.g. *Coprosma propinqua*, porcupine shrub and creeping pōhuehue *Muehlenbeckia axillaris*), and may prey on other reptiles.

ETYMOLOGY

Specific name (Latinisation) referring to the Waimate area, where the type specimen was collected. **Common name** is a reference to the scree habitats often inhabited by this species.

Canterbury

Grand skink

Oligosoma grande (Gray, 1845)

Endemic

Eastern

DESCRIPTION

Up to 115 mm SVL; up to 30 g weight

A large and handsome skink from Otago. **Dorsal surface** black and heavily flecked with fine cream, yellow, gold, green or grey markings. Sometimes with thin pale dorsolateral stripe. **Lateral surfaces** black with pale flecking becoming heavier towards ventral surface. **Ventral surface** uniform cream or with sparse black flecking. Chin and throat faintly speckled with black. **Eye** colour brown or cream. **Intact tail** tapering and long (much longer than body length/SVL). **Toes** particularly long. **Subdigital lamellae** 25–28. **Soles of feet** black.

DISTRIBUTION

South Island only. Occurs only in the Otago Region, around Lindis Pass and Lake Hawea (western populations) and Macraes Flat and Middlemarch (eastern populations).

VARIATION AND SIMILAR SPECIES

Two variants recognised, as populations in west and east parts of range (although it probably formerly occupied a much larger area around and between these surviving populations).

1. ***Western population***: Individuals slightly smaller (90–105 mm SVL). Dorsal surface generally with thin yellow or golden longitudinal stripes; a black upper lateral band; and tail more uniform or without patterning.
2. ***Eastern population***: Individuals larger (95–115 mm SVL). Dorsal surface with short longitudinal streaks; dorsolateral stripes, where present, broken, fragmented or indistinct; a black upper lateral band; lower lateral surface with black flecking; tail markings bold and similar to those present on rest of body.

Unlikely to be confused with any other skinks within its current natural range. Similar to **scree skink** (*O. waimatense*), but differentiated by its predominately black dorsal surface with yellow flecks, stripes and streaks (vs. grey or pale brown dorsal surface with transverse black markings or bands). **Barrier skink** (*O. judgei*) has similar colour patterning (short longitudinal rows of fine yellowish spots on a dark background) but is smaller, with a relatively smaller ear opening that is separated from the primary temporal scale by 6 scale rows (vs. separated by 4 scale rows).

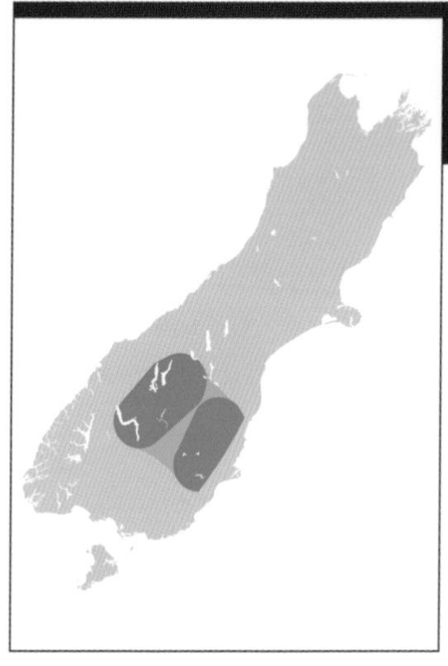

HABITAT

Lowland, Montane/subalpine, Alpine

Strongly associated with schist rock outcrops, particularly those surrounded by tussock grassland or native scrub. Inhabits rock crevices and fissures and may use tussock grassland or shelter beneath loose rocks among tussock.

NATURAL HISTORY

Diurnal; terrestrial and saxicolous. Strongly heliothermic, sun-basking either at crevice entrances or in the open on rock faces. Annual reproduction. Sexual maturity at 3–5 years; mating occurs in late summer (February–March), possibly into early autumn, followed by sperm storage until ovulation occurs in spring. Gestation period 4–5 months; 2–4 young born in late summer (February–March). Longevity recorded at 23 years (up to 30 years in captivity). Young may sun-bask close to or in contact with (e.g. on top of) the mother. Diet consists of invertebrates, fleshy fruits (e.g. berries), flowers (*Hieracium* species) and other lizards. An important seed disperser of low-growing shrubs (e.g. creeping pōhuehue, bush snowberry (*Gaultheria antipoda*)).

ETYMOLOGY

Specific name (Latin) meaning 'large'. **Common name** also refers to the large size of this skink (i.e. total length up to 240 mm).

Western

Burgan skink

Oligosoma burganae Chapple et al., 2011

Endemic

TONY JEWELL

DESCRIPTION

Up to 70 mm SVL

A small rare skink restricted to inland Otago. Has suffered significant population declines since the mid-1980s. **Dorsal surface** dark brown, with olive overtones (occasionally black) and irregular light or golden flecks. Dark mid-dorsal stripe (complete or broken), often with olive and dark brown flecks either side. Pale yellow or cream dorsolateral stripes extending from behind eye to partially down intact tail. **Lateral surfaces** with a wide dark brown lateral band with notched edges above and below, and often flecked with small pale markings; grey-yellow mid-lateral stripe immediately below, passing beneath eye through ear and over limbs, terminating along tail. **Ventral surface** grey or murky yellow, and often speckled with small black spots. Chin and throat grey with black flecks. **Eye** colour dark brown, almost black. **Intact tail** equal to or slightly longer than body length (SVL). **Subdigital lamellae** 18–23. **Soles of feet** dark brown or black.

DISTRIBUTION

South Island only. Known only from inland Otago, in the Rock and Pillar and Lammermoor Ranges, but could also occur in other locations in eastern and Central Otago.

VARIATION AND SIMILAR SPECIES

Differentiated from closely related and similar-looking species by having: 3, sometimes 4, supraocular scales (vs. always 4 in most other species); much blunter snout (vs. **Nevis skink** (*O. toka*) and **Eyres skink** (*O. repens*)); and a higher subdigital lamellae count (18–23 vs. 16 in **Te Kakahu skink** (*O. tekakahu*)). May also be confused with the sympatric **southern grass skink** (*O.* aff. *polychroma* Clade 5) and **McCann's skink** (*O. maccanni*), but differentiated by its grey or yellow ventral surface, and no pale stripe on upper surfaces of forelimb (vs. stripe usually present in those taxa). Neonate and juvenile Burgan skinks with an unmarked dorsal surface, and uniform light brown colouration between the cream dorsolateral stripes, similar to southern grass skinks. McCann's skink from eastern Otago has a more strongly chequered dorsal pattern; McCann's skink, throughout its range, has a more greyish basal colour (vs. glossy brown in the Burgan skink).

HABITAT

Montane/subalpine, Alpine

High-altitude montane or alpine habitats only, with an apparent strong affiliation with low-growing dense herbfields, montane grassland and shrubs (*Coprosma* species, snowberry (*Gaultheria depressa*) and *Olearia* species), rather than open tussock grasslands and rocky environments. Typically associated with damper gully systems in montane and alpine zones.

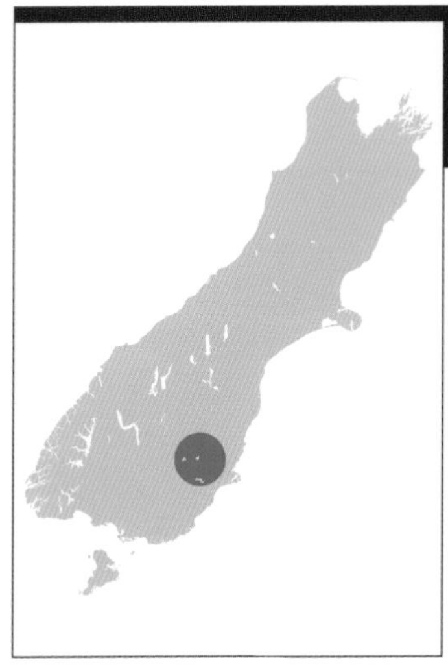

NATURAL HISTORY

Diurnal; terrestrial. Heliothermic and actively sun-basks. Females sexually mature at 49 mm SVL; up to 6 young born late January–early February. May use subterranean invertebrate (e.g. worm, spider, wētā) burrows as refuge sites to escape both predators and extreme low temperatures. Feeds on invertebrates (e.g. spiders) and berries (e.g. snowberry).

ETYMOLOGY

Specific name (Latinisation) and **common name** referring to the Burgan Stream, the type locality for the species.

Eyres skink

Oligosoma repens Chapple et al., 2011 **Endemic**

TRENT BELL

DESCRIPTION

Up to 62 mm SVL

More slender in build than its closest relatives (e.g. *O. inconspicuum*). **Dorsal surface** yellow-brown with a distinctive dark brown mid-dorsal stripe extending from behind head to base of tail, where it breaks up. Narrow pale yellow dorsolateral stripes, edged in black. **Lateral surfaces** have a broader brown lateral band, extending from behind eye to hind leg. Edged below by another narrow black-edged cream-yellow stripe. **Ventral surface** yellow, and chin and throat white-grey, often with black speckles. **Eye** colour tan or light brown. **Intact tail** longer than body length (SVL). **Toes** long and slender. **Subdigital lamellae** 19–23. **Soles of feet** dark brown to black.

DISTRIBUTION

South Island only. True extent of distribution unknown. Currently known from the Eyre, Thompson and Hector Mountains of western Otago, Borland Saddle (Fiordland), and Takahe Valley in the Murchison Mountains; likely to be more widespread in Fiordland.

VARIATION AND SIMILAR SPECIES

Little variation across its range. May be confused with **McCann's skink** (*O. maccanni*), but distinguished by its warm-brown glossy dorsal surface (vs. duller, greyer basal colouration), and yellow ventral colour (vs. pale grey). Can be distinguished from McCann's skink, **cryptic skink** (*O. inconspicuum*), and **southern skink** (*O. notosaurus*) by its 3 supraocular scales (vs. 4 in the other species). Differs from **southern grass skink** (*O.* aff. *polychroma* Clade 5), which has similar colour patterning, by its brighter yellow ventral surface (vs. dull yellow buff). Has more subdigital lamellae than **Te Kakahu**

skink (*O. tekakahu*) (i.e. 19–23 vs. 16). Top of head usually unmarked, unlike in **Nevis skink** (*O. toka*) and **southern skink** (*O. notosaurus*). More slender than closely related taxa. Distinguished from **Burgan skink** (*O. burganae*) by its longer shallower head.

HABITAT

Montane/subalpine, Alpine
Lives amongst eroding schist and greywacke rock piles and screes in mountain foothills and valley flats, as well as low-growing shrubs on alpine ridges.

NATURAL HISTORY

Diurnal. Terrestrial, often saxicolous. Heliothermic. Little known of its ecology and reproductive biology (viviparous). Sympatric with several other local skink and gecko species. Curls its tail above body when threatened (e.g. by predator), placing the most disposable body part between its torso and predator. Insectivorous.

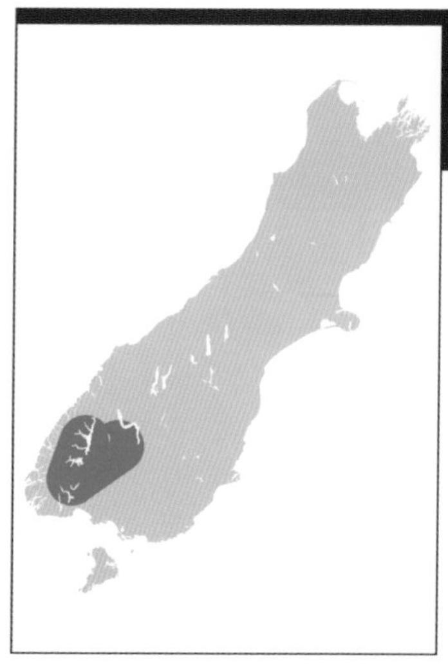

ETYMOLOGY

Specific name (Latin) meaning 'unexpected', referring to the unexpected discovery of this species in the Eyre Mountains. **Common name** refers to the Eyre Mountains where this species was first discovered.

JAMES REARDON

Nevis skink

Oligosoma toka Chapple et al., 2011

Endemic

TRENT BELL

DESCRIPTION

Up to 71 mm SVL

A poorly known, rock-dwelling species from the Otago Region. **Dorsal surface** black to varying shades of brown, often with pale or dull flecks either side of midline. Black flecks may continue down dorsal surface of tail. Top of head with or without black markings and flecks. Distinct dark mid-dorsal stripe with smooth edges extending from behind head to base of tail, bordered on either side by a thin pale grey-yellow stripe. Prominent pale cream or yellowish dorsolateral stripe running from snout over eye and continuing to tail base, or partially down tail. **Lateral surfaces** with a wide brown smooth-edged lateral band bordered above and below by a thin black line; lower black line may have white-yellow flecks. A second prominent pale yellow or whitish stripe below lateral band, running from below eye, through ear to hind limb. **Ventral surface** yellow and usually with light speckling. Chin and throat white with black speckling. **Eye** colour cream or pale brown. **Supraocular scales** 3. **Intact tail** longer than body length (SVL). **Subdigital lamellae** 17–23. **Soles of feet** cream or brown.

DISTRIBUTION

South Island only. Occurs in the Nevis Valley in Central Otago, between the Hector Mountains and the Old Woman Range, and in the area around Lindis Pass.

VARIATION AND SIMILAR SPECIES

Variation poorly known. A single individual with unusual colour pattern (i.e. poorly defined pale dorsolateral stripes and heavily flecked with white over dorsal and lateral surfaces) has been reported from Carrick Station (Central Otago).

May be confused with **McCann's skink** (*O. maccanni*), but distinguished by its glossy warm-brown dorsal surface (vs. duller surface and greyer colouration in McCann's skink) and yellow ventral colour (vs. pale grey). Also has 3 supraocular scales (vs. 4 in McCann's skink, **cryptic skink** (*O. inconspicuum*), and **southern skink** (*O. notosaurus*)). Distinguished from **southern grass skink** (*O.* aff. *polychroma* Clade 5), which can have similar colour markings, by absence of pale stripe on forelimb (vs. usually present) and a bright yellow ventral surface (vs. dull yellow-buff). Has more subdigital lamellae than **Te Kakahu skink** (*O. tekakahu*) (17–23 vs. 16). Dark head markings, mid-dorsal stripe and dorsolateral stripes distinguish Nevis skink from **Eyres skink** (*O. repens*). Distinguished from **Burgan skink** (*O. burganae*) by its longer shallower head.

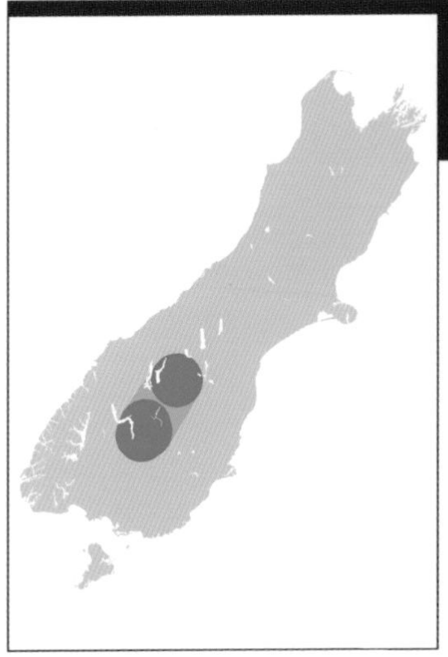

HABITAT

Lowland, Montane/subalpine, Alpine

Strongly associated with rock piles (both natural and human-made, e.g. gold mine tailings), river terraces, stone walls, screes and terrace edge tumbles that are generally associated with tussockland, grassland, and low-growing shrubs (e.g. *Coprosma*, *Melicytus* and *Muehlenbeckia* species).

NATURAL HISTORY

Diurnal; terrestrial and saxicolous. Strongly heliothermic (avid sun-basker). Nothing known about reproductive biology; little known of its ecology. Curls its tail above body when threatened (e.g. by predator), placing the most disposable body part between its torso and predator. Feeds on small invertebrates and may consume fruits (e.g. berries).

ETYMOLOGY

Specific name (Māori) meaning 'rock' or 'boulder', referring to the rocky habitats this species occupies across its range. **Common name** refers to the Nevis Valley, where this species occurs.

TRENT BELL

Okuru skink

Oligosoma "Okuru"

Endemic

TONY WHITAKER

DESCRIPTION

65 mm SVL

A very poorly known species, known from a single individual. Distinguished by unique combination of 3 **supraocular scales**, strongly keeled scales on tail, absence of markings on front limbs, and presence of lobules in ear. **Dorsal surface** brown with sparse black spots, and indistinct darker brown mid-dorsal stripe. Narrow pale cream dorsolateral stripes. **Lateral surfaces** have a broad chocolate-brown upper lateral stripe running from nostril down body and to tip of tail; stripe edged above and below with black. Narrow white notched mid-lateral line extending from below eye through ear opening to hind limb. **Ventral surface** bronze, continuing down tail; tinged with pale yellow at edge of throat. Chin and throat white. **Subdigital lamellae** unknown. **Soles of feet** grey or yellow, with black toes.

DISTRIBUTION

South Island only. Known from a single location near Okuru, south of Haast, in south Westland.

VARIATION OR SIMILAR SPECIES

Variation unknown. Most similar to the **small-eared skink** (*O. stenotis*), but geographically separated (i.e. south Westland vs. Stewart Island/Rakiura); lacks greenish colour tone; and occurs in lowland rather than alpine habitats. Resembles the **cryptic skink** (*O. inconspicuum*) but differentiated by the same characters described above.

HABITAT

Lowland

Only known specimen was collected in pākihi (i.e. sphagnum) swamp habitat by a moss picker.

NATURAL HISTORY

Nothing known of its ecology or reproductive biology.

ETYMOLOGY

Common name and **tag name** referring to the collection location of the only known specimen.

TONY WHITAKER

Te Kakahu skink

Oligosoma tekakahu Chapple et al., 2011

Endemic

JAMES REARDON

DESCRIPTION

Up to 79 mm SVL; up to 10 g weight

A small, robustly built and glossy skink from Te Kakahu/Chalky Island in Fiordland. **Dorsal surface** pale, chestnut or olive-brown, occasionally darker brown, with irregular black flecks. Black flecks may be present on top of head. Dorsolateral stripe running from behind eye to base of tail, of a single row of scales; each scale divided longitudinally, with upper half yellow or cream and lower half black giving the appearance of black triangular markings. **Lateral surfaces** with a broad brown lateral band edged below by broken narrower white stripe, or frequently with white and black flecks and irregular markings. **Ventral surface** generally bright uniform yellow. Chin grey. **Eye** colour brown to black. Small **ear opening**. **Intact tail** approximately equal to or slightly longer than body length (SVL). **Subdigital lamellae** 16–17. **Soles of feet** dark brown, sometimes with a yellow flush.

DISTRIBUTION

South Island only. Naturally restricted to Chalky Island in Fiordland, but a translocated population present on Anchor Island.

VARIATION AND SIMILAR SPECIES

Variable shades of brown colouration. Geographically isolated from similar species, but can be distinguished from **McCann's skink** (*O. maccanni*) by its glossy warm-brown dorsal surface (vs. duller, greyer base colour), and fewer subdigital lamellae (16 vs. 19–28 in McCann's skink). Differs from **southern grass skink** (*O.* aff. *polychroma* Clade 5) by the absence of a pale stripe on forelimb and lack of a mid-dorsal stripe. Low number of subdigital lamellae (16) also differentiates this species from other closely related taxa.

HABITAT

Coastal

Occurs in open coastal herbfield and prostrate shrubs growing on chalk chip strata at one location on Chalky Island. Associated with windswept grasses, coastal vegetation and shrubs (*Olearia*, *Coprosma* and *Carex* species, and other complex prostrate plants).

NATURAL HISTORY

Diurnal; terrestrial. Heliothermic. Little known about its reproductive biology; females become sexually mature at c. 60 mm SVL, and are gravid January–March. Viviparous; parturition likely from late January. Exists in high densities, and frequently sun-basks on chalk flakes. Nothing known of diet; presumably feeds on small invertebrates.

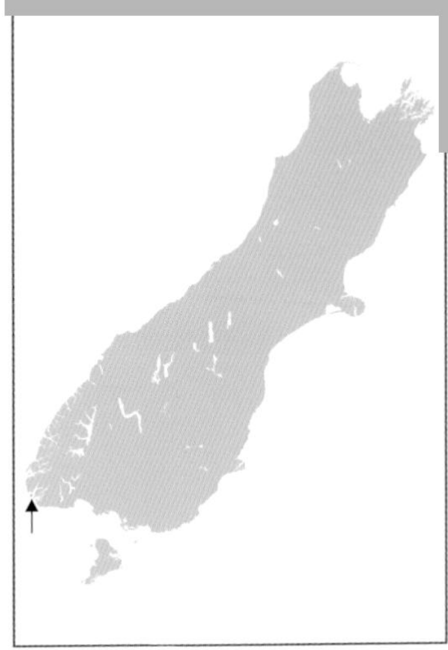

ETYMOLOGY

Specific name (Māori) and **common name** referring to Te Kakahu/Chalky Island, the type locality of this species.

JAMES REARDON

Cryptic skink

Oligosoma inconspicuum (Patterson & Daugherty, 1990)

Endemic

TRENT BELL

DESCRIPTION

Up to 75 mm SVL; c. 6 g weight

A relatively common species found in southern regions of the South Island. **Dorsal surface** red- or chestnut-brown, or very dark brown, with or without a dark mid-dorsal stripe. If present, stripe may be continuous or broken along tail. Top of head may be flecked with black or uniformly brown. **Lateral surfaces** with broad brown lateral band, bordered above and below by pale narrower stripes with notched edges. Lower surface more grey-brown, with dark flecks. **Ventral surface** grey-brown or bronze to vivid yellow, often without dark flecking. Chin and throat grey or occasionally yellowish, and usually heavily flecked with black. **Eye** colour brown, olive or with a bluish tinge. **Intact tail** equal to or longer than body length (SVL). **Subdigital lamellae** 17–23. **Soles of feet** black or brown.

DISTRIBUTION

South Island only. Occurs in south Westland, northern Fiordland, Otago and Southland, including small islands in northern Foveaux Strait.

VARIATION AND SIMILAR SPECIES

Somewhat variable, with three other noticeably distinct variants:

1. ***"Big Bay skink"***: (up to 74 mm SVL). From Big Bay and nearby areas on southern West Coast. Dorsal surface very dark, copper-brown; chin and throat distinctive uniform grey; and ventral surface coppery brown or golden bronze.
2. ***"Mahogany skink"***: (up to 65 mm SVL). A distinctive taxon according to some herpetologists. Occurs in alpine Fiordland. A uniform deep mahogany brown. Occasionally with a discernible mid-dorsal stripe or dark flecking on head, and a broad brown upper lateral band edged above and below by narrow lighter brown stripes. Ventral surface yellow, usually heavily flecked with black, and chin and throat very dark brown or black. Has noticeably longer toes than those from lower altitudes. Soles of feet black.
3. ***"Oteake skink"***: (c. 65 mm SVL). A distinctive taxon according to some herpetologists. Confined to alpine

zone in north-east Otago; lives among creviced rock bluffs and deep boulder piles that are overgrown with prostrate herbaceous vegetation. Robust, with a long tail; has more pronounced black spotting on edge of throat, and more intense black dorsal flecking (such that each scale has a solid black perimeter with a brown patch in middle). 'Flighty' and rapidly flees and takes refuge when disturbed or approached. Soles of feet black.

Has been confused taxonomically with **Eyres skink** (*O. repens*), **Nevis skink** (*O. toka*) and **Burgan skink** (*O. burganae*), but these usually (Burgan skink), or always (Eyres and Nevis skinks) have 3 supra-ocular scales (cryptic skink always with 4 scales). Distinguished from the **Te Kakahu skink** (*O. tekakahu*) by its greater number of subdigital lamellae (17–23 vs. 16). Can be distinguished from the sympatric **McCann's skink** (*O. maccanni*) by its much more glossy brown (vs. greyish) dorsal colouring, and grey-brown or yellow ventral surface (vs. pale grey). Distinguished from sympatric **southern grass skink** (*O. polychroma* Clade 5) by its colour patterning (i.e. less pronounced longitudinal striping), and absence of pale stripe on forelimb (vs. almost always present in southern grass skink).

HABITAT

Montane/subalpine, Alpine

Occupies tussock grasslands, scrublands, herbfields, sand dunes, wetlands and rocky areas such as cobble beaches, boulder fields, screes and vertical rock walls. Favours damp gully systems. Sun-basks

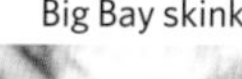

Big Bay skink

TONY WHITAKER

and forages among rock piles and dense low-growing vegetation.

NATURAL HISTORY

Diurnal. Terrestrial, or partially arboreal (e.g. climbs low-growing shrubs). Reproduction poorly known; females produce 1–3 young annually in summer (January–March). Feeds on invertebrates (e.g. spiders, millipedes, centipedes, insects, crustaceans, worms, molluscs and flatworms), and may also consume berries and prey on other reptiles.

ETYMOLOGY

Specific name (Latin) meaning 'not readily visible'. **Common name** refers to both its cryptic behaviour and the difficulty in distinguishing this species from other sympatric skinks.

Oteake skink

CAREY KNOX

Alpine shrubland, Stewart Island, habitat of the southern skink

Southern skink

Oligosoma notosaurus (Patterson & Daugherty, 1990) **Endemic**

DESCRIPTION

Up to 90 mm SVL

A very common species on Stewart Island/ Rakiura and its outlying islands, and readily seen in a variety of habitats. **Dorsal surface** dark walnut or lighter chestnut brown, with or without complete or broken darker mid-dorsal stripe that does not continue down tail. Lighter yellow, or golden flecks often present either side of midline. Pale dorsolateral stripe with irregular or notched edges. **Lateral surfaces** have a broad dark chocolate lateral band, edged below with a fine black line (often with white flecks along toothed margins), running from tip of snout through eye and to past base of tail. A thin lighter stripe immediately below lateral band. **Ventral surface** (including chin and throat) grey brown to yellow, uniform or flecked with black, particularly on throat. **Eye** colour olive or brown. **Intact tail** longer than body length (SVL). **Subdigital lamellae** 17–24. **Soles of feet** brown or black, sometimes with yellow.

DISTRIBUTION

Stewart Island archipelago only. Confined to Stewart Island and outlying islands (e.g. Codfish Island/Whenuahou, Kundy Island).

VARIATION AND SIMILAR SPECIES

Little variation but may vary in tone of brown colouration. Difficult to distinguish from closely related species. For example, closely resembles **cryptic skink** (*O. inconspicuum*), but a combination of distribution, presence of throat speckling, ventral colouration, and absence of mid-dorsal stripe down tail differentiate this species. Distinguished from **small-eared skink** (*O. stenotis*) by its fewer mid-body scale rows (26–29 [usually 26] vs. 26–30 [usually 28] in the small-eared skink), and presence of notched (vs. smooth-edge) dorsolateral and lateral stripes.

HABITAT

Montane/subalpine

Inhabits a broad range of habitat types from coastal sand dunes to alpine herbfields and exposed rock, and takes cover beneath granite rock slabs.

NATURAL HISTORY

Diurnal. Terrestrial, but may climb into low shrubs to sun-bask or forage. Heliothermic. Up to 4 young born in February–March. Can be very abundant and quite conspicuous. Feeds on small invertebrates (e.g. *Hemiandrus* ground wētā, other insects, amphipods), and may consume the small fruits (e.g. berries) of subalpine plants.

ETYMOLOGY

Specific name (Greek) meaning 'southern lizard'. **Common name** a reference to the species' extreme southern distribution.

McCann's skink

Oligosoma maccanni (Patterson & Daugherty, 1990) **Endemic**

Otago

DESCRIPTION

Up to 73 mm SVL

A very common, predominantly dryland inhabitant of the South Island. Highly variable in colour patterning and sometimes difficult to distinguish from other local taxa. **Dorsal surface** light brown or grey-brown, with longitudinal stripes and/or chequered patterning. Stripes smooth or notched. Mid-dorsal stripe, when present, may be broken, notched or wavy on tail. **Lateral surfaces** with a broad dark brown band, bordered above by a thin pale dorsolateral stripe, and below by a thin pale greyish mid-lateral stripe, both smooth edged or notched. Brown lateral band may have pale flecks or smudges interiorly. **Ventral surface** white-grey to muddy yellow, either uniform or with fine black speckling. Chin and throat white-grey, with fine black speckling. **Eye** colour cream to dark brown. **Intact tail** equal to or slightly longer than body length (SVL). **Subdigital lamellae** 19–28. **Soles of feet** white or cream.

DISTRIBUTION

South Island only. Occurs east of the Main Divide, ranging widely from Canterbury to Southland.

VARIATION AND SIMILAR SPECIES

Seven distinct genetic clades recognised, with large variation in colour and patterning across the range. Rare melanotic (uniform very dark grey-black) variants occur in Otago. May be confused with **grass skinks** but distinguished by a more grey or grey-brown basal colour (vs. 'warm' brown) on dorsal surface; mid-dorsal stripe (where present) broken, notched or wavy on tail (vs. continuous and smooth-edged down tail); chin and throat lighter white-grey (vs. grey-brown); and cream-coloured soles of feet (vs. brown or black). Potentially confused with **Nevis skink** (*O. toka*), **Eyres skink** (*O. repens*) and **cryptic skink** (*O. inconspicuum*) but differs by having a white-grey or muddy yellow belly (vs. bright, vivid yellow belly) and greyer overall tone.

HABITAT

Coastal, Lowland, Montane/subalpine

Inhabits open habitats, usually occupying dry rocky environments, using rock outcrops and frequently taking refuge beneath rocks. Especially abundant in montane grassland, and is found among herbs and shrubs.

NATURAL HISTORY

Diurnal; terrestrial. Strongly heliothermic (avid sun-basker). Annual reproduction, with mating occurring in late summer and autumn (March–May), gestation lasting 2.5–5 months, and 2–6 young, c. 25 mm SVL, born December–late February. Reaches sexual maturity in 2–3 years. Longevity reported at 8 years in the wild. Diet includes invertebrates (e.g. spiders, centipedes, millipedes, insects, crustaceans, worms, molluscs, and flatworms), small berries and other smaller lizards.

ETYMOLOGY

Specific name and **common name** referring to Charles McCann (1899–1980), a former vertebrate zoologist at the Dominion Museum (Wellington) and author of the first major modern revision of the New Zealand lizards.

Canterbury

Small-eared skink

Oligosoma stenotis (Patterson & Daugherty, 1994) **Endemic**

TONY WHITAKER

DESCRIPTION

Up to 75 mm SVL; up to 6 g weight

A distinctive and poorly known, brightly coloured species from Stewart Island/ Rakiura. Snout relatively short and angular. **Dorsal surface** yellow-brown to greenish brown with a distinctive black mid-dorsal stripe extending from behind head to base of tail, sometimes edged with yellow; stripe broken, indistinct or absent on tail. Pale cream or yellowish smooth-edged dorsolateral stripes from nostril to tail base, becoming indistinct thereafter. Dorsal scales on intact tail form longitudinal ridges either side of midline, beginning at hind limb and continuing to tail tip. **Lateral surfaces** have a broad brown lateral band, bordered below with a relatively smooth-edged or notched pale or yellowish mid-lateral stripe. **Ventral surface** (including chin and throat) uniform grey-brown, yellow-green or yellow, occasionally with sparse dark flecks. **Eye** colour green or pale blue. **Ear opening** minute (< 0.9 mm wide). **Intact tail** equal to or longer than body length (SVL). **Tail scales** keeled. **Subdigital lamellae** 15–21. **Soles of feet** black.

DISTRIBUTION

Stewart Island only; confined to open subalpine areas above the treeline.

VARIATION AND SIMILAR SPECIES

Little variation in colour patterning. May be confused with the syntopic **southern skink** (*O. notosaurus*) but differentiated by its straight-edged longitudinal stripes, green or yellowish colour tone, tiny ear opening, and presence of keeled scales on dorsal surface of intact tail. Distinguished from **southern grass skink** (*O.* aff. *polychroma* Clade 5) by black mid-dorsal stripe; small ear opening; and keeled scales on dorsal surface of intact tail.

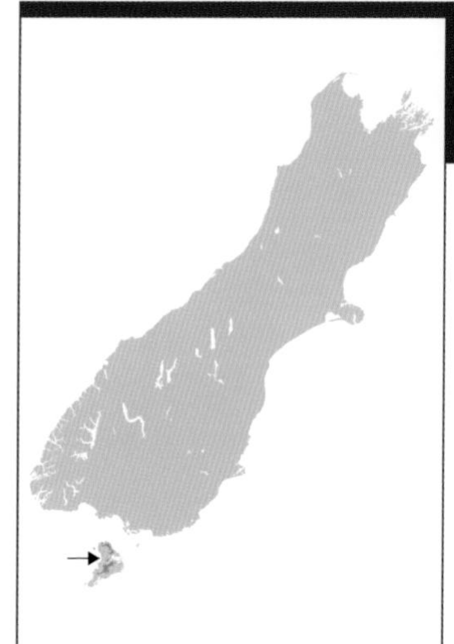

HABITAT

Montane/subalpine, Alpine

Occurs above treeline in subalpine zone, where it is frequently associated with rocks, granite boulders, tussock grassland and low-growing herbs and shrubs.

NATURAL HISTORY

Diurnal; terrestrial. Very little known about its natural history and reproductive biology. Births of 2 young have been reported in November (captive specimen), neonates measuring 26 mm SVL and 0.2 g in weight. Primarily insectivorous, but likely to also consume small berries from alpine shrubs.

ETYMOLOGY

Specific name (Greek) meaning 'narrow ear', and **common name** referring to the very small ear opening, scarcely larger than a pinhead in some individuals.

Green skink (Southland green skink)

Oligosoma chloronoton (Hardy, 1977) **Endemic**

DESCRIPTION

Up to 125 mm SVL; up to 23.3 g weight

Head shallowly convex when viewed laterally, and snout relatively blunt. **Dorsal surface** pink- or copper-brown, to green (green can be strikingly iridescent, especially on top of head), with numerous black and light green ocelli running from behind head to tip of intact tail. Indistinct thin golden dorsolateral stripes with notched edges. **Lateral surfaces** with a broad dark (almost black) lateral band, with relatively indistinct margins, and usually heavily flecked with gold, brown and white. Lower lateral surface mottled, flecked or speckled with black, golden brown and white. Occasionally dark lateral band partially bordered below by a pale mid-lateral stripe. **Ventral surface** (including chin and throat) light to dark grey, often with pinkish hue, and either uniform or flecked with black. Juvenile colouration similar to adults, but sometimes very dark laterally and ventrally. **Eye** colour very dark brown. **Intact tail** slightly longer than body length (SVL). **Subdigital lamellae** c. 16–24 (usually ≤ 22). **Soles of feet** coppery brown to black.

DISTRIBUTION

South Island only. From Te Anau to Southland, including the Catlins, Hokonui Hills, Takitimu Mountains, Awarua wetlands, Tiwai Point and some islands in Foveaux Strait (e.g. Ruapuke Island).

VARIATION AND SIMILAR SPECIES

Little variation in colour patterning. Distinguished from **Otago green skink** (*O.* aff. *chloronoton* "Eastern Otago") and **lakes skink** (*O.* aff. *chloronoton* "West Otago") by its much shorter, blunter snout and stouter body; and from **Stewart Island green skink** (*O.* aff. *chloronoton* "Stewart Island") by its smaller size, and numerous ocelli (vs. usually absent in the Stewart

Island green skink). Distinguished from all members of ***O. lineoocellatum* species complex** by 3 anterior subocular scales of similar size (vs. 2 anterior subocular scales, or 3 where third is much smaller than first two).

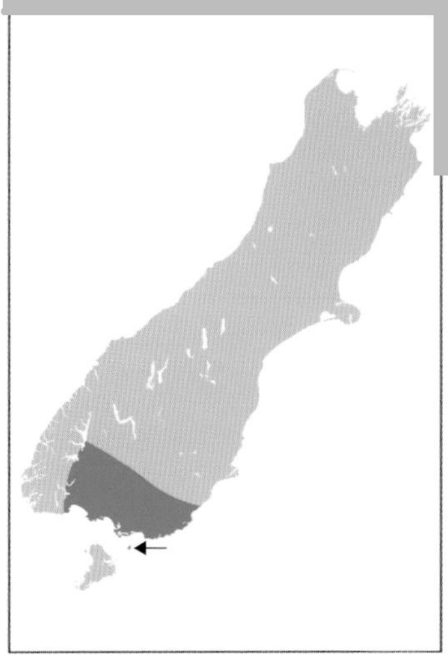

HABITAT

Coastal, Lowland, Montane/subalpine, Alpine Occupies scrubland, herbfields, tussock grassland, flaxland and wetlands; favours dense vegetation and rock piles.

NATURAL HISTORY

Diurnal; terrestrial. Heliothermic and actively sun-basks, but seldom strays far from cover. Annual reproduction, 1–4 young produced late summer (February–March). Primarily insectivorous but will consume fruit (berries).

ETYMOLOGY

Specific name (Greek), meaning 'green-backed'. **Common name** referring to the green colouration on the dorsal surface.

Lakes skink

Oligosoma aff. *chloronoton* "West Otago"

Endemic

DESCRIPTION

Up to 110 mm SVL

Snout long and slender, and head dorso-ventrally flattened. **Dorsal surface** brown to iridescent green, commonly light grey-green, and sparsely flecked with black, green or gold ocelli. Prominent pale cream dorsolateral stripes, well defined and smooth edged, and often outlined in black. **Lateral surfaces** with a broad light brown lateral band running from nostril through eye and down to hind limb, flecked or with prominent ocelli. A light brown mid-lateral stripe that fades to grey ventrally, also with ocelli or light and dark flecking. **Ventral surface**, including chin, throat and belly, uniform pale grey or flushed with pink-red or pale orange. Ventral scales may be outlined in black. **Eye** colour dark brown. **Subocular scales** 2 or 3. **Intact tail** longer than body length (SVL). **Subdigital lamellae** 20–22. **Soles of feet** black.

DISTRIBUTION

South Island only. Occurs south of the Pukaki River in south Canterbury, through the Lindis Pass area and the Crown and Pisa Ranges, to the Eyre Mountains in western Otago. May occur elsewhere.

VARIATION AND SIMILAR SPECIES

Minor variation in dorsal colouration. Distinguished from **green skink** (*O. chloronoton*) by its more slender body form; longer and more flattened snout; more definitive brow over eye; and a more well-defined pale dorsolateral stripe, with smooth edges. Resembles **Mackenzie skink** (*O. prasinum*) but distinguished by its dorsal, lateral and ventral markings extending to tip of tail (vs. patternless tail).

Distinguished from **Otago green skink** (*O.* aff. *chloronoton* "Eastern Otago") by its longer snout; absence of lateral banding; and a brown, or heavily flecked with brown, lateral stripe.

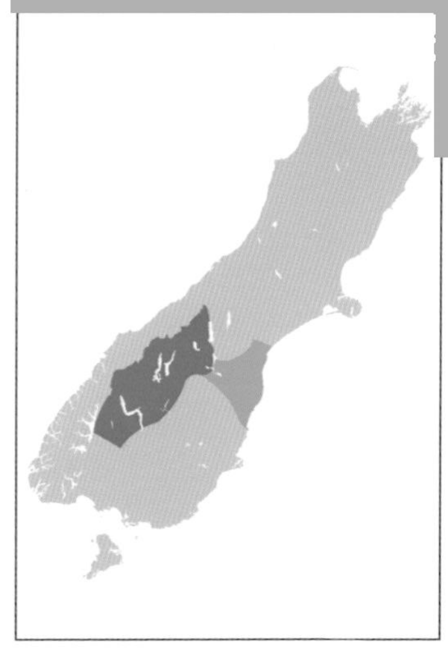

HABITAT

Lowland, Montane/subalpine

Inhabits tussock grassland, eroding river terraces, screes and alpine ridges, usually among rock piles or areas with low-growing woody vegetation and shrubs.

NATURAL HISTORY

Diurnal. Terrestrial and saxicolous. Strongly heliothermic (avid sun-basker). Little known of its ecology and reproductive biology, although probably an annual breeder; gravid females have been reported in February. Feeds on invertebrates and probably small berries.

ETYMOLOGY

Common and **tag names** referring to the lakes region of north-west and western Otago, where this species occurs.

Otago green skink

Oligosoma aff. *chloronoton* "Eastern Otago" **Endemic**

TRENT BELL

DESCRIPTION

Up to 110 mm SVL

Slender body form, and with a shallow head and long snout. **Dorsal surface** shades of green (often iridescent), olive or brown, with prominent ocelli and/or black flecking running from behind head to tip of intact tail. Pale brown or cream dorsolateral stripes from behind eye to hind limb, and often continuing down intact tail. **Lateral surfaces** with a broad black band running from behind eye to tip of intact tail. Bands flecked interiorly with white or pale brown, and lower margin graduates into a grey-brown or white lower lateral surface, heavily flecked and mottled with black, cream and white. **Ventral surface** uniform light grey, and chin and throat light grey with sparse dark flecking. **Eye** colour dark brown. **Intact tail** longer than body length (SVL). **Subdigital lamellae** usually ≤ 22. **Soles of feet** black.

DISTRIBUTION

South Island only. Occurs in Otago and possibly northern Southland, from the Hawkdun Range southwards through the Dunstan Mountains and possibly the Old Man Range and Garvie Mountains, and eastwards to the Otago Peninsula.

VARIATION AND SIMILAR SPECIES

Variation limited to dorsal colouration (brown to various shades of green). May be confused with **Stewart Island green skink** (*O.* aff. *chloronoton* "Stewart Island") or **green skink** (*O. chloronoton*) but distinguished by its more slender body form, and distinctively longer slender head and snout. Distinguished from **Lakes skink** (*O.* aff. *chloronoton* "West Otago") by its brighter dorsal colouration, and lateral markings.

HABITAT

Coastal, Lowland, Montane/subalpine

Inhabits tussock grassland, eroding river terraces, screes and alpine ridges, usually among rock piles or areas with low-growing woody vegetation and shrubs. Favours damp retreat sites and will move beneath dense vegetation, leaf litter or even burrows between retreat and sun-basking sites.

NATURAL HISTORY

Diurnal; terrestrial. Strongly heliothermic (avid sun-basker) but typically remains close to cover. Little known of its reproductive biology but likely to be similar to that of green skink. Feeds on invertebrates and soft fruits (i.e. berries).

ETYMOLOGY

Common and **tag names** referring to the Otago Region, where this taxon occurs.

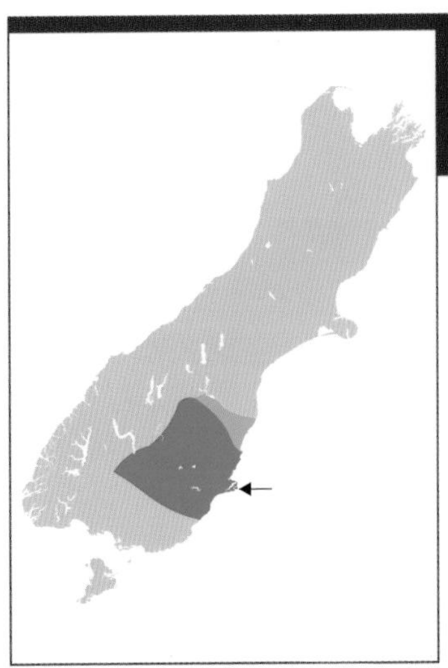

CAREY KNOX

Stewart Island green skink

Oligosoma aff. *chloronoton* "Stewart Island"

Endemic

TONY JEWELL

Stewart Island

DESCRIPTION

Up to 125 mm SVL

The only large skink on Stewart Island/Rakiura and its surrounding islands. Head shape convex in side profile, and relatively short or blunt snout. Very robust body. **Dorsal surface** brown to olive-green, usually with boldly marked crescent-shaped ocelli that continue down tail, but occasionally poorly marked. In most specimens, top of head distinctly olive-green. **Lateral surfaces** black, and heavily flecked with pale or golden markings that may link to form short transverse bands. Lateral surface gradually fades into grey, overlaid with dark mottling on lower lateral surface. **Ventral surface** grey, usually with dark flecks. Chin and throat grey, with or without dark flecking. **Eye** colour dark brown, almost black. **Intact tail** equal to or longer than body length (SVL). **Subdigital lamellae** usually ≤ 22. **Soles of feet** brown to black.

DISTRIBUTION

Stewart Island and associated offshore islands only. Occurs sparsely on mainland Stewart Island, where it is becoming increasingly rare, but common on Codfish Island/Whenuahou.

VARIATION AND SIMILAR SPECIES

Variable in colour (brown to olive-green), and degree of dorsal, lateral and ventral black flecking. Most similar to **green skink** (*O. chloronoton*), but distinguished by its more robust body, very blunt and convex head shape, more crescent-shaped ocelli usually with less prominent central pale area, and being found only on the Stewart Island archipelago.

HABITAT

Coastal, Lowland

Occupies grassland, wetlands, scrubland and forest edges, and found in smaller numbers in light gaps in forest. On Codfish Island, occupies vegetated back-dunes near the coast, open shrublands and forest edge close to pākihi habitat.

NATURAL HISTORY

Diurnal; terrestrial. Heliothermic (readily sun-basks). Little known about the ecology and reproductive biology, but presumably similar to that of green skink. Diet consists of invertebrates and fruits (berries).

ETYMOLOGY

Common and **tag names** referring to the Stewart Island archipelago, where this species is found.

Habitat of the Stewart Island green skink

SARAH J. WELLS

Canterbury spotted skink

Oligosoma lineoocellatum (Duméril & Duméril, 1851) **Endemic**

TRENT BELL

DESCRIPTION

Up to 107 mm SVL

A large and handsome skink with a spotted dorsum from the Canterbury Region. **Dorsal surface** olive-green with light and dark ocelli, which continue along dorsal surface of tail almost to tip. Mid-dorsal stripe absent. Pale dorsolateral stripes extending from above eyes to base of tail and then becoming indistinct. **Lateral surfaces** with a broad brown lateral band, running from in front of eye towards tail tip. Band heavily flecked with white and margins notched. Thinner pale mid-lateral line below, graduating into irregular cream and dark brown mottling on lower lateral surface. **Ventral surface** uniform grey, flushed with pink or orange. Chin and throat pale cream or grey with dark speckling. **Eye** colour dark brown. **Intact tail** longer than body length (SVL). **Subdigital lamellae** 21–25. **Soles of feet** grey or cream.

DISTRIBUTION

South Island only. Occurs from Mt Grey/ Maukatere southwards to the Rangitata River, and eastwards to Banks Peninsula. May occur further south in Canterbury.

VARIATION AND SIMILAR SPECIES

Colouration and patterning variable among specimens. Most similar to **Mackenzie skink** (*O. prasinum*), **Marlborough spotted skink** (*O. elium*), and **northern spotted skink** (*O. kokowai*), but distinguished from former two species by usually having < 24 subdigital lamellae, and dorsal ocelli markings usually continuing down tail (vs. > 24 and ocelli absent or fading on tail). Distinguished from the northern spotted skink by its uniformly grey belly (vs. red-orange), its larger SVL to head-width ratio and by the two taxa having widely separated ranges. Also similar to members of the ***O. chloronoton* species complex**, but typically has only 2 anterior subocular scales, or if 3, third much smaller than first two (vs. 3 all of similar size), and usually > 22 subdigital lamellae (vs. usually < 22).

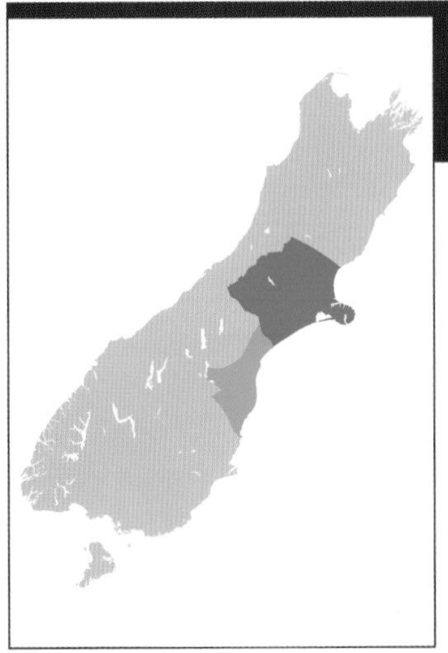

HABITAT

Coastal, Lowland, Montane/subalpine, Alpine
Inhabits boulder and cobble beaches, dune shrublands, open grassy areas, rocky coasts, flaxlands, vinelands and tussock grasslands. In montane/subalpine and alpine areas, occupies scree slopes, rock piles and fellfield habitats.

NATURAL HISTORY

Diurnal; terrestrial. Strongly heliothermic (avid sun-basker). Females produce 1–3 young in summer (February–March). Omnivorous, feeding on invertebrates (e.g. spiders, millipedes, insects, crustaceans, worms and molluscs), soft fruits (e.g. berries) and nectar, and will also consume smaller lizards (including members of the same species).

ETYMOLOGY

Specific name (Latin) referring to the rows of ocelli on the dorsal surface. **Common name** refers to the Canterbury Region, where this species occurs.

MARIEKE LETTINK

Northern spotted skink

Oligosoma kokowai Melzer et al., 2017

Endemic

Nelson

DESCRIPTION

Up to 95 mm SVL

A robust and beautifully marked skink with a bright red belly from central New Zealand. **Dorsal surface** olive-green or shades of brown, with regular light and dark ocelli that continue down intact tail. Mid-dorsal stripe absent. Pale dorsolateral stripes, with wavy or relatively straight margins, running from behind eye to base of tail, becoming indistinct on tail. **Lateral surfaces** with a broad dark brown lateral band, with light and dark speckling, running from nostril through eye to base of tail, then becoming indistinct. Lateral band bordered below by an indistinct pale mid-lateral 'stripe' made up of closely spaced pale flecks. Lower lateral surface mottled with creams, greys and dark browns. **Ventral surface** red-orange, and chin and throat uniform grey. **Eye** colour dark brown. **Intact tail** slightly longer than body length (SVL). **Subdigital lamellae** 21–24. **Soles of feet** grey or brown.

DISTRIBUTION

North and South Islands. In the North Island, an isolated population near Napier, sparse populations along Wairarapa coast, and also around Wellington, including on Matiu/Somes Island (introduced from there to Mana Island). In the South Island, found in the Marlborough Sounds (including The Brothers and Stephens Island (Takapourewa)) and Nelson, southwards to about St Arnaud.

VARIATION AND SIMILAR SPECIES

Colouration can be variable, from pale straw-brown to mid-dark brown, or olive to bright or even dark green dorsally. Sexually dimorphic, with females significantly larger than males on Matiu Island and in St Arnaud. Differs from **Mackenzie skink** (*O. prasinum*), **Marlborough spotted skink** (*O. elium*) and **Canterbury spotted skink** (*O. lineoocellatum*) by its often bright red-orange belly and genetics. Distinguished from Mackenzie skink and Marlborough spotted skink by having usually < 24 subdigital lamellae (vs. usually > 24) and by ocelli continuing down tail (vs. fading out at base of, or partway down, tail). Northern spotted skink often has 1 nuchal scale pair (vs. always > 1 pair in Canterbury spotted skink, and usually > 1 pair in Marlborough spotted skink). Similar to members of the ***O. chloronoton* species complex**, but distinguished by having 2 anterior subocular scales, or if 3, third is much smaller than first two (vs. 3 all of similar size); and usually > 22 subdigital lamellae (vs. usually < 22).

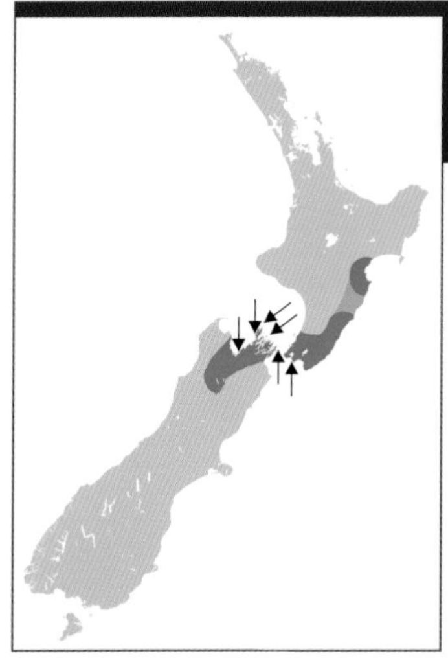

HABITAT

Coastal, Lowland

Inhabits open habitats in littoral zone, as well as grassland, shrubland, open coastal forest, boulder beaches, talus slopes, river terraces and screes. Uses seabird burrows on offshore islands.

NATURAL HISTORY

Diurnal; terrestrial but may climb into low shrubs to sun-bask or forage. Females produce 1–4 young in summer (February–March). Longevity in the wild estimated at 8–14 years. Omnivorous, feeding on invertebrates, soft fruits (e.g. berries) and nectar, and will also consume smaller lizards (including members of the same species).

ETYMOLOGY

Specific name (Māori), meaning 'red' or 'auburn', referring to the colour of the ventral surface. **Common name** refers to its more northerly distribution (i.e. southern North Island and northern South Island), compared to other members of the *O. lineoocellatum* species group, which are found further south.

Mackenzie skink

Oligosoma prasinum Melzer et al., 2017

Endemic

MARIEKE LETTINK

DESCRIPTION

Up to 94 mm SVL

A large, heavy-bodied and drably coloured skink from the Mackenzie Basin of inland Canterbury. **Dorsal surface** olive-green, green-grey or light brown, with irregular light and dark ocelli, that become indistinct or absent on tail. Dorsal surface of head usually olive-green, with or without black flecking. Dorsal surface of tail usually unmarked but may have dark speckling. A light cream or golden brown dorsolateral stripe, occasionally flecked with black, extending from behind eye towards base of tail, becoming indistinct thereafter. **Lateral surfaces** with a broad dark brown band, speckled with light and dark, gradually fading into grey lower lateral surface, which may be uniform or speckled with black. Lateral surface of tail either uniform or sparsely flecked with light and dark. **Ventral surface** uniform grey, or occasionally flushed with pink. Chin and throat uniform grey. **Eye** colour dark brown. **Intact tail** longer than body length (SVL). **Subdigital lamellae** 23–28. **Soles of feet** dark grey.

DISTRIBUTION

South Island only. Restricted to the Mackenzie Basin, between the Rangitata River (northern limit of the range) and Lake Pukaki (southern limit). May occur further south in Canterbury.

VARIATION AND SIMILAR SPECIES

Colour varies among individuals. Most similar to **Marlborough spotted skink** (*O. elium*) but species are geographically isolated from each other. Also similar to **Canterbury spotted skink** (*O. lineoocellatum*) and **northern spotted skink** (*O. kokowai*) but distinguished by having (usually) > 24 subdigital lamellae (vs. usually < 24), and absence of ocelli on tail. Similar to members of the ***O. chloronoton*** **species complex**, but with 2 anterior subocular scales, or if 3, third much smaller than first 2 (vs. 3 all of similar size); and usually > 24 subdigital lamellae (vs. usually < 22).

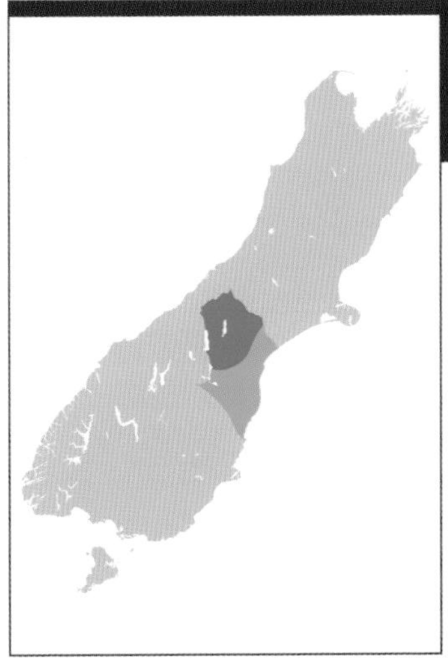

HABITAT

Lowland, Montane/subalpine

Inhabits open grassy areas, rocky river terraces, and tussock grasslands, scree, rock piles and fellfield habitats.

NATURAL HISTORY

Diurnal; terrestrial. Strongly heliothermic (avid sun-basker). Reproductive biology unknown, but likely to be similar to that of Canterbury spotted skink. Omnivorous, feeding on invertebrates, and probably soft fruits (including berries).

ETYMOLOGY

Specific name (Latinisation of Greek word) meaning 'green', referring to the olive-green dorsal colouration. **Common name** is a reference to the Mackenzie Basin in the central South Island, where this species occurs.

TONY JEWELL

Marlborough spotted skink

Oligosoma elium Melzer et al., 2017

Endemic

MARIEKE LETTINK

DESCRIPTION

Up to 89 mm SVL

A large and poorly known species from Marlborough and northern Canterbury. **Dorsal surface** pale green, with distinctive light and dark ocelli usually continuing down tail (less commonly may fade out down tail). Mid-dorsal stripe absent. Pale dorsolateral stripes, with notched edges, running from behind head to base of tail but becoming indistinct on tail. **Lateral surfaces** with a broad brown lateral band running from behind eye towards tail tip; interior of lateral band heavily flecked and blotched with pale cream or white; a pale cream mid-lateral stripe below, also notched. Lower lateral surface mottled with cream and dark brown. **Ventral surface** grey or occasionally suffused with pink; may have black flecking. Chin and throat uniform cream or grey, although throat may be heavily speckled with black. **Eye** colour dark brown. **Intact tail** slightly longer than body length (SVL). **Subdigital lamellae** 23–29. **Soles of feet** light grey or cream.

DISTRIBUTION

South Island only. Restricted to the Marlborough and north Canterbury regions, from Ward southwards to about Hawarden, and also present on Motunau Island.

VARIATION AND SIMILAR SPECIES

Colour varies among individuals. Similar to **northern spotted skink** (*O. kokowai*) and **Canterbury spotted skink** (*O. lineoocellatum*) but can be distinguished by usually having > 24 subdigital lamellae (vs. usually < 24 in the other two species). Most similar to **Mackenzie skink** (*O. prasinum*) but species are geographically isolated from each other. Similar to members of the ***O. chloronoton* species complex**, but has 2 anterior subocular scales, or if 3, third much smaller than first 2 (vs. 3 all of similar size); and usually has > 24 subdigital lamellae (vs. usually < 22).

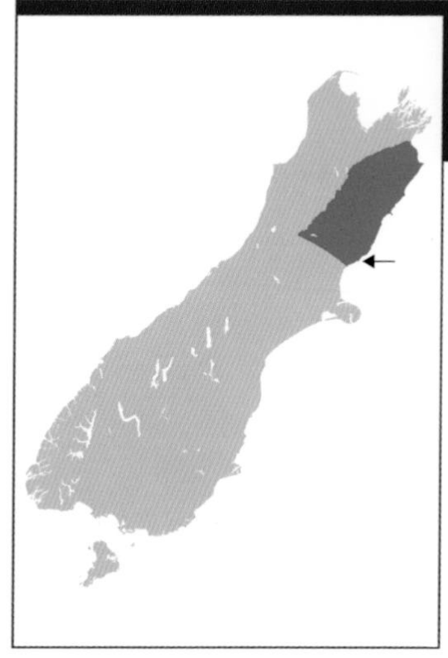

HABITAT

Coastal, Lowland, Montane/subalpine, Alpine
Found in open habitats such as tussock grassland, shrubland, scree slopes, rock piles and fellfields.

NATURAL HISTORY

Diurnal; terrestrial. Strongly heliothermic (avid sun-basker). Reproductive biology poorly known, but may be similar to that of other members of the *O. lineoocellatum* species group. Omnivorous, feeding on invertebrates and probably fruits (e.g. berries).

ETYMOLOGY

Specific name (Greek) meaning 'olive', referring to the general pale or olive-green colour. **Common name** refers to the Marlborough Region, where this species occurs.

Northern long-toed skink

Oligosoma longipes Patterson, 1997 **Endemic**

BRUCE THOMAS

DESCRIPTION

Up to c. 75 mm SVL

An active skink from dry rocky habitats in inland Marlborough. Characterised by very small scales on body (i.e. high mid-body scale count), long toes and long tail. **Dorsal surface** grey-brown to grey, with faint or indistinct pale grey and darker brown markings or blotches. With or without rudimentary brown mid-dorsal stripe. Thin pale dorsolateral stripe running from above ear down body to hind limb, becoming indistinct on tail. **Lateral surfaces** with a broad brown lateral band with notched edges, bordered below by a thin pale stripe beginning on lower lip, running through ear and to hind limb, becoming indistinct on tail. **Ventral surface** grey, either uniform or with dark flecks or speckles, especially under chin. **Mid-body scales** 40–44 rows. **Eye** colour tan or brown. **Intact tail** noticeably longer than body length (SVL). **Toes** relatively long. **Subdigital lamellae** 26–28. **Soles of feet** grey-brown and undersurface of digits black.

DISTRIBUTION

South Island only. East of the Southern Alps in scattered populations throughout inland and southern Marlborough, perhaps into northern Canterbury.

VARIATION AND SIMILAR SPECIES

Extremely similar to **roamatimati skink** (*O.* aff. *longipes* "southern"); separation based entirely on genetic evidence (detailed morphometric comparisons yet to be done). Unlikely to be confused with **white-bellied skink** (*O. hoparatea*) given wide separation of distributions, but distinguished by its notched (vs. smooth-edged) dorsolateral stripes, and usually lacking mid-dorsal stripe (vs. frequently present). Separated from sympatric **South Marlborough grass skink** (*O.* aff. *polychroma* Clade 3) by (typically) its more finely speckled colour patterning, more greyish tone, higher scale row counts (i.e. smaller scales), and longer toes and tail. Outwardly similar in appearance to some populations of **McCann's skink** (*O. maccanni*) but geographically separated from that species, and distinguished by its much longer toes and tail, absence of mid-dorsal stripe and smaller and more numerous scales on body (i.e. higher mid-body scale count). A recently discovered skink living in boulder fields at Lonely Lake in the Douglas Range resembles both long-toed skink species and the white-bellied skink in many respects, but has a considerably longer tail and different markings. Further research is required to determine the status of this population; it may represent an entirely new species.

HABITAT

Montane/subalpine, Alpine

Occupies screes, gravel or boulder talus slopes, eroding river terraces, dry streambeds and rock piles within dry open grassland, and montane tussockland or shrubland environments.

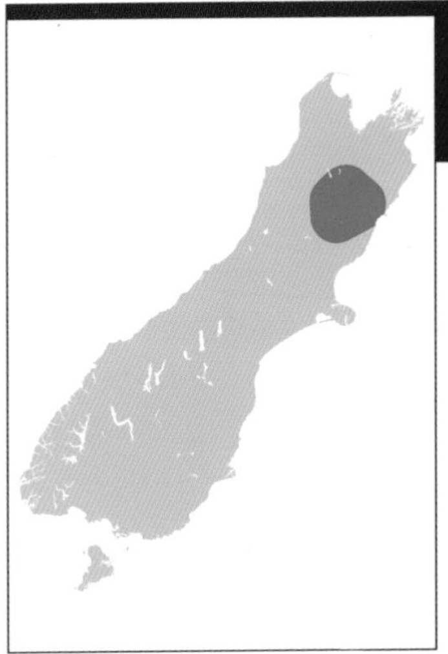

NATURAL HISTORY

Diurnal; terrestrial and saxicolous. Strongly heliothermic (avid sun-basker). Reproductive biology unknown. Actively forages for invertebrates among rocks and shrubs. Can be difficult to detect, as it readily disappears beneath vegetation or rocks, or into crevices within screes, when approached.

ETYMOLOGY

Specific name (Latin) means 'long foot'. **Common name** refers to the characteristic long toes in this species.

Lonely Lake skink

WARWICK BRIGGS & ALEC MILNE

WARWICK BRIGGS & ALEC MILNE

Roamatimati skink

Oligosoma aff. *longipes* "southern"

Endemic

TONY JEWELL

DESCRIPTION

Up to c. 75 mm SVL

Very similar to northern long-toed skink (*O. longipes*) in appearance and behaviour. **Dorsal surface** grey-brown to grey with faint or indistinct pale grey and darker brown blotches. With or without rudimentary brown mid-dorsal stripe. Thin pale dorsolateral stripe running from above ear and down body to hind limb, and then becoming indistinct on tail. **Lateral surfaces** with a broad brown lateral band with notched edges, and bordered below by thin pale stripe that begins on lower lip, runs through ear and continues to hind limb; band and stripe becoming indistinct on tail. **Ventral surface** grey, either uniform or with dark flecks or speckles, especially under chin. **Scales** on body small (i.e. mid-body scales. 40–44 rows). **Eye** colour tan or brown. **Intact tail** noticeably longer than body length (SVL). **Toes** relatively long. **Subdigital lamellae** 26–28. **Soles of feet** grey-brown and under-surface of digits black.

DISTRIBUTION

South Island only. Scattered populations occur throughout inland Canterbury and southwards to the Mackenzie Basin.

VARIATION AND SIMILAR SPECIES

Extremely similar to **northern long-toed skink** (*O. longipes*) and at this stage, with detailed morphometric comparisons still to be done, separation based entirely on genetic evidence; taxa geographically isolated and thus misidentification unlikely. May be confused with **McCann's skink** (*O. maccanni*) but distinguished by its significantly longer toes and tail, and smaller and more numerous scales on body (i.e. higher number of mid-body scale rows). Syntopic populations of McCann's skinks usually have a distinct mid-dorsal stripe, which is absent or rudimentary in the roamatimati skink. Also similar to the syntopic **white-bellied skink** (*O. hoparatea*) but distinguished by its notched (vs. smooth-edged) dorsolateral stripes, and usually lacking mid-dorsal stripe (vs. frequently present).

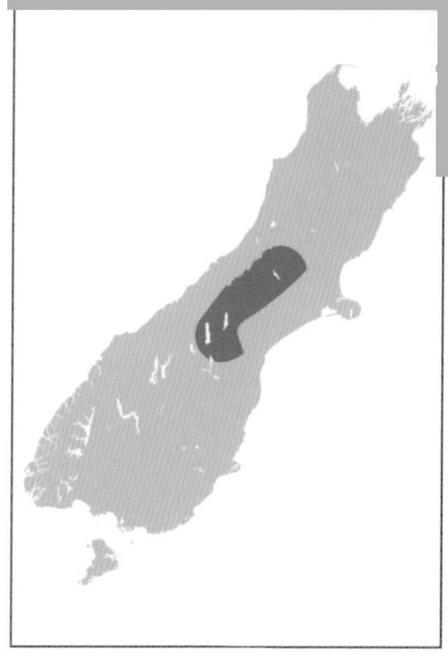

HABITAT

Montane/subalpine, Alpine

Occupies screes, gravel or boulder talus slopes, eroding river terraces, dry streambeds and rock piles within dry open grassland, tussockland or shrubland environments.

NATURAL HISTORY

Diurnal; terrestrial and saxicolous. Strongly heliothermic (avid sun-basker). Reproductive biology unknown. Can be difficult to detect as it readily disappears beneath vegetation or rocks, or crevices within screes, when approached. Actively forages for invertebrates among rocks and in low-growing shrubs.

ETYMOLOGY

Common name deriving from the Māori words roa and matimati meaning 'long' and 'fingers, claws or toes,' respectively, referring to this taxon's characteristic long toes. **Tag name** refers to its more southern distribution compared to its closely related sister taxa, *O. longipes*.

CAREY KNOX

White-bellied skink

Oligosoma hoparatea Whitaker et al., 2018

Endemic

MARIEKE LETTINK

DESCRIPTION

Up to 91 mm SVL

A handsome skink that often sun-basks in a distinctive upright posture. Rare and highly threatened. **Dorsal surface** mid- to dark brown with a dark mid-dorsal stripe becoming indistinct anteriorly. Dorsolateral stripe pale, smooth edged, extending from behind head to base of tail, becoming indistinct thereafter. **Lateral surfaces** with a broad dark brown lateral band bordered below by a thin pale mid-lateral stripe running from below eye through ear and above forelimbs, stopping just before hind limbs; stripe becoming indistinct on intact tail. **Ventral surface** (including chin and throat) white or cream, and unmarked. **Eye** colour hazel or light brown. Small, numerous **scales** on body (i.e. mid-body scale rows > 38). **Intact tail** noticeably longer than body length (SVL). **Toes** long and narrow. **Subdigital lamellae** 26–28. **Soles of feet** brown or dark brown.

DISTRIBUTION

South Island only. Found in the Ashburton Basin of inland Canterbury, in mountains near the Rangitata Gorge and Mt Somers.

VARIATION AND SIMILAR SPECIES

Little variation. Superficially similar to **McCann's skink** (*O. maccanni*), but distinguished by its more robust body form, proportionally longer toes and tail, smaller and more numerous scales on body (i.e. higher mid-body scale count), and more erect, head-up posture, resting up on its forelimbs when sun-basking. May be confused with syntopic **roamatimati skink** (*O.* aff. *longipes* "southern"), but larger and more robust in build; dark flecks absent from dorsal surface; stripes smooth edged (vs. notched); 2 or more nuchal scales (vs. 1 or none); and ventral surface uniform white (vs. white or greyish, often with dark flecking). White-bellied skink also with a more erect, head-up posture when sun-basking compared to other congeners. Geographically isolated from the **northern long-toed skink** (*O. longipes*), but can be distinguished by the same characters as described for the roamatimati skink.

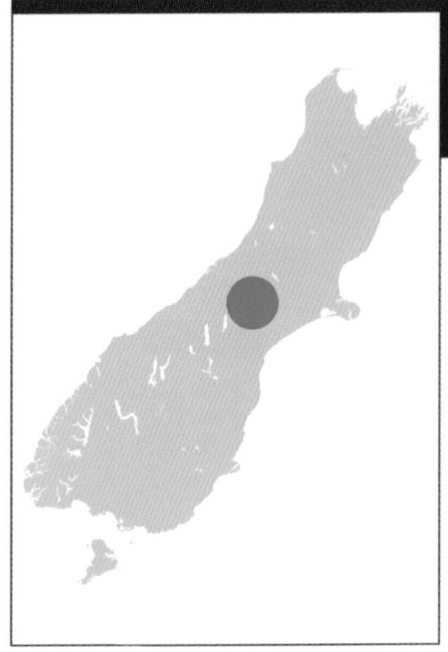

HABITAT

Alpine

Inhabits unstable greywacke screes and talus slopes in lower alpine zone, usually remaining close to vegetation such as divaricating shrubs and vines (e.g. creeping pōhuehue; matagouri, *Discaria toumatou*; porcupine shrub). Takes refuge from predators and inclement alpine weather deep within the scree.

NATURAL HISTORY

Diurnal; terrestrial and saxicolous. Strongly heliothermic (avid sun-basker), but active for only short periods of morning when temperatures are most suitable (c. 12–14 °C). Nothing known of its reproductive biology. Omnivorous, feeding on small invertebrates (e.g. flies), fruits of divaricating shrubs and vines, and other, smaller skinks (e.g. McCann's skink).

ETYMOLOGY

Specific name (Māori) from hōpara, meaning 'belly' or 'underside', and tea, meaning 'white'. **Common name** refers to the uniform pale white ventral surface.

Habitat of white-bellied skink, Canterbury

Northern grass skink

Oligosoma polychroma (Patterson & Daugherty, 1990) **Endemic**

Nelson

Wellington

DESCRIPTION

Up to 80 mm SVL

A common and conspicuous skink throughout its range, and readily encountered in suburban areas. Blunt snout and relatively large ear opening. **Dorsal surface** tan to dark brown with prominent pale cream dorsolateral stripes that may be smooth edged or notched. Dark brown mid-dorsal stripe usually present and extending down intact tail. **Lateral surfaces** with a prominent brown lateral band with wavy or smooth edges; bordered by a fine pale cream mid-lateral line on lower margin. Forelimb with pale stripe. **Ventral surface** uniform grey, brown, cream, white or yellow; usually dull yellow. Chin and throat light brown to grey. **Eye** colour hazel to light brown. **Intact tail** usually slightly longer than body length (SVL). **Subdigital lamellae** 16–24. **Soles of feet** brown or grey (sometimes flushed with yellow) or black.

DISTRIBUTION

North and South Islands. Central North Island from Gisborne to the Central Plateau southwards to Wellington and across Cook Strait. Occurs on Stephens Island/ Takapourewa and other islands in the western Marlborough Sounds. In the South Island, occurs in Nelson, Tasman and West Coast regions, from Nelson southwards along the west coast to about Hokitika.

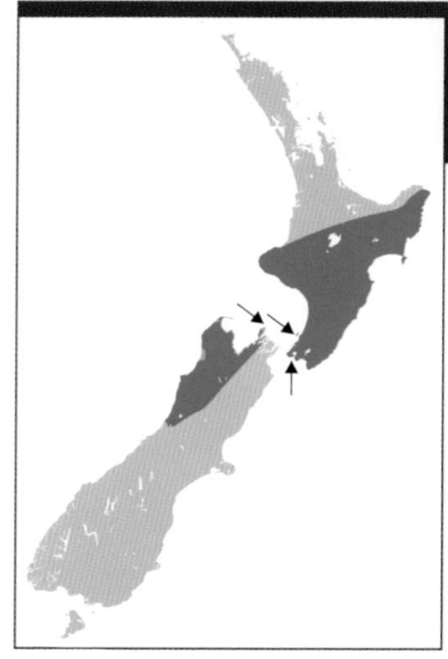

VARIATION AND SIMILAR SPECIES

Variable in colouration (i.e. light to darker shades of brown) and degree of smoothness or notching along margins of dorsolateral and mid-lateral stripes. Sometimes individuals with smooth-edged stripes and those with notched stripes in same population. Currently no morphological characters available to distinguish northern grass skink from other four genetically distinct members of **grass skink complex**, i.e. Waiharakeke grass skink (*O.* aff. *polychroma* Clade 2); South Marlborough grass skink (*O.* aff. *polychroma* Clade 3); Canterbury grass skink (*O.* aff. *polychroma* Clade 4); and southern grass skink (*O.* aff. *polychroma* Clade 5). Thus, determining which grass skink an individual is requires information on individual's origin. May be confused with **glossy brown skink** (*O. zelandicum*) but distinguished by absence of denticulate markings along jawline and lower scale counts. Similar to **speckled skink** (*O. infrapunctatum*) and related taxa, but lacks ventral speckling; pale lateral stripe does not go straight through ear opening; pale lateral stripe is continuous (vs. usually broken) above forelimb; and forelimb has a pale stripe (vs. spots). Northern grass skink and **McCann's skink** are geographically isolated from each other, thus misidentification unlikely.

HABITAT

Coastal, Lowland, Montane/subalpine
Occupies a wide range of habitats including littoral zones, duneland, wetlands, grassland, shrublands, forest edges, small rocky islets, offshore islands, screes and talus slopes, rocky or boulder areas, shrublands, subalpine tussockland and even suburban gardens. Also persists in areas of exotic forestry.

NATURAL HISTORY

Diurnal; terrestrial. Strongly heliothermic (avid sun-basker). Annual reproduction. Matures at 1.5–2 years; mating reported in March; gestation period 3 months; and 3–6 young born in summer (January–February). Longevity reported at c. 3–4 years (6 years in captivity). Feeds on small invertebrates (e.g. spiders, insects, molluscs and worms, including nematodes), and actively pursues prey. Also consumes soft fruits (including berries).

ETYMOLOGY

Specific name (Greek) meaning 'many colour', referring to the geographically variable colouration. **Common name** refers to its northerly distribution compared to the other grass skinks.

Waiharakeke grass skink

Oligosoma aff. *polychroma* Clade 2

Endemic

JOZEF POLEC

DESCRIPTION

Up to c. 80 mm SVL

A common and conspicuous skink throughout its range, and readily encountered in suburban areas. Blunt snout and relatively large ear opening. **Dorsal surface** tan to dark brown with prominent pale dorsolateral stripes that are typically notched but may be smooth edged. Dark brown mid-dorsal stripe (often finely edged in black) usually present, extending down intact tail. **Lateral surfaces** with a prominent brown lateral band with wavy (typical) or smooth (occasionally) edges, bordered below by a fine pale cream mid-lateral line. Pale stripe present on forelimb. **Ventral surface** uniform grey, brown, cream, white or yellow. Chin and throat light brown to grey. **Eye** colour hazel to light brown. **Intact tail** usually slightly longer than body length (SVL). **Subdigital lamellae** 16–24. **Soles of feet** brown or grey (sometimes flushed with yellow) or black.

DISTRIBUTION

South Island only. Eastern Marlborough Sounds, including The Brothers island group, and southwards to the Wairau Valley and Kaikoura Coast.

VARIATION AND SIMILAR SPECIES

Variable in colouration (i.e. light to darker shades of brown) and degree of smoothness or notching along margins of dorsolateral and mid-lateral stripes. Sometimes individuals with smooth-edged stripes and those with notched stripes in same population. Currently no morphological characters available to distinguish Waiharakeke grass skink from other four genetically distinct members of **grass skink species complex**, i.e. northern grass skink (*O. polychroma*); South Marlborough grass skink (*O.* aff. *polychroma* Clade 3); Canterbury grass skink (*O.* aff. *polychroma* Clade 4); and southern grass skink (*O.* aff. *polychroma*

Clade 5). Thus, determining which grass skink an individual is requires information on individual's origin. May be confused with **glossy brown skink** (*O. zelandicum*) but distinguished by absence of denticulate markings along jawline. Similar to **speckled skink** (*O. infrapunctatum*) and related taxa, but lacks ventral speckling; pale lateral stripe does not go straight through ear opening; pale lateral stripe continuous (vs. usually broken) above forelimb; and forelimb has a pale stripe (vs. spots). Also similar to **McCann's skink** (*O. maccanni*) but can be distinguished from northern populations of McCann's skink by its notched (vs. smooth-edged) dorsolateral and lateral stripes; a more brown (vs. grey-brown) basal colouration; and, where present, mid-dorsal stripe continuing down intact tail (vs. breaking up on tail). Smooth-striped Waiharakeke grass skinks can be distinguished from McCann's skink by: an overall more golden brown rather than greyish tone; soles of feet dark brown or black (vs. white, cream or pale yellow); absence of patchy markings on dorsal surface; and mid-dorsal stripe continuing down intact tail (vs. breaking up on tail). Waiharakeke grass skink and McCann's skink are geographically isolated from each other, thus misidentification unlikely.

HABITAT

Coastal, Lowland

Occupies a wide range of habitats including littoral zones, duneland, wetlands, grassland, shrublands, forest edges, small rocky islets, offshore islands, screes and talus slopes, rocky or boulder

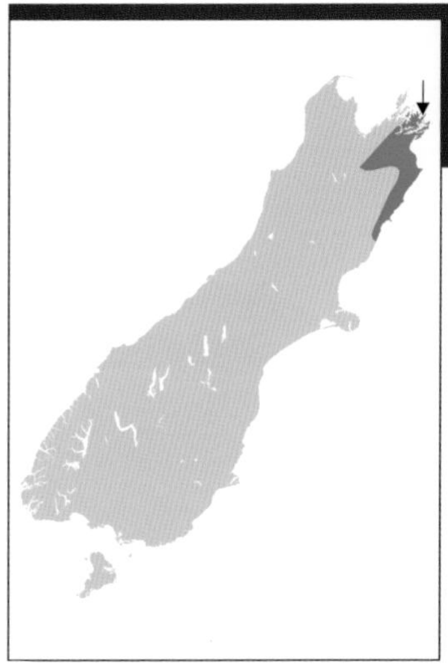

areas, shrublands, tussockland and even suburban gardens. Also persists in areas of exotic forestry.

NATURAL HISTORY

Diurnal; terrestrial. Strongly heliothermic (avid sun-basker). Annual reproduction. Matures at 1.5–2 years; mating reported in March; gestation period 3 months; and 3–6 young born in summer (January–February). Feeds on small invertebrates (e.g. spiders, insects, molluscs and worms, including nematodes), and actively pursues prey. Also consumes soft fruits (including berries).

ETYMOLOGY

Specific name (Greek) meaning 'many' 'colour', referring to the geographically variable colouration. **Common name** (Māori) is after the South Island town, Blenheim (Te Waiharakeke), referring to the geographic area of New Zealand where this taxon occurs.

South Marlborough grass skink

Oligosoma aff. *polychroma* Clade 3

Endemic

TRENT BELL

DESCRIPTION

Up to c. 80 mm SVL

One of the lesser-known members of the grass skink complex, with a restricted geographical range. Blunt snout and relatively large ear opening. **Dorsal surface** tan to dark brown with prominent pale cream dorsolateral stripes that may be smooth edged or notched. Dark brown mid-dorsal stripe usually present and extending down intact tail, bordered below by a fine pale cream mid-lateral line. **Lateral surfaces** with a prominent brown lateral band with wavy or smooth edges. Pale stripe present on forelimb. **Ventral surface** uniform grey, brown, cream, white or yellow. Chin and throat light brown to grey. **Eye** colour hazel to light brown. **Intact tail** usually slightly longer than body length (SVL). **Subdigital lamellae** 16–24. **Soles of feet** brown or grey (sometimes flushed with yellow) or black.

DISTRIBUTION

South Island only. Occurs in inland southern Marlborough and mountainous regions of north Canterbury, and the Seaward and Inland Kaikōura Ranges.

VARIATION AND SIMILAR SPECIES

Variation poorly known; likely to be variable in colouration (i.e. light to darker shades of brown) and degree of smoothness or notching along margins of dorsolateral and mid-lateral stripes. Sometimes individuals with smooth-edged stripes and those with notched stripes in same population. Currently no morphological characters available to distinguish South Marlborough grass skink from other four genetically distinct members of the **grass skink species complex**, i.e. northern grass skink (*O. polychroma*); Waiharakeke grass skink (*O.* aff. *polychroma* Clade 2); Canterbury grass skink (*O.* aff. *polychroma* Clade 4); and southern grass skink (*O.* aff. *polychroma* Clade 5). Thus, determining which grass skink an individual is requires information on individual's origin. May be confused with **glossy brown skink** (*O. zelandicum*) but is geographically isolated from that species, and denticulate markings along jawline are absent (vs. present in glossy brown skink). Similar to **speckled skink** (*O. infrapunctatum*) and related taxa, but lacks ventral speckling; pale lateral stripe does not go straight through the ear opening and is continuous (vs. usually broken) above forelimb; and forelimb has a pale stripe (vs. spots). Range does not overlap with McCann's skink.

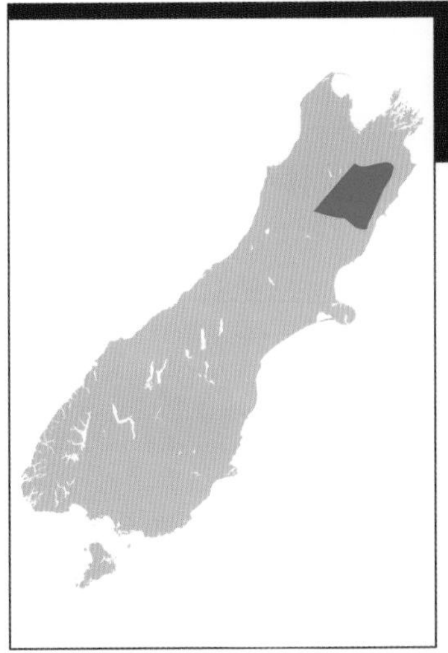

HABITAT

Coastal, Lowland, Montane/subalpine

Occupies a wide range of habitats including wetlands, grassland, shrublands, forest edges, offshore islands, screes and talus slopes, rocky or boulder areas, shrublands and subalpine tussockland.

NATURAL HISTORY

Diurnal; terrestrial. Strongly heliothermic (avid sun-basker). Ecology and reproduction poorly known. Likely to breed annually and mature at c. 2 years. In summer (January–February), 3–6 young born. Feeds on small invertebrates (e.g. spiders, insects, molluscs and worms, including nematodes), and actively pursues prey. Also consumes soft fruits (including berries).

ETYMOLOGY

Specific name (Greek) meaning 'many' 'colour', referring to the geographically variable colouration. **Common name** refers to the southern Marlborough Region where this taxon occurs.

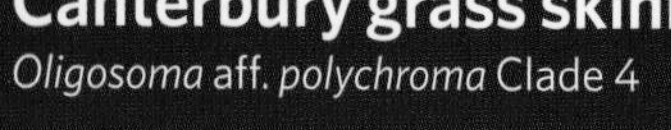

Canterbury grass skink

Oligosoma aff. *polychroma* Clade 4

Endemic

TRENT BELL

DESCRIPTION

Up to c. 80 mm SVL

Widespread in inland Canterbury and not hard to find, but less common and conspicuous than other members of the complex. Blunt snout and relatively large ear opening. **Dorsal surface** tan to dark brown with prominent pale cream dorsolateral stripes that may be notched (typically) or smooth edged (sometimes). Dark brown mid-dorsal stripe usually present and extending down intact tail. **Lateral surfaces** with a prominent brown lateral band with wavy or (rarely) smooth edges, bordered below by a fine pale cream mid-lateral line. Pale stripe present on forelimb. **Ventral surface** uniform grey, brown, cream, white or yellow. Chin and throat light brown to grey. **Eye** colour hazel to light brown. **Intact tail** usually slightly longer than body length (SVL). **Subdigital lamellae** 16–24. **Soles of feet** brown or grey (sometimes flushed with yellow) or black.

DISTRIBUTION

South Island only. Occurs in the foothills and inland valleys of northern and central Canterbury, across the central South Island to the West Coast, south of Hokitika. Some populations in the Mackenzie Basin and Lindis Pass area may also belong to this species.

VARIATION AND SIMILAR SPECIES

Variable in colouration (i.e. light to darker shades of brown) and degree of smoothness or notching along margins of dorsolateral and mid-lateral stripes. Currently no confirmed morphological characters available to distinguish Canterbury grass skink from other four genetically distinct members of **grass skink species complex**, i.e. northern grass skink (*O. polychroma*); Waiharakeke grass skink (*O.* aff. *polychroma* Clade 2); South Marlborough grass skink (*O.* aff. *polychroma* Clade 3); and southern grass skink (*O.* aff. *polychroma* Clade 5). Thus, determining which grass skink an individual is requires information on individual's origin. Similar to **speckled skink** (*O. infrapunctatum*) and related taxa, but lacks ventral speckling; pale lateral stripe does not go straight through ear opening and is continuous (vs. usually broken) above forelimb; and forelimb has a pale stripe (vs. spots). May be confused with **McCann's skink** (*O. maccanni*) but can be distinguished from northern populations of McCann's skink by the typically notched (vs. smooth-edged) dorsolateral and lateral stripes; a more warm-brown (vs. grey-brown) basal coloration; and where present, mid-dorsal stripe continuing down intact tail (vs. breaking up on tail). Smooth-striped Canterbury grass skinks can be distinguished from McCann's skink by an overall more golden brown rather than greyish tone; soles of feet dark brown or black (vs. white, cream or pale yellow); absence of patchy markings on dorsal surface; and mid-dorsal stripe continuing down intact tail (vs. breaking up on tail).

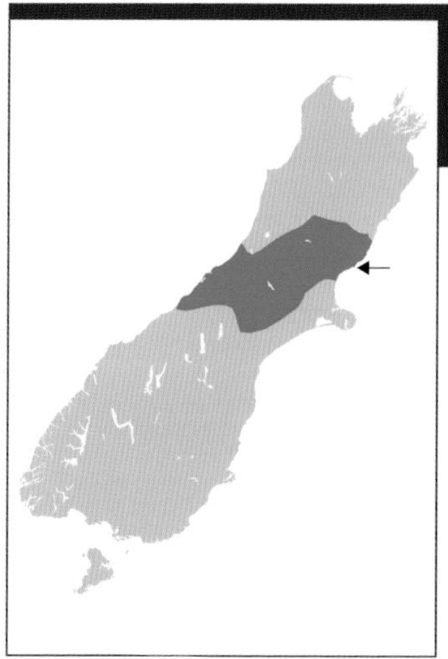

HABITAT

Lowland, Montane/subalpine

Occupies a wide range of habitats, including wetlands, grassland, shrublands, forest edges, screes and talus slopes, rocky or boulder areas, shrublands, and subalpine tussockland.

NATURAL HISTORY

Diurnal; terrestrial. Strongly heliothermic (avid sun-basker). Annual reproduction. Matures at 1.5–2 years; gestation period 3 months; and 3–6 young born in summer (January–February). Feeds on small invertebrates (e.g. spiders, insects, molluscs and worms, including nematodes), and actively pursues prey. Also consumes soft fruits (including berries).

ETYMOLOGY

Specific name (Greek) meaning 'many colour', referring to the geographically variable colouration. **Common name** refers to the Canterbury Region, where this species occurs.

Southern grass skink

Oligosoma aff. *polychroma* Clade 5 **Endemic**

TRENT BELL

DESCRIPTION

Up to c. 80 mm SVL

A common and conspicuous skink throughout its range. Blunt snout and relatively large ear opening. **Dorsal surface** commonly very warm tan, occasionally dark brown, with prominent pale cream dorsolateral stripes that may be notched or smooth edged. Dark brown mid-dorsal stripe usually present and extending down intact tail. **Lateral surfaces** with a prominent brown lateral band with wavy or smooth edges, bordered below by a fine pale cream mid-lateral line. Pale stripe present on forelimb. **Ventral surface** uniform grey, brown, cream, white or yellow, usually dull yellowish buff. Chin and throat light brown to grey. **Eye** colour hazel to light brown. **Intact tail** usually slightly longer than body length (SVL). **Subdigital lamellae** 16–24. **Soles of feet** brown or grey (sometimes flushed with yellow) or black.

DISTRIBUTION

South Island only. Widespread in central and southern Canterbury (including around Christchurch and on Banks Peninsula), Otago and Southland, and across the Foveaux Strait to Stewart Island/Rakiura. A population in Milford Sound is believed to have been introduced; not otherwise known from Fiordland or southern Westland.

VARIATION AND SIMILAR SPECIES

Variable in colouration (i.e. light to darker shades of brown) and the degree of smoothness or notching along margins of dorsolateral and mid-lateral stripes. Sometimes, individuals with smooth-edged stripes and those with notched stripes in same population. Currently no morphological characters available to distinguish southern grass skink from other four genetically distinct members of **grass skink species complex**, i.e. northern grass skink (*O. polychroma*); Waiharakeke grass skink (*O.* aff. *polychroma* Clade 2); South Marlborough grass skink (*O.* aff. *polychroma* Clade 3); and Canterbury grass skink (*O.* aff. *polychroma* Clade 4). Thus, determining which grass skink an individual is requires information on individual's origin. A uniform brown variant is known from populations at Awarua and in northern Otago. May be confused with **McCann's skink** (*O. maccanni*) but can be distinguished from northern populations of McCann's skink by its notched (vs. smooth-edged) dorsolateral and lateral stripes; a more brown (vs. grey-brown) basal

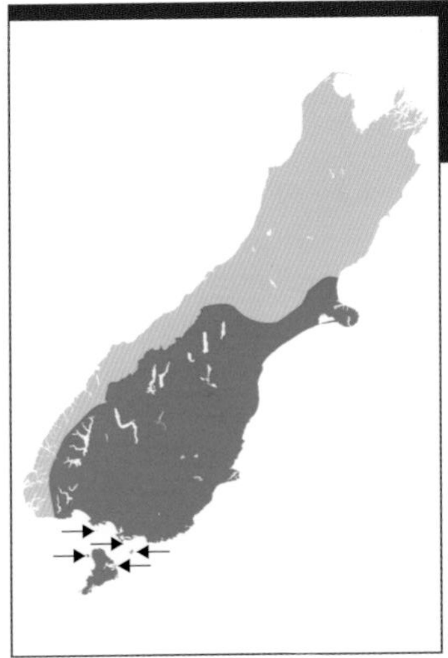

coloration; and, where present, mid-dorsal stripe continuing down intact tail (vs. breaking up on tail). Distinguished from McCann's skink by its overall more golden

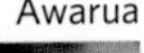

Awarua

TONY JEWELL

brown rather than greyish tone; soles of feet dark brown or black (vs. white, cream or pale yellow); absence of patchy markings on dorsal surface; and mid-dorsal stripe continuing down intact tail (vs. breaking up on tail). Generally, in areas where McCann's skinks have blotched or speckled dorsal markings, southern grass skinks are uniformly striped, and vice versa.

HABITAT

Coastal, Lowland, Montane/subalpine

Occupies a wide range of habitats including littoral zones, duneland, wetlands, grassland, shrublands, forest edges, small rocky islets, offshore islands, screes and talus slopes, rocky or boulder areas, shrublands, subalpine tussockland and even suburban gardens. Also survives in areas of exotic forestry.

NATURAL HISTORY

Diurnal; terrestrial. Strongly heliothermic (avid sun-basker). Annual reproduction. Matures at 2–3 years; mating reported in March; gestation period 3 months; and 3–6 young born in summer (January–February). Longevity reported at c. 3–4 years (6 years in captivity). Known to use burrows of subterranean invertebrates (e.g. worms, spiders and weta) as refuge sites, probably to escape predators and shelter from extreme low temperatures during winter. Feeds on small invertebrates (e.g. spiders, insects, molluscs and worms, including nematodes), and actively pursues prey. Also consumes soft fruits (including berries).

ETYMOLOGY

Specific name (Greek) meaning 'many colour', referring to the geographically variable colouration. **Common name** refers to its southerly distribution compared to other grass skinks.

Awarua

Central Otago

Habitat of southern grass skink, Otago

Speckled skink

Oligosoma infrapunctatum (Boulenger, 1887)

Endemic

Stephens Island

DESCRIPTION

Up to at least 86 mm (mainland) and up to 106 mm SVL (islands); at least 10 g weight (mainland)

Snout short and rounded. A variable species with several distinct sub-populations, requiring more work to determine their taxonomic significance. **Dorsal surface** light to dark brown and heavily speckled with small light and dark flecks. Black spots or blotches may be present on head. With or without mid-dorsal stripe. Distinctive pale dorsolateral stripes with notched edges, usually outlined in black. **Lateral surfaces** with a broad brown lateral band, bordered below by pale narrower stripes, outlined in black, with notched edges. Lateral striping breaking up at hind limb and not continuing down intact tail. **Ventral surface** bright yellow to salmon, and heavily spotted with black. Chin grey and throat grey fading abruptly to yellow or pink-red, both with black speckling. Ventral surface of intact tail grey or yellow with sparse black flecking. **Eye** colour light to dark brown. **Intact tail** equal to or slightly longer than body length (SVL). **Subdigital lamellae** 15–22. **Soles of feet** brown.

DISTRIBUTION

South Island only. Occurs on Stephens Island/Takapourewa in the Marlborough Sounds, southwards to St Arnaud, through Kahurangi National Park (including Mt Arthur) and northern West Coast to Hokitika; also introduced from Stephens Island to Maud and Mana Islands.

VARIATION AND SIMILAR SPECIES

Large morphological variation, particularly in size and build. Stephens Island individuals very large, heavily built, with large heads; adults more tan in colour. A morphologically aberrant individual found in Paparoa Mountains had dorsal markings arranged into narrow longitudinal stripes. Another aberrant population occurs on Denniston Plateau on the West Coast, with individuals heavily speckled with dark flecks above, such that dorsal and lateral stripes are almost indiscernible. Ventral surface pale yellow with black flecks forming short longitudinal striations. Individuals from around St Arnaud, and from various high-altitude locations in Kahurangi National Park, form a distinct genetic cluster, often having a pink-red (St Arnaud) or bright yellow (Mt Arthur) ventral surface. Individuals from Mt Arthur have long pointed snouts and dorso-ventrally flattened heads; are slender and petite in body form; and inhabit argillite screes and tussock grassland. An individual from Brown Hill, also in Kahurangi National Park, is also somewhat separated genetically from all other members of the species and has a longer tail.

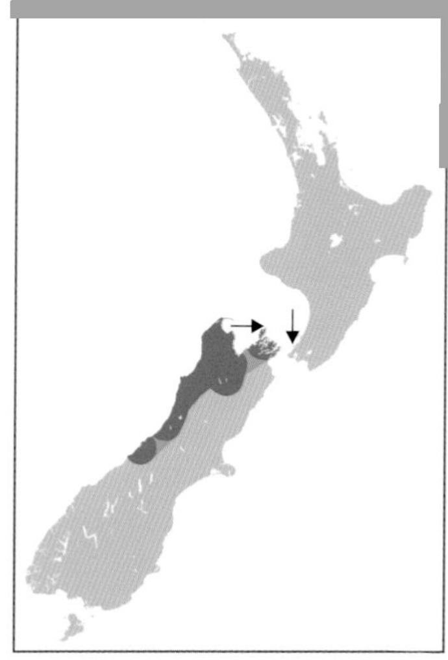

Distinguished from other closely related taxa by its stockier build, and more domed and more ridged scales, which give a rougher and less glossy appearance. Formerly found together with **cobble skink** (*O.* aff. *infrapunctatum* "cobble") at Granity; distinguished by its larger body size at all ages, and by proportionally smaller eye (i.e. distance from mouth to bottom of eye equal or greater than height of eye). Overlaps with **Chesterfield skink** (*O.* aff. *infrapunctatum* "Chesterfield") and **Hokitika skink** (*O.* aff. *infrapunctatum* "Hokitika") between Greymouth and Hokitika; superficially very similar but distinguished from both by adults' more robust build, slightly larger size, and more domed and striated scales giving a less smooth and glossy appearance.

West Coast

Distinguished from Chesterfield skink by absence of salmon-pink and blue-grey blotches under tail, and from Hokitika skink by absence of strong denticulate markings around mouth.

HABITAT

Coastal, Lowland, Montane/subalpine, Alpine Inhabits coastal cobble and boulder beaches, densely vegetated or shrubland habitats, open grassland, fernland and open forest. During day, sun-basks and forages on stones, boulders, cobbles, driftwood and low-growing vegetation. Retreats beneath rocks or dense vegetation at night. On Stephens Island, known to use burrows of fairy prions (*Pachyptila turtur*) as refuges.

NATURAL HISTORY

Diurnal; terrestrial. Strongly heliothermic (avid sun-basker). Has suffered catastrophic declines in some parts of its range (e.g. St Arnaud). Reproductive biology poorly known but is viviparous. Primarily insectivorous but may consume soft fruits (berries) of native shrubs (e.g. *Coprosma* species).

ETYMOLOGY

Specific name (Latin) meaning 'dotted or spotted below'. **Common name** refers to the speckled ventral surface.

Mt Arthur

Mt Arthur

Ventral surfaces of *Oligosoma infrapunctum* species complex and *Oligosoma kokowai*

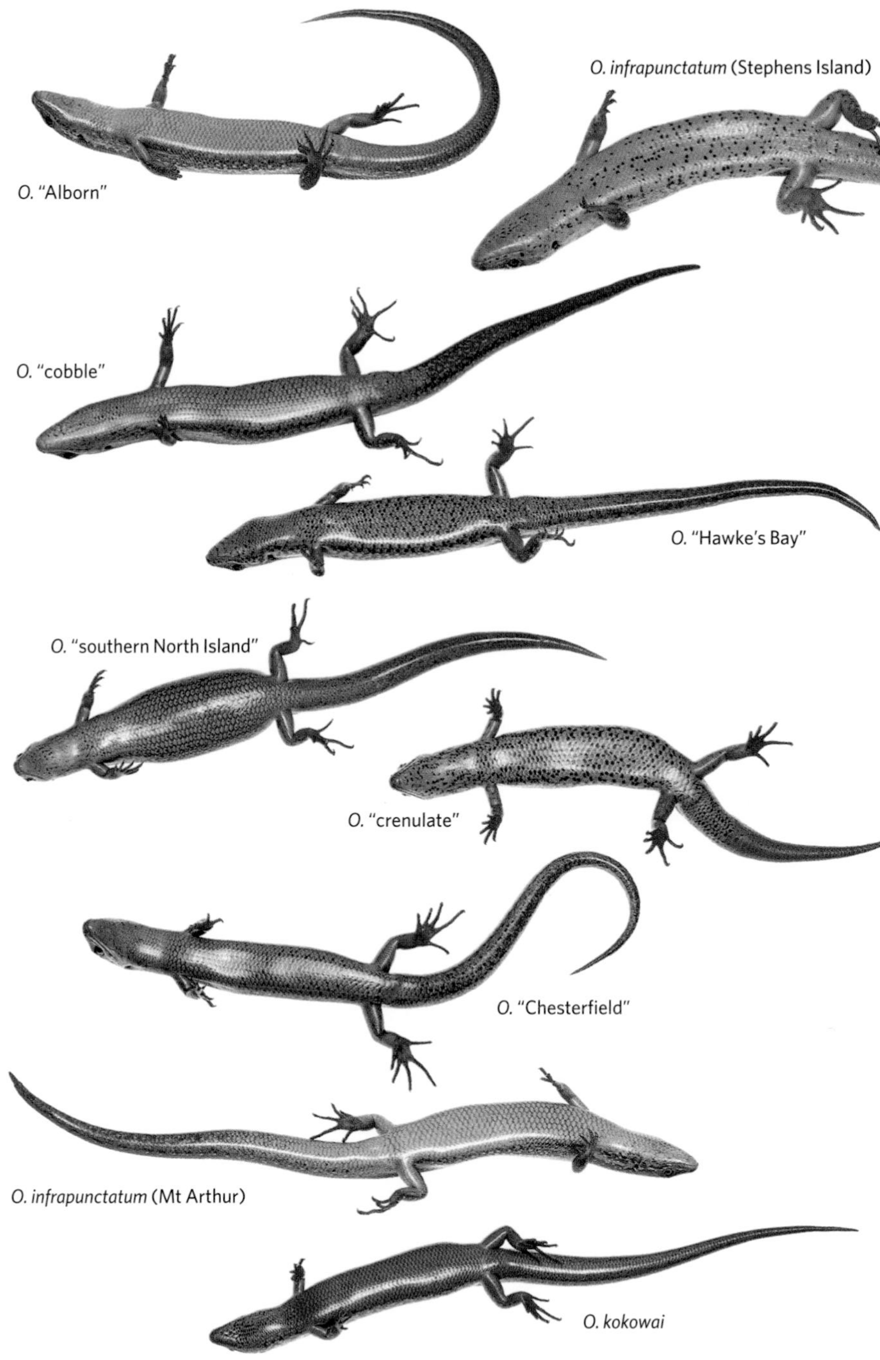

Alborn skink

Oligosoma aff. *infrapunctatum* "Alborn"

Endemic

DESCRIPTION

Up to at least 87 mm SVL; 11.5 g weight

A rare and poorly known skink, with a single known population occurring at a remote site in Westland. Snout medium length, wedge shaped. **Dorsal surface** light brown and heavily speckled with small light and dark flecks. Head sometimes with black spots between eyes. Mid-dorsal stripe may be present. Distinctive pale dorsolateral stripes with notched edges, usually outlined in black. **Lateral surfaces** with a broad darker brown lateral band that may have light flecks within, bordered below by a thinner pale mid-lateral stripe with notched edges, also usually outlined in black. Lateral band and stripe not continuing down intact tail. **Ventral surface** uniform ochre-yellow, gradually fading into darker grey about halfway along underside of tail. Chin uniform grey and throat uniform grey fading abruptly to ochre-yellow. **Eye** colour dark brown. **Intact tail** equal to or longer than body length (SVL). **Subdigital lamellae** 18–20. **Soles of feet** brown, sometimes ochre-yellow on palms.

DISTRIBUTION

South Island only. Known only from a small area near Reefton on the West Coast. Full extent of its range unknown.

VARIATION AND SIMILAR SPECIES

Variation poorly known. Very similar to **speckled skink** (*O. infrapunctatum*), occurring along the West Coast coastline, but distinguished by its lack of speckling on belly, more slender build and glossier scales. Also very similar to closely related **Chesterfield skink** (*O.* aff. *infrapunctatum* "Chesterfield"), but distinguished by its larger size, differing body proportions (e.g. position of ear opening) and lack of colourful blotched undersurface of tail.

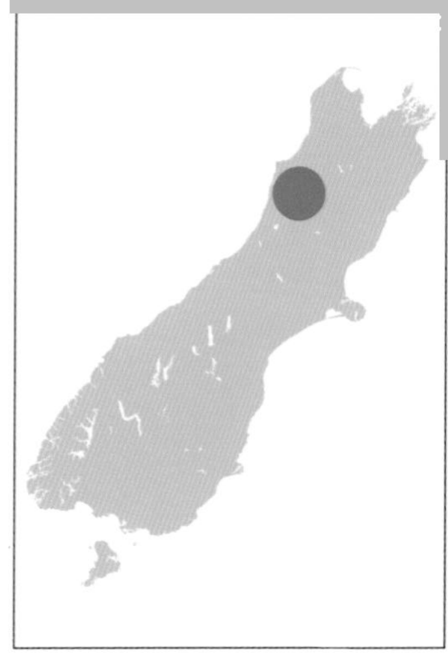

HABITAT

Montane/subalpine

Occupies artificial clearings in beech forest, pākihi, wetlands and regenerating shrubland. May also occur in forest, or small wetlands within a forest matrix.

NATURAL HISTORY

Diurnal; terrestrial. A poorly known species; life history and reproductive biology unknown. Occurs in pākihi, and when these flood after heavy rains, uses high points and logs to escape the water.

ETYMOLOGY

Common and **tag names** referring to the only known location (around Alborn Coal Mine) of this taxon.

Chesterfield skink

Oligosoma aff. *infrapunctatum* "Chesterfield" **Endemic**

DESCRIPTION

Up to 85 mm SVL (usually < 75 mm); 10.5 g weight

Another rare and highly threatened skink from the South Island's West Coast. Snout medium length; wedge shaped. **Dorsal surface** red-brown with distinctive golden glossy sheen, and sparse or dense black flecking that may extend onto head. Mid-dorsal stripe absent. **Lateral surfaces** with a distinct red-brown lateral band, edged in black, running from behind eye, down body and continuing down intact tail. Bordered above and below by pale golden brown stripes with notched margins. **Ventral surface** yellow, either uniform or sparsely flecked with small black spots. Chin and throat yellow or grey with a pink or orange hue, usually uniform or occasionally with few black speckles. Ventral surface of tail yellow at base, abruptly changing to a unique mosaic of blue-grey, black and distinctive pink-orange scales. **Eye** colour dark brown, almost black. **Intact tail** distinctly prehensile; longer than body length (SVL). **Subdigital lamellae** 17–22. **Soles of feet** brown, sometimes ochre yellow on palms.

DISTRIBUTION

South Island only. Restricted to a small area between Hokitika and Greymouth on the West Coast.

VARIATION AND SIMILAR SPECIES

Very similar to **speckled skink** (*O. infrapunctatum*), but distinguished by its more slender build, glossier scales and colourful blotched undersurface of tail. Fewer ventral scales than all other closely related taxa (e.g. speckled skink,

Alborn skink (*O.* aff. *infrapunctatum* "Alborn")).

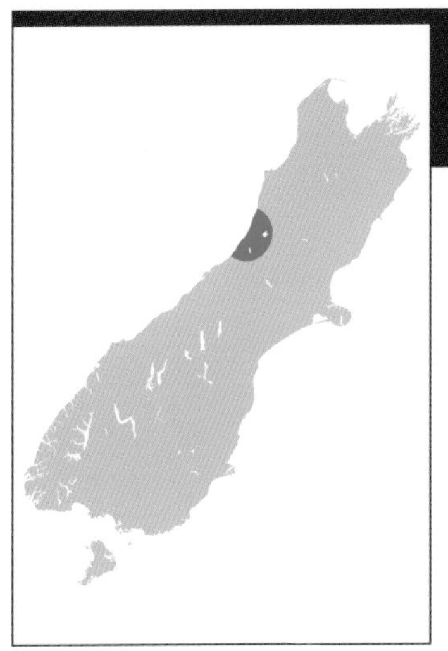

HABITAT

Coastal

Restricted to a narrow (c. 1 km x 5 m) strip of rank exotic grassland between managed pasture and coastal sand dunes. Lives among vegetation and takes refuge under logs, driftwood and discarded inorganic material (e.g. corrugated iron) on farmland.

NATURAL HISTORY

Diurnal; terrestrial. Heliothermic, cryptic sun-basker. Sexual maturity probably reached at 4 years; births reported in late summer (early February). Prehensile tail suggests arboreal tendencies (i.e. may have inhabited coastal forest behind the beach before it was cleared for agriculture). Primarily insectivorous but may consume other small invertebrates (e.g. isopods and amphipods), and probably ate berries before clearance of native vegetation.

ETYMOLOGY

Common and **tag names** referring to Chesterfield on the West Coast, the only known locality for the taxon.

Cobble skink

Oligosoma aff. *infrapunctatum* "cobble"

Endemic

DESCRIPTION

Up to 67 mm SVL; c. 6 g weight

A highly threatened skink; suffering significant decline owing to the ocean eroding its habitat, such that taxon is probably extinct in the wild. Short rounded snout; large round eyes (i.e. distance from mouth to bottom of eye slightly less than height of eye). **Dorsal surface** mid- to dark brown, either uniform or finely flecked with back. When a darker mid-dorsal stripe is present, there may be pale flecks either side. Dorsal surface of intact tail with pale flecks, sometimes forming transverse bands that continue to tip. Scales on top of head may be completely or partially outlined in black. **Lateral surfaces** with a broad darker brown band running from behind eye down to and along intact tail, with irregularly spaced small pale cream spots, and bordered above by a heavily crenulated cream or pale brown stripe, and below by a thinner pale notched stripe. Pale stripes indistinct on intact tail but notched edges of brown lateral band remain distinct. **Ventral surface** muddy to bright yellow, either uniform or with prominent black speckling or spots, latter often joining to form short angular rows. Chin and throat grey or washed brown, and usually finely speckled with black. Ventral surface of intact tail yellow anteriorly, and heavily flecked with black, gradually becoming very dark (almost black) posteriorly. **Eye** colour dark to mid-brown. **Intact tail** longer than body length (SVL). **Subdigital lamellae** c. 16. **Soles of feet** grey or brown, occasionally washed with murky yellow.

DISTRIBUTION

South Island only. Restricted to a short stretch of coastline near Granity, northern West Coast, but probably now extinct in the wild. A captive population has been established.

VARIATION AND SIMILAR SPECIES

Variation poorly known, but degree of black flecking on dorsal surface variable. Much smaller-bodied than other closely related taxa (i.e. up to 67 mm SVL, vs. up to about 85 mm SVL or more). Extremely similar to sympatric **speckled skink** (*O. infrapunctatum*), but distinguished by its small size, glossier scales, larger eye (i.e. distance from mouth to bottom of eye slightly less than height of eye, vs. that distance being equal to height of eye in speckled skink), darker colour of ventral surface of intact tail, and more numerous ventral scales.

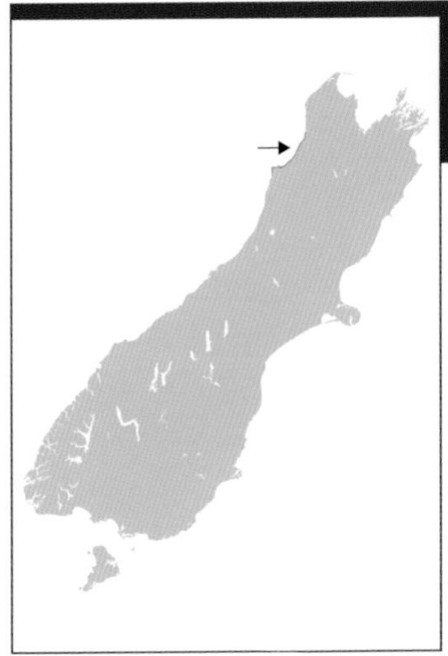

HABITAT

Coastal

Preference for deep cobble over a base of sand, smooth semi-flat stones with a sparse to dense cover of pōhuehue.

NATURAL HISTORY

Diurnal, terrestrial and saxicolous. Heliothermic, and sun-basks cryptically from beneath or between cobbles. Syntopic with the larger speckled skink (*O. infrapunctatum*). Typically gives birth to 2 offspring, presumably annually. Insectivorous, feeding on small invertebrates.

ETYMOLOGY

Common and **tag names** referring to the cobble boulder habitat in which this taxon lives.

Crenulate skink

Oligosoma aff. *infrapunctatum* "crenulate" **Endemic**

Waikato

DESCRIPTION

Up to 90 mm SVL; c. 8.2 g weight

A distinctive skink from the central North Island. **Dorsal surface** brown with fine black and pale speckles, flecks or striations, sometimes also on upper surface of head. A distinctive brown mid-dorsal stripe may be present but usually fades, becoming indistinct from hind limbs and down intact tail. **Lateral surfaces** with a broad dark brown lateral band flecked with golden cream spots, band extending from nostril through eye and down sides of body and tail, with smooth or crenulated edges; band bordered above and below by thinner cream-coloured stripes with relatively smooth or notched edges; area below bottom-most thin pale stripe weakly flecked with grey-brown. **Ventral surface** cream, pale to bright yellow or flushed with pale orange; occasionally uniform but usually densely speckled with black flecks and small spots continuing down undersurface of intact tail. Regenerating tail may be flushed with orange-red. Chin and throat cream or grey, and heavily speckled with black. **Eye** colour orange-brown. **Intact tail** usually longer than body length (SVL). **Subdigital lamellae** 17–22. **Soles of feet** brown or dark grey.

DISTRIBUTION

North Island only. Occurs in the central North Island from Rotorua (including Mokoia Island) southwards to Tokoroa and Taumaranui. A population also on Moutohorā (Whale Island) in the Bay of Plenty.

VARIATION AND SIMILAR SPECIES

Variable in body form, and the degree of notched edges along lateral band.

Individuals from central North Island particularly heavy bodied, with broad head and robust limbs. Those from islands (Mokoia and Moutohorā) smaller and more slender. Geographically isolated from closely related and similar-looking taxa.

HABITAT

Coastal, Lowland

Occupies dense grassland, scrub, shrubands, fernland (bracken), and more open areas on edges of forest. On Moutohorā, found on the coast, among boulder beaches and beneath logs and rocks in grassed areas behind beach. Takes refuge beneath logs and rocks and in dense foliage overnight.

NATURAL HISTORY

Diurnal; terrestrial. Heliothermic but may sun-bask cryptically. Reproductive biology poorly known, but females of Mokoia Island population gravid in spring and summer (November), give birth December–March. Feeds on invertebrates.

ETYMOLOGY

Common and **tag names** referring to the crenulated or notched brown lateral band.

Waikato

Hokitika skink

Oligosoma aff. *infrapunctatum* "Hokitika" **Endemic**

LES MORAN

DESCRIPTION

Up to 85 mm SVL

A very poorly known taxon, known only from two museum specimens and photographs of one additional subadult specimen. Snout blunt, with very distinct denticulate markings around mouth. **Dorsal surface** grey-brown, heavily speckled with dark and light scales. Pale dorsolateral stripes with notched edges continuing along length of body and intact tail. **Lateral surfaces** with a broad dark upper lateral band extending from nostril along length of body and continuing down intact tail, often heavily speckled. Mid-lateral stripe pale cream and narrow (one scale wide). **Ventral surface** cream, with fine black speckles arranged in longitudinal streaks, particularly under tail. **Eye** colour brown. **Intact tail** longer than body length (SVL). **Subdigital lamellae** 18–21. **Soles of feet** grey.

DISTRIBUTION

South Island only. Known from only isolated localities along the South Island's West Coast near Hokitika.

VARIATION AND SIMILAR SPECIES

Variation poorly known. Similar to other closely related taxa but differs in having strongly denticulate lip markings, and belly spots arranged into longitudinal streaks, particularly at base of tail. Also, most specimens have an additional scale separating prefrontal scales on head.

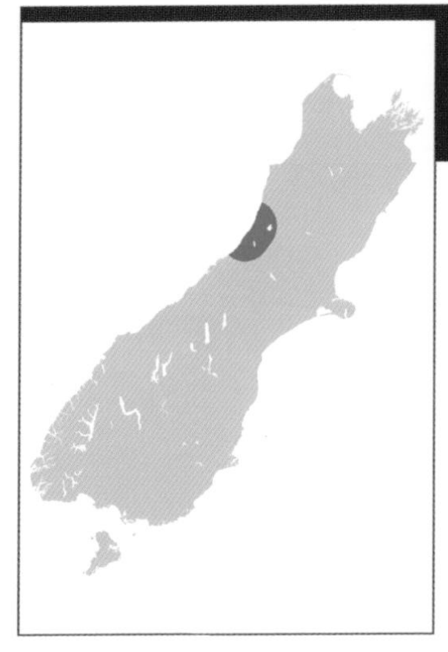

HABITAT

Coastal, Lowland

Occupies exotic and rank grassland, river terraces and banks, and pasture.

NATURAL HISTORY

Diurnal; terrestrial. Heliothermic. Nothing known of its ecology or reproductive biology. Feeds on small invertebrates.

ETYMOLOGY

Common and **tag names** referring to the Hokitika area of the West Coast, where this taxon occurs.

LES MORAN

Westport skink

Oligosoma aff. *infrapunctatum* "Westport"

Endemic

JEAN-CLAUDE STAHL, TE PAPA

DESCRIPTION

Up to 75 mm SVL

Known from a single museum specimen collected in Westport in the late 1990s. Distinguished mainly by genetics; additional specimens needed for an accurate morphological description. Short, blunt, and rounded snout. **Dorsal surface** mid-brown and sparsely flecked with pale and black speckles. Mid-dorsal stripe absent. **Lateral surfaces** have a broad dark brown lateral band overlaid with small irregular pale spots; band edged above by a thin notched pale cream-gold dorsolateral stripe, and below by a creamy white crenulated mid-lateral stripe. A series of small pale blotches continuing along dorsolateral margin of intact tail. Lower lateral surface grey with dark and light flecking. **Ventral surface** (including chin and throat) uniform grey or with faint dark speckling. **Eye** colour brown. **Intact tail** length unknown, but probably equal to or longer than body length (SVL). **Subdigital lamellae** 18. **Soles of feet** brown.

DISTRIBUTION

South Island only. Known only from Westport on the West Coast.

VARIATION AND SIMILAR SPECIES

Variation unknown, but colouration and patterning may differ in live individuals. Outwardly similar to other closely related taxa (e.g. **speckled skink** (*O. infrapunctatum*); **Chesterfield skink** (*O.* aff. *infrapunctatum* "Chesterfield"); **Hokitika skink** (*O.* aff. *infrapunctatum* "Hokitika")). Sister taxon to **Hawke's Bay skink** (*O.* aff. *infrapunctatum* "Hawke's Bay").

HABITAT

Costal, Lowland

No details known other than that specimen was collected from Westport.

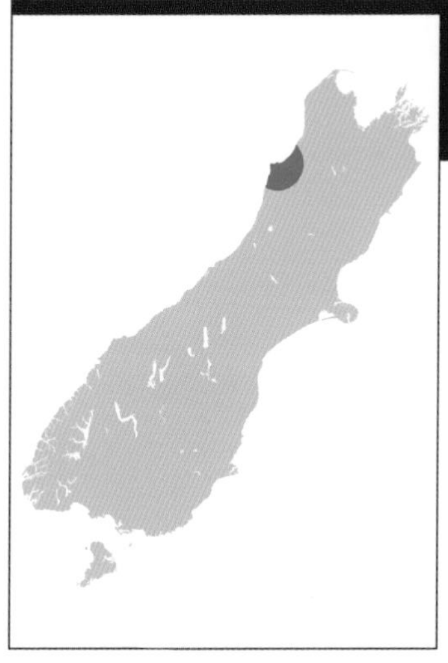

NATURAL HISTORY

Presumably diurnal and terrestrial like other closely related taxa. Ecology and reproductive biology unknown.

ETYMOLOGY

Common and **tag names** referring to the Westport area of the West Coast, from where this taxon is known.

Hawke's Bay skink

Oligosoma aff. *infrapunctatum* "Hawke's Bay" **Endemic**

DESCRIPTION

Up to 92 mm SVL

A robust, heavily built skink from the North Island's south-east coast. **Dorsal surface** light to mid-brown, and heavily speckled or blotched with light and dark markings. Top of head sometimes with black spots or scales outlined with black. A continuous, broken or indistinct mid-dorsal stripe usually present, continuing down tail. **Lateral surfaces** have a broad darker brown lateral band with sparse pale flecks interiorly, and bordered above and below by prominent pale stripes with lightly notched margins. Brown band continuing down intact tail but bordered above and below by only indistinct or broken pale blotches (i.e. no distinct stripes). **Ventral surface** cream or pale yellow and speckled with black flecks. Chin and throat uniform grey and under-surface of tail uniform grey. **Eye** colour light brown. **Intact tail** longer than body length (SVL). **Subdigital lamellae** 18–22. **Soles of feet** light brown.

DISTRIBUTION

North Island only. Known only from central Hawke's Bay (Cape Kidnappers), but may occur elsewhere.

VARIATION AND SIMILAR SPECIES

Variable in tone of brown and degree of black speckling and blotches on dorsal and lateral surfaces. Geographically isolated from all other closely related taxa, but distinguished by longer tail and usually more uniformly striped markings.

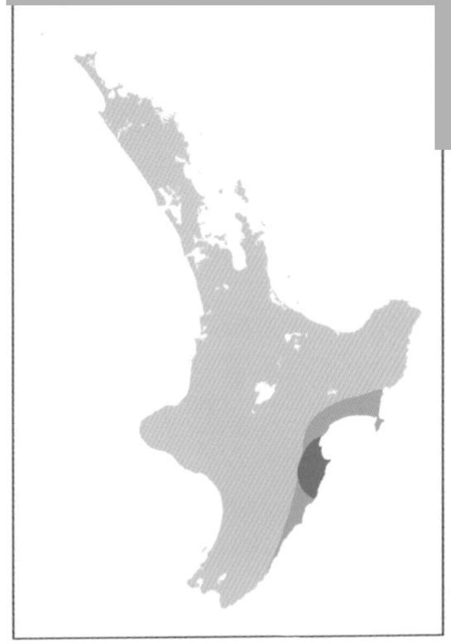

HABITAT

Coastal, Lowland

Occurs in coastal dunes, grassland, low shrubland, scrubland and the fringes of coastal forest. Remains close to cover or refuge when sun-basking, and readily flees when approached. Takes refuge beneath dense vegetation (e.g. grasses) and logs or rocks.

NATURAL HISTORY

Diurnal; terrestrial. Strongly heliothermic (avid sun-basker). Ecology and reproductive biology unknown. Feeds on invertebrates.

ETYMOLOGY

Common and **tag names** referring to the Hawke's Bay Region, where this taxon occurs.

Kupe skink

Oligosoma aff. *infrapunctatum* "southern North Island" **Endemic**

Whanganui

DESCRIPTION

Up to about 75–80 mm SVL

A medium-sized skink from the lower North Island's west coast and the Kaimanawa Mountains. Until recently, populations were considered conspecific with *O.* aff. *infrapunctatum* "Hawke's Bay", but now considered a distinct taxon due to discovery of substantial genetic separation. No museum specimens, so remains poorly known. **Dorsal surface** light to mid-brown, largely uniform in coastal populations and heavily speckled or blotched with light and dark markings in inland ones. Top of head sometimes with black spots or scales outlined with black. A continuous, broken or indistinct mid-dorsal stripe usually present, continuing down tail. **Lateral surfaces** have a broad darker brown lateral band with sparse pale flecks interiorly, and bordered by prominent pale stripes having lightly notched margins. Lateral band continuing down intact tail but borders reduced to indistinct or broken pale blotches (i.e. no distinct stripes). **Ventral surface** cream or pale yellow and speckled with black flecks. Chin and throat uniform grey and undersurface of tail uniform grey. **Eye** colour mid-brown. **Intact tail** longer than body length (SVL). **Subdigital lamellae** 20. **Soles of feet** brown, sometimes with yellow on palms or dark brown toes.

DISTRIBUTION

North Island only. From coastal grassy areas between Whanganui and Patea in southern Taranaki, Ngamatea Station in the Kaimanawa Mountains, and in the Wairarapa.

VARIATION AND SIMILAR SPECIES

Details of morphology poorly documented, but likely variable in brown colour tone, and degree of black speckling and blotches on dorsal and lateral surfaces. Geographically isolated from other closely related taxa.

HABITAT

Coastal, Lowland, Montane/subalpine

Occurs in coastal dunes, grassland, low shrubland, scrubland and the fringes of coastal forest. Remains close to cover or refuge when basking, and readily flees when approached. Takes refuge beneath dense vegetation (e.g. grasses) and logs or rocks.

NATURAL HISTORY

Diurnal; terrestrial. Strongly heliothermic (avid sun-basker). Ecology and reproductive biology unknown. Feeds on invertebrates.

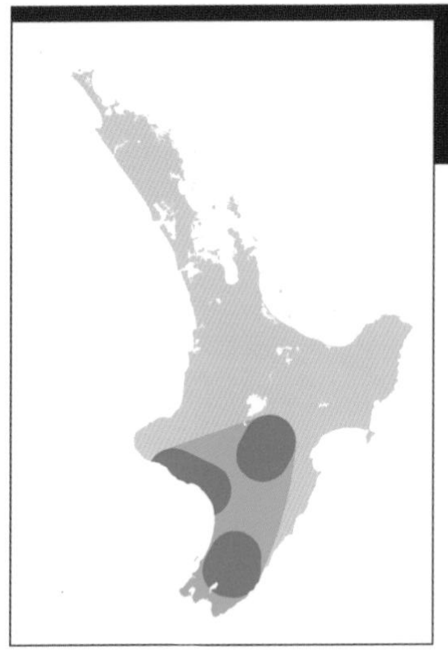

ETYMOLOGY

Common name (Māori) referring to Kupe, the Polynesian discoverer of New Zealand, or to the Kupe oil field in South Taranaki. **Tag name** refers to its distributional range.

Whanganui

Falla's skink

Oligosoma fallai (McCann, 1955)

Endemic

DESCRIPTION

Up to 145 mm SVL; up to 86 g weight

A large and robust skink found only on Manawatāwhi/Three Kings Islands. **Dorsal surface** golden brown, pink-brown or olive-brown, often heavily flecked with dark and light markings that may form short longitudinal striations. Sometimes with a brown mid-dorsal stripe extending from neck to base of tail. **Lateral surfaces** with a narrow golden dorsolateral stripe above a broad brown lateral band, running from behind eye to hind limb. Below brown band, lateral surface grey. Entire lateral surface speckled with brown or grey. **Ventral surface** cream or murky yellow with darker flecks, streaks and blotches. Chin and throat grey. **Eye** colour very dark olive-green to dark brown. **Intact tail** thick, particularly at base; equal to or slightly longer than body length (SVL). **Subdigital lamellae** 21–27. **Soles of feet** dark brown to black.

DISTRIBUTION

North Island only. Confined to the Manawatāwhi/Three Kings Islands, including Manawatāwhi/Great Island, Oromaki/North East Island, Moekawa/South West Island and Tutanekai Rock.

VARIATION AND SIMILAR SPECIES

Little variation, although colour and patterning may fade with age. Unlikely to be confused with syntopic or any other skinks owing to large size and robust body, even in juveniles.

HABITAT

Coastal, Lowland

Occupies a wide range of habitats from the seashore to coastal shrubland, fernland, low-growing vegetation and coastal forest. Favours more open habitats; particularly common under pōhutukawa and puka (*Meryta sinclairii*) canopy, but also inhabits dense scrubland. Uses seabird burrows as refuge sites.

NATURAL HISTORY

Cathemeral. Primarily terrestrial but will also climb tree branches to forage above ground (up to 3 m). Very fast-moving species, especially after basking in sun. Mating occurs in early autumn, with 4 (occasionally 5 or 6) young born in summer and into autumn (January–April), each c. 35–40 mm SVL. Females may not reproduce every year (biennial). Omnivorous, diet consisting of invertebrates (e.g. spiders, millipedes and centipedes, insects and crustaceans), fruits (e.g. berries and fruit of kawakawa (*Piper excelsum*)), and fish and bird carrion. Probably preys on smaller lizards too.

ETYMOLOGY

Specific name and **common name** in recognition of the prominent New Zealand naturalist, Sir Robert Falla (1901–1979).

Chathams skink

Oligosoma nigriplantare (Peters, 1873) **Endemic**

SARAH J. WELLS

DESCRIPTION

Up to 98 mm SVL

A relatively heavily built skink from the Chatham Islands, with variable colour patterns. Snout comparatively blunt. **Dorsal surface** highly variable, ranging from jet black to dark and lighter shades of brown or green with darker and lighter flecks, with or without a dark mid-dorsal stripe. **Lateral surfaces** with a broad dark brown lateral band extending from nostril through eye, along body, and onto anterior portion of intact tail, although some individuals uniformly coloured. Upper and lower edges of band notched, and band bordered above and below by a series of pale flecks or thin cream stripes that usually break up about halfway along body. Lateral surfaces heavily flecked with light and dark brown. **Ventral surface**, including chin and throat, uniform pale brown or yellow-green. **Eye** colour light to dark brown. **Intact tail** longer (up to 1.5x) than body length (SVL). **Subdigital lamellae** 14–21. **Soles of feet** yellow, brown or black.

DISTRIBUTION

Chatham Islands only. Restricted to the Chatham Island group, including Pitt Island (Rangiauria) and nearby small islands and The Pyramid (Tarakoikoia) and The Sisters (Rangitatahi). No longer present on the main Chatham Island.

VARIATION AND SIMILAR SPECIES

Highly variable in colour, and boldness of patterning. Individuals living on the barren, rocky outlying Pyramid and Sisters larger, and typically dark brown or black in colour. Unlikely to be confused with any other lizard owing to geographical isolation from all other species. Most similar to **northern grass skink** (*O. polychroma*) but larger and more robust in body form.

HABITAT

Coastal, Lowland

Inhabits open grassland, shrubland, fernland, forest edges and steep rocky platforms on remote pinnacle islands.

NATURAL HISTORY

Diurnal; terrestrial and strongly heliothermic, often basking out in the open on logs, low-growing vegetation or rocky platforms. Mating occurs in autumn, and up to 4 young born in late January–February. Diet includes invertebrates (e.g. spiders, centipedes, millipedes, insects and crustaceans), soft fruits (including berries) and fish regurgitated by seabirds. Occurs at incredibly high densities on remote rocky islands (e.g. 10 individuals per square metre on The Pyramid).

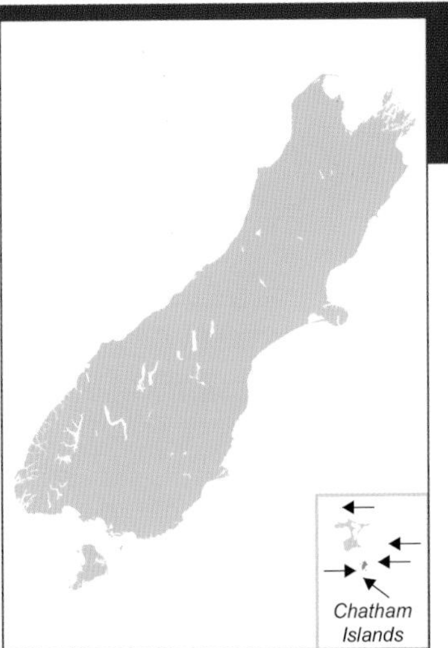

ETYMOLOGY

Specific name (Latin) meaning 'black soled', referring to the colour of the soles of the feet. However, the soles may not necessarily be black. **Common name** refers to the Chatham Islands, where this species occurs.

SARAH J. WELLS

SARAH J. WELLS

Shore skink

Oligosoma smithi (Gray, 1845)

Endemic

Northland

DESCRIPTION

Up to 82 mm SVL; up to 10.3 g weight

One of New Zealand's species restricted to coastal areas, which can be abundant in duneland and rocky shoreline habitats. Snout distinctively pointed. Highly variable in colour patterning. **Dorsal surface** pale creamy white to shades of grey, brown, green, gold and uniform glossy black. Dark mid-dorsal stripe may be present but does not extend down length of intact tail. Frequently heavily speckled or with distinctive cream or golden dorsolateral stripes. Some Northland individuals with markings on upper lip, vaguely reminiscent of a teardrop. **Lateral surfaces** with an indistinct broad brown lateral band, often lightly speckled. **Ventral surface** cream, grey, black or occasionally pink-red, often flecked with darker speckles. Chin and throat usually cream or white. **Eye** colour brown. **Intact tail** often strongly tapering and short, less than or equal to body length (SVL). **Subdigital lamellae** 14–22. **Soles of feet** grey or black.

DISTRIBUTION

North Island only. Widely distributed across the North Island's east coast, from the east coast of Aupouri Peninsula to the Gisborne Region, including many offshore islands. Translocated populations on several islands in Hauraki Gulf and off Whangarei and East Cape.

VARIATION AND SIMILAR SPECIES

Colour patternings vary considerably within and between populations. Animals on many offshore islands glossy jet black (sometimes with iridescent green or white flecks), a variety apparently associated with boulder beach habitats and seaweed piles. Populations from white sandy beach sites and duneland habitats often paler. Striped and speckled specimens associated with more heavily vegetated habitats. Similar to **tātahi skink** (*O.* aff. *smithi* "Three Kings, Te Paki, Western Northland") of west coast but distributions are not known to overlap. May be confused with **egg-laying skink** (*O. suteri*) but distinguished by its lighter build; smaller eyes and less pronounced brow; smaller feet; and shorter toes.

HABITAT

Coastal

Largely restricted to the coast, including sandy, shelly or boulder beaches, and littoral zone. Rarely found more than 100 m from shoreline, but can occur up to 1 km from shore. Forages amongst and takes refuge beneath seaweed, driftwood and other debris, and will enter rock pools.

NATURAL HISTORY

Diurnal; terrestrial. Strongly heliothermic (avid and conspicuous sun-basker) but readily flees for cover, or into rock pools, when disturbed. Able to remain under water, holding its breath, for several minutes. Mating occurs in spring (from about October), and 4–6 young born annually in January–February. Has a high tolerance for salt. Primarily insectivorous, feeding on small shoreline invertebrates (e.g. amphipods, earwigs, beetles, flies), but also known to consume fruits (berries), and scavenge fish and bird carrion.

ETYMOLOGY

Specific name (Latinisation) in recognition of Lieutenant Alexander John Smith of the British Royal Navy, who visited New Zealand in early 1840s and collected type specimens for John Edward Gray of the British Museum. **Common name** refers to its occurrence in coastal or shoreline habitats.

Poor Knights Islands

Tātahi skink

Oligosoma "Three Kings, Te Paki, Western Northland" **Endemic**

West Auckland

DESCRIPTION

Up to 80 mm SVL, but usually smaller; up to c. 10 g weight

A shoreline inhabitant that is similar-looking to and closely related to the shore skink. Snout very pointed. **Dorsal surface** variable in shades of golden sandy brown, grey, greenish or almost black and heavily flecked with gold, white, black or green. Mid-dorsal stripe may be present. A pair of pale or golden dorsolateral stripes extending from above eye and body; may break up and become indistinct about midway between limbs or may continue down intact tail. **Lateral surfaces** with a broad dark brown band running from nostril though eye and onto intact tail, flecked interiorly with gold or white and edged below with an indistinct wavy white line. Lower lateral surface heavily flecked and mottled with white, gold, brown or grey. **Ventral surface** cream, pink, pale yellow or orange, or dark grey; usually uniform but may be speckled with black. Chin and throat grey or cream and lightly or heavily speckled. **Eye** colour olive, light brown or reddish. **Intact tail** slender and long, longer than body length (SVL). **Subdigital lamellae** 14–22. **Soles of feet** black, grey or creamy yellow.

DISTRIBUTION

North Island only. Occurs on the west coast of the upper North Island from Muriwai Beach, northwards to North Cape (Otou). Also on several far northern offshore islands, including Motuopao and Manawatāwhi/Three Kings Islands.

VARIATION AND SIMILAR SPECIES

Highly variable in colour and patterning within and between populations. Very similar to **shore skink** (*O. smithi*) but distributions are not known to overlap; morphological differences between these genetically distinct species yet to be determined. May be confused with **egg-laying skink** (*O. suteri*) but distinguished by its lighter build; smaller eyes and less pronounced brow; smaller feet; and shorter toes.

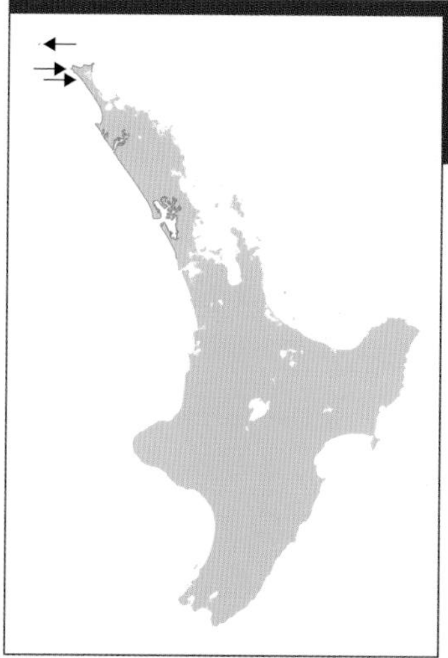

HABITAT

Coastal

Inhabits the shoreline, and vegetation behind beaches, including sand dunes, boulder beaches, coastal rock talus, rock platforms, vineland, scrubland and rank pasture. Occasionally found several hundred metres from the coast in scrubland or rocky habitats.

NATURAL HISTORY

Diurnal; terrestrial, strongly heliothermic (avid sun-basker). Nothing known of the reproductive biology, but presumed to be similar to that of its east coast relative, the shore skink. Primarily insectivorous but will also consume amphipods, potentially soft fruits, and may scavenge carcases of fish and birds on shoreline.

ETYMOLOGY

Common name (Māori) meaning 'beach', referring to the shoreline or beach habitat where this taxon is found. **Tag name** refers to the taxon's geographic range.

West Auckland

Small-scaled skink

Oligosoma microlepis (Patterson & Daugherty, 1990) **Endemic**

DESCRIPTION

Up to 73 mm SVL; c. 5 g (up to 13 g) weight

An inland skink that evolved from shore skink ancestors, probably following closure of the Pliocene sea strait that once ran through the lower North Island. Distinctive white teardrop marking below eye, edged in black. **Dorsal surface** brown or grey-brown with a darker mid-dorsal stripe that breaks up or fades down intact tail. Distinctive pale (cream) dorsolateral stripes with toothed margins. Lighter blotches over dorsal surface. **Lateral surfaces** with a broad dark brown lateral band running from snout down body and intact tail, usually speckled with pale flecks. **Ventral surface** (including chin, throat and tail) uniform pale cream or white. **Eye** colour black; yellow scales surrounding eye. **Mid-body scales** 38–44 rows. **Intact tail** frequently exceeding body length (SVL). **Subdigital lamellae** 22–25. **Soles of feet** grey.

DISTRIBUTION

North Island only. Occurs only in the central North Island, from around Lake Taupō, including on Motutaiko Island, southwards to just north of Taihape, and eastwards through Rangitikei River catchment to Ruahine Range. Also a population on the eastern side of Ruahine Range, at Whanawhana (western Hawke's Bay).

VARIATION AND SIMILAR SPECIES

Little variation in colour patterning, but clear differences in body size across range (larger in southern subpopulations). Superficially similar to **Kupe skink** (*O.* aff. *infrapunctatum* "southern North Island") and **Hawke's Bay skink** (*O.* aff. *infrapunctatum* "Hawke's Bay") but smaller; has a teardrop marking below eye; smaller scales (and more mid-body scale rows); a greyer basal colour; and larger pale blotches on dorsal surface. Distinguished from all other skinks by higher mid-body scale count (38–44 rows). Most closely related to **shore skink** (*O. smithi*) but does not resemble it morphologically; easily distinguished by its larger size, presence of a teardrop marking, and higher counts for mid-body scale rows.

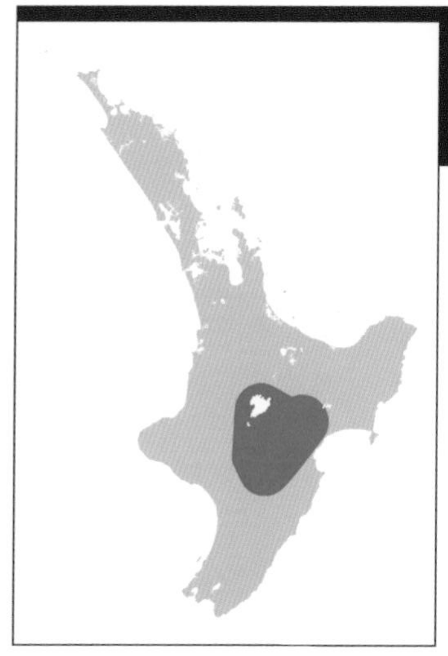

HABITAT

Lowland, Montane/subalpine

Strongly associated with exposed rocky substrate, including rock screes and outcrops, boulder riverbanks, and cliff-faces. Also found among shrublands and vinelands on edges of rock screes. Much of habitat now surrounded by intensively grazed pasture.

NATURAL HISTORY

Diurnal; terrestrial and saxicolous. Strongly heliothermic (avid sun-basker). Reproductive biology poorly known, but 2–3 young born late summer (January–March). Feeds primarily on small invertebrates and possibly eats fruit (i.e. berries).

ETYMOLOGY

Specific name (Greek) meaning 'small scales'. **Common name** also refers to scales being smaller than those of most other New Zealand skinks (i.e. higher number of scales around the body).

Striped skink

Oligosoma striatum (Buller, 1871) **Endemic**

DESCRIPTION

76 mm SVL

A secretive and poorly known species with strong arboreal tendencies. Shallow head with a pointed snout. **Dorsal surface** mid- to light brown, with small irregular pale flecks of white or black. Often with an indistinct dark brown mid-dorsal stripe. Broad pale cream dorsolateral stripes, with smooth margins, running from above eye and along entire length of body; either continuing as separate stripes or converging on intact tail. **Lateral surfaces** with a broad brown mid-lateral band graduating into paler brown on lower lateral surface. **Ventral surface** (including chin and throat) pale grey, brown or yellowish, and heavily speckled with dark brown or black. **Eye** colour orange or orange-brown. **Intact tail** longer than body length (SVL). **Subdigital lamellae** 18–24. **Soles of feet** brown or grey-brown.

DISTRIBUTION

North Island only. Widely distributed from Northland to inland Taranaki, but occurs in scattered locations including Kaipara Flat (Northland); Waitakere Ranges; inland Bay of Plenty around Rotorua; central North Island; Waikato; inland Taranaki. Also known from two large offshore islands in Hauraki Gulf: Great Barrier Island (Aotea Island) and Hauturu/Little Barrier Island.

VARIATION AND SIMILAR SPECIES

Little variation. May be confused with **moko skink** (*O. moco*) or **northern grass skink** (*O. polychroma*), but distinguished by its much broader dorsolateral stripes, a more pointed snout, lighter brown dorsal surface, shorter tail and red eye colour (vs. gold or dark).

HABITAT

Coastal, Lowland

Inhabits dense native lowland podocarp forest (usually dominated by tawa (*Beilschmiedia tawa*)), where it is probably largely arboreal; takes refuge under bark, in epiphytes and under leaf litter and logs on forest floor. Also found in rank pasture, under rotting logs and in weed-dominated (e.g. pampas) shelterbelts in pastoral farmland that was formerly covered with podocarp-hardwood forest. Prefers humid or moist microhabitats.

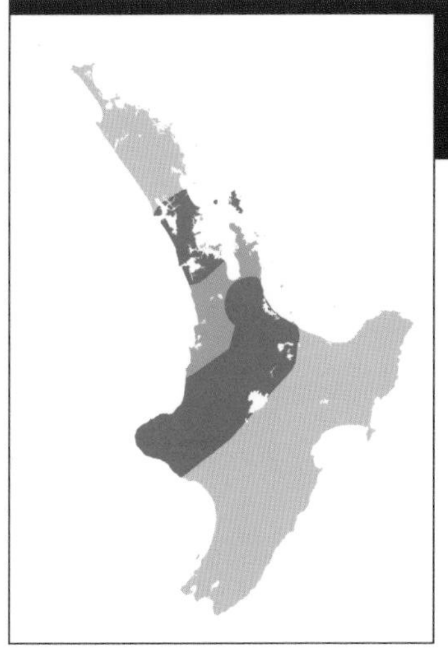

NATURAL HISTORY

Diurnal; arboreal and terrestrial. Heliothermic (active sun-basker, including at extreme heights on large trees and epiphytes, e.g. 22 m up on a rimu tree trunk). Very cryptic, at least partially due to its arboreal habits. Females give birth to 3–8 young in late summer (February–March), but births as late as early autumn in captivity. May occur in social groupings, with adults and juveniles sharing same refuge site. Colonies of 30–40 individuals have been reported from epiphyte clusters in large trees. Primarily insectivorous but may consume soft fruits.

ETYMOLOGY

Specific name (Latin) meaning 'striped'. **Common name** refers to the pale dorsolateral stripes, characteristic of this species.

Moko skink

Oligosoma moco (Duméril & Bibron, 1839) **Endemic**

DESCRIPTION

Up to 81 mm SVL; c. 8 g weight

An active and conspicuous skink at sites where it is abundant. Snout short and rather blunt. **Dorsal surface** various shades of brown (e.g. light, dark or coppery brown); typically with a dark brown mid-dorsal stripe that may be edged in black, and may continue down intact tail or become indistinct. Prominent pale cream dorsolateral stripes extending from nostrils over eyes and to base of tail. A pale cream stripe usually present on forelimb. **Lateral surfaces** with a distinct broad mid- or dark brown smooth-edged band, bordered below by a thinner pale cream mid-lateral line (similar to dorsolateral stripe) that begins beneath nostril and continues through ear, over shoulder to hind limb and typically down intact tail. **Ventral surface** (including chin and throat) pale grey or cream and unmarked. **Eye** colour black. **Intact tail** slender, tapering and long; usually much longer than body length (SVL). **Subdigital lamellae** 17–25. **Soles of feet** black.

DISTRIBUTION

North Island only. Occurs on numerous islands off northern and eastern coasts of the North Island, and also present in scattered populations on the mainland from Northland to Coromandel and Bay of Plenty.

VARIATION AND SIMILAR SPECIES

Little variation, although some individuals may be very dark brown with less distinct stripes. May be confused with **Whirinaki skink** (*O.* "Whirinaki"; syntopic at Bream Head) but distinguished by absence of teardrop marking below eye (vs. present). Similar to **northern grass skink** (*O. polychroma*) but geographically separated, and with smooth-edged stripes that are continuous from nostril and down intact tail (vs. typically notched and becoming indistinct on tail). May resemble **glossy brown skink** (*O. zelandicum*) but geographically isolated and lacking teardrop marking.

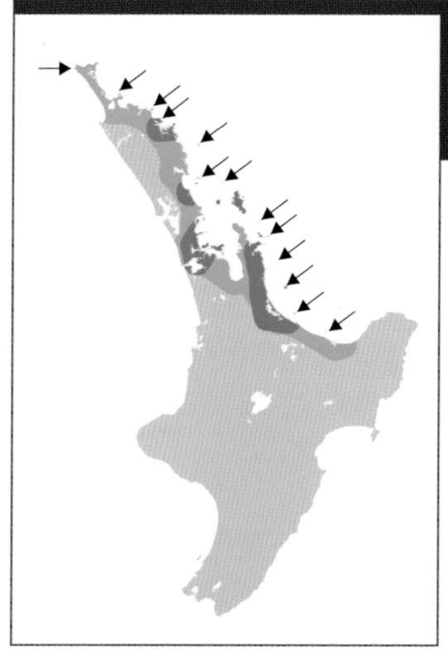

HABITAT

Coastal, Lowland

Occurs in a variety of open sunny habitats, but particularly common in coastal grassland, vineland, boulder beaches and rocky platforms. Also occurs in scrubland, rank grassland, rock jumbles, and the edges and clearings in open forest.

NATURAL HISTORY

Diurnal. Terrestrial, but may climb tree trunks and low branches to forage or find suitable basking sites or feed. Strongly heliothermic (avid sun-basker). Highly alert, and can move quickly when actively foraging. Gravid females recorded in October–January; 2–6 young born February–March. Omnivorous, feeding on small invertebrates (e.g. spiders, millipedes, centipedes, insects and crustaceans), fruit (e.g. berries) and other skinks (e.g. rainbow skink (*L. delicata*)). Also known to take nectar from flowers (e.g. ngaio (*Myoporum laetum*)). Often abundant on offshore islands, especially mammal-free islands, but rare and declining on the mainland.

ETYMOLOGY

Specific name (Latinisation) and **common name** from the Māori word moko, meaning 'lizard'.

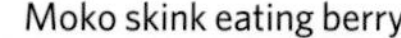

Moko skink eating berry

Whirinaki skink

Oligosoma "Whirinaki" **Endemic**

Whangarei

DESCRIPTION

c. 70 mm SVL

A distinctive skink with a disjunct distribution. Known from a single individual sighted in the central North Island and from a small population in Northland. Snout blunt, head short and broad. Prominent teardrop marking below eye. **Dorsal surface** brown, occasionally with black flecks especially on top of head. No mid-dorsal stripe. A pale dorsolateral stripe extending to just behind forelimb, then gradually fading away. White stripe down forelimb. **Lateral surfaces** with a broad uniform dark brown band extending from nostril, through eye and down body and intact tail; band edged below by a thin cream-coloured mid-lateral stripe, running from eye, through ear, broken over forelimb, and then breaking up into a series of flecks on flanks. **Ventral surface** brown or dark red-orange, and speckled with black. Chin heavily speckled. **Eye** colour dark brown. **Intact tail** slender, prehensile and long; longer than body length (SVL). **Subdigital lamellae** 19–24. **Soles of feet** dark brown to black.

DISTRIBUTION

North Island only. Known only from a single individual found inside a tramping hut in the Whirinaki Te Pua-a-Tāne Conservation Park in the Huiarau Range of western Urewera (central North Island), and from a small population at Bream Head Scenic Reserve, near Whangarei (Northland). True extent of distribution unknown.

VARIATION AND SIMILAR SPECIES

Variation unknown, and the genetic relationship between the Northland and Whirinaki populations also not known. Most similar to **glossy brown skink** (*O. zelandicum*) but distinguished by its greater degree of speckling on ventral surface; higher subdigital lamellae count (usually 23 [19–24] vs. usually 19 [16–23]); and more scale rows across the back (6.5 vs. 8.5 rows). Also resembles **moko skink** (*O. moco*) and **northern grass skink** (*O. polychroma*) but distinguished by teardrop marking below eye, and dorsolateral and mid-lateral stripes being notched or broken (vs. continuous).

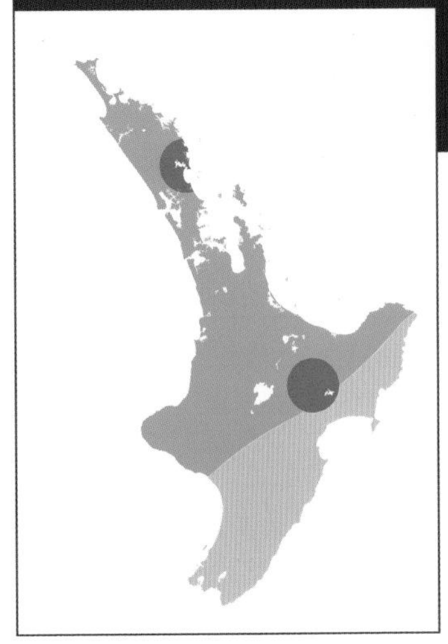

HABITAT

Lowland

Occurs in podocarp, tawa and silver beech (*Lophozonia menziesii*) forests, where it presumably favours open areas that receive sunlight (forest clearings, slips, river terraces), or potentially the canopy of tall trees. On Bream Head, occurs in clearings in coastal broadleaved forest, scrubland and exposed rock outcrops on high ridges.

NATURAL HISTORY

Diurnal. Terrestrial, with arboreal tendencies. Strongly heliothermic, freely sun-basking out in the open but usually close to cover. A poorly known taxon, with nothing known of its reproductive biology. Feeds on small invertebrates.

ETYMOLOGY

Common and **tag names** referring to the Whirinaki Te Pua-a-Tāne Conservation Park where this taxon was first discovered.

Huiarau Range, Bay of Plenty. MARK JEFFERSON

Whangarei

Glossy brown skink

Oligosoma zelandicum (Gray, 1843) **Endemic**

Kapiti Coast

DESCRIPTION

Up to 75 mm SVL; up to 8 g weight

A patchily common skink in shrubland and forest habitats in the south-western North Island and north-western South Island. Shallow head, with a very pointed snout. Denticulate markings along jaws; sometimes with an indistinct white teardrop marking, edged in black, below eye. **Dorsal surface** light to dark brown, with or without darker brown mid-dorsal stripe. Some individuals with fine dark and/or white flecking on upper surface and top of head. **Lateral surfaces** with a broad dark brown band running from nostril, through eye to hind limb, with smooth or notched edges, usually becoming indistinct on tail (occasionally continuing partway down lateral sides of tail). Lateral band bordered above and below by fine pale stripes, complete or broken (fragmented). Lateral surfaces and intact tail sometimes flushed with pink. Continuous white stripe on forelimb. **Ventral surface** (including chin and throat) grey, cream or (more usually) flushed with orange or red, and either uniform or finely flecked with black. **Eye** colour reddish. **Intact tail** longer than body length (SVL). **Subdigital lamellae** 16–23. **Soles of feet** grey, dark brown or black.

DISTRIBUTION

North and South Islands. Occurs from Taranaki across to southern Hawke's Bay, and southwards to Wellington. Also occurs on islands in Cook Strait and in the Marlborough Sounds. In the South

Island, rare on the mainland around the Marlborough Sounds, and occurs from Nelson southwards down the west coast to north Westland.

VARIATION AND SIMILAR SPECIES

Some geographic variation in colour and degree of notching or smoothness of lateral band's edges (e.g. Wellington populations typically smooth edged; South Island individuals can have heavy notching). Some individuals associated with shoreline habitats almost entirely black. May be confused with **northern grass skink** (*O. polychroma*) or **Waiharakeke grass skink** (*O.* aff. *polychroma* Clade 2), but differentiated by having orange or red flush on belly; denticulate markings on jawline; and 8.5 (vs. c. 6) scale rows across back. Similar to **ornate skink** (*O. ornatum*) and **copper skink** (*O. aeneum*) but more slender in build; longer toes and intact tail; more pointed snout; and continuous white stripe down forelimb (vs. always absent). Distinguished from **Whirinaki skink** (*O.* "Whirinaki") by uniform or fine flecking on ventral surface (vs. heavily flecked); lower subdigital lamellae count (usually 19 [16–23] vs. 23 [19–24]); and by differences in scale counts (i.e. 8.5 vs. 6.5 scale rows across the back).

TRENT BELL

Wellington

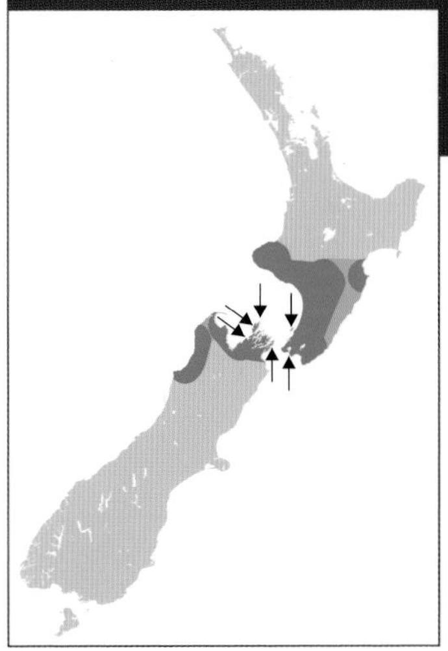

HABITAT

Coastal, Lowland

Occupies a wide range of habitats from more open sites such as the littoral zone, boulder beaches, shingle riverbeds, grassland and wetlands, to more densely vegetated scrubland and damp forests. Also occurs in suburban areas, residential gardens and farmland.

NATURAL HISTORY

Diurnal; terrestrial. Heliothermic. Annual reproduction; up to 7 young (usually 1–5) born in summer (January–March). Diet consisting of smaller invertebrates (e.g. spiders, insects, crustaceans and molluscs); known to feed on smaller lizards, including young of the same species and juvenile geckos.

ETYMOLOGY

Specific name (Latinisation) referring to New Zealand. **Common name** refers to shiny brown colouration.

Copper skink

Oligosoma aeneum (Girard, 1857)

Endemic

Waikato

DESCRIPTION

Up to 76 mm SVL; c. 5 g weight

A small secretive but common skink from the North Island. Snout blunt, and jawline flecked with alternating black and white stripes (denticulate markings). Short limbs and toes. **Dorsal surface** uniform brown or with small black or golden flecks, and narrow copper dorsolateral stripes, particularly obvious above shoulder. **Lateral surfaces** brown but often heavily flecked with black and/or white. **Ventral surface** uniform cream, yellow-green to bright yellow, and tail may be flushed with orange-red. Throat pale, usually with black spots. **Eye** colour orange. **Intact tail** equal to or slightly longer than body length (SVL). **Subdigital lamellae** 13–23. **Soles of feet** off-white or cream.

DISTRIBUTION

North Island only. Widely distributed throughout the North Island from southern Aupouri Peninsula to Wellington, including many offshore islands.

VARIATION AND SIMILAR SPECIES

Variable in shades of brown on dorsal and lateral surfaces, as well as the degree of black flecking. Amelanotic individuals a uniform light pink (almost transparent). May be confused with introduced **plague (rainbow) skink** (*L. delicata*), but differs by having divided or paired frontoparietal scales (divided along the midline), and alternating black and white markings along jawline. Distinguished from **ornate skink** (*O. ornatum*) by its narrower head, denticulate markings on jawlines (vs. the presence of a teardrop marking under eye), smaller ear opening and smaller adult body size. Can be separated from **Hardy's skink** (*O. hardyi*) by its continuous row of subocular scales (vs. subocular row broken below eye), and from **slight skink** (*O. levidensum*) by a combination of higher scale counts and more heavily built body and limbs. Does not overlap in distribution with latter two species.

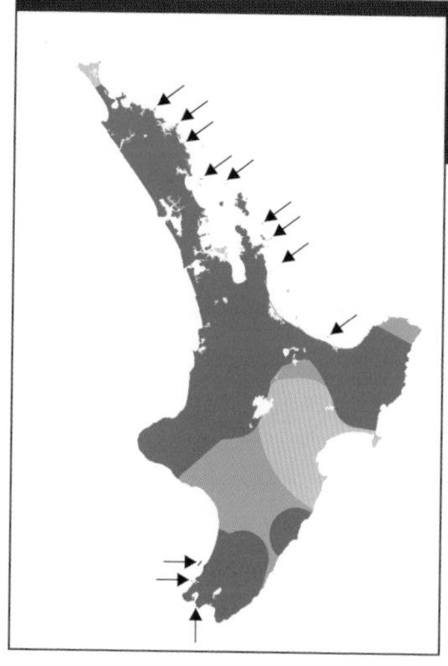

HABITAT

Coastal, Lowland

Generalist; inhabits sandy beaches, coastal vegetation, grassland, dry scrubland, closed forest and even managed agricultural land and urban gardens. Lives among leaf litter, under rocks and logs, in flax and dense herbage. Can be abundant in habitats with dense vegetation, and is one of the most common species found in urban and peri-urban landscapes in the North Island.

NATURAL HISTORY

Predominantly diurnal and occasionally crepuscular; terrestrial but may climb low vegetation. Cryptic, and seldom emerges from cover (cryptozoic), but will sun-bask cryptically or in the open in predator-free areas. Mating occurs September–November. Gravid females recorded in October–January (up to April), and up to 7 young (usually 1–4) born, mainly in January–March. Primarily insectivorous, feeding on smaller leaf litter-dwelling invertebrates (e.g. spiders, insects, crustaceans, molluscs and worms, including nematodes) but will consume smaller members of the same species. Also known to feed on soft fruits.

ETYMOLOGY

Specific name (Latin) meaning 'copper'. **Common name** also refers to the copper or bronze colouring.

Auckland

Waikato

Slight skink

Oligosoma levidensum (Chapple et al., 2008) **Endemic**

DESCRIPTION

Up to 51 mm SVL

A small slight skink from far northern New Zealand; indeed, the smallest native skink. Snout pointed, and limbs somewhat reduced. **Dorsal surface** uniform brown, occasionally with fine pale flecking, particularly on tail. **Lateral surfaces** with copper dorsolateral stripes bordered below by a wider darker stripe; dorsolateral stripes prominent from behind head and over shoulder but fade towards base of tail. Distinct black and white denticulate patterning on upper and lower jawlines. **Ventral surface** uniform white, cream or straw-yellow. Undersurface of tail may be flushed with orange. Chin and throat straw-yellow with or without black flecking. **Body scales** relatively large (i.e. low mid-body scale count, 24–26). **Eye** colour red. **Intact tail** shorter than body length (SVL). **Subdigital lamellae** 16–18. **Soles of feet** orange-brown.

DISTRIBUTION

North Island only. Restricted to northern areas of the Aupouri Peninsula and Motuopao Island Nature Reserve off Cape Maria van Diemen.

VARIATION AND SIMILAR SPECIES

Little variation in colour and patterning. Similar to **copper skink** (*O. aeneum*) but smaller, more slightly built, and with limbs more reduced and lower mid-body scale count; and taxa are geographically isolated.

HABITAT

Coastal, Lowland

On the mainland, found in native kauri (*Agathis australis*) forest and scrubland, beneath damp leaf litter, logs, rocks and shed kauri bark on forest floor. On Motuopao Island, lives among dense flaxland that provides a suitably moist environment.

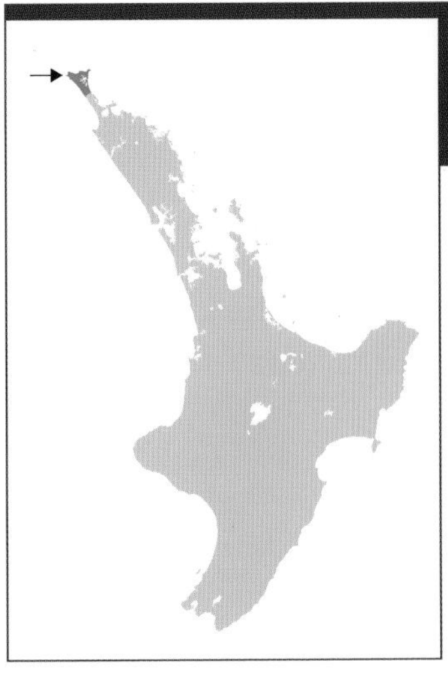

NATURAL HISTORY

Diurnal; terrestrial, semi-fossorial. Very cryptic and sun-basks close to retreat sites or between gaps in leaf litter. Nothing known of its reproductive biology, but almost certainly viviparous. Feeds on small leaf litter invertebrates. Appears to survive at low abundance; becoming increasingly rare on the mainland (unknown causes).

ETYMOLOGY

Specific name (Latin) meaning 'thin, slight'. **Common name** refers to the thin, petite and elongate body, and reduced limbs of this skink.

Hardy's skink

Oligosoma hardyi (Chapple et al., 2008)

Endemic

DESCRIPTION

Up to 62 mm SVL, up to c. 5.1 g weight

Snout sharply pointed. Ear opening small. **Dorsal surface** golden brown, with irregular white and black speckling. Copper dorsolateral line over shoulder, occasionally edged below by a thin black line. **Lateral surfaces** brown above and fading to greyish or yellow-brown below, with irregular light and dark flecks. Alternating dark and pale markings (i.e. denticulate markings) along jawline. **Ventral surface** uniform cream, and chin and throat cream with or without dark flecking. Belly and tail may be flushed with yellow or orange-red. **Eye** colour red. **Subocular scale** row discontinuous. **Intact tail** equal to or slightly longer than body length (SVL). **Subdigital lamellae** 19–23. **Soles of feet** grey.

DISTRIBUTION

North Island only. Restricted to the two largest islands in the Poor Knights Island group: Aorangi and Tawhiti Rahi.

VARIATION AND SIMILAR SPECIES

Little variation in colour and patterning within populations. May resemble the sympatric **Aorangi skink** (*O. roimata*) and juvenile **marbled skink** (*O. oliveri*) but easily distinguished by its denticulate markings on jaw (vs. teardrop marking below eye). Similar-looking to **copper skink** but geographically isolated; Hardy's skink snout much sharper, and subocular scale rows incomplete (vs. complete).

HABITAT

Coastal

Found in coastal forest and scrubland beneath leaf litter, rocks, logs, boulders and small screes, and in flaxland around the coastal fringe. Probably uses seabird burrows as refuge sites.

NATURAL HISTORY

Cathemeral or crepuscular. Terrestrial. Rarely emerging from beneath cover, but may sun-bask cryptically by exposing only part of its body to sunlight. Nothing known of its life history or reproductive biology.

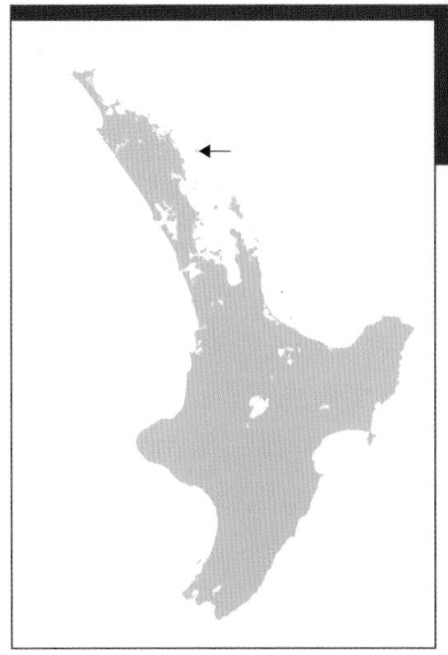

ETYMOLOGY

Specific name (Latinisation) and **common name** in recognition of Graham Hardy, a herpetologist and taxonomist who undertook a comprehensive revision of the New Zealand skink fauna. Hardy recognised that this species showed some significant differences from the related copper skink (*O. aeneum*) but did not separate it formally.

Aorangi skink

Oligosoma roimata Patterson et al., 2013

Endemic

DESCRIPTION

Up to 65 mm SVL

A small but robustly built skink with a pointed snout, which can be relatively cryptic. Distinctive white teardrop marking below eye, edged with black. **Dorsal surface** uniform brown, with or without dark or golden flecks. Black spots or speckles on head. Bronze or golden dorsolateral stripe running from behind head, over shoulder, with a darker chocolate brown smudge below, fading towards hind limb. **Lateral surfaces** brown above and fading to cream on lower lateral surfaces; golden flecks or short streaks may be present. **Ventral surface** white or cream with some dark speckling. **Eye** colour orange. **Intact tail** approximately equal to or shorter than body length (SVL). **Subdigital lamellae** 21–23. **Soles of feet** grey.

DISTRIBUTION

North Island only; island endemic. Known only from the two largest islands in the Poor Knights Island group: Aorangi and Tawhiti Rahi.

VARIATION AND SIMILAR SPECIES

Little variation. May be confused with **Hardy's skink** (*O. hardyi*) but differentiated by its white teardrop marking below eye, and moderately larger ear opening. Similar to **ornate skink** (*O. ornatum*), but geographically isolated from it, and ventral surface is white (vs. usually flushed with orange-red, cream or yellow).

HABITAT

Coastal, Lowland

Occupies coastal forest and forest edges, living among dense ground cover (e.g. flax, scrub), rocks and logs. Often found near seabird colonies and may take refuge in seabird burrows.

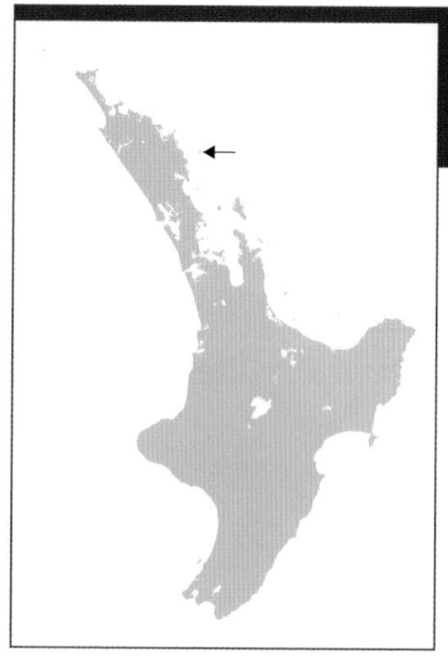

NATURAL HISTORY

Cathemeral, or crepuscular; terrestrial (possibly sub-fossorial). Very cryptic but may sun-bask close to refuge sites. Feeds on small invertebrates. Nothing else known of its ecology or reproductive biology.

ETYMOLOGY

Specific name (Māori) meaning 'tears', referring to the teardrop markings under the eyes. **Common name** refers to Aorangi Island in the Poor Knights Island group, where this species occurs.

Ornate skink

Oligosoma ornatum (Gray, 1843)

Endemic

Auckland

DESCRIPTION

Up to 84 mm; up to 11.5 g weight

A common but secretive skink that prefers damp or humid environments. Short blunt snout. A distinctive white or yellowish teardrop marking, bordered with black on both sides, below eye. Heavily built body, square in cross-section; relatively short limbs and digits. **Dorsal surface** light to dark brown, either uniform or with small pale blotches edged with black flecks. **Lateral surfaces** grey-brown or red-brown, often with distinctive black markings on neck and shoulder. May have intense orange colouration on side of neck and shoulder, and upper surface of forelimb. Tail often flecked with pale blotches along dorsal and lateral surfaces. **Ventral surface** orange-red, cream, green-tinged or yellow, often with less speckling compared to chin and throat, which are heavily flecked with black. **Eye** colour red or orange. **Intact tail** thick and tapers abruptly; equal to or slightly longer than body length (SVL). **Subdigital lamellae** 15–23. **Soles of feet** grey.

DISTRIBUTION

North Island only. Widespread across the North Island mainland, from Northland to Wellington, including many offshore islands. Notable islands include Manawatāwhi/Three Kings Islands, Great Barrier Island (Aotea Island) and Hauturu/Little Barrier Island.

VARIATION AND SIMILAR SPECIES

Variable shades of brown on body and extent of patterning, particularly degree of blotching and flecking. Manawatāwhi/Three Kings Islands individuals morphologically distinct, having a much more slender build, a longer snout and dull or less contrasting dorsal surface markings. Northland individuals often highly patterned with contrasting black and pale-white markings. Similar to **copper skink** (*O. aeneum*), **slight skink** (*O. levidensum*) and **Hardy's skink** (*O. hardyi*), but larger, with distinctive teardrop marking below eye, moderately large ear opening and more heavily built.

Also outwardly similar to **Aorangi skink** (*O. roimata*) but geographically isolated from it, and ventral surface is orange-red, cream or yellow (vs. white). May also be confused with **Hauraki skink** (*O. townsi*), **marbled skink** (*O. oliveri*) and **Whitaker's skink** (*O. whitakeri*), but the lesser degree of black blotching on head, neck, shoulders and ventral surfaces distinguishes ornate skink from these. Juveniles can be distinguished from juvenile **chevron skink** (*O. homalonotum*) by blunter snout, absence of chevron markings on dorsal surface, shorter limbs and more stout body.

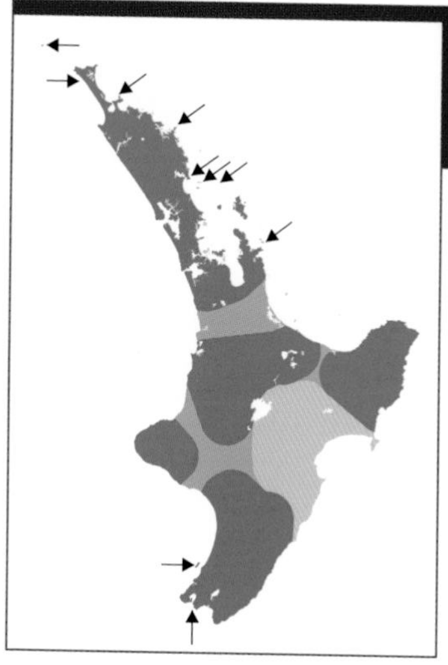

HABITAT

Coastal, Lowland

Inhabits forests, shrublands and grasslands, where damp thick leaf litter and stable cover such as piles of rock or logs, dense vegetation or cracks in the ground (e.g. clay soil) occur. Also found on some smaller offshore islands, in low scrub and sedges. Persists in rural and urban areas. Can occur at high abundance at some sites.

NATURAL HISTORY

Predominantly crepuscular, but can be active at other times of day. Heliothermic and sun-basks cryptically. Secretive (cryptozoic), seldom emerging from beneath cover. Annual reproduction; mating occurs in spring; gestation period 3–4 months; and 4–6 young are born in summer (January–February). Longevity in captivity up to 13 years. Diet consisting of smaller invertebrates (e.g. spiders, insects, crustaceans, worms and molluscs). Adults aggressive and territorial, and have small home ranges.

ETYMOLOGY

Specific name (Latin) meaning 'adorned, decorated, embellished, or ornate'. **Common name** refers to the ornate patterns on the body and tail.

Juvenile, Northland

Three Kings Islands

Whitaker's skink

Oligosoma whitakeri (Hardy, 1977)

Endemic

Kapiti Coast

DESCRIPTION

Up to 101 mm SVL; up to 20 g weight

An exceptionally rare nocturnal species, confined to a few small offshore islands and presumed to have become extinct on the mainland in the last decade. Snout short and blunt. A pale teardrop marking on upper lip below eye. **Dorsal surface** coppery or yellow-brown, usually with dense yellow and black flecking that continues down intact tail. **Lateral surfaces** dark or lighter brown, with heavy yellow and black blotching. Side of head to forelimb very dark brown or black, with large yellow or cream blotches. **Ventral surface** yellow or orange (rarely cream), usually uniform or may be heavily spotted with black. Chin and throat grey, dark brown or black with irregular pale spots, flecks or blotches. **Eye** colour orange or reddish. **Intact tail** equal to or slightly longer than body length (SVL). **Subdigital lamellae** 17–23. **Soles of feet** pale brown or grey-brown.

DISTRIBUTION

North Island only. Restricted to islands in the Mercury Island group and Castle Island off Coromandel Peninsula, and a single (likely extinct) population on the southern Kapiti Coast, north of Wellington. Subfossil evidence indicates that it was once continuously distributed across the majority of the North Island.

VARIATION AND SIMILAR SPECIES

Little variation, although colour patterning may fade significantly with age. Easily confused with **marbled skink** (*O. oliveri*) and **Hauraki skink** (*O. townsi*) but distinguished by its more slender build, and a greater degree of black colouration on side of head, neck, chin and throat. Distinguished from **ornate skink** (*O. ornatum*) by larger adult size; black colouration on head, neck, chin and throat; and conspicuous yellow flecking.

HABITAT

Coastal

On offshore islands strongly associated with thick leaf litter and areas littered with seabird burrows beneath the coastal forest canopy. Kapiti Coast population known from a single greywacke scree or talus slope, partly covered by dense pōhuehue and low-growing *Coprosma* species.

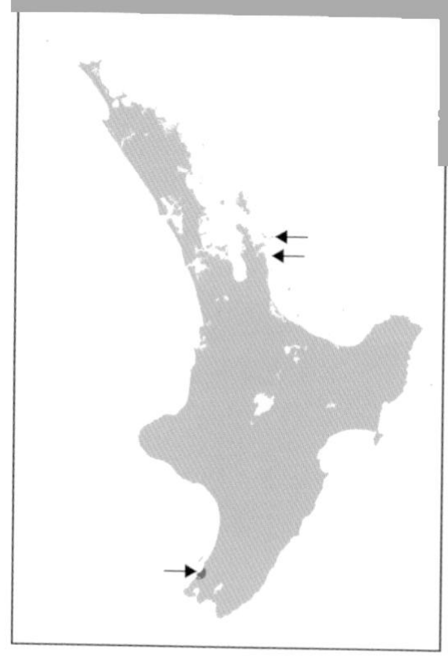

NATURAL HISTORY

Nocturnal, but may rarely sun-bask by day. Terrestrial and semi-fossorial, but may climb lower branches. Requires warm moist environments - highly susceptible to evaporative water loss, so surface activity limited to warm humid nights (especially during or following rainfall) during summer and autumn. At other times, forages in burrows or under rocks. Biennial reproduction; 1-4 young born in February-April. Sexual maturity reached at 5-8 years. Longevity recorded at 18 years (c. 50 years in captivity). Omnivorous, diet consisting of invertebrates (e.g. spiders, millipedes, centipedes including *Cormocephalus rubriceps*, crustaceans and molluscs), and fruits (e.g. American black nightshade (*Solanum americanum*); kawakawa).

ETYMOLOGY

Specific name (Latinisation) and **common name** in recognition of the late Anthony Hume Whitaker (1944-2014), a renowned New Zealand herpetologist.

Coromandel

Marbled skink

Oligosoma oliveri (McCann, 1955) **Endemic**

Poor Knights Islands

DESCRIPTION

Up to 116 mm SVL

A robustly built skink from the northern offshore islands. A white black-edged teardrop marking below eye; may have light and dark denticulate patterning on lips. **Dorsal surface** light to dark brown, uniform or flecked with black. **Lateral surfaces** grey-brown with black blotches, occasionally entirely black with grey-white blotches along length of body, usually lessening in intensity towards ventral surface. Distinctive dark blotches on neck and above forelimb. **Ventral surface** pale cream with black markings and spots, especially on chin and throat but also on belly. Juvenile colouration similar to adult's but more uniform brown on dorsal surface and more contrasting colours. **Eye** colour orange. **Primary temporal scales** 2. **Mid-body scales** 34–42 rows. **Intact tail** equal to or longer than body length (SVL). **Subdigital lamellae** 17–24. **Soles of feet** grey- or pink-brown.

DISTRIBUTION

North Island only. Restricted to northern offshore islands, including the Poor Knights Islands, Mercury Islands, Ohinau Island, and Alderman Island group. Subfossil evidence indicates a more widespread historic distribution across the North Island mainland, from Northland to Hawke's Bay.

VARIATION AND SIMILAR SPECIES

Little variation but dorsal and lateral colours may fade with age. Northern (Poor Knights Islands) animals much larger, with minor morphological differences from southern populations (Mercury and Alderman Islands), but differences not reflected in levels of genetic divergence. Southern population previously considered a separate species (*C. pachysomaticum*). May be confused with **Hauraki skink** (*O. townsi*) but taxa are geographically isolated and marbled skink distinguishable by its more robust body form, speckled or blotched ventral surface and 2 primary temporal scales (vs. 1). May be confused with **Whitaker's skink** (*O. whitakeri*), but differentiated by its larger size and more thickset body proportions. Juveniles can be distinguished from **ornate skink** (*O. ornatum*) by colour pattern, particularly dark speckling and blotches on ventral surface.

HABITAT

Coastal, Lowland

Lives among leaf litter and rock piles beneath coastal forest and scrubland. Frequently takes refuge in seabird burrows and will escape predators (e.g. tuatara and giant centipedes) by rushing into burrows.

NATURAL HISTORY

Primarily nocturnal, but can also be active during the day; terrestrial. Occasionally sun-basks cryptically. Reproductive

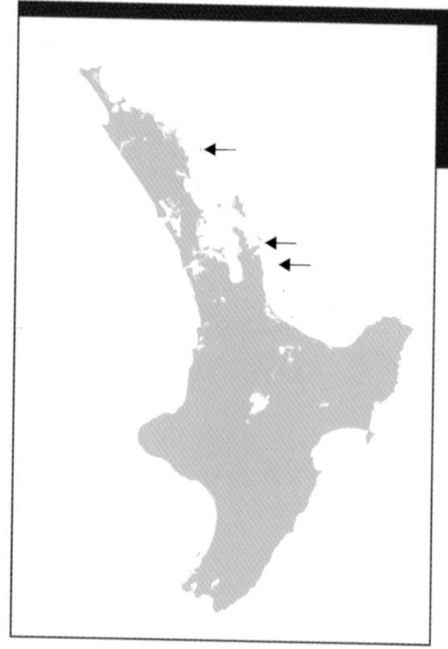

biology poorly known, but 2–4 young born in late summer (March–April). Breeding may not occur every year (i.e. possibly biennial reproduction). Omnivorous, actively seeking out and feeding on invertebrates (spiders, millipedes and centipedes, crustaceans and molluscs), fruits (i.e. berries such as American black nightshade), and likely to prey on smaller lizards. Also known to scavenge on the carcases of fish and seabirds.

ETYMOLOGY

Specific name recognising Dr W. R. B. Oliver (1883–1957), former director of the Dominion Museum (now Museum of New Zealand Te Papa Tongarewa). **Common name** refers to the 'marbled' patterning on the ventral surface.

Hauraki skink

Oligosoma townsi (Chapple et al., 2008) **Endemic**

Little Barrier Island

DESCRIPTION

Up to 95 mm SVL

A distinctive white black-edged teardrop marking beneath eye; alternating black and white (denticulate) patterning on lower jaw. **Dorsal surface** light to darker brown with irregular dark and light spots or flecks. **Lateral surfaces** dark brown and heavily blotched with light and dark markings, brown colour fading to cream or grey ventrally. Black mottling and blotches particularly prominent from behind head and over shoulder. **Ventral surface** cream or grey, sometimes with an orange tinge; usually uniform but may be lightly flecked with black. Chin and throat heavily flecked with black. Juvenile colouration similar to adult's but usually more contrasting. **Eye** colour orange. **Primary temporal scales** 1 (occasionally 2). **Mid-body scales** 38–44 rows. **Intact tail** approximately equal to body length (SVL). **Subdigital lamellae** 19–25. **Soles of feet** grey or brown.

DISTRIBUTION

North Island only. Occurs only on offshore islands, including Great Barrier Island (Aotea Island) and Hauturu/Little Barrier Island; the Hen and Chickens Island group; and Mokohinau Islands in Northland. Subfossil evidence indicates a more widespread historic distribution across the North Island mainland from Northland to Hawke's Bay, although this is tentative as bones are difficult to distinguish from those of **marbled skink** (*O. oliveri*).

VARIATION AND SIMILAR SPECIES

Little variation, although colour and patterning in older individuals may be more faded or dull. Resembles **marbled skink**, **Whitaker's skink** (*O. whitakeri*) and **ornate skink** (*O. ornatum*). Distinguished from marbled skink by its more slender body form, uniform or lightly speckled ventral surface, and 1 primary temporal scale (vs. 2); species are geographically isolated (i.e. not sympatric). Distinguished from Whitaker's skink by absence of yellow and copper colouration, and uniform or lightly speckled ventral surface. Although syntopic with ornate skink on Great and Little Barrier Islands and the Chickens group, Hauraki skink is much larger and has more black colouration on head, dorsal and lateral surfaces.

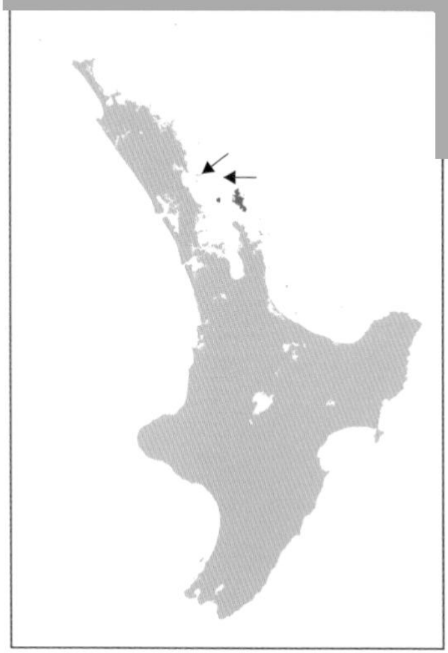

HABITAT

Coastal, Lowland

Occurs from the littoral zone inland into flaxland, low scrubland and coastal forest, inhabiting boulder beaches covered in prostrate vines (e.g. pōhuehue), dense leaf litter and rock screes below the forest canopy. May also use seabird burrows.

NATURAL HISTORY

Nocturnal; terrestrial. Occasionally moves around during day, but rarely sun-basks. Primarily insectivorous but will consume small fruits (e.g. berries). Nothing known about its reproductive biology but likely to be similar to that of marbled skink.

ETYMOLOGY

Specific name (Latinisation) in recognition of David R. Towns, a prominent New Zealand herpetologist and conservation scientist. **Common name** refers to the Hauraki Gulf, which encompasses the distributional range of this species.

Little Barrier Island

Robust skink

Oligosoma alani (Robb, 1970) **Endemic**

Northland

DESCRIPTION

Up to 150 mm SVL; up to 100 g weight

A large distinctive skink, with large eyes and a very stout build. Snout very short. Bold pale yellow teardrop marking below eye, edged with black. Body almost square in cross-section. Limbs short and stout, with short digits. **Dorsal surface** brown, copper-brown or pink-brown with irregular pale yellowish blotches, often edged in black, mid-dorsally and dorsolaterally. **Lateral surfaces** light brown-grey, cream, salmon pink or pale yellow, with irregular pale blotches that fade towards belly. A series of dark markings or blotches over shoulder. **Ventral surface**, chin and throat cream, pale yellow or red with darker flecks. **Eye** colour black; eye large and ringed with yellow scales. **Intact tail** almost square in cross-section and taping sharply; shorter than body length (SVL). **Subdigital lamellae** 16–21. **Soles of feet** cream or light grey with a pink hue.

DISTRIBUTION

North Island only. Currently restricted to small islands off northern and north-eastern coastline of the North Island from Coromandel to the Aupouri Peninsula. Subfossil evidence indicates a past distribution throughout low-elevation forests across the North Island mainland.

VARIATION AND SIMILAR SPECIES

Substantial genetic and morphological divergences exist between the Northland and Coromandel populations.

1. ***Northland:*** Often strikingly patterned, with rich brown dorsal surface and lemon-yellow blotches. Ventral colouration varies from cream to yellow or crimson. Cheeks often bright salmon-pink, with a pale teardrop marking usually present beneath eye. Generally larger than Coromandel individuals (i.e. up to 150 mm SVL; approximately 100 g in weight).
2. ***Coromandel:*** Comparatively plain in colouration, with a grey-brown dorsum with darker flecks, and large dark-edged cream-yellow blotches. Flanks also blotched and have a lighter background colour. Noticeably smaller than northern individuals.

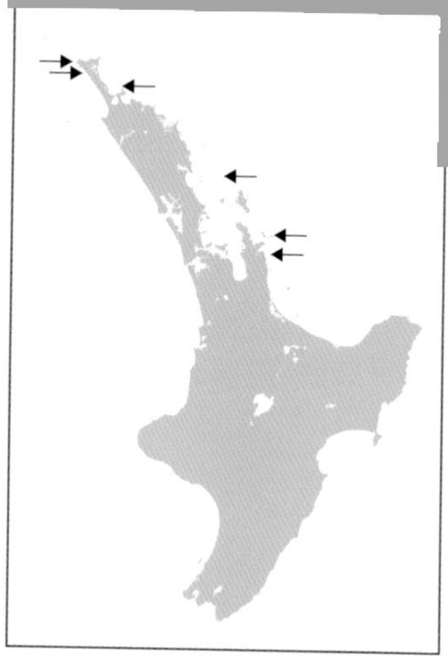

Unlikely to be confused with other species owing to its distinctive thickset body proportions and very large dark eye. Neonate or juvenile robust skinks may be confused with **ornate skink** (*O. ornatum*), but can be distinguished by the large irregular-shaped yellow blotches on dorsal surface (vs. absent in *O. ornatum*).

HABITAT

Coastal

A forest inhabitant, preferring deep moist leaf litter: often found in association with seabird burrows. Found in flaxland, where it takes refuge beneath dead flax fronds. Susceptible to evaporative water loss, and particularly active after heavy rain.

NATURAL HISTORY

Nocturnal; terrestrial. Annual or biennial reproduction. Females reach sexual maturity at 5–6 years, and 6–8 young are born February–April. Lifespan likely to exceed 20 years. Feeds on large ground-dwelling invertebrates (e.g. wētā, spiders, centipedes including *Cormocephalus rubriceps*, millipedes, beetles, crustaceans and molluscs), other lizards (geckos and probably skinks) and fruits (e.g. American black nightshade, kawakawa and *Coprosma* species). Also known to scavenge the carcases of fish and seabird chicks.

ETYMOLOGY

Specific name a reference to Alan Robb, the nephew of the late Joan Robb (1921–2017), former Associate Professor of Zoology at the University of Auckland, who described this species. **Common name** refers to this skink's large and robust body shape.

McGregor's skink

Oligosoma macgregori (Robb, 1975)

Endemic

Mana Island

DESCRIPTION

Up to 114 mm SVL

A large, heavily built and aggressive skink, with distinctive colour patterns. Triangular-shaped head with blunt snout. Pale black-edged teardrop marking below eye. **Dorsal surface** light to dark shades of brown, with 3 irregularly broken darker stripes (vary in intensity) or darker flecks from neck to base of tail, or may fade to a more uniform brown colour. **Lateral surfaces** pale grey-brown with irregular pale and dark markings or smudges. Large irregular black blotches, frequently outlined in cream or white, on side of neck and above shoulder. Dark longitudinal streaks may be present on lateral surface of tail. **Ventral surface** uniform grey-white or pale pink, occasionally with dark speckling on throat and chin. **Eye** colour orange. **Intact tail** equal to or longer than body length (SVL). **Subdigital lamellae** 20–26. **Soles of feet** sooty grey.

DISTRIBUTION

North Island only. Restricted to several offshore islands, including the Cavalli and Bream groups, Sail Rock in the Chickens group, and Mana Island off the Kapiti Coast. Historically, distributed widely throughout the North Island (evidence based on subfossil remains).

VARIATION AND SIMILAR SPECIES

Little variation; however, extent of dark blotches on neck may vary. Colouration may fade or dull with age. Very distinctive and unlikely to be confused with other taxa. Most similar to **Hauraki skink** (*O. townsi*) and **marbled skink** (*O. oliveri*), but distinguished by its uniform greyish ventral surface; geographically isolated from these two species.

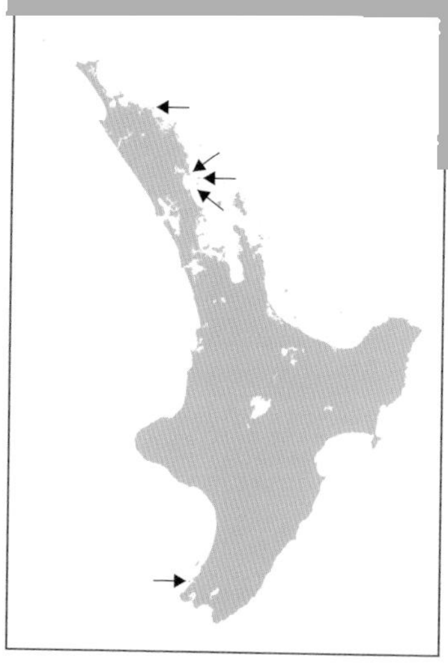

HABITAT

Coastal

Occurs from the shoreline up into forest, occupying rocky shore platforms, rock crevices, rocky ledges covered in prostrate herbs, boulder beaches, leaf litter beneath coastal shrubland, flaxland and coastal forest.

NATURAL HISTORY

Nocturnal and/or crepuscular; terrestrial. Reproductive biology poorly known but 2 young born usually in late summer (February–March). Feeds on small to large invertebrates. Aggressive towards other lizards, including its own kind, and preys upon smaller species (e.g. **moko skink** (*O. moco*)). Does not appear to be able to coexist with mammalian predators.

ETYMOLOGY

Specific name and **common name** in honour of the former head of the Department of Zoology at the University of Auckland, the late Professor William Roy McGregor (1895–1975).

Plague (rainbow) skink

Lampropholis delicata (De Vis, 1888)

Exotic; introduced and naturalised

'Unwanted Organism' under the Biosecurity Act 1993. It is illegal to knowingly move, spread, release, breed, display or sell this species without permission from the Ministry for Primary Industries.

DESCRIPTION

Up to 55 mm SVL; up to 1.9 g weight

A small fast moving sun-loving skink, frequently seen in gardens and parks in northern regions of the North Island. **Dorsal surface** grey or grey-brown to dark brown, occasionally lightly speckled, and may shimmer with iridescence in sunlight. A faint narrow mid-dorsal stripe occasionally present. **Lateral surface** with a broad dark band from shoulder to base of tail, often bordered above and below by thin pale stripes. **Ventral surfaces** pale grey, white or pale yellow. Chin and throat whitish, with or without dark brown speckles or striations. **Eye** colour hazel brown. **Frontoparietal scale** 1 (vs. divided frontoparietal scales in all *Oligosoma* skinks). **Intact tail** thin and long, noticeably longer than body length (SVL). **Subdigital lamellae** 21–23. **Soles of feet** black.

DISTRIBUTION

North Island. Introduced from Australia in the 1960s, now naturalised and widespread in the upper North Island from Northland (central Aupouri Peninsula) to central Waikato. Established 'satellite' populations occur in Palmerston North, New Plymouth, Whanganui and Hawke's Bay, and a small population found near Blenheim (South Island) (but eradication of this population is underway). Generally absent from offshore islands, although there are populations on several islands in the Hauraki Gulf (e.g. Rangitoto and Motutapu Islands, Kawau Island, Waiheke Island and Great Barrier Island (Aotea Island)). Dispersal to new sites is generally assisted by humans, who inadvertently move individuals or eggs with freight, building materials, soil, gravel and pot plants. Distribution expected to expand significantly over time.

VARIATION AND SIMILAR SPECIES

Typically little variation, but degree of dorsolateral striping varies. Some individuals finely speckled with black on dorsal surface. May be confused with **copper skink** (*O. aeneum*), but differs by being more slight in body form; having a single frontoparietal scale (vs. divided or paired frontoparietal scales in all native *Oligosoma* skinks); and lacking black and white denticulate markings along jaws (vs. markings clearly visible). Southern outlying populations may be confused with **glossy brown skink** (*O. zelandicum*) or **grass skink species complex**, i.e. northern grass skink (*O. polychroma*); Waiharakeke grass skink (*Oligosoma* aff. *polychroma* Clade 2); South Marlborough grass skink (*O.* aff. *polychroma* Clade 3); Canterbury grass skink (*O.* aff. *polychroma* Clade 4); and southern grass skink (*O.* aff. *polychroma* Clade 5), but are considerably smaller as adults, and distinguished by their single frontoparietal scale.

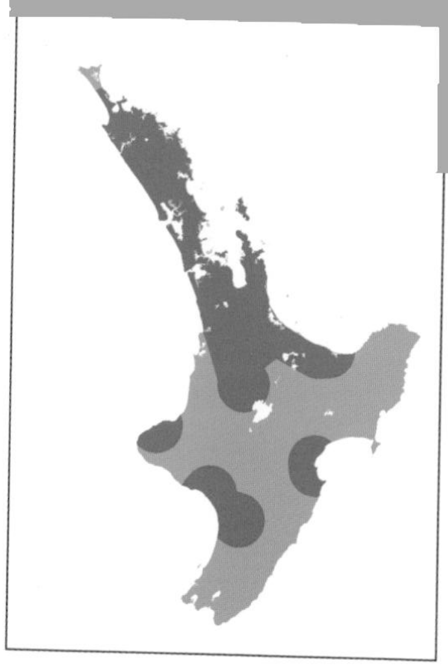

Eggs

HABITAT

Coastal, Lowland

Primarily inhabits open landscapes, including littoral zone, boulder beaches, sandy beaches, farmland, urban and suburban areas, open shrubland, forest edges and clearings, but can occur in dense native forest. Frequently occurs in disturbed habitats (e.g. industrial sites, public walkways), and beneath organic or inorganic debris and wood or rock piles.

NATURAL HISTORY

Diurnal; terrestrial. Alert and moves rapidly, especially after basking in the sun. Strongly heliothermic, conspicuous sun-basker. Oviparous (egg-laying); females can lay 2–8 white oval eggs per clutch; egg 8–10 mm long with tough leathery shell. Up to 3 clutches per year; communal nests with 20–250 eggs reported in New Zealand. Eggs hatch in late summer (February–March); eggs in their late development stage can hatch in response to disturbance (e.g. vibration or movement). Lifespan 2–4 years. Can rapidly attain high population densities and, thus, is expected to have negative impacts on native lizards or other native fauna through resource competition (food and habitat), predation of native invertebrates, and/or by artificially elevating the abundance of lizard predators (e.g. kingfishers (*Todiramphus sanctus*)), which in turn may result in greater predation pressure on native lizards.

ETYMOLOGY

Specific name (Latin) meaning 'delicate', referring to the slender body form.
Common name(s) respectively reflect either the huge abundance in which this species can occur (plague proportions), and the iridescent rainbow sheen of the scales on the dorsal surface.

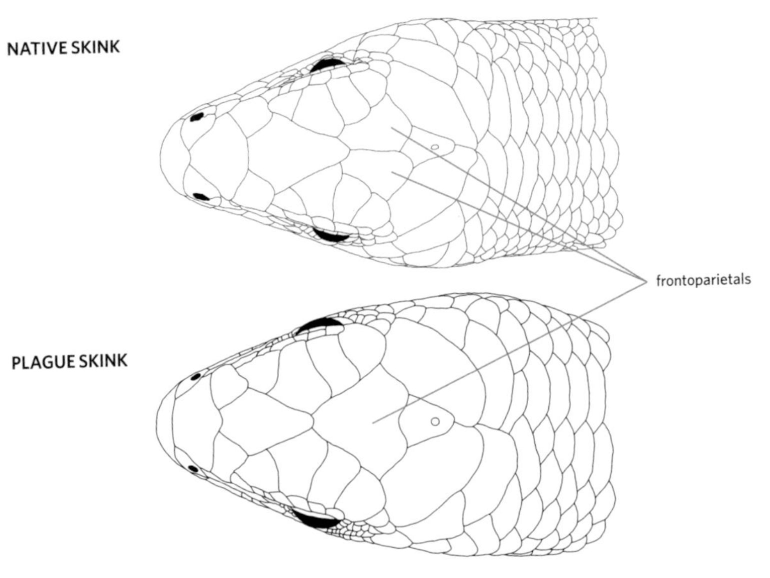

Key to New Zealand skinks

1	**Body** squarish in cross-section; **limbs and toes** relatively short; lower **eyelid** scaly or covered by 1 or 2 opaque scales; **head** relatively deep and blunt	2
	Body oval in cross-section; **limbs and toes** relatively long; lower **eyelid** with 1 transparent disc; **head** relatively shallow and pointed	13
2	Lower margin of eye without pale **teardrop** marking; **mid-body scale rows** ≤ 34; **ear** opening small (scarcely larger than pinprick)	11
	Lower margin of eye with distinct pale **teardrop** marking; **mid-body scale rows** > 32; **ear** opening moderate/large	3
3	**Eye** colour black; eye large relative to head; **snout** short, rounded; **body** very thickset and particularly squarish in cross-section	***O. alani***
	Eye colour red or orange; eye relatively small; **snout** elongate or blunt; **body** less thickset but squarish in cross-section	4
4	**Dorsal surface** with 3 irregularly broken darker stripes (vary in intensity) from neck to base of tail; large black irregular-shaped marking on lateral surface of neck and shoulder (often outlined with a pale line), and distinctive from rest of grey-brown lateral surface of body	***O. macgregori***
	Dorsal surface without stripes; where present, black markings on neck and shoulder merge gradually into lateral surface of the body	5
5	**Dorsal surface** with numerous black and yellowish flecks; lateral surface dark brown to black from ear to hind limbs, interrupted with small yellowish blotches; **ventral surface** yellow-orange	***O. whitakeri***
	Dorsal and lateral surfaces without yellowish flecks or blotches	6
6	**Throat** creamy to reddish, variously flecked with dark grey to black; dorsolateral surface with narrow, continuous dark brown to black stripe from above ear to forelimb insertion; **dorsal surface** often with small pale patches	7
	Throat white, heavily marked with black; dorsolateral surface with broad dark brown band interrupted with paler blotches from above ear to forelimb insertion or further; **dorsal surface** light to dark brown, sometimes flecked with black	8
7	**Ventral surface** white; Poor Knights Islands only	***O. roimata***
	Ventral surface usually flushed with orange, red, pink or yellow	***O. ornatum***
8	**Mid-body scale rows** < 38	***O. oliveri***
	Mid-body scale rows 38–44	9

9	1 primary **temporal scale**	***O. townsi***
	2 primary **temporal scales**	**10**
10	**Throat** heavily speckled or blotched with black; **ventral surface** heavily speckled	***O. oliveri***
	Throat heavily speckled with black; **ventral surface** lightly speckled or flecked with black	***O. townsi***
11	**Subocular scale** row discontinuous under eye	***O. hardyi***
	Subocular scale row continuous under eye	**12**
12	**Mid-body scale rows** 24–26; **dorsolateral lines** prominent; **body and limbs** slender	***O. levidensum***
	Mid-body scale rows usually > 26; **dorsolateral lines** indistinct or absent; **body and limbs** stout	***O. aeneum***
13	**Frontoparietal scale** single; **dorsal surface** uniform brown, occasionally with sparse black speckles; mid-dorsal stripe absent; nasal scales widely separated when viewed from above; egg laying	***Lampropholis delicata***
	Frontoparietal scale divided (paired)	**14**
14	South Island or Stewart Island/Rakiura only	**15**
	North Island, South Island or Stewart Island	**21**
15	**Dorsal surface** very dark with many greenish or yellowish flecks giving an overall greenish tinge; occurs on or very near exposed rocky shoreline platforms; Fiordland only	***O. acrinasum***
	Not as above	**16**
16	**Mid-body scale rows** ≥ 40	**17**
	Mid-body scale rows < 40	**25**
17	Distinctive brown **lateral band**, bordered above and below by narrow pales stripes; **toes** long relative to body size; **body size** < 91 mm SVL	**18**
	No brown **lateral band** or obvious stripes; **toes** not long relative to body size (but may still be long); **body size** > 91 mm SVL	**19**
18	**Lateral band** with smooth edges	***O. hoparatea***
	Lateral band with notched (crenulated) edges	***O. longipes*** **O. aff. *longipes* "southern"**
19	**Dorsal and lateral surfaces** dark (almost black) with large cream, pale yellow or pale green blotches, extending down tail; **ventral surface** mottled with large black and white blotches	***O. otagense***
	Dorsal surfaces speckled or flecked; **ventral surface** uniform or finely flecked with black	**20**
20	**Dorsal surface** pale cream or grey with dark speckling or markings that often form transverse bands; **mid-body scale rows** ≥ 50	***O. waimatense***
	Dorsal surface base colour dark (black) with light speckling or flecks, that may form short longitudinal striations; **mid-body scale rows** < 54	***O. grande***

21	Broad pale cream-coloured **dorsolateral stripes** (1 and 2.5 scales wide) that come close together at base of tail; **belly** heavily spotted. North Island only	***O. striatum***
	Not as above	**22**
22	**Dorsal surface** with distinct chevron markings; bold black and white markings across lips; known only from Great Barrier Island (Aotea Island) and Hauturu/Little Barrier Island	***O. homalonotum***
	Not as above	**23**
23	**Dorsal and lateral surfaces** coloured with black, cream, grey or gold blotches (sometimes almost entirely black or pale cream), never striped; glossy in appearance; **snout** pointed, with prominent **brow**; restricted to boulder or shingle beaches and rocky platforms; nocturnal	***O. suteri***
	Not as above	**24**
24	**Dorsal surface** with regularly scattered white or green flecks edged with black (ocelli or 'eye-spots')	**25**
	Not as above	**29**
25	**Dorsal surface** brown, olive or grassy-green or iridescent green with regular pale flecks edged with black (ocelli); 3 **anterior subocular scales**, of similar size; **subdigital lamellae** usually ≤ 22; south Canterbury, Otago, Southland and Stewart Island only	***O. chloronoton* complex**
	Dorsal surface with scattered white or pale green ocelli; 2 **anterior subocular scales**, or if 3, third much smaller than first two; **subdigital lamellae** > 22; **ventral surface** grey or orangey red; eastern areas of Hawke's Bay to south Canterbury only	**26**
26	**Subdigital lamellae** usually < 24; occasionally 3 **anterior subocular scales**; central Canterbury and Banks Peninsula	***O. lineoocellatum***
	Subdigital lamellae usually > 24; always with 2 **anterior subocular scales**	**27**
27	**Dorsal ocelli** continue down tail; **ventral surface** often red-orange; North or South Island	***O. kokowai***
	Dorsal ocelli usually do not continue down tail; **ventral surface** grey, often suffused with pink or orange; South Island only	**28**
28	**Mid-body scale rows** always > 33; throat occasionally speckled; Marlborough Region only	***O. elium***
	Mid-body scale rows usually < 33; throat unmarked; Mackenzie Basin only	***O. prasinum***
29	**Mid-body scale rows** ≥ 38; North Island only	**30**
	Mid-body scale rows < 38	**31**
30	**Body size** small (up to 73 mm SVL); **dorsal surface** grey or grey-brown with regular patches of pale grey either side of midline; distinctive pale **dorsolateral stripes** with notched edges; central North Island only	***O. microlepis***
	Body size large (up to 145 mm SVL); Three Kings Islands only	***O. fallai***

31	**Body size** 60–106 mm SVL; **dorsal surface** mid- or chestnut-brown, often distinctively flecked with black and white; with or without mid-dorsal stripe (where present, breaks up on tail); **lateral band** brown and boldly crenulated, edged above and below by thin pale stripes; **ventral surface** red or yellow with dense black spots or flecks (occasionally uniform); chin and throat grey (sometimes pinkish); central North Island to upper South Island (including Westland)	***O. infrapunctatum* complex**
	Body size Usually < 80 mm SVL (never > 98 mm); **ventral surface** uniform or flecked; not fitting all characters above	**32**
32	**Body** generally more speckled than striped; **dorsal surface** light brown with small irregular pale blotches (some populations may be uniform jet black); **snout** very pointed; never found far from shoreline	**33**
	Not as above	**34**
33	East coast of upper North Island from northern Aupouri Peninsula to Gisborne	***O. smithi***
	North-western coast of North Island, from top of Aupouri Peninsula, including Manawatāwhi/Three Kings Islands, to Muriwai Beach, west Auckland	**O. aff. *smithi* "Three Kings, Te Paki, Western Northland"**
34	**Ear** opening minute (not more than 0.9 mm across); few **mid-body scale rows** (26–29); longitudinal ridges on **tail**; Stewart Island only	***O. stenotis***
	Not as above	**35**
35	**Teardrop marking** present below eye	**36**
	Teardrop marking absent below eye	**37**
36	**Snout** relatively blunt; **subdigital lamellae** usually 23 (19–24); 6.5 **scale rows** across back; belly and chin heavily speckled and may be flushed with red; brown **lateral band** with notched edges	**O. "Whirinaki"**
	Snout sharply pointed; **subdigital lamellae** usually 19 (16–23); 8.5 **scale rows** across back; belly and chin uniform cream or creamy orange, or lightly flecked with black; brown **lateral band** either with notched or smooth edges	***O. zelandicum***
37	**Eye** black or very dark brown	**38**
	Eye coloured (cream to brown, blue, or olive)	**42**
38	Pale cream **dorsolateral stripes**; long tail (c. 1.5x SVL); North Island only	***O. moco***
	Not as above; Fiordland and Southland	**39**
39	**Dorsal surface** black with fine cream, greeny-cream or golden flecks; with or without dorsolateral stripes	***O. judgei***
	Dorsal surface brown, dark brown, greyish-brown or green, with flecking or stripes	**40**

40	**Dorsal surface** patched with iridescent green; **ventral surface** bright red	***O. pikitanga***
	Dorsal surface brown; **ventral surface** yellow or greyish yellow, with flecking	**41**
41	**Dorsal surface** brown, with or without black flecking; **lateral surfaces** flecked and with weakly or strongly defined stripes; **ventral surface** grey to yellow with black flecking; throat light grey with black flecking, through to blackish; **eye** round, more or less as tall as long; 3 **anterior subocular scales**; from islands off South Westland	***O. taumakae***
	Dorsal surface brown with much black flecking on back; **lateral surfaces** heavily flecked with black-edged cream spots, and an indistinct pale dorsolateral stripe; **eye** oblong, distinctly longer than tall; 2 **anterior subocular scales**; alpine Fiordland	***O. awakopaka***
42	**Ventral surface** yellow, with or without fine flecking	**43**
	Ventral surface grey, white, cream, brown or muddy yellow	**51**
43	Stewart Island	**44**
	Not as above	**45**
44	Pale **stripe on forelimb**; **dorsal surface** mid-brown	***O.* aff. *polychroma* Clade 5**
	Usually no pale **stripe on forelimb**; **dorsal surface** deep brown; Stewart Island archipelago only	***O. notosaurus***
45	**Dorsal surface** dark brown with rudimentary or weakly defined dorsolateral stripes, flecked with black; mid-dorsal stripe may be visible; **ventral surface** deep yellow, often with black flecking; throat mid-grey to black; Llawrenny Peaks in Fiordland only	***O. inconspicuum* "Mahogany skink"**
	Clearly defined or discernible stripes (dorsolateral, mid-dorsal, lateral, mid-lateral)	**46**
46	Brown **lateral band** not clearly bordered by cream dorsolateral stripes; without mid-dorsal stripe; irregular black flecks or spots on back; Te Kakahu (Chalky) Island only	***O. tekakahu***
	Brown **lateral band** bordered above and below by cream dorsolateral and mid-lateral stripes; mid-dorsal stripe may be present	**47**
47	Black spots on **dorsal surface**, longitudinal ridges along **tail**; 3 **supraocular scales**; Okuru in South Westland	***O.* "Okuru"**
	Not as above	**48**
48	White **stripe on forelimb**	***O. polychroma* complex**
	No **stripe on forelimb**	**49**
49	**Lateral band** notched	***O. inconspicuum***
	Lateral band smooth edged	**50**
50	East of Lake Wakatipu (Hawkdun Range across to Lake Hawea, and Nevis Valley)	***O. repens***
	Mt Burns (Fiordland), Murchison Mountains and the Livingstone, Thomson and Eyre Mountains	***O. toka***

51	Chatham Islands or Stewart Island	**52**
	Mainland New Zealand	**53**
52	Restricted to Chatham Islands; **variable** in colour and degree of striping and flecking	***O. nigriplantare***
	Restricted to Stewart Island and associated offshore islands; no **stripe on forelimb**; **dorsal surface** deep brown; with or without black flecks and prominent whitish spots on lower **lateral surfaces**	***O. notosaurus***
53	**Dorsal scales of intact tail** with longitudinal ridges; black spots on dorsal surface; Okuru in south Westland	**O. "Okuru"**
	Dorsal scales of intact tail smooth	**54**
54	**Dorsal surface** grey or grey-brown base colour; pale dorsolateral stripes usually present; with or without mid-dorsal stripe or checkerboard pattern on dorsal surface; mid-dorsal stripe, if present, breaks up or becomes heavily notched on tail; **ventral surface** grey; **subdigital lamellae** 19–28	***O. maccanni***
	Dorsal surface brown base colour; with dorsolateral stripes (notched or smooth edged); with or without mid-dorsal stripe, may continue or break up down tail; **ventral surface** grey, brown or yellow	**55**
55	Pale **stripe on forelimb**; not highly glossy; **ventral surface** dull yellow-buff	***O. polychroma* complex**
	Lacking pale **stripe on forelimb**; **ventral surface** bright yellow or bronze	**56**
56	3 (sometimes 4) **supraocular scales**; ventral surface pale brown; known only from Rock and Pillar and Lammermoor Ranges	***O. burganae***
	Always 4 **supraocular scales** and not as above	***O. inconspicuum***

FROGS

Hochstetter's frog, *Leiopelma hochstetteri*, in natural habitat, Great Barrier Island

Contents

Archey's frog *Leiopelma archeyi* 308
Hochstetter's frog *Leiopelma hochstetteri* 310
Hamilton's frog *Leiopelma hamiltoni* 312
Green and golden bell frog *Ranoidea aurea* 314
Southern bell frog *Ranoidea raniformis* 316
Brown (whistling) tree frog *Litoria ewingii* 318
Key to New Zealand frogs 320

Archey's frog, *Leiopelma archeyi*, Whareorino. LISA KEENE

Green and golden bell frog, *Ranoidea aurea*

Archey's frog, *Leiopelma archeyi* (male) with eggs. SARAH J. WELLS

NEW ZEALAND FROGS

The New Zealand frog fauna includes three extant native species (family Leiopelmatidae) and three introduced species (family Hylidae). The native species all belong to the genus *Leiopelma*, an ancient lineage of primitive frogs found only in New Zealand. Their closest relatives are the North American tailed frogs in the genus *Ascaphus* (family Ascaphidae). The *Ascaphus* frogs (of which there are two species) share the primitive traits of Leiopelmatidae, distinguishing both families from all other species of frogs: vestigial tail-wagging (caudalipuboischiotibialis) muscles; cartilaginous inscriptional ribs (elongate cartilages in the muscles of the abdominal wall); amphicoelous vertebrae; and nine presacral vertebrae (most frogs have eight). In addition, *Leiopelma* frogs lack tympana (eardrums), eustachian tubes and vocal sacs. This limits their ability to vocalise; most other frogs usually emit loud social calls during the mating period. Instead, New Zealand's native frogs probably communicate in a similar way to salamanders, using chemosignals that convey information about size and individuality of conspecifics.

Leiopelma frogs are all strictly nocturnal, and highly cryptic. They predominantly live in dense damp native forest, and/or close to small streams. Two species (Hamilton's (*L. hamiltoni*) and Archey's frogs (*L. archeyi*)) are primarily terrestrial but Hochstetter's frog (*L. hochstetteri*) is semi-aquatic, usually living in and on the edges of small, shaded stream tributaries (although also sometimes found away from streams on the forest floor). The reproduction of the two terrestrial species is quite specialised – there is no free-living tadpole stage, and development occurs entirely within the egg capsule (i.e. there is no free-feeding larval stage). Eggs are unpigmented, about 5 mm in size, and contain a large yolk. During spring, females lay the eggs in clusters (of up to 19 eggs) in dark, damp

SVL AND FLASH MARKINGS

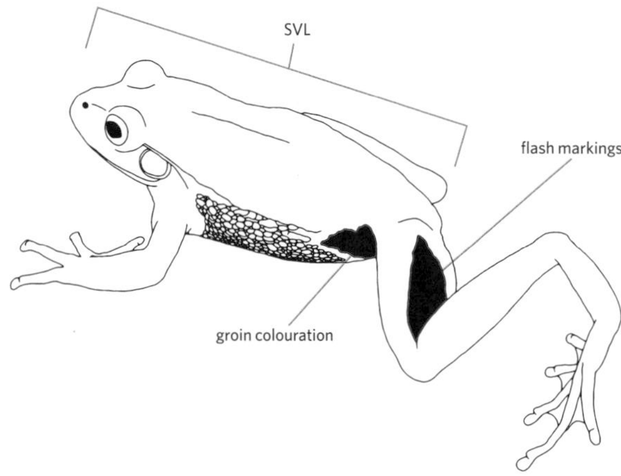

BODY FORM

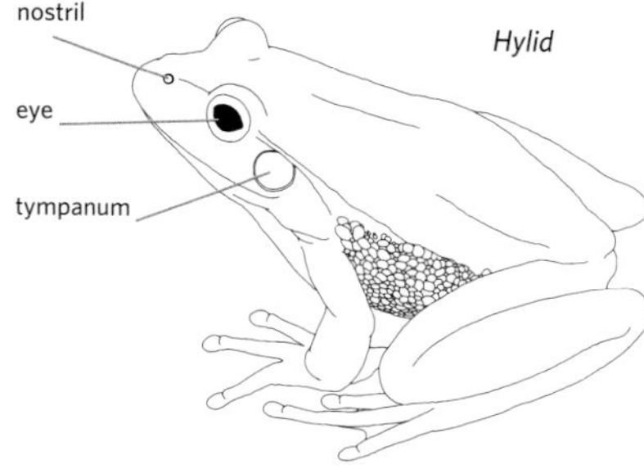

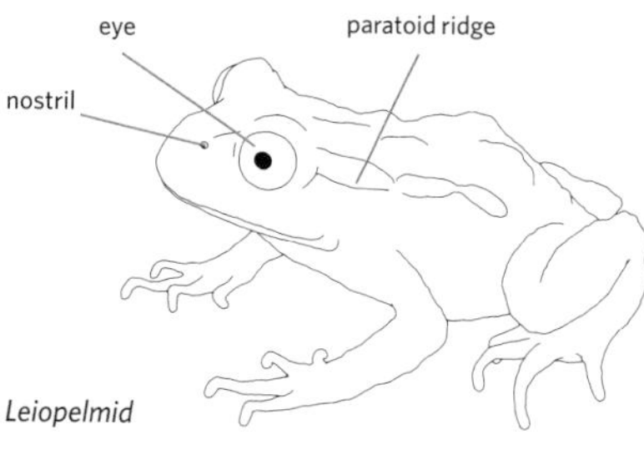

sites such as under logs and rocks. The male guards the eggs until they hatch. The tiny, tailed froglets then climb onto the back of the male, who continues to guard these offspring for several weeks while they complete their development. The reproductive strategy of Hochstetter's frog differs markedly, with strings of eggs (up to 22) laid in shallow depressions with trickling water. Eggs hatch at a relatively early development stage into larvae with partially developed limbs and well-developed tail fins that enable them to swim. They do not feed, and remain in the shallow water while they develop into small frogs.

All *Leiopelma* frogs persist in small fragmented populations on the North Island's mainland, or on islands in Cook Strait and the Marlborough Sounds. Two of the three New Zealand native frogs (both of the terrestrial species, Hamilton's and Archey's frogs) are listed as threatened on the IUCN Red List. All three species are listed in the top 100 Evolutionarily Distinct and Globally Endangered (EDGE) amphibians, with Archey's frog topping the list as the world's most evolutionarily distinct and globally endangered amphibian species.

All three introduced species are from Australia. The two *Ranoidea* bell frogs - green and golden bell frog (*R. aurea*) and southern bell frog (*R. raniformis*) - were deliberately introduced by acclimatisation societies during the 1860s, and the brown (whistling) tree frog (*Litoria ewingii*) by a private individual in 1875. These species have adapted well to New Zealand conditions, and are now widespread and common. The green and golden bell frog has become very rare in its native Australian range, following significant declines in distribution and abundance since the 1960s, to the degree that it is now listed as 'Vulnerable A2ace ver 3.1' on the IUCN Red List.

The introduced species are easily distinguished from the native frogs by the clearly visible tympanum, their loud mating calls and a large (60–100 mm long) free-living tadpole stage. The spread of these species is of concern because of their potential to transmit pathogens (e.g. chytridiomycosis) to native frogs, and they are also known to prey upon native frogs and lizards.

HIND FOOT SHAPES

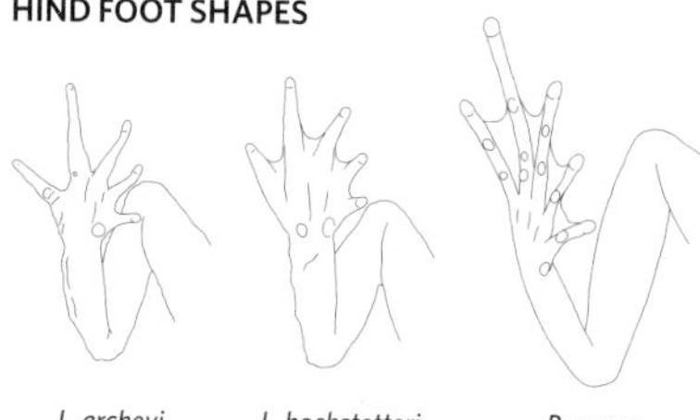

Archey's frog

Leiopelma archeyi Turbott, 1942

Endemic

Coromandel

DESCRIPTION

Males up to 31 mm, females up to 37 mm SVL

New Zealand's smallest and most beautifully marked frog; vulnerable to extinction. **Dorsal surface** generally light to dark brown, green-brown or completely green (uncommon); most with scattered dark blotches. Dorsolateral glandular ridges on both sides, protruding from tip of snout over edge of eye to upper surface of hind limbs. Black dorsolateral stripes (either continuous or broken) below dorsolateral ridges. **Lateral surfaces** often pink or orange-brown, with black or green blotches and flecks. Some black stripes or markings on dorsal surface of fore- and hind limbs. Black markings under each eye; black upper lip (continuous or discontinuous). **Ventral surface** black or dark brown and heavily speckled with green, and sometimes blue or yellow, flecks. **Skin** generally smooth; some individuals have scattered tubercles on dorsal surface of legs. **Eye** mostly black in colour with a lighter golden arch in upper surface; large. **Feet** unwebbed; digits slender, lacking enlarged distal pads. Lacking true vocal sacs and tympana.

DISTRIBUTION

North Island only. Occurs on the Coromandel Peninsula, and in Whareorino Forest, west of Te Kuiti.

VARIATION AND SIMILAR SPECIES

Highly variable in colour and patterning. Whareorino individuals often with pink or orange-brown patches on body. Distinguished from sympatric **Hochstetter's frog** (*L. hochstetteri*) by its smoother skin, more slender body, longer digits, smaller (but overlapping) body size and lack of webbing between toes on hind feet.

HABITAT

Lowland, Montane/subalpine

Occupies damp native (cloud) forest, often on mist-shrouded ridges away from creeks. Takes refuge under rocks or rock piles and beneath logs during the day; emerges at night, moving over the ground, short-stature vegetation and logs to feed.

NATURAL HISTORY

Nocturnal; terrestrial, but may climb several metres up trees or shrubs. Unable to call but can squeak or chirp when disturbed. Terrestrial reproduction; mating occurs September–November, fertilisation via amplexus. Females lay 4–15 large unpigmented eggs (8–11 mm diameter) per clutch over summer (December–February) in damp soil beneath rocks or logs, or in hollow ponga (*Cyathea dealbata*) trunks. Eggs guarded (brooded) by male, hatched as froglets (with tails) that climb onto and cling to back of adult male. Froglets remain with male for several weeks until metamorphosis complete; mature in 3–4 years. Long-lived species (> 35 years). Relies on body colouration for camouflage. Poor jumping (hopping) abilities, but may assume rigid stance, with raised body and extended legs when disturbed or threatened. Coromandel population declined significantly during 1996–2001, perhaps from virulent fungal disease chytridiomycosis (*Batrachochytrium dendrobatidis*), although surviving population now seems to have low susceptibility.

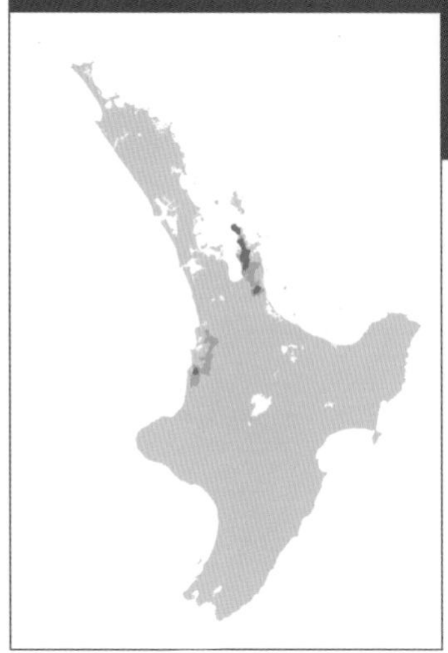

Waikato

ETYMOLOGY

Specific and **common names** in recognition of Sir Gilbert Edward Archey (1890–1974), the former director of the Auckland Institute and Museum, who worked on New Zealand's primitive frogs.

Hochstetter's frog

Leiopelma hochstetteri Fitzinger, 1861

Endemic

Great Barrier Island

Northland

DESCRIPTION

Males up to 38 mm, females up to 47 mm SVL
The most widespread *Leiopelma* species, and only native frog with a free-swimming larval stage. Body robust. **Dorsal surface** mostly red-brown or green-brown, with or without dark bands. **Lateral surfaces** brown or red-brown, often with sparse pale flecks. **Ventral surface** yellow-brown. **Skin** granular and covered with raised glandular tubercles, especially on dorsal and lateral surfaces, and limbs. **Eye** colour olive-green, hazel or golden brown; large. **Feet** with short fingers and toes; distinctive webbing on hind toes. Lack true vocal sacs and tympana.

DISTRIBUTION

North Island only. Fragmented populations occur from Northland (south of Whangarei) to Waikato (Maungatautari) and the Coromandel Peninsula, and on East Cape. Also on Great Barrier Island (Aotea Island).

VARIATION AND SIMILAR SPECIES

Morphological variation limited, but 13 genetically distinct populations. Syntopic with **Archey's frog** (*L. archeyi*) at some sites, but can be distinguished by its more granular (vs. smoother) skin covered in tubercles, more robust body form and shorter, webbed (vs. unwebbed) digits.

HABITAT

Coastal, Lowland, Montane/subalpine

Semi-aquatic; usually found in or near small streams and tributaries, within shaded native forest. Occasionally found long distances away from streams in damp native forest. Able to survive in some modified habitats (e.g. shaded streams in farmland and exotic plantation forests), but very sensitive to sedimentation. Takes refuge in damp crevices, and under stones, rock piles or logs, and thick leaf litter.

NATURAL HISTORY

The only semi-aquatic native species (others completely terrestrial). Nocturnal, with very limited daily movements (e.g. travelling c. 0.5 metres per day). Dispersal behaviour unknown. Does not produce mating calls but can squeak or chirp when disturbed. Relies on cryptic camouflage to avoid predators, but will jump into streams or swim (alternate leg kicks) to escape. Insectivorous, feeding on spiders, beetles and mites. Sexually dimorphic: males more muscular and with more robust forelimbs than females. Females lay small (5–6 mm) unpigmented eggs in strings of 10–13 (possibly up to 22) eggs in shallow depressions with trickling water (e.g. seeps), in underground cavities or in small open pools. Egg-laying period at least late September–May; hatching after c. 40–60 days; larvae with partially developed limbs and well-developed tail fins, capable of swimming. Larvae remain in shallow water 4–8 weeks while developing into froglets, but do not feed. Maturity reached at 3–4 years: adult longevity > 30 years. Of the 13 genetically distinct populations, Otawa forest frogs (Bay of Plenty) are the most isolated, with the smallest area of occupancy, and most genetically distinct.

ETYMOLOGY

Specific and **common names** in recognition of Ferdinand von Hochstetter (1829–1884), an Austrian geologist who carried the first specimens of this frog to Europe.

Hamilton's frog

Leiopelma hamiltoni McCulloch, 1919

Endemic

KEN MILLER

Maud Island

DESCRIPTION

Males up to 43 mm, females up to 52 mm SVL

New Zealand's largest native frog, and the most threatened. **Dorsal surface** variable in colour, ranging from uniform dark blackish brown to light brown with irregular darker patches, blotches or mottling. A dark band extending from tip of snout to nostril, continuing through eye and over shoulder, below dorsolateral ridge. Some light-coloured individuals with a dark backwards-pointing triangular marking on head between eyes. Rarely with small green flecks on dorsal surface. **Lateral surfaces** brown, either uniform or flecked with black. Hind legs may be marked with oblique dark bands. **Ventral surface** typically shades of brown, and may be uniform or patterned or blotched with dark brown or black. **Skin** on dorsal surface smooth with sparsely scattered tubercles on hind limbs. **Eye** mostly black in colour with a lighter golden arch in upper surface; large. **Feet** unwebbed; digits are slender and without enlarged distal pads. Lacking true vocal sacs and tympana.

DISTRIBUTION

South Island only. Restricted to islands in the Marlborough Sounds (Maud Island, Motuara Island and Long Island, although the success of the Long Island translocation remains uncertain) and Cook Strait (Stephens Island Takapourewa). A small population was translocated to a fenced mainland sanctuary in Wellington.

VARIATION AND SIMILAR SPECIES

Until recently, population from Maud Island was considered a separate species (*L. pakeka*). Reassessment of morphological and genetic differentiation resulted in two species now being regarded as one (*L. hamiltoni*), with each population a separate evolutionarily significant unit. Distinguished from **Hochstetter's**

frog (*L. hochstetteri*) by the less robust body form, longer digits, lack of toe webbing (or if present, only rudimentary) and completely terrestrial (vs. partially aquatic) habit. Distinguished from **Archey's frog** (*L. archeyi*) by drabber and less varied colouration, and larger and more robust body.

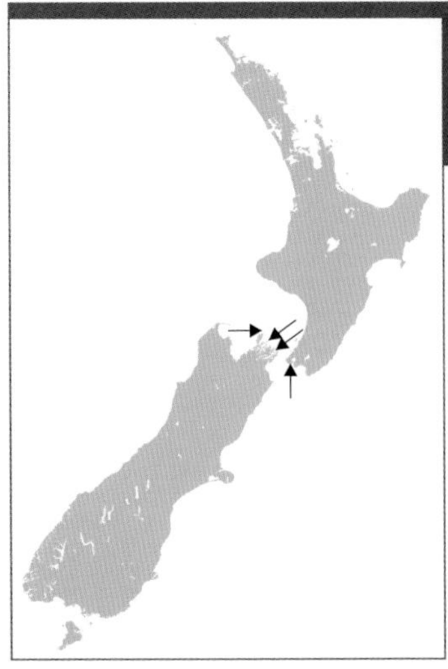

HABITAT

Coastal, Lowland

Occupies vegetated boulder banks beneath the forest canopy. Shelters in damp crevices, and beneath rocks during the day, emerging at night to feed.

NATURAL HISTORY

Nocturnal; terrestrial. Relatively sedentary (can remain motionless for long periods), and generally ranges over just a few metres (up to 5 m) over entire life. Terrestrial reproduction; mating occurs October-December. Male occupies oviposition sites prior to female laying eggs. Male clasps female around waist (inguinal amplexus), and fertilises 1-19 unpigmented eggs as they are laid in damp ground. No tadpole stage, so froglets hatch out, with a small tail. High parental care provided by males, guarding eggs for 14-21 weeks, and then froglets carried on male's back; presumably this keeps young moist, protected from predators, and reduces fungal or microbial infections. Froglets mature in 3-4 years; adults long lived (> 40 years). Primarily insectivorous but will consume other invertebrates. Population on Maud Island with very high densities (c. 1000 frogs per hectare).

ETYMOLOGY

Specific and **common names** in recognition of Harold Hamilton (1885-1937), who first discovered the species on Stephens Island.

KEN MILLER

Maud Island

Green and golden bell frog

Ranoidea aurea (Lesson, 1829) **Exotic; introduced and naturalised**

Auckland

DESCRIPTION

Males up to 60 mm, females up to 80 mm SVL
A striking green and golden-brown frog in decline in its native country of Australia, but thriving in New Zealand. **Dorsal surface** relatively smooth and emerald and/or golden brown, with irregular and variable golden bronze blotches. A cream-coloured dorsolateral stripe, edged below by a narrower black line, extending from nostril to eye and over tympanum towards groin. Another cream-coloured stripe runs over upper lip to base of forelimb. Tympanum distinct and clearly visible. **Lateral surfaces** brown with cream-coloured spots and flecks; limbs green or bronze with golden blotches. **Ventral surface** creamy white. Breeding males may have dark olive throat. Armpits and groin bright blue; **flash markings** on thighs also blue. Front **feet** lack webbing but hind feet almost fully webbed; finger and toe discs expanded but only slightly wider than digits. **Tadpoles** with olive-green to black dorsal surface, and silvery-white ventral surface.

DISTRIBUTION

North and South Islands. Native to Australia; eastern and south-eastern New South Wales and eastern (coastal) Victoria. Introduced to New Zealand in 1860s by the Auckland Acclimatisation Society. Occurs in the North Island, from Northland to East Cape and south Taranaki; a few small isolated populations occur in Southland.

VARIATION AND SIMILAR SPECIES

Variable in basal colour, from green to yellow to uniform brown. Capable of dramatic colour changes from light to dark, and vice versa, in minutes. Xanthic (entirely yellow) forms with red eyes occur in captivity. Often confused with **southern bell frog** (*R. raniformis*) but distinguished by its wider toe pads, smoother dorsal surface, and absence of a thin pale green mid-dorsal stripe. Also, lighter blotches on dorsal surface frequently cross midline (vs. do not cross the midline in *R. raniformis*). Calls of the two species also distinctive.

HABITAT

Coastal, Lowland, Montane/subalpine
Found in farmland and other settled areas close to swamps, lakes, ponds and slow-flowing streams.

NATURAL HISTORY

Cathemeral (primarily active at night but frequently active by day); terrestrial, arboreal and semi-aquatic. Commonly found perched on vegetation near water. Spawns in spring–early summer, females depositing 100s–1000s of eggs in a floating gelatinous mat in still water. These sink after 6–10 hours. Tadpoles hatch in c. 2 days (tadpole length c. 60–100 mm), and froglets appear after 2 months. Males produce deep growling call from water: a long growl of several seconds followed by a series of short croks – *cr-a-aw-a-a-awk cra-a-a-awk crok crok*. Tadpole feeds on bacteria, algae and organic detritus. Adult forages at night, especially in warm damp evenings, feeding on almost anything, from insects to other frogs and lizards.

ETYMOLOGY

Specific name (Latin) meaning 'golden'.
Common name refers to its colouration.

Tadpole

Xanthic form

Southern bell frog

Ranoidea raniformis (Keferstein, 1867) **Exotic; introduced and naturalised**

DESCRIPTION

Males up to 65 mm, females up to 95 mm SVL
A large and common frog, with a loud growling call, that occurs in most regions of New Zealand. **Dorsal surface** green (bright emerald to dark olive) or brown (golden to almost black), with varying degrees of brown spots, blotches or longitudinal streaks. Usually with a visible pale green mid-dorsal stripe. Numerous large tubercles, warts and skin folds on dorsal and lateral surfaces. Dorsolateral cream-coloured stripe (often fragmented), bordered below by a thin black line, extending from nostril to eye and over tympanum towards groin. Another cream stripe runs over upper lip to base of forelimb. Tympana distinct and clearly visible. **Lateral surfaces** brown with cream spots and flecks; limbs blotched with green or brown. **Ventral surface** creamy white. Breeding males may have dark olive throat. Armpits and groin bright blue; **flash markings** on thighs also blue, may be overlaid with white spots in some North Island populations. Front **feet** lack webbing but hind feet almost fully webbed; finger and toe discs generally not wider than digits. **Tadpoles** with olive-green to black dorsal surface, and creamy white ventral surface.

DISTRIBUTION

Native to Australia; south-eastern areas of New South Wales, Victoria, South Australia and Tasmania. Introduced to New Zealand from Tasmania in 1867 by the Canterbury Acclimatisation Society, but now distributed widely across the North and South Islands of New Zealand.

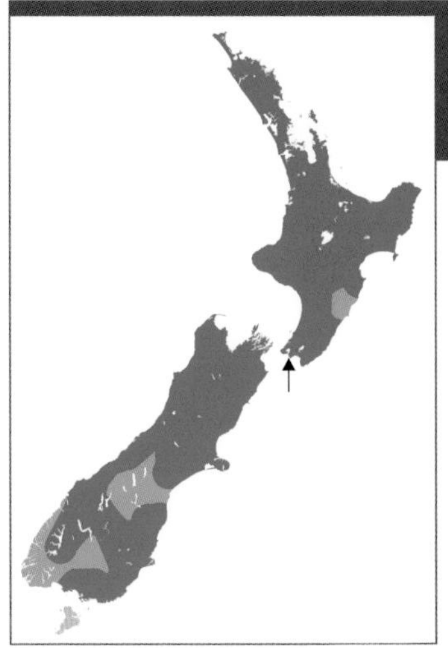

VARIATION AND SIMILAR SPECIES

Variable in basal colour from green to yellow or uniform brown. Capable of dramatic colour changes, from light to dark, and vice versa, in minutes. Often confused with **green and golden bell frog** (*R. aurea*), but can be distinguished by its narrower toe pads; more abundant and pronounced tubercles and warts on dorsal and lateral surfaces (vs. smooth); and a green or yellowish mid-dorsal stripe, or lighter colour blotches on dorsal surface that never cross midline. The calls of the two species are distinctive.

HABITAT

Coastal, Lowland, Montane/subalpine, Alpine
Associated with bodies of still water (e.g. dams, ponds, swamps, marshes) and terrestrial vegetation on the edges of bushland, farmland or residential areas.

NATURAL HISTORY

Cathemeral, and avid sun-basker. Found in vegetation close to water sources, but in water bodies without vegetated margins, frogs may be fully aquatic. Spawning occurs in spring–early summer, with egg masses (100s–1000s of eggs) sinking in water after initially floating for several hours. Tadpoles hatch in 2–4 days (tadpole length c. 60–100 mm); froglets appear after 2–3 months. Males produce deep growling call from the water. Call: a short but deep guttural growl – *crawark crok crok crawk*. Tadpoles feed on bacteria, algae and organic detritus. Adults opportunistic predators, feeding on invertebrates, other frogs and lizards.

ETYMOLOGY

Specific name (Latin) meaning 'rana-like', referring to the Ranid (family Ranidae) frogs, also called the true frogs. **Common name** refers to its southerly distribution in both its native range in Australia and in New Zealand, although the species occurs widely across the North and South Islands. Also known (in Australia) as the growling grass frog, after its growling call.

Brown (whistling) tree frog

Litoria ewingii (Duméril and Bibron, 1841) **Exotic; introduced and naturalised**

DESCRIPTION

Males up to 37 mm, females up to 49 mm SVL
A small brown tree frog with a loud harsh call. **Dorsal surface** varies from pale fawn to brown or olive-green; a broad darker brown band of same width as distance between eyes, running longitudinally over length of body. Light brown or golden triangular marking on anterior region of head; a dark brown stripe running from nostril through eye and tympanum to axilla, with a pale cream or white stripe below extending over upper lip towards forelimb. Tympana distinct and clearly visible. **Lateral surfaces** light greyish brown or fawn, and throat and **ventral surface** uniform white or cream. **Flash markings** on thighs bright orange, and armpits and groin yellow-green. Fingers and **toes** with expanded distal pads, scarcely wider than digit width, and all partially webbed. **Tadpole** dorsal surface green to brown, or black; ventral surface metallic bronze.

DISTRIBUTION

Native to Australia; from south-eastern South Australia, southern Victoria, south-eastern and central New South Wales, and Tasmania. Introduced to Greymouth (Westland) from Tasmania in 1875; currently distributed widely across the South Island, and patchily distributed across the North Island – but well established in the lower North Island. Also present on the Chatham Islands.

VARIATION AND SIMILAR SPECIES

Little variation, although individuals may differ in shades of brown on dorsal surface.

Capable of dramatic colour change, from light to dark, and vice versa, in minutes. Unlikely to be confused with other frogs in New Zealand.

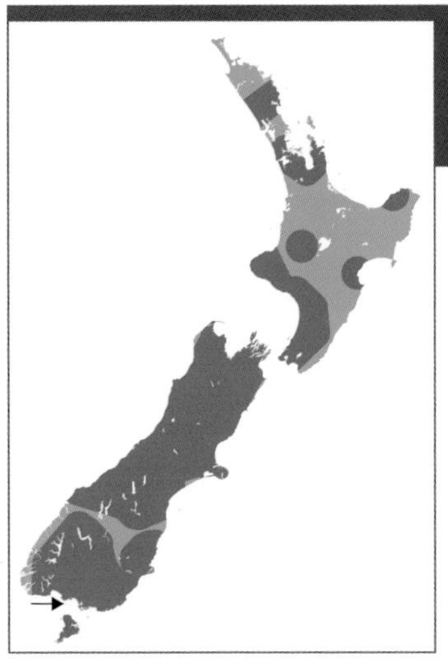

HABITAT

Coastal, Lowland, Montane/subalpine, Alpine
Found in temporary and permanent water in urban areas, farmland, vegetated sand dunes, and bush including tussock grasslands, alpine herbfields and pavement. Adults found < 2 m above ground, in low dense vegetation, rocks or logs. Frogs may live around breeding ponds or up to 1 km away.

NATURAL HISTORY

Nocturnal, but commonly sun-basks. Terrestrial and arboreal. Occurs in high densities around breeding ponds. Breeding may occur at any time of year, including winter, and most water bodies (except fast-moving streams) can be used for breeding. Eggs laid in small clumps on submerged vegetation, and hatch in 7–29 days depending on temperature. Development (metamorphosis) 4–5 months. Tadpoles c. 50 mm long. Call: initially, a prolonged *creeeeee* followed by a series of similar, but rapid and harsh, pulsing notes usually repeated about 5–10 times – *creeeeeee creee creee cree cree cree*. Calling may occur throughout year (i.e. not just during breeding season). Adults feed on small invertebrates, including snails. Capable of surviving after being frozen.

ETYMOLOGY

Specific name (Latinisation) in recognition of Reverend Thomas James Ewing (c. 1813–1882) of England, an amateur naturalist and collector who moved to Tasmania in 1833. **Common names** refer, respectively, to the brown basal colouration and the frog's call.

Tadpole metamorphosing

Key to New Zealand frogs

1	**Tympana** (eardrums) absent; **pupil** round	2
	Tympana present; **pupil** horizontal	4
2	**Webbing on hind feet** extending to half length of toes; indistinct **parotoid ridge** behind eye; dorsum with raised **tubercles**	***Leiopelma hochstetteri***
	Webbing on hind feet greatly reduced or absent; distinct **parotoid ridge** behind eye; dorsum generally smooth or with few raised **tubercles**	3
3	Adult **size** generally ≤ 38 mm SVL; **dorsal or lateral surfaces** green, pink or orange-brown	***Leiopelma archeyi***
	Adult **size** > 39 mm SVL; **dorsal and lateral surfaces** typically brown	***Leiopelma hamiltoni***
4	**Distal pads** noticeably wider than digits; a broad **brown stripe** from eye through tympanum to shoulder; **posterior of thigh** yellow to reddish orange	***Litoria ewingii***
	Distal pads equal to or slightly wider than digits; a pale **yellow or white dorso-lateral stripe** running posteriorly from eye; groin and **posterior of thighs** bright blue (except juveniles)	5
5	**Distal pads** typically wider than digits; **mid-dorsal stripe** usually absent; **dorsal** colour blotches may cross midline; dorsum mostly smooth or finely granular above	***Ranoidea aurea***
	Distal pads about as wide as digits; **mid-dorsal stripe** (green, yellow or white) usually present; **dorsal** colour blotches do not cross midline; dorsum smooth or usually with raised tubercles and longitudinally aligned ridges	***Ranoidea raniformis***

MARINE TURTLES

Green turtle, *Chelonia mydas*. SIMON PIERCE

Contents

Loggerhead turtle *Caretta caretta* 326
Green turtle *Chelonia mydas* 328
Olive ridley *Lepidochelys olivacea* 330
Hawksbill turtle *Eretmochelys imbricata* 332
Leatherback turtle *Dermochelys coriacea* 334
Key to New Zealand marine turtles 336

Green turtle, *Chelonia mydas.* PATRICE PLICHON

MARINE TURTLES

Five species of marine turtle visit New Zealand. None breed here, and most are considered vagrants, arriving only occasionally and probably accidentally. The exceptions are the green turtle (*Chelonia mydas*), which is present in our waters year-round, and the leatherback turtle (*Dermochelys coriacea*), which visits each year in sufficient numbers to be considered a regular migrant. In New Zealand, marine turtles can be seen free-swimming especially in Northland waters. However, most observations are generally of stranded (washed ashore) individuals, or turtles tangled in fishing nets.

Marine turtles are well known for undertaking long migrations to feeding and nesting grounds. Mating occurs at sea, and females lay their eggs in sand at their natal nesting beaches. Once the eggs hatch, juveniles dig their way out of the sand and enter the ocean. There, they live a pelagic (open ocean) life for several years, before settling in juvenile feeding grounds for a number of decades. The Northland Region of New Zealand is a juvenile feeding ground for green turtles. Once sexual maturity is reached, the turtles establish a pattern of migration between nesting beaches and adult feeding grounds.

Marine turtles rarely leave the water other than to nest, and so are well adapted to life in the ocean. They have evolved some distinctive characters for a life of swimming (e.g. enlarged flippers and streamlined shells) and to secure prey (e.g. hooked beaks; backward-pointing projections in the mouth and throat to hold soft-bodied prey such as jellyfish; or large, powerful jaws to crush shellfish).

Nearly all species of marine turtle are threatened by habitat loss (particularly loss of nesting areas), predation and exploitation (human consumption of turtles and/or eggs), by-catch from human fishing practices, and ingestion of waste such as plastics. In recognition of their global plight, marine turtles are protected in many countries, and all species are listed in the CITES Appendices, which aim to prohibit or manage the international trade of marine turtles and their products (e.g. carapaces for ornaments and jewellery, and eggs and meat for food). In New Zealand, all five species are legally protected under the Wildlife Act 1953.

Leatherback turtle, *Dermochelys coriacea*

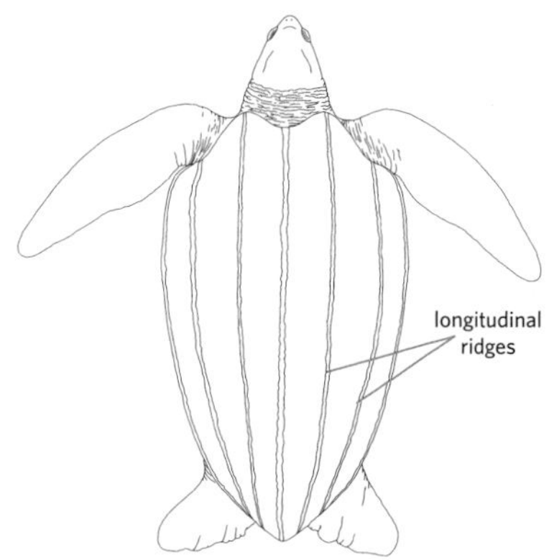

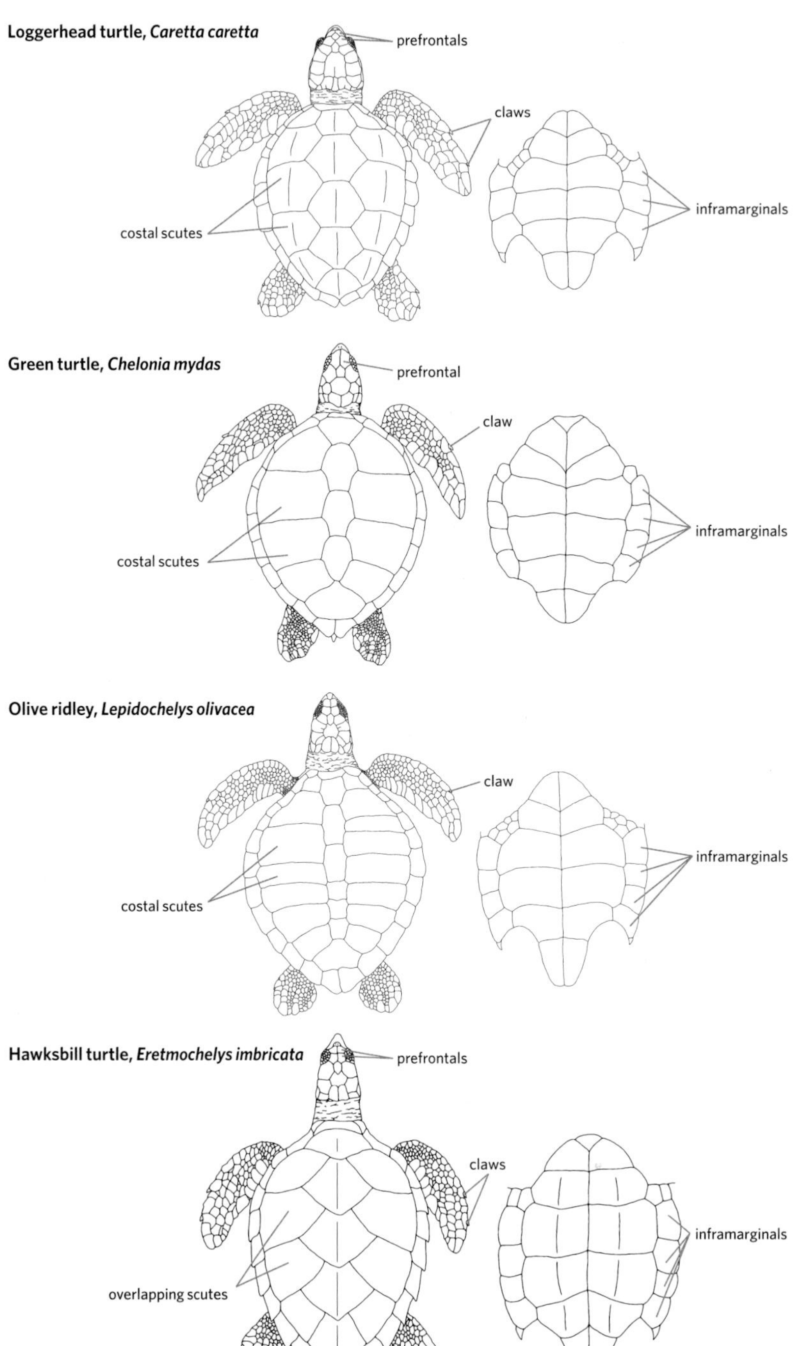
Loggerhead turtle, *Caretta caretta*
prefrontals
claws
inframarginals
costal scutes
Green turtle, *Chelonia mydas*
prefrontal
claw
inframarginals
costal scutes
Olive ridley, *Lepidochelys olivacea*
claw
inframarginals
costal scutes
Hawksbill turtle, *Eretmochelys imbricata*
prefrontals
claws
inframarginals
overlapping scutes

Loggerhead turtle

Caretta caretta (Linnaeus, 1758)

Native; vagrant

Juvenile

DESCRIPTION

Up to 1.2 m in length; 100–180 kg weight
Disproportionately large head and large beak. **Prefrontal scales** 2 pairs. **Carapace** ovoid or heart-shaped, and red-brown in colour, often with irregular blotching. **Plastron** cream to pale yellowish-brown. **Carapace scutes** not overlapping. **Vertebral scutes** 5. **Costal scutes** 5 (sometimes 6) pairs; first in contact with cervical scute. **Marginal scutes** 11–15. **Flippers** all short and thick; each with 2 **claws**.

DISTRIBUTION

Occurs throughout temperate and tropical regions of the Pacific, Indian and Atlantic Oceans. Nests in the Middle East, Japan, Australia, Florida (USA) and Mediterranean (Greece, Turkey and Israel). Few observations in New Zealand, most from off the northern North Island (both east and west coasts), with a few reports from off the West Coast and Stewart Island/Rakiura.

VARIATION AND SIMILAR SPECIES

Little variation in morphology but Atlantic, Pacific and Indian Ocean populations genetically distinct, and Mediterranean populations of mixed origin. Hatchlings with 3 dorsal ridges on carapace, which diminish with age. Colouration varies between populations. May be confused with **green turtle** (*Chelonia mydas*) or **olive**

ridley turtle (*Lepidochelys olivacea*), but distinguished by its larger head. Differs from green turtle by having 2 pairs of prefrontal scales (vs. 1 pair); from olive ridley turtle by having 5 vertebral scutes (vs. > 5); 5–6 pairs of costal scutes (vs. 5–10 pairs); and carapace longer than wide (vs. more circular).

HABITAT

Adults occur in coastal waters, bays and estuaries, as well as in shallow waters of continental shelves. Juveniles spend most of their time in open ocean, in major current systems (gyres) serving as open-ocean developmental grounds.

NATURAL HISTORY

Females nest at 2–4 year intervals, nesting several times per breeding season. Average of 120–150 white, spherical and soft-shelled eggs per nest, in sandy beaches. Incubation period c. 60–80 days; hatchlings emerge at about 40 mm in length. Does not breed in New Zealand. Primarily carnivorous, feeding mostly on shellfish (e.g. crabs, conches, mussels and whelks), as well as fish and jellyfish. Powerful jaws easily crush shellfish. Occasionally eats sponges and algae.

PATRICE PLICHON

ETYMOLOGY

Specific name (Spanish) meaning 'tortoise-shell'. **Common name** refers to its large head that supports powerful jaw muscles.

Green turtle

Chelonia mydas (Linnaeus, 1758) **Native; migrant**

DESCRIPTION

Up to 1.5 m in length; 110–200 kg (up to 300 kg) weight

The second largest marine turtle, and only species with resident juveniles consistently present in New Zealand waters. Head small and blunt, with sharp pointed beak and serrated jaw. **Prefrontal scales** 1 pair. **Carapace** oval in shape. Colour can undergo ontogenic colour change, from black at hatchling stage to dark brown or olive as juveniles, and brown or green with brown or yellow shades as adults. Each scute with radiating striations and spots or blotches. **Plastron** colour variable but generally off-white, yellow or dark grey-blue or grey-green. **Carapace scutes** smooth, not overlapping. **Vertebral scutes** 5. **Costal scutes** 4 pairs; first pair not in contact with cervical scute. **Inframarginal scutes** 4 pairs, on bridge. **Flippers** each with a single visible **claw**.

DISTRIBUTION

Occurs globally in temperate, subtropical and tropical waters. New Zealand is the southern distribution limit in the south-west Pacific. Juveniles occur in New Zealand waters year-round (previously thought to be occasional visitors or stragglers), mainly in waters of the northern North Island, with sparse records down to the South Island. Also resident (non-breeding) at the Kermadec Islands (Raoul Island).

VARIATION AND SIMILAR SPECIES

Some Northland juveniles are from the eastern Pacific population. Occasionally referred to as *Chelonia mydas agassizii*, not a currently recognised subspecies but still considered a separate population. These turtles have a narrower and more strongly elevated carapace, and darker skin pigmentation (giving them an overall darker appearance). Green turtle easily distinguished by its single pair of prefrontal scales on head (vs. 2 pairs in all other species). Distinguished from **hawksbill turtles** (*Eretmochelus imbricata*) by its blunt snout, unhooked beak and single claw on each flipper (vs. 2 claws). May be confused with **loggerhead turtle** (*Caretta caretta*) but distinguished by its smaller head and 1 pair of prefrontal scales (vs. 2 pairs); or with **olive ridley turtles** (*Lepidochelys olivacea*) but separated by its 1 pair of prefrontal scales (vs. 2 pairs), 5 vertebral scutes (vs. > 5) and 4 pairs of costal scutes (vs. 5–10 pairs).

HABITAT

Hatchlings found in oceanic waters as pelagic inhabitants, whereas immature juveniles and adults inhabit shallow waters near coastlines (e.g. bays and around islands), especially in areas with seagrass beds.

NATURAL HISTORY

Hatchlings spend 3–10 years in open ocean before migrating to shallower coastal waters as immature juveniles. Remain there for several decades until reaching maturity, then migrate back to natal nesting rookeries. Presence of immature juveniles and resident subadults in northern New Zealand coastal waters suggests New Zealand may be a transitional developmental area, with adult turtles migrating away on reaching sexual maturity. Nesting occurs year-round on sandy beaches in c. 80 countries (excluding New Zealand). Females nest solitarily every 2–4 years; c. 115 white spherical soft-shelled eggs per nest. Several clutches of eggs laid per season. Egg incubation c. 60 days, and hatchlings emerge at 45–50 mm in length. Does not breed in New Zealand. Diet varies with age: juveniles opportunistic omnivores (e.g. eating worms, jellyfish, salps, algae and seagrass); adults primarily herbivorous (e.g. seagrass, algae, seaweed, jellyfish, crustaceans and sea stars). Capable of diving to depths of 30 m, possibly deeper.

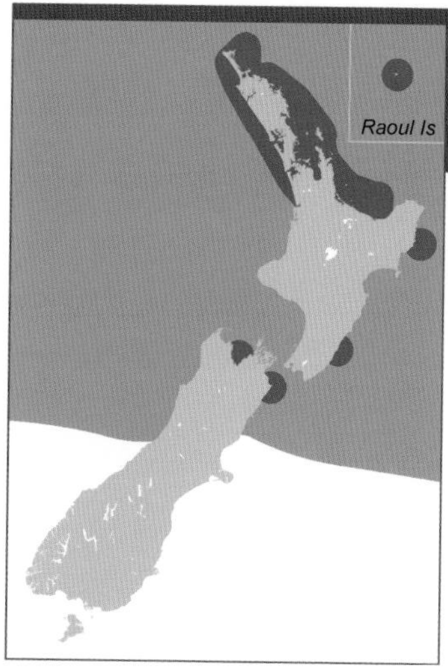

ETYMOLOGY

Specific name (Greek) meaning 'dampness, wetness', referring to aquatic lifestyle. **Common name** refers to the colour of its fat (adipose tissue), which turns green when cooked.

Olive ridley turtle

Lepidochelys olivacea (Eschscholtz, 1829) **Native; vagrant**

BERNARD GAGNON

DESCRIPTION

0.60–0.75 m in length; 35–45 kg weight

The smallest marine turtle in the Pacific region. Head relatively small but with large powerful jaws. **Prefrontal scales** 2 pairs. **Carapace** semicircular or wedge-shaped, and smooth without ridges; pale, olive or dark grey-green. **Plastron** off-white. **Vertebral scutes** ≥ 5. **Costal scutes** 5–10 pairs; first pair in contact with cervical scute. **Flippers** all with 1–2 **claws**.

DISTRIBUTION

Occurs in subtropical and tropical regions of the Pacific, Indian and South Atlantic oceans. Rare vagrant to New Zealand.

VARIATION AND SIMILAR SPECIES

Geographic variation in numbers of vertebral and costal scutes, carapace colour and carapace height. May be confused with **green turtle** (*C. mydas*) but differs by having more vertebral (≥ 5) and costal (5–10 pairs) scutes (vs. 4 vertebral and 4 pairs of costal scutes), and 2 pairs of prefrontals (vs. 1 pair). Distinguished from **loggerhead turtle** (*C. caretta*) by having more vertebral (≥ 5 vs. 5) and costal (5–10 pairs vs. 5-6 pairs) scutes, and smaller head.

HABITAT

Frequently occurs in near-shore waters, inhabiting bays, estuaries and continental shelves where it dives to 150 m to forage on the sea floor. Also pelagic, spending much of its time migrating across open ocean.

NATURAL HISTORY

Frequently referred to as most abundant species of marine turtle, perhaps reflecting large aggregations of females prior to nesting. Nesting annual, in c. 40 countries along continental coasts. Three breeding strategies. First, arribada, is most well known; 100s–1000s of females nest simultaneously on beaches over a few days or weeks. Second, dispersed nesting, is most common; females nest solitarily with no synchrony between individuals. Lastly, a mix of the two first strategies can occur in some locations. Many clutches laid per season, with c. 130 (range: 70–220) white, spherical, soft-shelled eggs per clutch. Incubation period 50–75 days. Hatchlings emerge at 35–45 mm in length (c. 17 g). Does not breed in New Zealand. Primarily carnivorous, feeding on various prey including crabs, lobster, shrimp, sea urchins, jellyfish, tunicates and fish, but will also consume algae.

ETYMOLOGY

Specific name (Latin) meaning 'olive green', referring to the colour of the carapace. **Common name** also refers to the colour of the carapace. The origin of 'ridley' is not known.

Hawksbill turtle

Eretmochelys imbricata (Linnaeus, 1766)

Native; vagrant

SIMON PIERCE

DESCRIPTION

0.4–1.1 m in length; 40–100 kg weight

A small, distinctive and beautifully marked turtle. Narrow head; distinctive pointed and sharp beak, without serrations on jaw. **Prefrontal scales** 2 pairs. **Carapace** heart-shaped, posterior edge of carapace strongly serrated. Brown or orange-brown with contrasting yellow and darker coloured mottling, spots, blotches and striations. **Plastron** white or pale yellow. **Vertebral scutes** 5. **Costal scutes** 4 pairs; first pair not in contact with cervical scute. **Inframarginal scutes** 4 pairs, on bridge. **Flippers** each with 2 visible **claws**.

DISTRIBUTION

Occurs in tropical and subtropical waters of the Atlantic, Pacific and Indian Oceans. Recorded only around the North Island of New Zealand, mostly off Northland and the Kermadecs, and a single individual from off Wellington (in Cook Strait).

VARIATION AND SIMILAR SPECIES

Variation limited to regional size differences and genetic profiles across global populations. Unlikely to be confused with other marine turtles owing to imbricate scutes on carapace.

HABITAT

Inhabits shallow coastal waters around coral reefs, rocky areas, lagoons, mangroves and oceanic islands.

NATURAL HISTORY

Adults undertake long migrations (up to 1000s of kilometres) between foraging and breeding grounds at 2–4 year intervals. Females return to natal rookery, and crawl over reefs and rocky areas to reach secluded beaches. Clutches of 70–200 white spherical soft-shelled eggs deposited in hole in sand; several clutches per season. Incubation period c. 60–75 days. Hatchlings 40–45 mm in length. Harvested – despite being legally protected – for their ornate scutes, used to make tortoiseshell jewellery. Does not breed in New Zealand. Adult mouth shape allows access to holes and crevices in coral reefs to feed on sponges (its primary food). Sponge diet results in accumulation of silica and toxins in turtles' tissues, making them harmful for human consumption. Also feeds on anemones, squid, shrimp, other crustaceans and molluscs. Small juveniles feed on free-swimming organisms and small benthic invertebrates.

ETYMOLOGY

Specific name (Latin) meaning 'overlapping like tiles', in reference to the overlapping scutes of the carapace. **Common name** refers to the beak-like jaw.

PATRICE PLICHON

Leatherback turtle

Dermochelys coriacea (Vandelli, 1761)

Native; migrant

U.S. FISH & WILDLIFE SERVICE/RABON DAVID

DESCRIPTION

1.2–1.6 m (up to 2.5 m) in length; up to 900 kg weight

The largest, deepest-diving and most wide-ranging of marine turtle species, regularly reported in New Zealand waters. Only sea turtle in the world without a hard bony shell. Instead, carapace soft, and leathery or rubbery, with 7 distinct longitudinal ridges covering a matrix of bone, giving a hydrodynamic profile. Large conical head with distinctive notched upper jaw. **Carapace** dark grey to black, with pale spots extending onto front flippers. **Plastron** pink-white to blue-black. **Flippers** proportionally longer than in other sea turtles; front flippers large wing-like, without **claws**.

DISTRIBUTION

Occurs widely throughout tropical and temperate waters in the Pacific, Atlantic and Indian Oceans. In Pacific, range extends as far north as Alaska and into the Southern Ocean, south of Stewart Island/Rakiura. Widespread distribution around almost the entire coastline of New Zealand, including the Chatham Islands.

VARIATION AND SIMILAR SPECIES

Some variation in morphology, life history traits and population trends within global population due to resource availability, and genetic structuring present between Atlantic, Pacific, Indian Ocean and South China Sea populations. Unlikely to be confused with other marine turtles because of leathery skin-covered carapace (vs. bony scutes).

HABITAT

Pelagic, but may feed in coastal waters. Females return to land only to lay eggs.

Able to dive to depths of over 1 km and can remain underwater for up to 85 minutes.

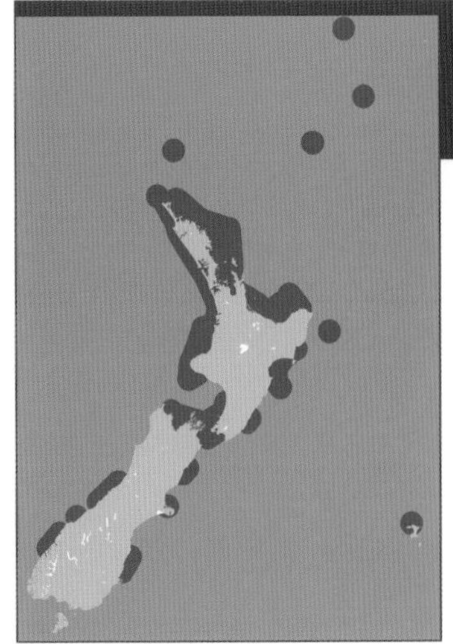

NATURAL HISTORY

Known for its long migrations (e.g. 19,000 km) to feed in cooler waters. Regular presence in New Zealand waters thought to represent regular, deliberate feeding excursions into temperate waters. Able to maintain core body temperature above ambient temperature so tolerates very cold waters (as low as 4 °C). Females congregate annually at nesting beaches along continental coasts in tropical areas, laying c. 80 (30–150) white spherical soft-shelled eggs in deep holes dug in sand on broad beaches. Incubation period 60–80 days; hatchlings emerge and dash into ocean trying to avoid predators. Does not breed in New Zealand. Unlike other marine turtles, with crushing chewing plates, has pointed tooth-like cusps and sharp-edged jaws for feeding, as well as backward-pointing spines in mouth and throat to retain soft-bodied prey, such as jellyfish, sea jellies, tunicates and salps.

ETYMOLOGY

Specific name (Greek) meaning 'leathery'. It and **common name** both refer to the leathery carapace.

U.S. FISH & WILDLIFE SERVICE/CLAUDIA LOMBARD

Key to New Zealand marine turtles

1	**Carapace** covered in leathery skin; carapace with distinctive longitudinal ridges; **limbs** without claws	***Dermochelys coriacea***
	Carapace covered in bony plates (scutes); carapace with single longitudinal ridge down midline; **limbs** with claws	**2**
2	4 **costal scutes** on either side of carapace; first pair of costal scutes excluded from nuchal scute	**3**
	5 or more **costal scutes** on either side of carapace; first pair of costal scutes in contact with nuchal scute	**4**
3	1 pair of **prefrontal scales** on head; **scutes on carapace** do not overlap; **upper jaw** not 'beaked' but serrated; 1 claw on front **limb**	***Chelonia mydas***
	2 pairs of **prefrontal scales** on head; **scutes on carapace** overlap; **upper jaw** with narrow projecting beak; 2 claws on front **limb**	***Eretmochelys imbricata***
4	5 (rarely 6) **costal scutes** on either side of carapace; **carapace** longer than wide; adult carapace reddish or yellowish brown; 3 enlarged **inframarginal scutes** on plastron	***Caretta caretta***
	6 or more **costal scutes** on either side of carapace (may be asymmetrical in number); **carapace** almost circular; adult carapace olive-grey; 4 enlarged **inframarginal scutes** on plastron	***Lepidochelys olivacea***

MARINE SNAKES

Saint Giron's sea krait, *Laticauda saintgironsi*. PATRICE PLICHON

Contents

Yellow-lipped sea krait *Laticauda colubrina* 342
Brown- (blue-) lipped sea krait *Laticauda laticaudata* 344
Saint Giron's sea krait *Laticauda saintgironsi* 346
Yellow-bellied sea snake *Hydrophis platurus* 348
Key to New Zealand marine snakes 350

Yellow-lipped sea krait, *Laticauda colubrina*. SIMON PIERCE

MARINE SNAKES

Four species of marine snake have been reported to visit New Zealand. Most of these records represent snakes washed ashore after heavy storms; there are very few observations of free-swimming individuals. Yellow-bellied sea snakes (*Hydrophis platurus*, family Hydrophiidae) are completely aquatic, never voluntarily coming ashore, not even to mate or give birth. They are primarily pelagic, and live in clumps of floating debris over very deep water far from land, where they prey on fish. The sea kraits (three species in the genus *Laticauda*, family Elapidae) are semi-aquatic, and spend a significant amount of time on land to rest, sun-bask, digest prey, slough their skin and reproduce. Unlike other marine snakes, which are viviparous (live-bearing), kraits lay white leathery-shelled eggs on land. They feed predominantly on eels in the coastal shallows, but are capable of crossing wide expanses of ocean. All four species of marine snake are dangerously venomous; their small fangs can deliver neurotoxic venom that immobilises prey.

SNAKE BODY FORM

***HYDROPHIS PLATURUS* HEAD SHAPE**

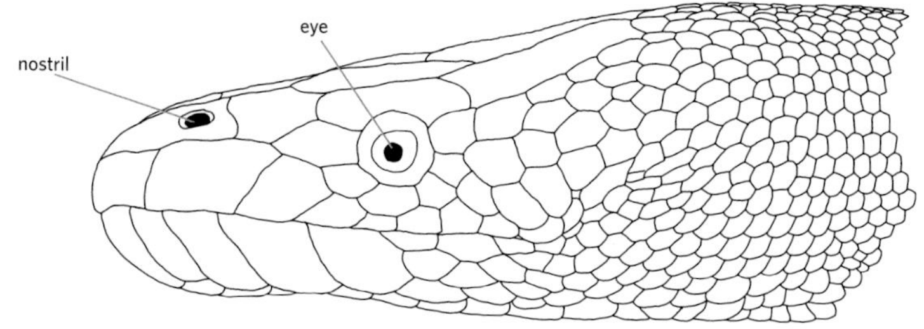

LATICAUDA HEAD SCALES (MIDDLE SHOWING AZYGOUS SCALE)

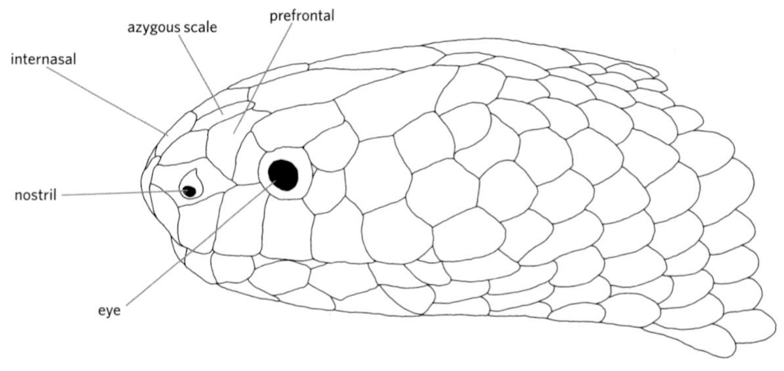

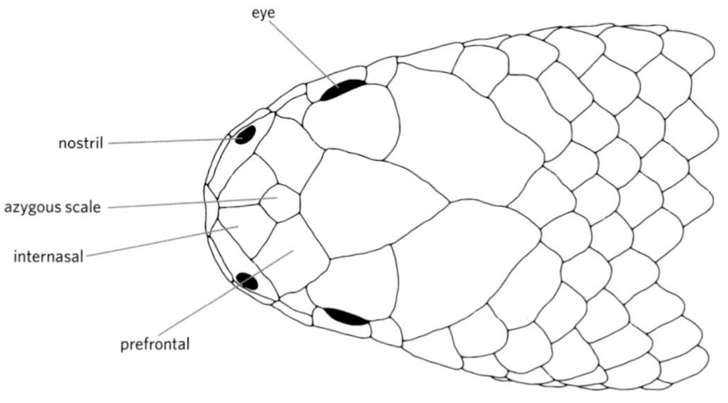

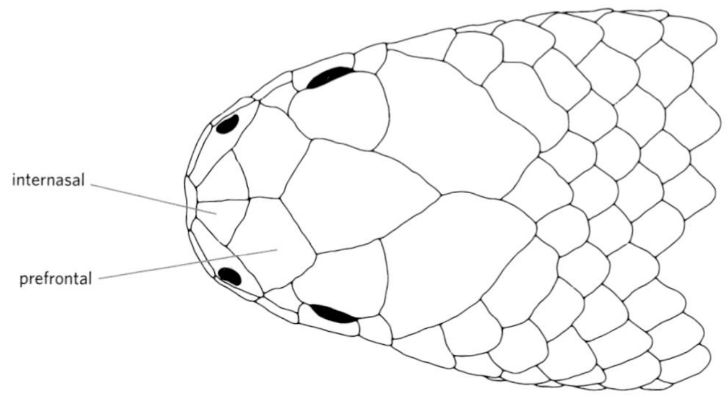

Yellow-lipped sea krait

Laticauda colubrina (Schneider, 1799)

Native; vagrant

Dangerously venomous but disinclined to bite.

HAL COGGER

DESCRIPTION

0.9–1.2 m (up to 1.7 m) total length; 0.4–1.2 kg weight

The second-most common marine snake reported in New Zealand, although sightings are rare. Strandings often associated with ocean storms. Head mostly black. Snout and **upper lip** yellow, pale cream or grey-yellow. A yellow band extending from above eye to temporal region. **Eye** colour grey-blue to black. **Dorsal surface** of body and tail light or dark steel-blue fading to pale yellow on **ventral surface**. Alternating transverse black or brown bands (narrower than steel-blue spaces between) along entire length of body. Dark bands on tail may be wider than those on body. Snout blunt and short, with laterally positioned nostrils. Body cylindrical and tail laterally flattened forming a paddle. **Rostral scale** entire. An azygous (single) scale present between 2 prefrontal scales. **Loreal scales** absent. **Body scales** smooth and overlapping. **Mid-body scales** 23–27 rows. **Ventral scales** enlarged (transversely elongate). **Anal scale** paired (divided). **Subcaudal scales** paired; number differs between sexes (i.e. 29–35 for females; 37–47 for males).

DISTRIBUTION

Most frequently recorded *Laticauda* species in New Zealand and most widely distributed *Laticauda* species globally, occurring throughout the Indo-Pacific from eastern coast of India through much of Asia and the Indo-Malayan Archipelago to New Guinea, and many islands of the western Pacific. Also reported from the western coast of Central America. In New Zealand, recorded only off the North Island, including at Northland, Auckland, Bay of Plenty, Gisborne and Wellington Regions.

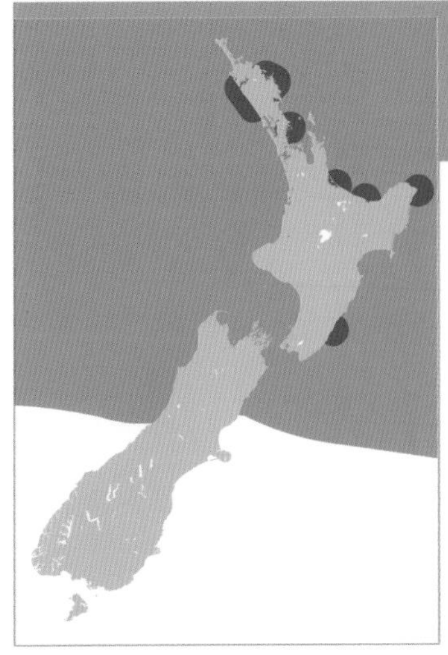

VARIATION AND SIMILAR SPECIES

Females significantly larger than males. Similar in appearance to **Saint Giron's sea krait** (*L. saintgironsi*) and **brown- (or blue-) lipped sea krait** (*L. laticauda*), but distinguished by its yellow upper lip (vs. black or dark brown upper lip), and more mid-body scale rows and higher ventral scale counts compared to Saint Giron's sea krait.

HABITAT

Found in warm tropical coastal waters around coral reefs, surrounding islands and mangroves, usually with sand or coral substrates. Usually in shallow waters (1–10 m depth) but can dive to 60 m, and hold its breath for extended periods of time. More terrestrial than the brown-lipped sea krait, spending up to 25–50% of its time on land in intertidal or littoral zone, taking refuge in crevices and caves, and below rocks or boulders (sometimes up to 100 m from the high-tide mark). Can climb trees but rarely does so.

NATURAL HISTORY

Primarily nocturnal but frequently thermoregulates on land during day. Frequently ventures onto land, often in large aggregations, to rest, slough skin, digest prey and reproduce. Oviparous, with breeding cycles and clutch sizes (4–20 eggs per clutch) varying geographically. Females deposit eggs in soil or rocky crevices, or in mangrove swamps. Sexual maturity reached at 18–24 months. Does not breed in New Zealand. Feeds primarily on eels but may consume small fishes. Larger females hunt conger eels, and smaller males predominantly feed on smaller moray eels.

ETYMOLOGY

Specific name (Latin) meaning 'serpent-like' or 'snake-like'. **Common name** refers to the yellow colour of the upper lip.

Brown- (blue-) lipped sea krait

Laticauda laticaudata (Linnaeus, 1758)

Native, vagrant

Dangerously venomous but inoffensive and docile in nature, and thus disinclined to bite.

HAL COGGER

DESCRIPTION

0.50–0.96 m (up to 1.36 m) total length

A blue and black banded krait from the Indian and western Pacific Oceans. Only one record from New Zealand. Broad black head with cream or pale yellow snout and above eyes. Upper **lips** brownish black. **Eye** colour dark brown to black. **Dorsal surface** light or dark steel-blue, with 39–50 transverse black or brown bands (approximately same width as pale bands) along body. **Ventral surface** yellowish. Snout short and blunt. Body cylindrical; tail laterally flattened, forming a paddle. **Nasal scales** laterally positioned, with 2 or more internasal scales. **Rostral scale** entire. **Prefrontal scales** 2 (i.e. azygous prefrontal shield absent). **Body scales** smooth and overlapping. **Mid-body scales** usually 17–21 rows. **Ventral scales** enlarged (transversely elongate). **Anal scale** paired (divided). **Subcaudal scales** paired; number differs between sexes (i.e. 30–35 for females; 38–47 for males).

DISTRIBUTION

Occurs along the coasts of India, Thailand and Malaysia; the Gulfs of Siam and Tongking; the coasts of China and southern Japan; the coastal waters of the Philippines, Indonesia, New Guinea, Solomon Islands and New Caledonia. The sole New Zealand record is from Auckland.

VARIATION AND SIMILAR SPECIES

Melanotic individuals known. Sexually dimorphic. Similar in appearance to the **yellow-lipped sea krait** (*L. colubrina*) and **Saint Giron's sea krait** (*L. saintgironsi*), but is distinguished by having a dark brownish-black upper lip.

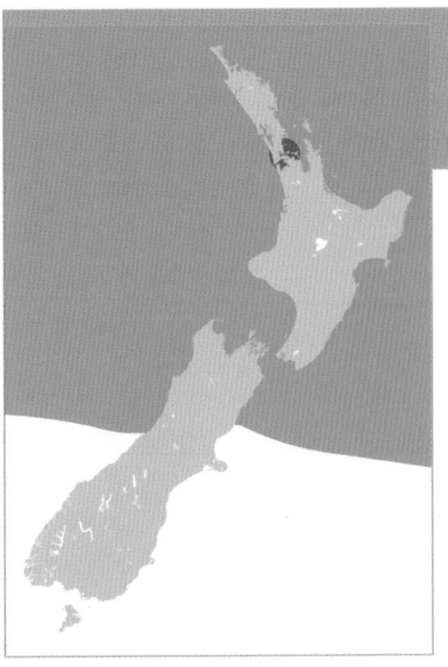

HABITAT

Occurs in coastal waters around rocky areas and coral reefs, usually at depths of 0–15 m, and can dive to > 80 m. Less terrestrial than other *Laticauda* species. Will use raised fossil reefs and rocky shorelines, but rarely travels more than 5 m from water's edge.

NATURAL HISTORY

Primarily nocturnal but may be active during the day. Oviparous reproduction. Females produce 1–7 eggs per clutch, laid in rocky crevices in littoral zone. Does not breed in New Zealand. Feeds predominantly on eels.

ETYMOLOGY

Specific name (Latin) meaning 'broad, flat tail', in reference to the broad, laterally flattened tail. **Common name** refers to the brown or dark blue upper lip.

PATRICE PLICHON

Saint Giron's sea krait

Laticauda saintgironsi Cogger & Heatwole, 2006

Native, vagrant

Dangerously venomous but disinclined to bite.

HAL COGGER

DESCRIPTION

0.80–1.12 m (up to 1.6 m) total length

A distinctive krait from New Caledonia, with russet-orange banding along the entire length of its body. Only one record from New Zealand. Head black, with yellow or cream snout and **upper lip**; black extending to below eye. **Eye** colour brown or blue-grey. **Dorsal surface** bright brown-orange (russet-orange), fading to pale cream or white on flanks. Alternating transverse pale and dark bands (28–32) along entire length of body, and often with light mid-ventral blotch inside each dark band. **Ventral surface** creamy-white, ventral scales edged with darker brown. Body cylindrical; tail laterally flattened, forming a paddle. **Rostral scale** entire. An azygous (single) scale present between 2 prefrontal scales. **Mid-body scales** 21–25 rows. **Anal scale** paired (divided). **Subcaudal scales** paired.

DISTRIBUTION

Occurs in the waters of New Caledonia and the Loyalty Islands. Represented in New Zealand by a single specimen. Precise locality unknown.

VARIATION AND SIMILAR SPECIES

Outwardly similar to **yellow-lipped sea krait** (*L. colubrina*) but pale bands on body russet-orange (vs. blue or steel-grey), and similar to **brown-lipped sea**

krait (*L. laticaudata*), but with a yellow upper lip (vs. black or dark brown) and pale mid-ventral blotches inside the dark bands.

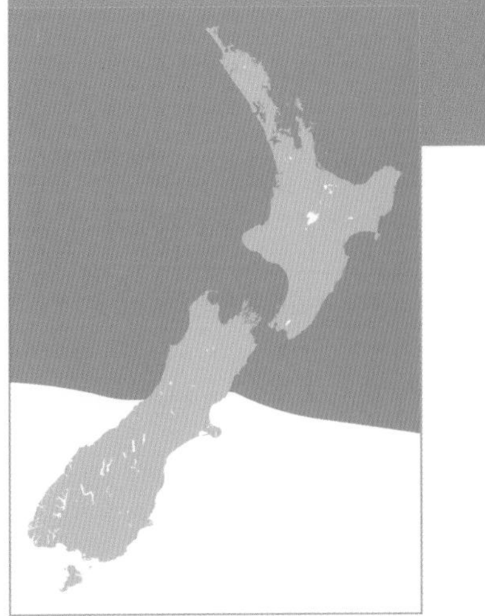

HABITAT

Inhabits shallow coastal waters (0–10 m depth) and reefs, and frequently ventures ashore, sheltering on shoreline, sandy beaches, coastal vegetation, rocky platforms and boulders,and in crevices or tree roots. Capable of travelling hundreds of metres inland, and > 100 m ASL in elevation.

NATURAL HISTORY

Nocturnal, but exhibits some diurnal activity. Readily sun-basks on shore, especially during winter and after feeding to digest prey. May form aggregations, with 30 or more individuals (up to 100s) in a single refuge. Mating occurs in the water; females lay 4–19 elongate white eggs in rock crevices in littoral zone. Incubation period 4.5 months. Does not breed in New Zealand. Feeds on eels in shallow reef waters and lagoons. Can dive and remain submerged for around an hour while hunting prey.

ETYMOLOGY

Specific name (Latinisation) and **common name** in recognition of the late Hubert Saint Girons (1926–2000), a renowned French herpetologist.

PATRICE PLICHON

Yellow-bellied sea snake

Hydrophis platurus (Linnaeus, 1766)

Native

Dangerously venomous but disinclined to bite, unless provoked.

HAL COGGER

DESCRIPTION

0.64 m total length (male), 0.79 m total length (female) (up to 1.1 m)

A distinctive species, and the most commonly observed sea snake in New Zealand. Dorso-ventrally flattened head. Tail laterally flattened to form paddle-like tail. **Eye** colour black or yellow. **Dorsal surface** black from head to beginning of tail, with sharply contrasting yellow **ventral surface**. Tail with longitudinally stretched black rhomboid or wedge-shaped patches, sometimes forming round spots. **Body scales** hexagonal and juxtaposed (non-overlapping). **Mid-body scales** 49–67 rows.

DISTRIBUTION

The world's most widely distributed snake. Occurs in tropical and subtropical waters, mostly in neritic zone in Indian and Pacific Oceans, but also along coasts of the Americas, from the Gulf of California to Chile. Also sightings in more southerly waters, including around Cape of Good Hope and New Zealand. Likely carried to waters around mainland New Zealand via warm tropical Pacific Ocean currents from Australia and the Pacific Islands. Records in New Zealand mostly from off Northland, Bay of Plenty and Taranaki but some sightings south (both east and west coasts) to Wellington, and Farewell Spit and near Westport (South Island). Most stranded individuals were alive, but mainland New Zealand waters considered too cold for year-round survival. Waters around the Kermadec Islands warm enough for year-round residence and breeding, but few records from that area.

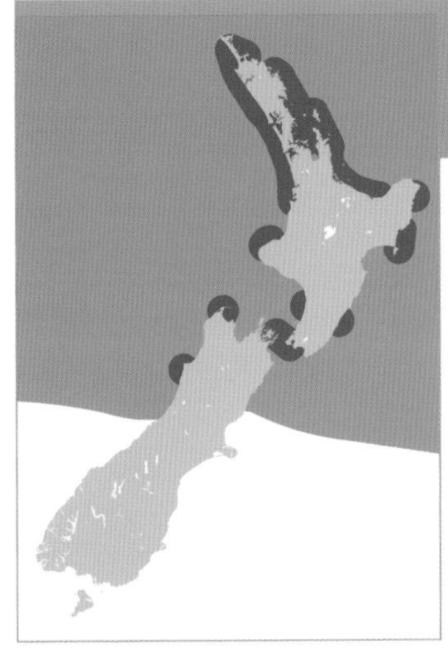

VARIATION AND SIMILAR SPECIES

Variation in general colour pattern in some populations. For example, xanthic (uniform yellow) and mottled variants known from around Costa Rica. Sexually dimorphic; females larger than males. Unlikely to be confused with any other marine snakes due to distinctive colouration (i.e. contrasting black upper and bright yellow lower body surfaces) and dorso-ventrally flattened head.

HABITAT

Occurs in marine pelagic environments but occasionally found in coastal waters and intertidal habitats. Often occurs in large aggregations along ocean slicks and around flotsam. Unable to move effectively on land, and thus often stranded ashore after large storm events.

NATURAL HISTORY

Diurnally active, spending the nights on ocean floor, surfacing only to breathe. Can dive to 50 m in depth, and remain underwater for up to 3.5 hours on single breath. Can tolerate cooler waters (12 °C) but only for short periods. Viviparous, breeding annually in waters ≥ 20 °C. Gestation period c. 6 months; females give birth to 1–8 live young in the water. No direct evidence of breeding in New Zealand, probably due to cold water temperatures around the mainland; however, breeding may occur in the warmer waters around the Kermadec Islands. Feeds on fishes and cephalopods (squid, cuttlefish).

ETYMOLOGY

Specific name (Greek) meaning 'flat tail', in reference to the broad laterally flattened tail. **Common name** refers to the colour of the ventral surface.

Key to New Zealand marine snakes

1	Alternating transverse light and dark **bands** around body; **head** short with blunt snout; enlarged **ventral scales**	2
	No alternating **bands**, dorsal surface black and ventral surface yellow (rarely, entire body yellow); **head** elongate and flattened; **ventral scales** similar size to dorsal scales	***Hydrophis platurus***
2	**Upper lip** (occasionally tip of snout) black or dark brown; 2 **prefrontal scales**	***Laticauda laticaudata***
	Upper lip and tip of snout white, or pale yellow or orange; azygous scale between **prefrontal scales**	3
3	Paler **bands** steel-grey or blue; dark bands meeting ventrally and uniform in width	***Laticauda colubrina***
	Paler **bands** predominantly orange-brown or russet; dark bands may not meet on ventral surface but if they do, bands become narrower and often have a pale mid-ventral blotch	***Laticauda saintgironsi***

Regional checklist of New Zealand herpetofauna

REGIONS	TERRESTRIAL REPTILES	FROGS	MARINE REPTILES
Northland	*Dactylocnemis* "Matapia" *Dactylocnemis* "North Cape" *Dactylocnemis pacificus* *Dactylocnemis* "Poor Knights" *Dactylocnemis* "Three Kings" *Hoplodactylus duvaucelii* *Lampropholis delicata* *Mokopirirakau granulatus* *Naultinus elegans* *Naultinus grayii* *Naultinus* "North Cape" *Oligosoma aeneum* *Oligosoma alani* *Oligosoma moco* *Oligosoma fallai* *Oligosoma hardyi* *Oligosoma levidensum* *Oligosoma macgregori* *Oligosoma oliveri* *Oligosoma ornatum* *Oligosoma roimata* *Oligosoma smithi* *Oligosoma* aff. *smithi* "Three Kings, Te Paki, western Northland" *Oligosoma suteri* *Oligosoma townsi* *Oligosoma* "Whirinaki" *Sphenodon punctatus* *Woodworthia maculata*	*Leiopelma hochstetteri* *Litoria ewingii* *Ranoidea aurea* *Ranoidea raniformis*	*Caretta caretta* *Chelonia mydas* *Dermochelys coriacea* *Eretmochelys imbricata* *Hydrophis platurus* *Laticauda colubrina* *Lepidochelys olivacea*
Auckland	*Dactylocnemis pacificus* *Dactylocnemis* "Mokohinau" *Hoplodactylus duvaucelii* *Lampropholis delicata* *Mokopirirakau granulatus* *Naultinus elegans* *Oligosoma aeneum* *Oligosoma homalonotum* *Oligosoma moco* *Oligosoma ornatum* *Oligosoma suteri* *Oligosoma smithi* *Oligosoma* aff. *smithi* "Three Kings, Te Paki, western Northland" *Oligosoma striatum* *Oligosoma townsi* *Sphenodon punctatus* *Woodworthia maculata* *Woodworthia* aff. *maculata* "Muriwai"	*Leiopelma hochstetteri* *Litoria ewingii* *Ranoidea aurea* *Ranoidea raniformis*	*Caretta caretta* *Chelonia mydas* *Dermochelys coriacea* *Eretmochelys imbricata* *Hydrophis platurus* *Laticauda colubrina* *Laticauda laticaudata* *Lepidochelys olivacea*

REGIONS	TERRESTRIAL REPTILES	FROGS	MARINE REPTILES
Waikato, including Coromandel	*Dactylocnemis pacificus* *Hoplodactylus duvaucelii* *Lampropholis delicata* *Mokopirirakau granulatus* *Naultinus elegans* *Oligosoma aeneum* *Oligosoma alani* *Oligosoma* aff. *infrapunctatum* "crenulate" *Oligosoma microlepis* *Oligosoma moco* *Oligosoma oliveri* *Oligosoma ornatum* *Oligosoma smithi* *Oligosoma striatum* *Oligosoma suteri* *Oligosoma whitakeri* *Sphenodon punctatus* *Toropuku* "Coromandel" *Woodworthia chrysosiretica* *Woodworthia maculata*	*Leiopelma archeyi* *Leiopelma hochstetteri* *Litoria ewingii* *Ranoidea aurea* *Ranoidea raniformis*	*Caretta caretta* *Chelonia mydas* *Dermochelys coriacea* *Eretmochelys imbricata* *Hydrophis platurus* *Lepidochelys olivacea*
Bay of Plenty	*Dactylocnemis pacificus* *Lampropholis delicata* *Mokopirirakau granulatus* *Naultinus elegans* *Oligosoma aeneum* *Oligosoma* aff. *infrapunctatum* "crenulate" *Oligosoma moco* *Oligosoma ornatum* *Oligosoma smithi* *Oligosoma striatum* *Oligosoma* "Whirinaki" *Sphenodon punctatus* *Woodworthia maculata*	*Leiopelma hochstetteri* *Litoria ewingii* *Ranoidea aurea* *Ranoidea raniformis*	*Caretta caretta* *Chelonia mydas* *Dermochelys coriacea* *Hydrophis platurus* *Laticauda colubrina* *Lepidochelys olivacea*
Gisborne	*Lampropholis delicata* *Mokopirirakau* "southern North Island" *Naultinus punctatus* *Oligosoma aeneum* *Oligosoma ornatum* *Oligosoma polychroma* *Oligosoma smithi* *Sphenodon punctatus* *Woodworthia maculata*	*Leiopelma hochstetteri* *Ranoidea aurea* *Ranoidea raniformis*	*Chelonia mydas* *Dermochelys coriacea* *Eretmochelys imbricata* *Hydrophis platurus* *Laticauda colubrina*
Hawke's Bay	*Lampropholis delicata* *Mokopirirakau* "southern North Island" *Naultinus punctatus* *Oligosoma aeneum* *Oligosoma* aff. *infrapunctatum* "Hawke's Bay"	*Litoria ewingii* *Ranoidea raniformis*	*Caretta caretta* *Chelonia mydas* *Dermochelys coriacea* *Hydrophis platurus*

REGIONS	TERRESTRIAL REPTILES	FROGS	MARINE REPTILES
Hawke's Bay (continued)	*Oligosoma kokowai* *Oligosoma ornatum* *Oligosoma microlepis* *Oligosoma zelandicum* *Sphenodon punctatus* *Woodworthia maculata*		
Taranaki	*Dactylocnemis pacificus* *Lampropholis delicata* *Mokopirirakau granulatus* *Naultinus elegans* *Naultinus punctatus* *Oligosoma aeneum* *Oligosoma* aff. *infrapunctatum* "southern North Island" *Oligosoma ornatum* *Oligosoma polychroma* *Oligosoma striatum* *Oligosoma zelandicum* *Woodworthia chrysosiretica*	*Litoria ewingii* *Ranoidea aurea* *Ranoidea raniformis*	*Dermochelys coriacea* *Hydrophis platurus*
Manawatu-Wanganui	*Dactylocnemis pacificus* *Lampropholis delicata* *Mokopirirakau granulatus* *Mokopirirakau* "southern North Island" *Naultinus elegans* *Naultinus punctatus* *Oligosoma aeneum* *Oligosoma* aff. *infrapunctatum* "southern North Island" *Oligosoma kokowai* *Oligosoma ornatum* *Oligosoma polychroma* *Oligosoma striatum* *Oligosoma zelandicum* *Woodworthia chrysosiretica* *Woodworthia maculata*	*Litoria ewingii* *Ranoidea raniformis*	*Caretta caretta* *Dermochelys coriacea* *Hydrophis platurus* *Lepidochelys olivacea*
Wellington	*Hoplodactylus duvaucelii* *Mokopirirakau* "southern North Island" *Naultinus punctatus* *Oligosoma aeneum* *Oligosoma infrapunctatum* *Oligosoma kokowai* *Oligosoma macgregori* *Oligosoma ornatum* *Oligosoma polychroma* *Oligosoma whitakeri* *Oligosoma zelandicum* *Sphenodon punctatus* *Woodworthia chrysosiretica* *Woodworthia maculata* *Woodworthia* "Marlborough mini"	*Leiopelma hamiltoni* *Litoria ewingii* *Ranoidea raniformis*	*Caretta caretta* *Chelonia mydas* *Eretmochelys imbricata* *Dermochelys coriacea* *Hydrophis platurus* *Laticauda colubrina* *Lepidochelys olivacea*

REGIONS	TERRESTRIAL REPTILES	FROGS	MARINE REPTILES
Tasman	*Mokopirirakau* "Cupola" *Mokopirirakau granulatus* *Mokopirirakau kahutarae* *Naultinus stellatus* *Naultinus tuberculatus* *Oligosoma infrapunctatum* *Oligosoma kokowai* *Oligosoma polychroma* *Oligosoma zelandicum* *Woodworthia maculata* *Woodworthia* "Marlborough mini" *Woodworthia* "Mount Arthur" *Woodworthia* "Southern Alps"	*Litoria ewingii* *Ranoidea raniformis*	*Chelonia mydas* *Dermochelys coriacea* *Hydrophis platurus*
Nelson	*Mokopirirakau granulatus* *Naultinus stellatus* *Oligosoma kokowai* *Oligosoma polychroma* *Oligosoma zelandicum* *Woodworthia maculata* *Woodworthia* "Marlborough mini"	*Litoria ewingii* *Ranoidea raniformis*	*Dermochelys coriacea* *Hydrophis platurus*
Marlborough	*Hoplodactylus duvaucelii* *Mokopirirakau granulatus* *Mokopirirakau kahutarae* *Naultinus manukanus* *Naultinus rudis* *Naultinus stellatus* *Oligosoma elium* *Oligosoma polychroma* *Oligosoma* aff. *polychroma* Clade 2 *Oligosoma* aff. *polychroma* Clade 3 *Oligosoma infrapunctatum* *Oligosoma kokowai* *Oligosoma longipes* *Oligosoma waimatense* *Oligosoma zelandicum* *Sphenodon punctatus* *Toropuku stephensi* *Woodworthia* "Kaikouras" *Woodworthia maculata* *Woodworthia* "Marlborough mini" *Woodworthia* "pygmy" *Woodworthia* "Southern Alps"	*Leiopelma hamiltoni* *Litoria ewingii* *Ranoidea raniformis*	*Chelonia mydas* *Dermochelys coriacea* *Hydrophis platurus* *Lepidochelys olivacea*
West Coast	*Mokopirirakau* "Cascades" *Mokopirirakau granulatus* *Mokopirirakau* "Okarito" *Mokopirirakau* "Open Bay Islands" *Naultinus stellatus* *Naultinus tuberculatus* *Oligosoma inconspicuum* *Oligosoma infrapunctatum* *Oligosoma* aff. *infrapunctatum* "Alborn"	*Litoria ewingii* *Ranoidea raniformis*	*Caretta caretta* *Dermochelys coriacea* *Hydrophis platurus*

REGIONS	TERRESTRIAL REPTILES	FROGS	MARINE REPTILES
West Coast (continued)	*Oligosoma* aff. *infrapunctatum* "Chesterfield" *Oligosoma* aff. *infrapunctatum* "Cobble" *Oligosoma* aff. *infrapunctatum* "Hokitika" *Oligosoma* aff. *infrapunctatum* "Westport" *Oligosoma* "Okuru" *Oligosoma polychroma* *Oligosoma* aff. *polychroma* Clade 4 *Oligosoma taumakae* *Oligosoma zelandicum* *Woodworthia maculata* *Woodworthia* unidentified species		
Canterbury	*Mokopirirakau granulatus* *Mokopirirakau kahutarae* *Naultinus gemmeus* *Naultinus rudis* *Oligosoma* aff. *chloronoton* "West Otago" *Oligosoma elium* *Oligosoma hoparatea* *Oligosoma lineoocellatum* *Oligosoma* aff. *longipes* "Southern" *Oligosoma maccanni* *Oligosoma* aff. *polychroma* Clade 2 *Oligosoma* aff. *polychroma* Clade 3 *Oligosoma* aff. *polychroma* Clade 4 *Oligosoma* aff. *polychroma* Clade 5 *Oligosoma prasinum* *Oligosoma waimatense* *Woodworthia* cf. *brunnea* *Woodworthia* "Kaikouras" *Woodworthia maculata* *Woodworthia* "Marlborough mini" *Woodworthia* "pygmy" *Woodworthia* "Southern Alps"	*Ranoidea raniformis*	*Caretta caretta* *Chelonia mydas* *Dermochelys coriacea*
Otago	*Mokopirirakau cryptozoicus* *Mokopirirakau kahutarae* *Mokopirirakau* "Roys Peak" *Mokopirirakau* "southern forest" *Naultinus gemmeus* *Oligosoma burganae* *Oligosoma* aff. *chloronoton* "Eastern Otago" *Oligosoma* aff. *chloronoton* "West Otago" *Oligosoma grande* *Oligosoma inconspicuum* *Oligosoma maccanni* *Oligosoma otagense*	*Litoria ewingii* *Ranoidea raniformis*	*Dermochelys coriacea* *Lepidochelys olivacea*

REGIONS	TERRESTRIAL REPTILES	FROGS	MARINE REPTILES
Otago (continued)	*Oligosoma* aff. *polychroma* Clade 5 *Oligosoma repens* *Oligosoma toka* *Oligosoma waimatense* *Sphenodon punctatus* *Woodworthia* "Central Otago" *Woodworthia* "Cromwell" *Woodworthia* "Otago/Southland large" *Woodworthia* "Southern Alps" *Woodworthia* "southern mini"		
Southland, including Fiordland	*Mokopirirakau* "Cascades" *Mokopirirakau cryptozoicus* *Mokopirirakau* "southern forest" *Naultinus gemmeus* *Oligosoma acrinasum* *Oligosoma awakopaka* *Oligosoma chloronoton* *Oligosoma* aff. *chloronoton* "Eastern Otago" *Oligosoma judgei* *Oligosoma inconspicuum* *Oligosoma maccanni* *Oligosoma pikitanga* *Oligosoma repens* *Oligosoma* aff. *polychroma* Clade 5 *Oligosoma tekakahu* *Woodworthia* "Otago/Southland large" *Woodworthia* "southern mini"	*Litoria ewingii* *Ranoidea aurea* *Ranoidea raniformis*	*Dermochelys coriacea*
Stewart Island	*Mokopirirakau nebulosus* *Naultinus gemmeus* *Oligosoma* aff. *chloronoton* "Stewart Island" *Oligosoma notosaurus* *Oligosoma* aff. *polychroma* Clade 5 *Oligosoma stenotis* *Tukutuku rakiurae*	*Litoria ewingii*	*Caretta caretta* *Lepidochelys olivacea*
Chatham Islands	*Oligosoma nigriplantare*	*Litoria ewingii*	*Dermochelys coriacea*

Glossary

Allopatric related taxa or populations occurring in separate non-overlapping geographical areas.

Amelanotic a pigmentation abnormality, characterised by the lack of the pigment melanin, resulting in a white, yellowish or pinkish appearance.

Amphicoelous referring to the vertebrae, where the central part of each vertebra is concave on both anterior and posterior surfaces.

Amphisbaenans a group of limbless, burrowing squamates, characterised by their long bodies, the reduction or loss of the limbs, and rudimentary eyes. Also referred to as 'worm lizards'.

Amplexus mating position of frogs and toads, in which the male clasps the female from above, around the waist (inguinal amplexus) or the armpits (axillary amplexus), and externally fertilises eggs as they are laid.

Anterior at or towards the front (head end) of the body.

Annulus a ring-shaped structure or region. Plural 'annuli'.

Apical plates/pads enlarged plates (pads) found at or near the tip of the digit (i.e. bordering the claw) in geckos.

Arboreal living, at least part of the time, above ground in trees.

ASL abbreviation for 'above sea level'. An altitudinal or elevational measurement.

Assemblage collection or gathering of taxa; collective name for all the species found in an area.

Autotomy loss of all or part of a body (e.g. tail) either spontaneously or because of pressure (e.g. grasped by a predator). Tail autotomy is commonly used as a predator escape mechanism by lizards.

Axilla region where forelimbs join the body (i.e. armpit). Plural 'axillae'.

Azygous a single organic structure; not in pairs.

Basal at or near the bottom or base of a particular structure.

Canthal at, near or relating to dorsolateral region or ridge on the snout, between the nostril and eye.

Cathemeral neither prescriptively nocturnal, nor diurnal, nor crepuscular. Irregularly active at any time of the night or day.

Caudal at, near or relating to the tail.

Chytridiomycosis an infectious disease in amphibians, caused by a fungus called *Batrachochytrium dendrobatidis*. Also known as 'chytrid'.

Clade genetic group of individuals or species all descended from one common ancestor.

Cloaca the common chamber into which the reproductive and excretory ducts open. The external opening of the cloaca is called the 'vent'.

Cloacal spurs one or more enlarged scales, lying ventrolaterally between the vent and the base of the tail.

Commensal animals living together with no mutual disadvantage.

Commensalism see 'commensal'.

Conspecific organism within the same species.

Congener organism within the same genus.

Conical triangular in shape (i.e. ending in a point).

Copulation the act of mating.

Costal plates rows of plates either side of the central row of plates on the carapace of turtles.

Crenulate scalloped, notched or wavy in shape. Used to describe a pattern or scale feature.

Crepuscular active during twilight hours, i.e. dawn and dusk.

Cryptic secretive or inconspicuous in nature (e.g. colour patterning or behaviour)

Cryptozoic living in hidden or darkened places, e.g. under leaf litter, stones or pieces of wood.

Density the number of individuals per unit area.

Denticulate small, tooth-like patterns or markings, e.g. alternating black and white pattern on the lips.

Digit a finger or toe.

Diurnal primarily active during day.

Distal away from the body or furthest from the point of attachment of a structure.

Distal pad suckers, the undersurface tip portion of the fingers or toe.

Distal phalange the tip portion of a finger or toe (smallest, outermost bone of the hands or feet), between the lamellar pad and the claw.

Dorsal the back or upper surface.

Dorsolateral the junction of the dorsal (back) and lateral (side) surfaces.

Ecdysis the action of shedding skin, or a shed skin. Also known as 'sloughing'.

Ectotherm animal in which body temperature is largely regulated by an external heat source and behavioural means.

Ectothermic see 'ectotherm'.

Egg the female reproductive cell; an ovum.

Egg capsule gelatinous layer that surrounds an oocyte (immature ovum, or egg cell).

Endemic animal (or plant) that is restricted to, or only found in, a certain place.

Epiphyte a type of plant that grows or perches on another plant or tree.

Eustachian tube a tube that links the nasopharynx to the middle ear.

Exotic organism originating in a foreign country or region. Exotic species may either have been accidentally or deliberately introduced, and may have negative impacts on native species through predation, competition or disease transmission. Also referred to as 'introduced' species.

Extant a species, family or group that is still existing or living.

Extinct a species, family or group with no living members.

Fellfield a treeless rock-strewn area of the subalpine or alpine zone, exposed to the dynamics of freezing and thawing, and frequent winds. Usually dominated by low-growing plants or grasses and sedges.

Femoral pores series of precloacal pores (hole or pit in a scale) extending onto the ventral surface or undersides of the thighs (especially obvious in geckos). Usually more well developed in males than females.

Filigree ornamental pattern of fine dark lines, e.g. over the surface of the eye as seen in many gecko taxa.

Flash marking brightly coloured region of an animal, usually concealed when animal is at rest. In frogs, markings are generally in the thigh; normally hidden when legs are folded in.

Fossil the hardened remains of a prehistoric organism embedded in rock and preserved in petrified form.

Fossorial burrowing, or living in burrows.

Frontal scale large median scale lying between the eyes.

Frontoparietal scales scales between the parietals and the frontal scales.

Gastralia dermal bones usually between sternum and pelvis, in the ventral body wall in crocodilians and *Sphenodon* species.

Genus taxonomic grouping of species (taxa) that are more similar to each other than to other species (taxa). Plural 'genera'.

Granular composed or appearing to be composed of granules or grains, i.e. small, convex, non-overlapping scales.

Gravid carrying eggs or developing young within the body of a female, i.e. pregnant.

Gyre referring to oceans, a large circulating ocean current system that is generally influenced by large wind movements.

Heliothermic obtaining heat from the sun by basking in direct sunrays.

Hemipenis copulatory organ found in male lizards and snakes. Usually paired and lying within a cavity in the base of the tail (hemipenal sac). One is usually extruded like an inverted glove for insertion into the cloaca of the female during mating. Plural 'hemipenes'.

Herpetofauna amphibian and reptile fauna.

Imbricate arrangement of scales with overlapping edges.

Indigenous occurring naturally within a country or specific region; 'native' or endemic species.

Infralabial scale one of a series of scales on the lower lips.

Inframarginal scale smaller scales lying between the marginal scales of turtles.

Inscriptional ribs elongate cartilages in the muscles of the abdominal wall.

Insectivore animal whose diet consists of insects.

Insectivorous see 'insectivore'.

Internasal scale single, paired or irregular group of scales on top of the snout between the nasal scales in snakes and lizards.

Interparietal scale the median scale on the top of the head lying between the parietal scales. Often containing the parietal eye in skinks.

Intraspecific existing or occurring within a species or between individuals of a single species.

Intromittent organ external organ of a male organism that is specialised to deliver sperm during copulation.

Iris surface of the eye surrounding the pupil.

Juvenile young animal that has not yet reached sexual maturity.

Keeled with a raised ridge. Usually refers to the ridge(s) on individual scales, or the body or caudal crest.

Labial of the lips. Refers to the scales bordering the lips.

Lamellae scales on the undersurface of the digits.

Lamellar pad widened or broad, flattened portion of a gecko's digit.

Larva organism at an independent and self-sufficient stage in development before acquiring the characteristics of its parents (adult), e.g. free-living tadpole of a frog. Plural 'larvae'.

Lateral at, near or relating to the sides of the body.

Lateroventral the region of conjunction between the lateral (side) and ventral (below) surfaces.

Leucistic having partial or fully white skin, fur or feathers due to lack of pigment. Leucistic animals can also be patchily white. Different from albinism, as leucistic individuals still have pigments in their eyes.

Littoral pertaining to the shoreline, including the intertidal zone that is cyclically inundated and exposed by water.

Loreal scale the scales along the lateral side of the head, between the nostril and eye.

Lower labial see 'sublabial scales'.

Marginals the outer series of shields in the turtle carapace.

Melanotic blackish, a result of exceptional development of black pigment (melanin).

Mental scale the single scale at the anterior tip of the lower jaw.

Meristic countable trait or character. Refers to anatomical features that can be counted, such as the number of scales or scale rows.

Metamorphosis change in body form from the larval to adult stage, e.g. tadpole to frog.

Mid-body scale rows the number of scales encircling the middle of the body in lizards and snakes (excluding the enlarged ventral scales in snakes). Usually abbreviated as 'MSRs'.

Mid-dorsal the area along the spine/middle of the body and tail.

Migrant taxon that predictably and cyclically visits New Zealand as part of the normal life cycle but does not breed here.

Morphological see 'morphology'.

Morphology pertaining to any aspect of the external anatomy (form and structure), including proportions, colouration and scales.

Morphotype an informal group of taxa with similar or identical morphology.

MSR see 'mid-body scale rows'.

Nape the dorsal surface of the neck.

Nasal scale a scale on the snout enclosing or bordering the nostril.

Naturalised a taxon that is established and living wild in a region where it is not indigenous.

Neonate a newborn.

Newt semi-aquatic amphibian with lungs and a well-developed tail.

Nocturnal	active at night.
Nuchal scale	relating to the enlarged scales on the nape (neck), behind the head.
Nuchal shield	in turtles, a single, small median scale between the first (anterior) marginals.
Ocelli	ring- or eye-shaped markings, usually spots formed of concentric rings of colour.
Omnivore	feeding on both animals and plants.
Omnivorous	see 'omnivore'.
Ontogenic	pertaining to the development and growth of an individual from early developmental stages to maturity (e.g. changes in colouration throughout its lifetime).
Oviparous	egg laying.
Pākihi	type of wet heath, characterised by very infertile soil with an impervious horizon and little or no peat.
Parasite	organism that lives, reproduces or feeds on another organism (host), and benefits by deriving nutrients at the other's expense.
Paratoid	external skin gland at the neck and shoulders (between the head and ear), usually in toads and frogs.
Parietal	pertaining to the part of the head in the region of the parietal body. May refer to particular scales on the head (e.g. two large scales at the posterior of the head in skinks) or bones in the skull.
Parietal eye	a structure on the top of the head, part of the pineal complex of some reptiles (probably light-sensitive). Often referred to as the 'third eye' in tuatara and some lizards.
Parturition	the action of giving birth.
Pelagic	inhabiting the open sea or ocean.
Phalanges	bones (joints) of digits (fingers, or toes).
Plastron	the lower (under) surface of the shell of a turtle.
Pleurodont	type of formation where sides of the teeth are fused to the inner surface of the jawbones.
Pore	hole or pit in a scale. See 'femoral', 'preanal' and 'precloacal'.
Posterior	toward the hind or tail end of the body.
Postmental	scales on the chin, lying immediately behind the mental scale.
Precloacal pores	series of pores on the lower surface, anterior of the vent (especially obvious in geckos). Pore series usually in triangular shape, and usually measured as the number of pore rows along the midline. Generally, more well developed in males than females. Can be present with or without femoral pores.
Prefrontal scale	scale on top of the head lying immediately in front of the frontal scale (i.e. between the nostril and eye).
Prehensile	capable of grasping, usually referring to an animal's tail or limb.
Rookery	a colony of breeding or nesting animals.
Rostral scale	scale found at the tip of the snout, its lower edge bordering the mouth.
Saxicolous	rock dwelling, inhabiting rocks
Scutes	body plates of a turtle shell.
Setae	microscopic hairs or bristles.
Sexual dichromatism	marked differences in body colouration between male and female of the same species/taxon.
Sexual dimorphism	marked differences in size or appearances between male and female of the same species/taxon.
Sister groups/taxa	closest relatives in an evolutionary tree; i.e. two descendants split from a phylogenetic node.
Slough	see 'ecdysis'.
Sloughing	see 'ecdysis'.
Snout-vent length	the distance between the tip of the snout and the anterior opening of the cloaca or vent. Usually abbreviated as 'SVL'.
Splash zone	the area above the high tide mark that is exposed to wave splash and ocean spray.
Squamate	members in the taxonomic order Squamata, which includes lizards and snakes.

Striate bearing lines or streaks of colour or texture, which are different from the base colour or texture.
Striation see 'striate'.
Subcaudal beneath the tail, often referring to scales.
Subdigital undersurface of the digits (fingers or toes).
Subfossil a bone or other part of an organism that has not fully fossilised.
Sublabial scale one of the scales along the lower lip. Also known as 'lower labial'.
Subocular scale one of the scales beneath the eye.
Supraciliary scale one of the scales above the eye that form the fringe or 'eyebrow'.
Supralabial scale one of the scales along the upper lip. Also known as 'upper labial'.
Supraocular scale one of the scales above the eye.
SVL see 'snout-vent length'.
Sympatric two or more populations or taxa that occur in the same or overlapping geographical area.
Syntopic two or more populations or taxa that occur in the same habitat or microhabitat.
Tag name a temporary name for a proposed, but undescribed species.
Tail annuli constrictions encircling the tail at regular intervals, marking the places where the tail can break off (autotomise) in lizards.
Tail autotomy see 'autotomy'.
Talus rock rubble at the bottom of a slope.
Taxa plural of 'taxon'.
Taxon any category in a system of classification, i.e. any taxonomic group. Plural 'taxa'.
Temporal scale one of the scales behind the eye, between the parietal and upper labial scales. Divided into three groups: primary, secondary and tertiary.
Terrestrial living on the ground.
Thigmothermic absorbing heat by contact with warm surfaces, e.g. rocks.
Tubercle any small, rounded protuberance on the skin or scales.
Tympanum eardrum. Plural 'tympana'.
Type locality the place where the type specimen was collected.
Type specimen the specimen used to describe a taxon/species.
Upper labial see 'supralabial'.
Uncinate hook-shaped.
Vagrant taxon whose presence is naturally transitory or which occurs unexpectedly in an area or region.
Vent transverse external opening of the cloaca.
Ventral pertaining to the lower surface or underside of an animal.
Ventrolateral junction between the lateral (side) and ventral (lower) surfaces.
Vestigial remnant, e.g. part of a body or organ that is rudimentary because it has become functionless over evolutionary time.
Viviparous live bearing.
Xanthic yellowish in colour.

Further reading

Chapple, D. G. (ed.) (2016). *New Zealand Lizards*. Cham, Switzerland: Springer International Publishing.

Cree, A. (2014). *Tuatara: Biology and conservation of a venerable survivor*. Christchurch: Canterbury University Press.

Gill, G., & Whitaker, T. (1996). *New Zealand Frogs and Reptiles*. Auckland: David Bateman Ltd.

Heatwole, H. (1999). *Sea snakes* (Australian Natural History Series). Sydney: University of New South Wales Press.

Hitchmough, R., Barr, B., Lettink, M., Monks, J., Reardon, J., Tocher, M., van Winkel, D., & Rolfe, J. (2016). *Conservation Status of New Zealand Reptiles, 2015* (New Zealand Threat Classification Series 17). Wellington: Department of Conservation.

Jewell, T. (2016). *Skinks of Southern New Zealand: A field guide*. First edition. Electronic document published by author, Invercargill.

Jewell, T., & Morris, R. (2008). *A Photographic Guide to Reptiles & Amphibians of New Zealand*. Auckland: New Holland Publishers (NZ) Ltd.

Lutz, P. L., & Musick, J. A. (1996). *The Biology of Sea Turtles*, vol. I. Boca Raton, Florida: CRC Press.

Robb, J. (1980). *New Zealand Reptiles and Amphibians in Colour*. Auckland: Collins.

Sharrell, R. (1975). *The Tuatara, Lizards and Frogs of New Zealand*. Auckland: Collins.

Whitaker, T. W., & Thomas, B. W. (1989). *New Zealand Lizards: An annotated bibliography*. Lower Hutt: Ecology Division, DSIR.

Websites

New Zealand Department of Conservation, www.doc.govt.nz
New Zealand Herpetological Society, www.reptiles.org.nz
Society for Research on Amphibians and Reptiles in New Zealand, www.srarnz.com
The Reptile Database, www.reptile-database.org

Index

ankylosaur, 9
Ascaphidae, 306
Ascaphus, 6, 306

Caretta, 3
caretta, 325-27, 336
Chelodina longicollis, 11
Chelonia, 3
mydas, 7, 321-25, 328-29, 336
Cheloniidae, 3, 7
crocodile, 9

Dactylocnemis, 3-4, 23, 43, 147, 151-52
"Matapia", 47, 102-3, 151
"Mokohinau", 36-37, 47, 110-11, 152
"North Cape", 104-5, 151
pacificus, 106-7, 151
"Poor Knights", 112-13, 152
"Three Kings", vi, 108-9, 151
Dermochelyidae, 3, 7
Dermochelys, 3
coriacea, 324-25, 334-36
Diplodactylidae, 1, 3-4, 9
dragon
bearded, 11, 17
eastern water, 11, 17

Eretmochelys, 3
imbricata, 324, 332-33, 336
Eugongylinae, 1, 5

frog, 1-3, 6, 9, 12, 15, 306-7, 320
African clawed, 12
Archey's, i, 3, 12, 15, 23, 304-9
brown (whistling) tree, 12, 307, 318-19
eastern banjo, 12
green and golden bell, 12, 305, 307, 314-15
Hamilton's, 15, 21, 306-7, 312-13
Hochstetter's, 2, 7, 23, 303, 306-7, 310-11
neobatrachian, 9
southern bell, 12, 307, 316-17
White's tree, 12

gecko, 1-2, 4-5, 16-18, 40-46, 147-54
Aupouri, 50-51
barking, 15, 56-57
black-eyed, iv, 25, 96-97
broad-cheeked, 80-81
Cascade, 84-85
cloudy, 94-95
Cupola, 78-79
Darwin's marked, 40
Delcourt's, 10
Duvaucel's, 2, 15, 39, 41, 46, 114-15
elegant, 15, 29, 54-55
forest, 2, 41, 47, 72-75
goldstripe, 144-46
harlequin, ii, 40, 48-49
jewelled, 17, 68-71
Kahurangi, 130-31
Kaikouras, 128-29
Kawarau, 136-37
korero, 138-141
Marlborough green, 58-59
Matapia, 47, 102-3
minimac, 126-27
Mokohinau, 36-37, 47, 110-11
Muriwai, 120-21
ngahere, 76-77
northern striped, 40, 98-99
Northland green, 5, 52-53
Open Bay Islands, 82-83
orange-spotted, 88-91
Pacific, 2, 106-7
Poor Knights, 112-13
pygmy, 124-25
Raukawa, 41, 116-19, 367
rough, 39, 60-61
rough-snouted giant, 40
schist, 134-35
short-toed, 142-43
Southern Alps, 25, 132-33
southern striped, 100-1
starred, 45, 62-65
Takitimu, 92-93
Tautuku, 86-87
Te Paki, 104-5
Three Kings, vi, 108-9
tough-snouted giant, 40
Waitaha, 122-23
West Coast green, 66-67
Gekkota, 3, 40

Homonata darwini, 40
Hoplodactylus, 3-4, 9-10, 43
delcourti, 10
duvaucelii, 2, 39, 46, 114-15, 147
Hydrophiidae, 3, 8, 340
Hydrophis, 3
platurus, 8, 340, 348-50

Hylidae, 3, 6, 306

Ichthyosaura alpestris apuanus, 11-12
Intellagama lesueurii lesueurii, 11

kawekaweau, 2, 10
krait, *see* marine snake
kumi, 2

Lampropholis, 3
    delicata, 5, 12, 160, 294-95, 298
Laticauda, 3, 340-41
    colubrina, 339, 342-43, 350
    laticaudata, 344-45, 350
    saintgironsi, 8, 337, 346-47, 350
Laticaudidae, 3, 8
Leiopelma, 1, 3, 6, 9, 15, 306-7
    archeyi, i, 3, 304-9, 320
    auroraensis, 9-10
    hamiltoni, 3, 306, 312-13, 320
    hochstetteri, 2, 7, 303, 306-7, 310-11, 320
    markhami, 9-10
    pakeka, 312
    waitomoensis, 9-10
Leiopelmatidae, 1, 3, 6, 306
Lepidochelys, 3
    olivacea, 325, 330-31, 336
Lepidosauria, 3, 32
Limnodynastes dumerilii, 12
Litoria, 3
    caerulea, 12
    ewingii, 12, 307, 318-20
lizard
    shingleback, 17
    see also gecko; skink

marine snake, 1, 3, 7-8, 16, 340-41, 350
    brown- (blue-) lipped sea krait, 344-45
    Saint Giron's sea krait, 8, 337, 346-47
    yellow-bellied sea snake, 8, 340, 348-49
    yellow-lipped sea krait, 339, 342-43
marine turtle, 1, 3, 6-7, 19, 324, 336
    green, 7, 321-25, 328-29
    hawksbill, 325, 332-33
    leatherback, 7, 324, 334-35
    loggerhead, 325-27
    olive ridley, 325, 330-31
moko, 2
    kākāriki, 2, 55, 71
    pirirākau, 2, 75
    taumaka, 83
Mokopirirakau, 3-4, 22, 43, 46, 147, 149-51
    "Cascades", 84-85, 150
    cryptozoicus, 92-93, 150
    "Cupola", 78-79, 150
    granulatus, 47, 72-75, 150
    kahutarae, iv, 25, 96-97, 149
    nebulosus, 94-95, 150
    "Okarito", 80-81, 150
    "Open Bay Islands", 82-83, 150
    "Roys Peak", 88-91, 149
    "southern forest", 86-87, 149
    "southern North Island", 76-77, 151

Naultinus, 3-4, 17, 22, 40, 43, 45-46, 147-49
    elegans, 15, 29, 54-55, 149
    gemmeus, 17, 68-71, 148
    grayii, 5, 52-53, 149
    manukanus, 58-59, 148
    "North Cape", 50-51, 149
    punctatus, 15, 56-57, 149
    rudis, 39, 60-61, 148
    stellatus, 45, 62-65, 148
    tuberculatus, 66-67, 148
newt, alpine, 11-12, 17
ngārara, 2
niho taniwha, 2, 163
non-maniraptoran coelurosaur, 8

Oligosoma, 1, 3, 5, 24, 158-60, 297-302
    acrinasum, 19, 158, 166-67, 298
    aeneum, 6, 156, 274-75, 298
    alani, 21, 290-91, 297
    awakopaka, 172-73, 301
    burganae, 182-83, 302
    chloronoton, 22, 202-3, 299
    chloronoton "Eastern Otago", 206-7, 299
    chloronoton "Stewart Island", 208-9, 299
    chloronoton "West Otago", 204-5, 299
    elium, 216-17, 299
    fallai, 256-57, 299
    gracilocorpus, 162
    grande, 15, 160, 180-81, 298
    hardyi, 278-79, 298
    homalonotum, 162-63, 299
    hoparatea, 222-23, 298
    inconspicuum, 22, 192-94, 301-2
    infrapunctatum, 236-39, 300
    infrapunctatum "Alborn", 239-41, 300
    infrapunctatum "Chesterfield", 239, 242-43, 300
    infrapunctatum "cobble", 239, 244-45, 300
    infrapunctatum "crenulate", 239, 246-47, 300
    infrapunctatum "Hawke's Bay", 239, 252-53, 300
    infrapunctatum "Hokitika", 248-49, 300
    infrapunctatum "southern North Island", 254-55, 300
    infrapunctatum "Westport", 250-51, 300
    judgei, 158, 170-71, 300
    kokowai, 212-13, 239, 299
    levidensum, 276-77, 298

lichenigera, 1, 158
lineoocellatum, 158, 210-11, 299
longipes, 218-19, 298
longipes "southern", 220-21, 298
maccanni, 198-99, 302
macgregori, 292-93, 297
microlepis, 264-65, 299
moco, 160, 268-69, 300
nigriplantare, 258-59, 302
northlandi, 9
notosaurus, 196-97, 301-2
"Okuru", 188-89, 301-2
oliveri, 157, 286-87, 297-98
ornatum, viii, 282-83, 297
otagense, 15, 174-75, 298
pikitanga, 25, 158, 168-69, 301
polychroma, 224-25, 301-2
polychroma Clade 2, 226-27, 301-2
polychroma Clade 3, 228-29, 301-2
polychroma Clade 4, 230-31, 301-2
polychroma Clade 5, 232-35, 301-2
prasinum, 214-15, 299
repens, 184-85, 301
roimata, 280-81, 297
smithi, 15, 161, 260-61, 300
smithi "Three Kings, Te Paki, Western Northland", 262-63, 300
stenotis, 200-1, 300
striatum, 155, 266-67, 299
suteri, 6, 158, 164-65, 299
taumakae, 176-77, 301
tekakahu, 190-91, 301
toka, 186-87, 301
townsi, 288-89, 298
waimatense, 25, 161, 178-79, 298
"Whirinaki", vi, 270-71, 300
whitakeri, 284-85, 297
zelandicum, 272-73, 300
ornithopod, 9

pepeke, 2
Phelsuma, 40
plesiosaur, 8-9
Pogona barbata, 11
pterosaur, 9

Ranoidea, 3, 12-13
aurea, 12, 305, 307, 314-15, 320
raniformis, 12, 307, 316-17, 320
Rhacodactylus
trachycephalus, 40
trachyrhynchus, 40
Rhynchocephalia, 1, 3-4, 9, 32

Scincidae, 1, 3, 5
sea krait, *see* marine snake
skink, 1, 5-6, 16, 158-60, 297-302
Alborn, 239-41
Aorangi, 280-81
Awakopaka, 172-73
Barrier, 158, 170-71
Big Bay, 192
blue tongue, 11
Burgan, 182-83
Canterbury grass, 230-31
Canterbury spotted, 158, 210-11
Chathams, 258-59
Chesterfield, 239, 242-43, 249
chevron, 162-63
cobble, 239, 244-45
copper, 6, 156, 274-75
crenulate, 239, 246-47
cryptic, 22, 192-94
egg-laying, 6, 19, 158, 160, 164-65
Eyres, 184-85
Falla's, 256-57
Fiordland, 19, 158, 166-67
glossy brown, 272-73
grand, 15, 160, 180-81
green, 22, 202-3
Hardy's, 278-79
Hauraki, 288-89
Hawke's Bay, 239, 252-53
Hokitika, 248-49
Kupe, 239, 254-55
lakes, 204-5
Lonely Lake, 219
Mackenzie, 214-15
mahogany, 192, 301
marbled, 157, 286-87
Marlborough spotted, 216-17
McCann's, 198-99
McGregor's, 292-93
moko, 160, 268-69
Nevis, 186-87
northern grass, 224-25
northern long-toed, 218-19
northern spotted, 212-13
Okuru, 188-89
ornate, viii, 282-83
Otago, 15, 174-75
Otago green, 206-7
Oteake, 192-93
plague (rainbow), 6, 12-13, 17, 160, 294-96
roamatimati, 220-21
robust, 21, 290-91
scree, 25, 161, 178-79
shore, 15, 19, 161, 260-61
Sinbad, 25, 158, 168-69
slight, 276-77
small-eared, 200-1
small-scaled, 264-65

skink (*cont.*)
south Marlborough grass, 228-29
southern, 196-97
southern grass, 232-35
Southland green, 202-3
speckled, 236-39
Stewart Island green, 208-9
striped, 155, 266-67
tātahi, 262-63
Taumaka, 176-77
Te Kakahu, 190-91
Waiharakeke grass, 226-27
Westport, 250-51
Whirinaki, vi, 270-71
Whitaker's, 284-85
white-bellied, 222-23
slider, red-eared, 11-13, 17
snake, *see* marine snake
Sphenodon punctatus, 2-4, 30-35
Sphenodontidae, 1, 3-4, 32
Squamata, 3
Stereospondyli, 9

Tiliqua
rugosa, 17
scincoides, 11
titanosauriform sauropod, 8-9
Toropuku, 3-4, 43, 147, 149
"Coromandel", 40, 98-99, 149
stephensi, 100-1, 149
Trachemys scripta elegans, 11, 13
tuatara, 1-4, 15-17, 21, 30-35
Tukutuku, 3-4, 43
rakiurae, ii, 40, 48-49, 147
turtle, *see* marine turtle

Woodworthia, 3-4, 23-24, 42-43, 46, 147, 152-54
brunnea, 122-23, 153
"Central Otago", 134-35, 154
chrysosiretica, 144-46, 152
"Cromwell", 136-37, 154
"Kaikouras", 128-29, 153
maculata, 116-19, 153, 367
maculata "Muriwai", 120-21
"Marlborough mini", 126-27, 153
"Mount Arthur", 130-31, 153
"Otago/Southland large", 138-41, 153-54
"pygmy", 124-25, 152
"Southern Alps", 25, 132-33, 153
"southern mini", 142-43, 152

Raukawa gecko, *Woodworthia maculata*

BLOOMSBURY WILDLIFE
Bloomsbury Publishing Plc
50 Bedford Square, London, WC1B 3DP, UK

BLOOMSBURY, BLOOMSBURY WILDLIFE and the Diana logo are trademarks of Bloomsbury Publishing Plc

First published in 2018 in New Zealand as *Reptiles and Amphibians of New Zealand* by Auckland University Press
This edition published in Great Britain 2019

A catalogue record for this book is available from the British Library

Library of Congress Cataloguing-in-Publication data has been applied for

ISBN: PB: 978-1-4729-7499-0; ePub: 978-1-4729-7498-3

2 4 6 8 10 9 7 5 3 1

Design by Katrina Duncan
Printed and bound in China by 1010 Printing International Ltd

Frogs *Leiopelmatidae*

Leiopelma

3 species. Small cryptic nocturnal frogs occurring in isolated populations in northern half of the North Island, and on islands in Marlborough Sounds. Subfossil evidence indicates a much wider historic distribution into the South Island. No visible tympana, unable to vocalise. Round pupils.

Pages 308–313

Frogs *Hylidae*

Ranoidea

2 species. Introduced from Australia. Distributed throughout New Zealand. Large, brightly coloured (green, yellow or brown, occasionally blackish) frogs with expanded terminal toe pads, visible tympana, horizontal pupils and ability to vocalise loudly. Toes half to fully webbed.

Pages 314–317

Litoria ewingii

1 species. Introduced from Australia and occurs throughout the South and North Islands. Small fawn or brown frogs with greatly enlarged terminal toe pads, visible tympana, horizontal pupils; vocalises loudly. Toes only half webbed.

Page 318

Marine turtles *Cheloniidae*

Caretta caretta

1 species. Mostly confined to tropical and warm temperate waters, but few observations in New Zealand mainly off the northern North Island. Breeds only in the tropics. Carapace covered in non-overlapping bony scutes (5 or 6 pairs of costal scutes); 2 pairs of prefrontal scales; large head and beak; and two claws on each flipper.

Page 326

Chelonia mydas

1 species. The second-largest marine turtle, and only species with resident juveniles consistently present in New Zealand waters. Breeds only in the tropics. Carapace covered in bony scutes, which are smooth and non-overlapping; a single pair of prefrontal scales; blunt snout with unhooked beak; and single claw on each flipper.

Page 328